LISTENING TO THE
SILENT MUSIC

The Memoir of a Journey in Place

Charlie & Mickey:
God's best to you on your journey.
LeRoy Friesen
Advent, 2009

LeRoy Friesen

Dedication

To the gritty citizenry
of the assuredly independent
and largely sovereign state of
Tylerton

To our thousands of overnight guests,
who brought the world
to our door, tables, and hearts

And to Sharryl Ann,
my spouse and "the other innkeeper,"
without whom
neither the Inn nor this book
would have been.

Epigraph

Horns in the high hall are piping Your splendor;
their expanse is bowing Your artistry.
Eons of days hum Your music,
epochs of nights chant Your *Gloria*.

Despite dearth of word, speech, and sound,
their cadence pulses in all that is,
their polyphony to the frontiers of the cosmos.

Amid the ensemble You have sequestered Sir Sol
who, ever singing, bursts forth as hankering lover;
eager as athlete 'fore the fray.

Twixt overture right and finale left,
his *chanson d'amour* burning bright,
I can no more escape Your sea of dark fire
than the inaudible torch song he sings!

—from Psalm 19:1–6

Contents

Foreword

Dear Reader,

To understand this extraordinary book, please close your eyes for a minute, and listen carefully. What do you hear? (Seriously, try it—I'll pause a moment).

Now, if you were at the Inn of Silent Music, in the village of Tylerton on remote Smith Island in the lower Chesapeake Bay, sitting on the dock early in the morning, here's what you would hear: waves lapping at the dock. Cries of countless gulls and shorebirds. The endless breeze playing in the marsh grasses and your hair. The faint motor and VHF radio chatter from a crab boat trolling by. The centuries-old Yorkshire-ish patois of the fewer than 60 remaining villagers, chatting up the crab harvest and the cursed "boitin' floys."

And if you were this book's author—LeRoy Friesen, former innkeeper of the Inn of Silent Music—you would hear far more. You also would hear *silent music*—the music that plays in your heart and soul and mind. This is the music of deep perception and tranquility, of oneness with the place you are in, of the human spirit attuned with what LeRoy calls the Uni-verse. (As his story unfolds, this will come clear.)

In the decade from 1997 to 2006, LeRoy and his wife Sharryl were participants in, and catalysts of, a priceless gift exchange that affected thousands. The gifts flowed back-and-forth among four entities: the innkeepers, the island's heaven-on-earth setting, its salt-of-the-sea villagers, and thousands of guests, including myself and wife Jeanne.

The priceless gifts: Bringing to all comers the vibrant heritage of a special hospitality that fully nourishes guests in body and soul (hospitality in varied senses—biblical, nurturing, service leadership), through operating a lovely one-of-a-kind Inn, in a magical setting where Earth's "four spheres" intersect (land—sea—air—life), and done in a manner that encouraged everyone to hear and feel the silent music playing within themselves.

During the decade when LeRoy and Sharryl operated the Inn, my wife and I spent seven memorable wedding anniversaries there (34th through 40th), each stay growing richer. On our first visit in 2000, we were children loosed in a magical kingdom. The romantic Inn, the tiny village of Tylerton with its very special citizens, the awesomely sensual setting on this flat speck of an island in the magnificent Bay, and most of all our extraordinary hosts, LeRoy and Sharryl—people of deep compassion, principle, intellect, humor, talent, charm. We were just beginning to understand the depth of the Inn's idyllic name: *Inn of Silent Music.*

As we departed the Inn to catch the ferry back to the mainland, we vowed to return, and did so six times.

On our second visit, a small book graced the nightstand: *Music of Silence: A Sacred Journey through the Hours of the Day,* by Brother David Steindl-Rast and Sharon Lebell. The book's topic—hours of the day—is not the 24, but the hours of prayer observed in monasteries, like *matins, lauds, vespers*—the *moods* or *seasons* of the day that we all feel, that anchor us to genuine reality (not society's contrived reality). Perception grew; the silent music played louder.

At table over Sharryl's glorious breakfasts and seafood dinners (the Inn also serves evening fare, since the village lacks a restaurant), talk roamed the universe, but innkeepers and guests alike always returned the conversation to the Inn, the fragile island, the tenuous lifeway of the villagers, the primal beauty surrounding us—and beneath it all, the silent music played.

Our seven visits to the Inn of Silent Music were, in the end, a spiritual revelation about life, living in the moment, valuing the truly valuable, a quiet ministry of the spirit. The experience awakened in me a soundtrack of silent music that now plays daily. It can play for everyone, but learning to hear it requires listening to what surrounds you—not to the diurnal noise, but to the real sounds of nature and the souls who populate your place.

Which takes us to the other half of this book's title, "The Memoir of a Journey in Place." A pun of course—the paradoxical image of journeying by running in place, but also a journey in *place* as geographers, sociologists, and religious know it: listening intently to a place to discover its impact on people, its meaning, insights, gifts—its silent music.

This book is LeRoy's memoir of how he and Sharryl chanced upon this lovely isle and its people, how they built an Inn that extended hospitality to nurture thousands of guests, and how they learned to listen to the silent music on their journey in place. The book is a gem with multiple facets, each a gift:

- A beautifully crafted memoir of a life well-lived, spirited, and spiritual—a life like no other.
- A *vade mecum* of the village of Tylerton and tiny Smith Island and the Chesapeake Bay, places like no other.
- A mind-expanding (almost mind-blowing) exposition on the concept of *place,* like no other.
- The creation myth of the Inn of Silent Music, a bed-and-breakfast like no other.
- A grimoire on the hospitality of innkeeping, a how-to guide like no other.

- Another grimoire on the physical and spiritual care of innkeepers, a how-to guide like no other.
- A concluding, spirited dialog in cosmology and prayer, like no other.

This book is from the pen (actually, Macintosh) of a master writer whose twin gifts for expression and substance offer countless well-turned and memorable phrases, a promenade of insights, and an engaging story, all peppered with very human anecdotes and humor.

Chance events led us to the Inn of Silent Music, a life-changing experience in which we grew in spirit. Thank you, LeRoy and Sharryl. And thank you, LeRoy, for sharing it with thousands.

Fred Schroyer
Low Gap, West Virginia
May 28, 2009

PART I
THE GENESIS OF THE BOOK

On Memorial Day weekend of 1997, my wife Sharryl and I, having embraced hope over realism, opened a small bed and breakfast. Called the Inn of Silent Music, it was located in the village of Tylerton on Smith Island, a lacework of marshy islets barely above sea level, astride the Maryland/Virginia border near the center of the Chesapeake Bay. One of three villages on Smith (total year-round population c. 260), Tylerton, both a village and islet, had fifty-eight year-round residents as of 2006, a size that often had me simply using "Friesen 21866" as my return address. Save for the two of us innkeepers, virtually all other year-round Tylertonians hailed from the culture residing on Smith for nearly 350 years. The term for this culture is "waterman": those deriving livelihood from the water, whether via harvest or conveyance.

Served by a twice-daily nonvehicular ferry linking our community across nine miles of Tangier Sound to Crisfield at the bottom of Maryland's Eastern Shore, Tylerton Island is tiny (less than half a square mile), remote (separated by water even from Smith's other two villages, North End and Rhodes Point), and arguably at the ends of the earth. This innkeeping project would extend to an even ten years, an unprecedentedly vital time for the two of us. This book is one innkeeper's account of an extraordinary experience in one place during that decade.

The Decision to Write

I had packed into Tylerton the possibility of putting thoughts to paper, perhaps about the island's culture or the adventure of innkeeping. I had not been here long before I jettisoned such notions, for two related reasons. First, it was complicated writing about either guests we received or locals among whom we lived. Besides, a definitive portrait on the latter, Tom Horton's *An Island Out of Time*, was published the year before we opened. The challenges he encountered writing about the community within which he and his family had lived (1987–1989) served to deter me. Second, I was uncomfortable with the way such a writing project could skew the living experience itself—life following art. I wanted to avoid the temptation to steer a conversation on the Inn porch in the interests of my writing about it that night.

Thus it was only with the emergence of a new focus, one that only secondarily included elements of my earlier plan, that the itch to write recurred during a day-long retreat I made in September 1999, courtesy of the alignment of dallying Hurricane Dennis and a serious case of poison ivy. Subsequent musing on the notion of "spiritually evocative landscapes" with guest Sanford Alwine, a spiritual director and father-in-law of my older son, served both to scratch and prolong the itch, as did exchanges with Fred Schroyer, a guest and professional editor, who first visited in 2000. A very different nudge was my awareness of the summer of 2008 as the 400th anniversary of Capt'n John Smith's historic cartographical exploration of the Chesapeake Bay, an endeavor that repeatedly had him in the precincts of our isle.

By the mid-point of our decade on Tylerton, I knew not only that our risky venture would survive, but that we were riding one tiger of a tale! Part of the story's power lay in the way it encompassed our unlikely locale, its sturdy people, the surrounding bay, and our varied guests. Part of its power resided in how this entire package was boring into my interior and becoming a component in my spiritual journey. But how could I tell these various stories as the single tale I knew them to be? Unknowingly in my prayer and spiritual journaling, a tad more intentionally as I played with various overviews amid my ongoing research of Tylerton's life, and amid encouragement from various guests and friends, the configuration of a book emerged. And throughout, it was as though the story itself was assuming a life of its own, one demanding to be told.

The Emergence of Memoir as My Genre

Probably implicitly so from the outset, the book's genre in time became explicit: memoir. My shorthand for *memoir* is "creative recollection." This means that rather than pure fiction, the account is based on facts that were arrived at via research, interviews, and, chiefly, living. However, these facts were selected from many others, creatively shaped, and embodied in text—all of this as I remembered and deemed their significance relevant to my project. Rather than a mere reconstructed chronicle, memoir is an objective/subjective "construct," to introduce a category developed in Part III and employed throughout the remainder of the book. Stated otherwise, the manner in which the facts are chosen, weighted, shaped, and arranged by the memoirist into the creative tapestry of narrative is not totally unlike that of a work of fiction. While I alone am responsible for any factual errors in this text, I seized my prerogative to bring facts to text as a creative work of art.

Depending on where the reader dips in, the resulting book might appear to be about the Chesapeake biosphere, or the role of faith in Tylerton's culture, or the art of hospitality, or self-care by the long-distance runner, or cosmogenesis, or the strictures on human language, or music as metaphor for the numinous. But above all of these—or more accurately, *below*—is my attempt to scratch out a few words for the Good amid the good, Beauty amid the beautiful, Love amid the loves, Truth amid the true, the One amid the many.

This is an audacious goal, one condemned to failure in any comprehensive sense; yet the process and the sharing of the story have already been my substantial rewards. The earliest meaning of the word *martyría* in the Christian tradition is that of "witness" (see Acts 6:13 and 7:58, for example). Although only indirectly so in Part II, I understand this memoir as bearing witness to the weightiness of what transpired in a slip of a place across a decade of time. Being in the September of my own life has seemed a propitious time to tackle such an ambitious project.

The decision to write something so autobiographical was not taken lightly; *hubris* and insignificance, fast friends, are but two of the pitfalls down this road. What finally warrants memoir—indeed, occasionally *demands* it—is the conviction, appropriately tested, that there is a story worthy of the telling which no one else is able to tell. While I acknowledged the danger of *hubris*, in the end I chose to deny it veto power.

Journey as Metaphor

One of the two metaphors central to this book is *journey*. Literature of wildly varied genres has repeatedly intertwined the geographical trek with a journey of an inward kind. Whether in Homer's *The Odyssey*, Augustine's *Confessions*, Dante's *The Divine Comedy*, Kazantzakis' *Report to Greco*, Merton's *The Seven Storey Mountain*, Pirzig's *Zen and the Art of Motorcycle Maintenance*, Hampl's *Virgin Time: In Search of the Contemplative Life*, and the very title of Hammarskjöld's *Markings*—to say nothing of the meanderings of the Israelites in both the Hebrew Pentateuch and Exile literature or that of Jesus in the Christian gospels—journeying *without* becomes a vehicle for communicating about journeying *within*.

In this book the external journey, its setting a tiny islet, is both simple and minuscule: rarely more than a quarter-mile per day, as the osprey flies. By contrast, the internal journey to which this image points is both more complex and far longer. Regarding time, it unfolds across a full decade. As to space, our worldwise guests facilitated my prowling of much of the planet in the internal journey, this requiring nary a packed suitcase nor crossing of the Sound. In Part VI even those bounds are blown wide open as my faith seeks greater engagement with science's farthest glimpses into both space and the early stages of cosmic time.

But the underlying internal theme to which the journey metaphor is pointing is my own, a peregrination increasingly spiritual as the decade progressed. And as a member of one of the "Abrahamic faiths"—the interrelated traditions of Judaism,

Christianity, and Islam—that journey is never merely from "here" to "there," from "now" to "then," but in the direction of, toward, and, increasingly, *into* the One for whom no name or image suffices.

Title and Organization

This book's title demands a tale, the telling of which is deferred until Part III. For now, the reader is invited to note that the title contains one paradox, the subtitle another. What is music that is silent? And is not "journey in place" also an oxymoron, analogous to a travel guide for the tethered life or Thoreau's comment "I traveled much in Concord"? Yet is not this title, a kind of Zen *koan* squared, appropriate to a project repeatedly squirming under the limitations of language, one in which as much effort is sometimes devoted to saying what *is not* as what *is*? The more mystical wings of the Abrahamic faiths are squatters in paradox in the face of this challenge. All language about the One needs to connote provisionality; nothing does this like paradox.

The themes of the five major sections of this work, and their sequence, evolved across the journey of writing. Parts II and III focus on the theme of "place" and require that order. Parts IV and V share the rubric of "hospitality," although their sequence is less crucial. Each of the four, while able to stand alone, is enriched by the other three. While Part VI's expansion of place into yet another dimension—the vertical under the lure of the night sky—is in continuity with Part II, discontinuity emerges in different grammatical persons (first person addressing the second) and mode (interrogative) as well as genre (prayer). The ordering of the six parts hints of the way the decade's experience ripened.

Spirituality as Substratum

In addition to being a Roman Catholic Christian, and an orthodox one in most respects, I am a secular in the Discalced Carmelite religious order. Both are noteworthy given the fact that virtually all of our villagers who are religious are conservative evangelicals with their roots in the Wesleyan tradition. Not generic United Methodists, but a peculiarly *Tylertonian* sort of Christian. That the experience that I as a Roman Catholic had could have unfolded in such a milieu is one of the grace notes in this story's music.

The substratum theme of the book is "spirituality," a term employed because of its breadth and nonsectarian quality. I introduce my working definition of the term here by stating what it is not (*via negativa*). First, "spirituality" is not the antithesis of the "physical," "material," or "natural," some sphere inaccessible to the sensorium. Rather, the Christian doctrine of the Incarnation forever views the part of reality accessible to the senses as the arena where spirit is operative. In the words of the poet

Gerard Manley Hopkins, SJ (1844–1889), "There lives the dearest freshness deep down things," one not fully accessible to the senses. While real, and often good as well as beautiful, the universe accessed via the senses is not all that there is; in addition to the *manifest* aspect of reality, there is its *implicit* depth. Thus, "spirituality" in this work refers to this larger material/spirit interplay wherever in the cosmos it is found. In theological language, the finite is *capax Dei*: capable of—indeed, equipped precisely for—reception of and embodiment by the divine. The sacramental possibilities are ubiquitous.

Nor, second, do I understand "spirituality" as synonymous with "religious" where institutional authority, boundary definition, and distinctives of dogma and liturgy hold much sway. The term "spirituality" is more open to the material/spirit interplay wherever it unfolds, including faith traditions other than Christian. I understand the term as equally at home in the secular and sacred spheres, a versatility I trust is evident in this book.

Finally, "spirituality" must also be contrasted with "theology," a methodical setting forth of, in my case, Scripture and the Roman Catholic tradition. While "spirituality" centers in the heart involving faith, prayer, and their implications for behavior, "theology" (or the "science of God"), as commonly understood, resides more in the head and consists of reflection upon these primary experiences. Despite remaining something of a theological junkie, I know well that theology can become distraction or even idol, usurping the place of the One to whom prayer gives itself. In short, "theology" is one row farther back than "spirituality" from the Main Event: encounter with God.

Thus, while "religion," "theology," or "spirituality" is each descriptive of an aspect of my life, and all are involved in what interests me most about Tylerton culture (see chapter 5), it is spirituality which, in addition to being most important in my present September season, is central to this book. Needless to say, none of these terms is understood as encompassing the reality of God.

Speaking of whom: since first reading Dag Hammarskjöld's *Markings* in 1965, I have been interested in the issues of "God-talk." How do I—or do I *not*—name the Whirlwind? What is my response to the contention that carelessness with words, particularly in the precincts of religion, often renders their power inversely proportional to the frequency of their use?

One expression of this interest in my book is the employing of names for the divine other than the overused and abused "God." Although when working with themes in the Hebrew Bible I often employ "YHWH" ("I AM WHO AM" [Ex 3:13, 14]), the text's most important divine name, otherwise I generally resort simply to "the One"

(Apoc 4:2, 9). To employ an oft-used metaphor, I am trying to improve the way we point toward the moon, rather than improve upon the moon itself. In Part VI, I explore how the bundling of the grammatical second person with the interrogative mode in the genre of prayer generated fresh names for the One.

The Places of Writing about Place

In what sort of places did I write this book about a place? Most research, prayer, and writing took place in the gable room and Oratory of the innkeepers' quarters on the third floor of the Inn. Through the glass door to the balcony off this space, I can see out over the quarter-mile of Tyler's Creek—or "the Crick," in Tylerton's vernacular shorthand that became my own. And from the balcony itself one is arrested by a vista of nearly 240 degrees of Smith Island and the Chesapeake Bay, including Virginia's Tangier Island to the south (seven miles) as well as the mainland of Virginia's Smith Point (thirteen miles) and Maryland's Point Lookout (seventeen miles), bookends of the wide Potomac. I am unable to exaggerate the inspirational power for the project of a full decade of this vista! Had I rather opted for the genre of fiction, this islescape would have been one of the major characters rather than mere setting.

During both the 2004 and 2005 off-seasons, to escape the prospect of ice sequestering Smith Island, Sharryl and I fled to Atlantic Coast climes offering mobility if not warmth. Serendipitously, both locations were also islands, each, however, with indulging causeway: Edisto Island in South Carolina, and nearby Ocean City, Maryland, respectively. Facing the Atlantic in the dead of winter, each also provided spiritually evocative seascapes. In short, the sea, whether Bay or Atlantic—by which I, together with millions of other Americans have been shamelessly seduced, with our eyes wide open—was the setting for virtually all aspects of the first five parts of the gestation of this child.

The final form of Part VI of this book, drawing upon experiences of the entire decade, emerged after we departed Tylerton for South Bend, Indiana, our retirement destination. Here I researched, prayed, and wrote not only adjacent to the water, now the St. Joseph River, but on another island of sorts, this one created by the late 1830s East Race hypotenuse cut across the inside of one of the river's many bends.

Appreciations

It is impossible to acknowledge all who contributed to this project. Room for a work on the spirituality/geography tectonic boundary was first shoehorned open for me and then energized by my encounter with the works of three authors, each fascinated by that interface. Introducing me to this boundary was Barry Lopez whose *Arctic*

Dreams: Imagination and Desire in a Northern Landscape I read shortly after its publication in 1986. The second was Kathleen Norris, notably her *Dakota: A Spiritual Geography* published in 1993, which I read shortly thereafter. A second reading after our first season at the Inn repeatedly raised tantalizing parallels between her experience in South Dakota (not so far from my southwestern Minnesota origins) and Tylerton.

The third writer was Belden C. Lane, a Presbyterian in the Jesuit nation of St. Louis University, whose *The Solace of Fierce Landscapes: Exploring Desert and Mountain Spirituality* (1998) proved most influential of all. Both Norris and Lane contributed profoundly to the kind of vision giving rise to this book. Even though this work is as much the fruit of prayer as of study, I doubt whether I would have either glimpsed the undergirding vision, or had the requisite tools, without these place-blazers. Late in my project, Philip Sheldrake's *Spaces for the Sacred: Place, Memory, and Identity* rose to complement Lane's analysis of the topography/spirituality frontier.

For very different reasons, another writer contributed significantly as well. Jessica Powers (1905–1988) was a poet of stature both before and after entering the Discalced Carmelite enclosure in 1941, to be known subsequently as Sr. Miriam of the Holy Spirit, OCD. In a manner not unlike *Variations on a Theme by Paganini* by Johannes Brahms (1833–1897), many of her poems are orchestrations both sensuous and spare on themes of John of the Cross. A troubadour within the cloister until her death, she continues to pipe the silent music in her incarnational poetry. Her work was my companion throughout the decade on the Crick, and is cited repeatedly in this book.

I am also indebted to more others than I can name for inspiration on various fronts. Conversations, often on the Inn's screened porch overlooking the Bay, took place about nearly everything in the book, and much, much more, with literally thousands of guests. In addition, there are family members who have been both supportive and interactive, especially my son Todd, a pastor, and brother Berry, Mennonite spiritual companions both. I am indebted as well to fellow members of the Discalced Carmelite order: secular Marianne Chapin in addition Fr. Kieran Kavanaugh and Br. Bryan Paquette. The latter two were my spiritual directors prior to and during the second half of our decade, respectively. There have also been friends with strong interest in and support for first the Inn and then this work: Bill and Teri Hocking as well as Jean and Jim Matlack.

Moreover, there were the longsuffering and forgiving folk of Tylerton by whom Sharryl and I, both papists and "foreigners" (pronounced *fúrr-ners*)), were improbably taken in, welcomed, and schooled. Joan Corbin, cultural interpreter, sole Inn staffperson, and our friend, heads any such list, but Dwight and Mary Ada Marshall, as well as Alan Smith, Sr., must be included as well. In a special category is North End's retired waterman Jennings Lee Evans, the isle's première historian and resident savant who is bad medicine to any dismissive use of the phrase "being in one's anecdotage."

And I am profoundly indebted to guest Fred Schroyer who, together with his wife Jeanne, risked badgering both early on and late to encourage me to take on, and then complete, this project, and then repeatedly offered his substantial editorial gifts toward its completion. His savvy, doggedness, therapy, and, on occasion, resuscitative skills in a strange land prevented this book from being still-born. Amazingly, he also became my friend.

I am also grateful to Tom Horton and Todd Friesen, each of whom read and offered feedback to portions of early drafts of the book; Valerie Weaver-Zercher who did the final edit; Jody L. Brown who generated the maps; and the team at BookSurge who oversaw the project to its completion.

Most importantly, I am indebted to my friend, co-constructor, co-innkeeper, and spouse, Sharryl Ann Lindberg: for her patience and support over the years of writing. For her amazing gift for generating beauty with smile, space, form, and celebratory food. For her creation of gardens of flowers and other plants around the Inn by sheer force of will in the face of arch-foes Wind, Salt, and Tide. For companionship in both prayer and theologizing. For the indomitability and buoyancy of her spirit apart from whom the music would have been profoundly diminished. And most tangibly, for a heart, like her face, predisposed to joy. That, aside from portions of chapters 16, 19, 23, and 26, I have not attempted to catalogue the extent of my indebtedness to her, particularly in Part V, should not be misunderstood. Lane's words nail the paucity of my own in this regard: "In the apophatic tradition, the one about whom the least is said is always the most important."

"One Brief Shining Moment"

Finally, I wrote this book, more an impressionist painting than a photograph, to catch some of the stark beauty and spiritual heft of Tylerton, even as it struggles for its very survival. The challenges it faces, whether economic, environmental, cultural, or demographic, to say nothing of hurricanes, are formidable. During the fourteen years between our first visit and the sale of the Inn in late 2006, Sharryl and I witnessed, and perhaps contributed inadvertently to, movement toward a tipping point. One way or another, the Tylerton we knew would one day be no more. In which case this book, in addition to being both a leave-taking love song to the place and its people, and a prayer of gratitude for it to the One, might also serve as a proleptic eulogy for, to use Alan Lerner's lyric, this "one brief shining moment."

Three Maps: The Bay, The Island, The Village

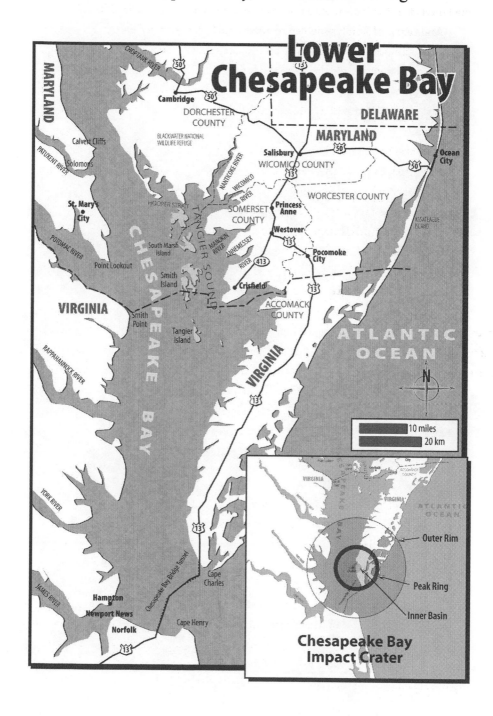

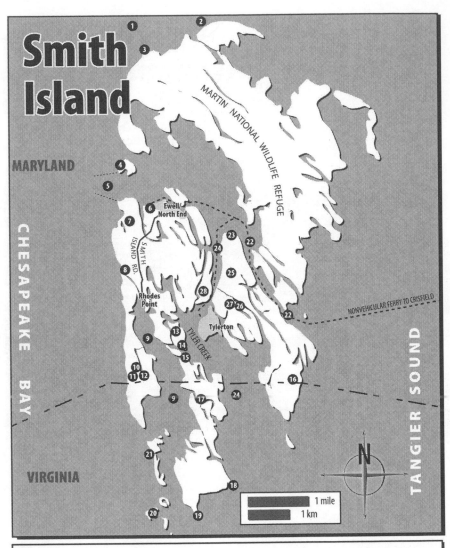

Smith Island

MARYLAND

MARTIN NATIONAL WILDLIFE REFUGE

CHESAPEAKE BAY

Ewell/North End

SMITH ISLAND RD.

Rhodes Point

Tylerton

TYLER CREEK

NONVEHICULAR FERRY TO CRISFIELD

TANGIER SOUND

VIRGINIA

1 mile
1 km

N

① Solomons Lump Lighthouse	⑧ Sheep Pen Gut	⑮ Hunter Gut	㉒ Big Thorofare
② Kedges Strait	⑨ Shanks Creek	⑯ Horse Hammock	㉓ Easter Point
③ Fog Point	⑩ Hog Neck	⑰ Fishing Creek	㉔ Tyler Ditch
④ Swan Island	⑪ Mill Gut	⑱ Peach Orchard Point	㉕ Longbranch
⑤ Jetty	⑫ Sassafras Hammock	⑲ Amen Corner	㉖ Juggling Creek
⑥ Pitchcroft	⑬ The Slough	⑳ Shanks Island	㉗ The Pines
⑦ Orchard Ridge	⑭ Parks Ditch	㉑ Cheeseman Island	㉘ Indian Creek

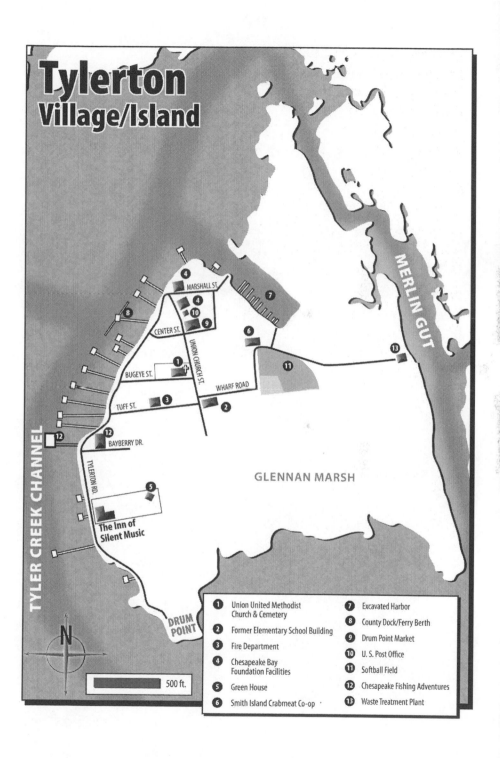

PART II
THE PLACE

"We must love life before loving the meaning of life . . ."
—attributed to Dostoyevsky by Albert Camus

"That? Why, that's Tylerton," he said dismissively. "Can't get there from here."
—a waterman from Rhodes Point

Since the fourth day of our marriage in January of 1990, Sharryl and I had been innkeepers. Preferring to work together rather than have a commuter relationship, as the continuing of our academic careers appeared to offer, we had accepted a shared position as resident managers of an international guesthouse, Davis House, operated by the American Friends Service Committee (AFSC) just off Dupont Circle in Washington, D.C.

Dupont Circle: Intro to Hospitality

There, amid one of America's most fascinating neighborhoods replete with the cuisine of the planet, satisfying architecture, glorious bookstores, and human diversity with an attitude, we received a dozen guests nightly from around the world as well as U.S. citizens on humanitarian forays to the capital. The list of countries represented might begin with Azerbaijan, Papua New Guinea, and Espiritu Santo Island in the Vanuatu in the south Pacific.

With the Quaker tradition of peace and justice coloring the ambience—AFSC shared the Nobel Peace Prize in 1947—we hosted players from innumerable conflict settings throughout the world, including Vietnam, North Korea, Northern Ireland, Palestine and Israel, the Balkans, Central America, and South Africa. Initially envisioning the Davis House placement as transitional, the two of us came to love the work and people as well as both the surprises and the challenges of hospitality. And, most of the time, we enjoyed working so closely together.

Because our predecessor at Davis House had experienced burnout as a result of carrying our shared responsibilities, the two of us were contractually obliged by AFSC to vacate the elegant brownstone one weekend monthly for restoration of body and spirit. Thus began a serendipitous cadence of compulsory forays, usually including a night in a bed and breakfast, into a mid-Atlantic ellipse bounded by Harpers Ferry, West Virginia, to Chincoteague, Virginia; Gettysburg, Pennsylvania, to Petersburg, Virginia.

Yonder Is Tylerton

Now, August of 1992, our weekend away found us in the hamlet of Ewell (North End to locals) on Smith Island, Maryland, in the private home of octogenarian Miss Bernice Guy. We were by that time already dimly aware of our pattern of heading for water—usually the Chesapeake—after a particularly stressful stretch. Indeed, in recent months we had been methodically exploring the Bayside of the Eastern Shore, also known as the Delmarva Peninsula (Delaware plus separated appendages of both Maryland and Virginia), river by river, neck by neck.

We had worked our way down from Chesapeake City to the bottom of Maryland's Eastern Shore and Smith Island, her one remaining inhabited isle lacking concrete umbilicus. Having rented bicycles from the North End home of Miss Frances Kitching, purveyor and popularizer of Smith Island's groaning table cuisine for more than thirty years, Sharryl and I rode the mile or so down the road through the verdant salt marsh garnished with Great Egrets beneath the sky blue to the even smaller settlement of Rhodes Point.

From there, we noted for the first time, less than a mile away across the expanse of green marsh and water, a third pod of buildings anchored by an imposing, towered church. Having been atypically careless in my research, I needed to ask a passing waterman what we were looking at. "That? Why that's Tylerton," he said. And when I pressed him as to how we could visit the place, he countered with "Can't get there from here." Rising to the challenge, I sought during the remainder of the weekend to arrange passage to Tylerton for the two of us. But alas, he had been right: we couldn't get here from there.

Upon our return to D.C., Sharryl gave me a copy of *Water's Way: Life Along the Chesapeake,* text by Tom Horton, photography by David Harp, with this inscription: "Falling in love with the Chesapeake . . . together. Smith Island, August, 1992." The hook had apparently already been set.

Three months later, having now discovered that Tylerton had never had houses of public accommodation, I made weekend reservations via telephone at a B&B in Crisfield, the port serving Smith. We would need to be content to walk about in Tylerton between the 1:30 PM arrival of the first ferry and the 3:30 PM departure of the second. But when at the end of our conversation the B&B owner, Becky Marshall, learned that our interest was Tylerton rather than Crisfield, her demeanor changed: "I can get teary with someone interested in Tylerton," she said, and then promptly did.

She did manage to inform me that she had grown up on Tylerton, and then announced that she would cancel the reservation and arrange for us rather to spend our October weekend there with her parents, Capt'n Romey (Jerome) and Miss Nanny Smith. And that is how we first arrived at the place that was very difficult to get to from there.

That October weekend of 1992 would prove to be an auspicious beginning. Capt'n Romey collected us at the dock, escorting us on foot past the village pump house and onto Center Street, a lane six feet wide, running between the flowered yards of Miss Meta Tyler and Ma Ginny Evans to the Smith bungalow across from the neatly kept Union United Methodist Church. Warnings that Smith Islanders were cold toward mainlanders proved spurious. Sharryl and I talked with Miss Nanny and Capt'n Romey about Tylerton, its history and culture and people, its language and tradition of faith, almost nonstop that weekend.

Between conversations, Capt'n Romey guided us through the village, including the old store, introduced us to the citizenry, and tossed in a walkthrough of two for-sale properties. Meanwhile, Miss Nanny's fare demonstrated why the village's cookbook was entitled *Cooking up a Storm on Tylerton*. The Smiths accepted modest payment when we reboarded the ferry, but made it clear that we should return soon as their personal guests. Years later I would re-discover my inscription in that year's Christmas gift of William Warner's Pulitzer-winning book *Beautiful Swimmers* (literal translation of *Callinectes sapidus*, the blue crab): "Dear Sharryl Ann, I give this gift to you as an expression of my hope that we shall someday live among the beautiful swimmers."

Following several shorter visits in the intervening two years, Sharryl and I, via the good offices of Miss Nanny, were able to vacation the entire month of August 1994 in a small Tylerton waterfront cottage owned by Arthur Sherwood, cofounder of the Chesapeake Bay Foundation, or CBF ("Save the Bay" to locals). It was a restorative month of reading, watching birds and working boats, catching our crab dinner nearly every day, and sipping wine on the porch as the sun disappeared into the Potomac across the Bay and Rhodes Point. I particularly relished our joint canoe explorations, one destination being what I called Necropolis Nauticus. This occluded cove was encircled by about a dozen work- and pleasure-boats, either by man or storm run hard aground to die. The Smiths continued to facilitate our meeting other Tylertonians, with whom we began to feel more comfortable.

The Seeds of the Inn

My journal reports that on the evening of August 20, 1994, Sharryl and I sat up late on Sherwood's porch putting to paper a fanciful list of the pros and cons for opening a B&B somewhere on Tylerton.

The next morning—the next morning!—the seasonal neighbor just north of us dropped in, inviting us to meet those in the second home to the south, owners of a gabled "Maryland house" who had just returned. And so we walked across *Spartina patens* (saltmeadow hay) in the intervening lot, a fig orchard in less saline times, to meet Margaret and Charlie Morgan, seasonal folk from Accomack County on Virginia's Eastern Shore. Within ten minutes, they had us prowling through their house, which, we learned, had been for sale for several years. Only after returning to D.C., chancing upon a crude floor plan and asking price in an old folder, did we determine that this had indeed been one of the houses Capt'n Romey had taken us through nearly two years before! The fact that the asking price now was 30 percent below what it had been in 1992 did not go unnoticed.

An explanatory word is in order. From the outset of our monthly forays from Washington, Sharryl and I had often drifted into fantasizing about an inn we might someday own. Most weekends, the B&B stay, sometimes enriched with walkthroughs of other properties having potential for the same, provided new fodder for this pattern—after which, come Monday morning, all would be promptly forgotten until the next month.

I had been particularly interested in sleuthing out the *niche* which the fine B&B filled, the quality which made it *sing*: was it proximity to the historical, the authenticity or antiquity of decorations and furnishings, the attention to detail, the personalities and life experiences of the innkeepers, the cuisine, or something less tangible yet fetching? In contrast to more conventional accommodations appearing in chains, the inimitable personality of the B&B was everything. Most months Sharryl and I had compared notes on the way home, accumulating quite a repository of questions, possibilities, insights, and knowledge of one another's dreaming. In retrospect, it is clear that neither of us made a conscious decision to pursue the purchase of a bed and breakfast. After all, the fantasizing was recreational diversion, an enjoyable and shared activity, and it entailed neither obligation nor cost!

When Sharryl and I returned to our cottage porch from the Morgans, we knew we faced a decision that could end our recreational fantasizing on the cheap. Indeed, we were immediately in the throes of a major discernment for which we both were and were not well-prepared. Our deliberations had strong faith components, insofar as both our ongoing hospitality work in Washington and a possible project on Tylerton were viewed as more than a mere livelihood.

As part of our further investigation, we arranged to rent the Morgans' house for a weekend in September of 1994 when they were absent. Upon our return to Washington after that experience, I called them, anxiously reporting that there had been water under the house from tides. Margaret, not a Tylertonian but incorrigibly of the Eastern

Shore, solemnly intoned Holy Writ, no less: "God gave to the sea its limit, that the waters shouldn't transgress his commands . . ." (Prv 8:29). Whether regarding island piety or tidewater realities, it would be the last good chance to turn back. We didn't. Just weeks later, in the face of puzzlement on the part of our five adult children and many friends, to say nothing of several huge unanswered questions on our burgeoning lists, we offered the Morgans what they were asking, and they accepted.

Frozen Pipes, Flat Champagne, and No Looking Back

Our return as new lord and lady of the manor proved to be less auspicious than our maiden voyage. Walking into the house on a brutally cold Friday afternoon in late January of 1995, on the occasion of both our new ownership and our fifth wedding anniversary, Sharryl and I were confronted with water and ice everywhere from frozen pipes. Frozen mustard-colored shag carpet undulating over buckled floors beneath a musty bouquet are among the sense memories. Our champagne followed our spirits to flat, and tears there were, but we resolutely activated our mutual buck-up dynamic and got to work.

When the ferry was nowhere in sight as we wearily waited on the dock that Sunday afternoon, a waterman ventured out into the cold to tell us that we, having forgotten about the return to standard time months earlier, had missed the boat. An additional night in the cold and wet house, this time without food, was thus the weekend bonus. Bright enough to recognize a bad omen when we saw one, we limped back to our amenitied life on fashionable Dupont Circle, wondering just what we had wrought.

Sharryl and I crafted a two-and-a-half-year plan to prepare the building to serve as an inn, with opening scheduled for Memorial Day 1997. During that interval, we would use our former respite weekends and summer vacations to do the needed renovation. Aside from sleeping briefly and attending local worship services, we would work flat out during those weekends before dashing back to Dupont Circle for another month of dreaming, scheming, list-making, and supply-purchasing.

We would only later become aware that this thirty-month interim served several other equally important functions: a gradual weaning from civilized amenities such as salary, health and retirement benefits, Kennedy Center concerts, afternoons with French impressionists in the National Gallery, dinner at the Ethiopian Red Sea restaurant, a matinee flick, April walks through the floral streets of Georgetown, and liturgy at our beloved Holy Trinity parish. A second derivative benefit of this timetable was getting to know villagers before we began receiving guests.

And thus on Memorial Day weekend of 1997, following a brief sprinkling ritual of blessing in and around the building which we had chosen to call the *Inn of Silent*

Music, Sharryl and I began chapter two of our lives as hospitaliers. Although the ardor of the love affair the two of us had begun with the islescape during that 1994 vacation occasionally cooled during the exhausting renovation process, it would flare up again as guests became a part of the experience.

As of this writing most of a decade later, Sharryl and I still agree that, from that flat champagne through first the renovation and then the decade of innkeeping, neither of us more than momentarily looked back. Our relationship was both complicated and reinforced by our competitive stubbornness. And although each of us wanted a somewhat different inn than that of the other, and for somewhat different reasons, the two visions overlapped—at least sufficiently to make it work. And that is how two former academics now in a strange land, all obstacles notwithstanding, barely avoided not getting to this place from there.

Telling the Tylertale

A foundational assumption of this book is the wisdom of Dostoyevsky's words beginning this chapter, here slightly edited: "We must love [a place] before loving the meaning [of the place]." However, preceding both of these steps is yet another: attentiveness, sensitivity to detail, awareness and valuing of nuance, commitment to the long haul of intimate familiarity. This initial step is nonnegotiable; its neglect sabotages all steps subsequently built upon it. Love of a place characterized by integrity is not based on an idea, a myth, or a vision. No, it is first grounded—albeit generally retrospectively—on the decision that a particular space actually warrants such attentiveness. (If you think the homogenization of America is nearly complete, visit Tylerton!) And, second, it is grounded upon what that space actually *is* physically and materially, as encountered primarily via the senses and secondarily via research and reflection.

Part II of this book, then, is the telling of the story of what Tylerton, both island and village, is, a story which begins in its remote cosmological and then geological past and extends into the present, including a peek at its precarious future. Stated otherwise, my approach here is movement from macro to micro: from the immensity of the cosmos to the concrete particulars of a tiny and jeopardized space in the present.

This interconnectedness or unity of, for example, our "Local Group" of galaxies on the macro side to such elementary particles as "quarks" on the micro, constitutes one of my paradigm shifts of this decade. I borrow here cosmologist Brian Swimme's hyphenating of the word "uni-verse" so as to accentuate this singularity and wholeness. In the words of William Blake:

To see a World in a Grain of Sand
And a Heaven in a Wild Flower,
Hold Infinity in the palm of your hand
And Eternity in an hour.

One of the strands woven into Part VI of this book is the further integration of this cosmic cohesion with my faith as a Catholic Christian. Here in Part II, I proceed assuming that the most promising way to convey the fruits of attentiveness to Tylerton and its Bay environs is to view it as an unfolding point in cosmological time, "one brief shining moment," birthed in a scarcely believable primordial past, on an adventure through the present, into a future shrouded in mystery.

1. The Cosmological Place

A. The Incendiary Inception

In the beginning, fire was the origin of this particular place we call Tylerton, like every other. It is the prevailing wisdom among scientists that approximately 13.7 billion years ago, the uni-verse was born when a tiny point of unimaginable density and temperature ignited, spraying out super-hot subatomic particles. This event—the "Big Bang," or what Swimme terms the "Flaring Forth"—did not take place within time or space: it *created* both time and space, to say nothing of the totality of energy, matter, and the embedded patterns that would characterize its evolution or unfolding. All the energy and matter making up Tylerton and its Bay environment is thought to have been present in that initial ignition.

To moderns accustomed to understanding everything in terms of context, the nascent cosmos was and remains unique: a "text" for which there was no "context," an "inside" lacking an "outside." Virtually all the energy and stuff that has been, is, or will be part of the uni-verse was present in the procession, both violent and delicate, of the debris of that ignition and the stunning differentiation process which followed. When we look up into the night sky we see, in the words of Jesuit poet Gerard Manley Hopkins, "all the fire-folk sitting in the air." And everywhere, elegance, equipoise, orderly procession, and beauty!

As what physicists call the "pre-atomic plasma" (ionized gases) expanded, its temperature diminished so as to allow for the formation first of subatomic particles and, later, the simplest atoms, hydrogen, together with traces of several other gases. It is thought that this atomic threshold triggered the release of brilliant light, which subsequent expansion of the uni-verse has stretched into the wavelengths of microwave radio. In 1965 scientists had their first glimpse into this threshold, with the detecting of faint and cool cosmic background energy, relic radiation, a kind of recollective hum or lingering glow of the Flaring Forth, as the seemingly homogenous expansion continued. The background radiation, present throughout the uni-verse, remains our earliest glimpse into the generating of cosmic structures.

From this atomizing threshold through the remainder of the first billion years, there was an absence of visual light in the expanding universe, an interval called the Dark Age. When visual light resumed—that milestone in time which today is being approached in "lookback time" by the Hubble project, to be followed by its more powerful siblings—voilà! The stars shone! Exactly how this new development unfolded is the enigma of the Dark Age, and it has in recent decades received enormous attention from astronomers and astrophysicists.

B. Gravity and Expansion: May We Tango?

In 1992, the *Explorer* satellite detected slight temperature ripples, irregularities in the cosmic background radiation of the newly atomic gaseous fabric, minute wiggles or clumpings both stretched by cosmic expansion and compacted by emerging gravity, a fructuous tension pivotal to all subsequent development. Some scientists suggest that the rate of expansion did and continues to accelerate, so as to offset gravity's impetus toward runaway collapse. In any event, it is thought that even before the onset of the Dark Age, gravity had already gained a tenuous foothold in these tiny irregularities in the otherwise smooth and expanding atomic fluid.

These footholds once gained, gravity quickly emerged as a formidable self-feeder, straining forward in its runaway impetus. Thus additional gaseous atoms were drawn into the primordial clumps, resultant increased gravity attracted yet more, and the growing mass of the aggregate body generating both increasing density and temperature, especially in the core. Gravity was a greedy well into which emerging aggregates were plummeting with the only check on the collapse of everything possessing mass being the equally relentless expansion of the nascent uni-verse.

In short, the dance—violent in a graceful sort of way—was between an expansion, in which everything was moving farther away from everything else, and gravity, with impetus toward attraction, compaction, and collapse. This dance was sculpting form out of formlessness, creation out of chaos, and crafting the engine on which would depend all that was to follow.

C. We Are Star-Stuff, Said the Astronomer

Sometime quite early in the Dark Age, a fateful tipping point was reached. The dynamic toward gravity-triggered compaction of these increasingly massive aggregates resulted in nuclear fusion at their cores, the conversion of hydrogen primarily into helium, with a tiny portion of matter transformed into energy. This threshold marks the beginning of the "main sequence phase" common to all true stars. The uni-verse had gone nuclear: hence shining stars!

Even as billions of yet-newer stars were birthed via similar gestation, the expansion/gravity dance, remaining in equipoise, was generating additional layers of organization and consolidating the vast portion of them into galaxies and a wide variety of galactic collectives. One might think of so many snowflake-like stars mysteriously appearing in a ripe moment when "meteorological" conditions were optimal, but then, unlike falling snow, astonishingly proceeding into innumerable systems called constellations, galaxies, and families of the same.

Most critical among first-generation stars spawned early in the Dark Age were gaseous massives, up to a thousand masses of our Sol, whose gravity-driven density triggered runaway fusion—"red supergiants" with lifetimes hot, luminous, violent, and short. These massives' crossing of the thermonuclear boundary served to expand the elemental menu, so that when they invariably immolated in spectacular explosions called "supernovae," with brief brightness billions of times that of our Sun, they disgorged this richness, including oxygen and carbon, back into the cosmic food chain for reconsumption. We know of no red supergiants of that first generation which have survived in their pre-supernova form.

In contrast, the destiny of stars closer in mass to that of our own Sun—the vast majority of which still exist today—is for their nuclear furnaces to consume all of their hydrogen after which their residual cores become dense and hot "white dwarfs." They then uneventfully drift toward that good night of entropy. This is the so-called "main sequence" of stars. Finally, there are "stars" with less than 8 percent of solar mass lacking the compaction density to achieve thermonuclear fusion. These are, in effect, orphan planets lacking a stellar parent.

So the nursery of raw materials from which could emerge the requisite building blocks for a hospitable environment such as Earth, the phenomenon of life, and finally a plentitudinous place and people called Tylerton about 13.7 billion years after the Flaring Forth, was the red supergiant of the primordial Dark Age. The multiplication of heavier elements after all hydrogen had been fused into helium, and then the supernova's violent disgorging of these enriched innards into the uni-verse's stellar foodchain, both took place in the relatively brief life and death of these massives. The elementally novel debris might then show up in a nebula where new stars, second generation or third or more, were incubated with thermonuclear fusion, throwing off ever-heavier elements. In fact, it is thought that the entire atomic chart was generated in and by stars of one generation or another.

As Carl Sagan stated pithily: we humans are "star stuff pondering the stars." We are all of the recyclings of the fire. It is estimated that eight or nine billion years of the above sequence, played out amid the tension between expansion and gravity, toward manifoldness and ever-richer variety, passed during which the elemental prerequisites for what would follow were put in place. On the issue of elemental differentiation alone, the generating of a biosphere such as is Tylerton and its environs, one teeming with life, would have been impossible apart from that lengthy period of preparation.

D. Here Comes the Sun

One collection of stellar aggregates, dating back nearly to the end of the Dark Age and unimaginatively dubbed simply "Local Group," is made up of about thirty galaxies including both Andromeda and the Milky Way, the galaxy which is our solar system's home. Our own galaxy, one of perhaps one hundred and thirty billion in the uni-verse, contains about four hundred billion stars similar to our own Sun. Measuring about one hundred thousand light years in diameter and twenty thousand light years at the hub, our spiral-shaped galaxy has curved arms that function as nurseries for star-birthing and greater elemental differentiation. By contrast, the hub and its enveloping halo are the retirement community for aging stars. In addition to moving as a gravity-bound unit through space, our galactic disk rotates once every 220 million years.

The system centered in our own star, Sun, together with her planetary progeny, is about two-thirds of the way out toward the edge of the disk, perhaps thirty thou-sand light years from the galactic nucleus. The view of the disk from Earth, as a river of light across the night sky, grows out of our edge-on perspective from *inside* that disk; we see our galaxy from the perspective of embedded constituents. The greatest concentration of stars in that river, the spiral's hub that is largely obscured by cosmic dust, is in the direction of the constellation Sagittarius.

The presence of relatively high amounts of heavier elements in the solar system emerging about five billion years ago indicates that its origin lies in the supernova explosion of perhaps a third-generation star. Much of the resulting debris was gradu-ally swept up into a nebula (cloud) that in time began rotating and became compacted within the complex dynamics of the parent galaxy. The emerging aggregate formed an "accretion disk," with its hub being our proto-Sun. In time, the accelerating rota-tion's effect on the density, and therefore heat within the hub, thrust that hub over the thermonuclear threshold and it became a star, in most respects unexceptional apart from its proximity to us today.

The proto-Sun's accretion disk simultaneously underwent individuation into at least eight planets and innumerable lesser orbiting objects. While accounting for less than .15 percent of the solar system's mass, remnants of Sun's disk nevertheless con-stituted a rich elemental cocktail to this day unknown elsewhere in the cosmos. This richness is particularly evident in the emerging "terrestrial planets" of smaller orbits, leaner atmospheres, and higher density that we call Mercury, Venus, Earth, and Mars. Not unlike the process that took place in the solar system itself, the sorting by density occurred—heavier metals to the core, lighter toward the surface, and even lighter gases to the atmosphere. Each planet, unique in size and distance from Sun, unfolded toward the state we know today.

The gravitational forces of the planets, particularly the much larger and gaseous Jupiter and Saturn, also swept their respective vicinities of most undedicated debris, resulting in further elemental enrichment and enhanced mass. Most of Sun's planets either emerged from the accretion process with satellites in tow or adopted orphans crashing in from without the solar pale; the system's known satellite family exceeds ninety. Some system debris from its earliest stages remains uncommitted: asteroids made of rocks and minerals between the orbits of Mars and Jupiter (the asteroid belt) and beyond Neptune (the Kuiper belt), and comets made of cosmic dust and ice originating both within and outside the system. Mercury as well as Earth's satellite, Moon, evidences to this day much bombardment by this debris in the system's early history. The solar system is thought to have attained its macro configuration much as we know it about four billion years ago, or nearly ten billion years after the Flaring Forth.

At this point, Tylerton was not a gleam in anyone's eye. Establishing Sun as energy source and Earth as a platform for land, water, air, and life were the first steps. The site for the musical production was readied, awaiting the carpenters, set designers, instruments, and players.

2. The Geological Place

A. The Anatomy of the Planet

Tylerton's planetary home, Earth, that was emerging from individuation within the solar system's accretion disk was and remains unique, both in its body and its atmosphere. In onion-like layers, Earth possesses a core of two heavy metals, iron and nickel (and thus a planetary density 7.9 times that of far-larger but gaseous Saturn), the inner portion of which is solid due to extreme pressure, the outer molten. Surrounding this two-part core is a mantle of dense rock.

Outside this mantle is the part of the planet with which we are most familiar: Earth's miles-thin crust of less-dense volcanic rock of two types: oceanic (primarily basalt covered with sediment) and continental (primarily granitic covered with sediment). The oceanic crust, in addition to being roughly 15 percent more dense than the continental, averages only a quarter of the thickness. The result is that the oceanic crust rests lower topographically, the continental being higher and more likely to rise even farther into mountains in response to subterranean events. Liquid water generally pools in the lower oceanic rock areas, its weight further compressing the crust beneath it.

Above Earth's crust lies the atmosphere, like the other geological layers retained by gravity. With the proliferation in time of flora and the crossing of the critical threshold of photosynthesis, oxygen became more plentiful. Accumulating in its atmosphere as both ozone (in tiny amounts that screen deadly ultraviolet radiation) and as oxygen gas necessary for life (nearly 21 percent), Earth's richness of oxygen to this day remains without known peer in either the solar system or the uni-verse beyond.

B. Whence Earth's Life-Giving Water?

The prevalence of water on Earth—71 percent of the surface—proved decisive for the unfolding of life, but the ratio of the two major sources remains uncertain. Much volcanic activity characterized the blue planet's early history, and we know that condensation of volcanic steam contributed to the surface water supply. Another source of Earth's water was imported via icy comets. About four billion years ago there was an extended bombardment by comets and asteroids, which brutally pocked the faces of Earth and its close neighbors, most visibly Mercury and Earth's Moon. (Mercury, lacking Earth's cosmetic brushes of water erosion and vegetation, today has three hundred thousand identifiable craters at least one kilometer in diameter!) Earth's strong gravity allowed it to hold much of its water, in contrast to its Moon, which did not.

Those comets originating beyond the planetary orbits constitute a kind of paleofreezer, which offers glimpses into the earliest stages of the formation of the solar system. Some, including meteoric material, have been shown to contain scores of amino acids, building blocks for life, which could have survived impact on Earth. Thus the multifaceted role of these frigid visitors in shaping life on this planet appears to have been very significant.

Abundant water existed on planet Earth very early, as evidenced by glacial erosion, water-deposited sedimentary rock, and the remains of primitive life, all presupposing it and dating back to early stages of the planet. All are ubiquitously present in the Chesapeake neighborhood within which Tylerton came to be.

There is evidence of numerous ice ages separated by warmer interglacial periods recurring across planet Earth's life span. While much of this oscillation predates the present continental configuration, the last ice age was relenting only ten thousand years ago. Ice ages are thought to result from rhythmic variations in Earth's attitude and rotation around its star, which itself varies in radiation output; the factors vary in cycles from centuries to one hundred thousand years, so the combinations are many. Each such age resulted in major polar and mountain glaciation, tying up water and thus reducing sea level, topographical erosion and deposit, and dramatic change to bio-habitat, with the opposite conditions characterizing the milder interglacial phases. The earliest arrival of humans in the North American continent and the mid-Atlantic region appears to be calibrated to dynamics of the last ice age.

C. The Crafting of Continents

There is varied evidence that Earth's present continent/ocean configuration emerged quite late in the unfolding of both the planet and its residents. By a quarter billion years ago, existing landmasses had converged, collided, and consolidated to form but one supercontinent, *Pangaea* (Greek for "all land"). In time, this continent divided into a northern component we know as Laurasia (Europe/Asia/North America) and a southern called Gondwana (Africa/South America/Australia/Antarctica).

This ponderous "continental drifting" has proceeded at centimeters per year ever since, driven by multimillion-year cycles of convection in Earth's mantle. North America's mid-Atlantic coastal concavity, including what would be the Chesapeake, retained the memory of its embrace with the convex of northwestern Africa. Further fragmentation and movement would continue until the present continental arrangement emerged around fifty million years ago.

According to tectonic theory, a dozen mammoth and numerous smaller miles-thick rocky slabs called "plates," each combining both oceanic and continental crust, are ever bumping and grinding about, colliding to raise mountains, separating to create low sea basins, and repositioning, all moving on a grudgingly plastic portion of the mantle. This endless dynamism produces continental drift, generating countless earthquakes, volcanoes, mountain ranges, and ocean basins and trenches, with most action at the plate boundaries. It is difficult to exaggerate the variety and violence of the saga of the mid-Atlantic region (and everywhere else) preceding the appearance of the first humans here.

D. The Bolide and the Bay

We cannot speak of a Chesapeake Bay we would recognize as such until perhaps three thousand years ago, about seven millennia after the most recent ice age was moving toward recession. In fact, if geologic time is viewed as a single twenty-four-hour day, Tylerton island and its Chesapeake environs would not have been recognizable until an eyeblink before midnight. That is, three thousand years ago, as compared to the 4.5 billion-year age of Earth, is equivalent to 0.05 second before midnight (23:59:59.95)!

But a key event that helped to form the Bay's environs occurred long before (around 23:59:49). Only recently have we stumbled upon evidence of it dating to thirty-five million years ago. The context of this event was an interglacial phase during which the ice packs retreated far to the north, melting to raise sea level much higher than at present, with the ocean covering the entire sedimentary continental shelf to the Piedmont or Fall Line. This line remains as a gracefully curved ridge of volcanic granitic rock passing just west of Wilmington, Baltimore, Washington, and Richmond, the approximate route of I-95 today. The Tylerton location on the continental shelf at the time of this event would thus have been about eighty miles into the Atlantic and under several hundred feet of saltwater.

Into this offshore environment about thirty-five million years ago in the late Eocene Epoch, a bolide—a comet or more probably an asteroid—plummeted, centering forty-five miles due south of what would be Tylerton. First detected only in 1983, and its study still in infancy, the Chesapeake Bay Impact Crater (C.B.I.C.), its outer rim fifty-five miles in diameter, its depth about a mile but with fractured granite continental basement as much as four miles below that, was made by an extraterrestrial body up to several miles in diameter traveling at perhaps thirty thousand miles per hour. This impact, like that in the Yucatan thirty million years earlier, possible cause of the extinction of dinosaurs and many other species, had consequences that are difficult to imagine. Billions of tons of water, like the bolide itself, vaporized; firestorms, earthquakes, and tsunamis; voluminous debris blasted into the atmosphere; meteorological change; and the extermination of all nearby flora and fauna.

The longer-term geological consequences were similarly vast. Although the crater, twice the size of Rhode Island and partially filled with impact debris, would subsequently be hidden by hundreds of feet of soft sediment deposited by the ebb and flow of ice ages, its footprint would remain a topographical depression prone to earthquakes, subsidence, and scrambled rock strata as deep as five miles. (I would ponder this instability during the minor earthquake and innumerable tremors we experienced during the decade.) Formerly enigmatic salty groundwater in shallow coastal plain wells is now thought to be another long-term consequence of the impact. Geologists have great interest in the site for several reasons: it is the largest crater in the United States, sixth-largest known on the planet; both the impacted sediment rock and underlying bedrock tell tales; the continental shelf location, while "wet," is accessible; and the crater is both young and relatively intact.

In subsequent epochs, the coastline oscillation between the Piedmont and the edge of the continental shelf, each about eighty-five miles from the north/south line between Tylerton and the impact crater epicenter, would have repeatedly crossed that axis, each time depositing sediment as sea level indexed the ebb and flow of glaciation. As each ice age began to wane, growing amounts of meltwater from retreating ice packs, bearing debris from the continent's interior, would have swollen existing river beds, further deepening their courses through relatively soft sediment and building up the surrounding alluvial valleys before emptying into the ocean at the continental shelf.

In time, the glacial melting would have resulted in rising sea level and the drowning of the shelf as the coastline made its way back toward the Piedmont. The process was reversed as each new ice age loomed. Each such cycle further cosmeticized the impact's blemish with additional sediment. Incidentally, we can surmise that with 71 percent of Earth's surface covered with water, there remain many undetected crater sites yet to be added to the confirmed global list of around 175 (and counting).

The question about the relationship between the bolide's impact and the formation of the Bay is intriguing. There is no consensus for any simple answer, in part because the crater is nearly twelve thousand times older than the Bay as we know it. While by the end of the last ice age (ten thousand years ago) hundreds of feet of sediment covered all evidences of the crater and its debris field, the impact's shattering and scrambling of strata far below caused the area to remain unstable and subject to subsidence—in short, a geological sinkhole.

This instability has almost certainly contributed to the shaping of the Bay in several ways. First, there is evidence that while the Susquehanna channel's left turn toward the ocean has migrated from north to south across the last half million years, the corner has always been in the vicinity of the crater rim. Second, the east-southeast direction of what we know as the James and the York turns, in each case, to the northeast at the crater rim before emptying into the Susquehanna. Third, the crater depression would have been where rising global sea level would first have begun to flood the alluvial valley. Although Tylerton island is twenty-five miles outside the crater's rim, it is well within the parameters of the broader impact of this awesome event thirty-five million years ago.

One window into this ebb-and-flow process midway between the crater event and the present is provided by the Calvert Cliffs, thirty-five miles northwest of Tylerton, on the Bay's western shore. For nearly thirty miles, rising more than a hundred feet against the flat topography of the Bay's waistline, these cliffs are the eroded remains of heavy sediments deposited on the continental shelf about seventeen million years ago. Interestingly, climate, sea level, coastline location, and behavior of the proto-Susquehanna passing just to the east of the cliffs then were quite similar to conditions at the time of the bolide impact eighteen million years earlier.

Calvert Cliffs, thought to have been a marine calving ground at a time of much higher sea level, contains the fossils of about six hundred species. These include rays, porpoises, sea cows, whales, crocodiles, turtles, sharks, and mollusks, in addition to a range of primitive mammals including mastodons, wooly rhinos, and camels. It is a vivid glimpse into one pole in the sea level oscillation. Several Tylerton watermen have collections of Calvert Cliffs shark teeth and other fossils. The geological drama continues as the cliffs are eroded by both weather and the sea, daily exposing new fossils.

E. The Bay Basin as Child of Its Parent River

Sea level as recently as eighteen thousand years ago, the height of the most recent ice age, may have been 325 feet lower than today, far *below* the continental shelf. At that time the southern reach of the Laurentide Ice Sheet, pushing before it rocky debris called moraines, extended near to what is now the northern end of the Bay. The relatively rapid receding of the glacier during subsequent millennia caused global sea level to rise toward present levels. The width and depth of the now-drowned Susquehanna channel still witness to the size and fury of this meltwater torrent, estimated by some to have been equivalent in volume to the Mississippi today. Inexorably flooded were first the shelf beyond our present coastline, and then valleys formed by rivers like the Susquehanna and Delaware.

The Chesapeake valley would become and remain a drowned river system, modestly covering evidence of its remarkable geological journey. The tops of a north/south spine of low hills just east of the axis of the central Bay have remained barely above sea level as an archipelago, including the marshy islets that comprise Smith Island. The lower elevations of the alluvial valley formed by the extraordinary network of river gorges draining the midsection of the continent's east coast following ice age after ice age were again drowned, with the result being an estuary. The river channels they generated in sediment they deposited, repeatedly deepened and enlarged by meltwater on the waning slopes of past ice ages, are all present today just under the surface of the Bay.

On many occasions I have been reminded of those submerged channels and how they came to be: while looking west from our balcony at the tall ships sailing from Norfolk to Baltimore or at a gaily lighted Baltimore cruise boat headed south for clement Caribbean climes; or while crossing east over the rougher water of "Puppy Hole," the locals' name for the eighty-five-foot deep confluence of the drowned rivers Nanticoke, Wicomico, Manokin, and Annemessex in Tangier Sound. The violent and oscillating geological story of the Bay's coming of age is everywhere just below the surface.

3. The Estuarial Place

But what is so significant about a drowned river system artfully creasing the floor of a valley that it had previously birthed? This Bay is inimitably what it is because it is an estuary, a term for a partially enclosed body where saltwater from the ocean encounters freshwater from rivers and the two mix incrementally to produce a salinity gradient. This Bay's elongated configuration—with the Atlantic Ocean entering at the bottom, and the dominant Susquehanna at the top, and with numerous additional freshwater lateral streams flowing in from east and particularly west—might be likened to a horizontal ladder.

A. This Estuary's Amazing Statistics

The Chesapeake, largest of 130 estuaries in the United States, while less than two hundred miles long, includes an astonishing 11,600 miles of crenulated shoreline if the tidewater portion of its tributaries is included. Even the Bay's shoreline figure with all tributaries excluded—four thousand miles—is well over twice that of the entire West Coast of the contiguous United States!

The Bay is about thirty miles wide at the broadest point several miles below Tylerton, and perhaps four miles at the Chesapeake Bay Bridge connecting Annapolis and Kent Island. It averages slightly more than twenty feet in depth, with the deepest point off Kent Island being 175 feet. Its watershed of more than sixty-four thousand square miles—ranging from the source of the James on the western slope of the Shenandoah Valley in southwestern Virginia up to Lake Otsego at Cooperstown, New York, also including portions of Delaware, Maryland, Pennsylvania, West Virginia, and District of Columbia—is the largest on the east coast. Although the Bay has more than 150 direct or indirect tributaries, fully half of the fresh water flows from the mighty Susquehanna, the birth parent of the entire configuration.

Were global sea level thirty feet higher—but a small fraction of what it has been between numerous ice ages past—the major portion of the Delmarva Peninsula would be covered, the estuary's requisite enclosure would not exist, and its delicate features would not be here discussed. Nor would this book be written. On the other hand, were the sea level only fifteen feet lower—only 5 percent of the drop during the last ice age—more than 75 percent of the present Bay would be dry land, and few of us would have heard of the estuarial stump remaining.

The cosmos is strewn with windows, the closing of any one of which could have shut down the entire show as we know it. It is not otherwise here on Tylerton, setting

4.5 feet or less above sea level, where in cosmological time the estuarine window has opened for a twinkling of the eye of less than 0.02 second, imminently to close again. Not unlike those that caused the galaxies to form, the solar system to individuate, and life itself to begin, Tylerton's geological story includes a delicately and elegantly calibrated tension involving a host of variables, the intertwined temperature and sea level most obviously.

An estuary is a salinity ladder or gradient, ranging from the oceanic salt concentration of thirty-five parts per thousand (ppt) at the interface with the Atlantic (Cape Henry and Cape Charles, on Tylerton, a.k.a. "Hank and Chuck") to freshwater at the Bay's northern end, approaching zero ppt. One of the reasons an estuary is so teeming with life—H. L. Mencken called the Bay's wetlands a "giant protein factory"—is that each rung or zone, in shallow water energized by the sun and in proximity to abundant biospheric nourishment delivered by the mechanics of tide, provides the optimal salinity/temperature environment for a narrow slice of aquatic flora and fauna. In short, the Bay consists of a succession of rare bio-zones, the sum total of which is unmatched on the continent. While the estuarine ladder was not central to the initial seventeenth-century Smith Island economy of tilling the land, it most certainly has made possible the island's second economic chapter, the mid-nineteenth century shift to harvesting of the sea, a notable *regression* from agriculture to a form of hunting/gathering.

B. What Tweaks the Salinity Gradient?

The estuarial plot thickens, however. Because of a delicious deck of variables, the mixing of the salt and fresh waters in the Bay is not uniform. First, tide enters the Chesapeake every twelve hours and twenty-five minutes, increasing salinity everywhere within the reach of its surge. A high tide does this more, a lower one less.

Second, tides are strongest every two weeks when the Moon is new or full and, being thus aligned with the Sun, exerts the strongest gravitational force. These are "spring" tides, so-called because they appear to "spring forth"; in between are the low or "neap" tides.

Third, a strong easterly wind blows more water into the Bay's mouth, elevating salinity, tide levels, and the vigor of mixing; a westerly wind, on the other hand, reduces seawater entering the Bay and thus its salinity.

Fourth, there are seasonal variations in freshwater entering the Bay by virtue of common precipitation, storms including hurricanes, and, in particular, melting snow flowing down the rivers. Thus the entire Bay has a lower salinity after heavy winter snowfalls in Pennsylvania are followed by freshets descending the Susquehanna than, for example, in a heat wave drought in August when surface evaporation is high.

Fifth, each tidewater tributary to the Bay has its own micro-salinity span, replicating the Bay's dynamics as well as altering both its mixing patterns and overall salinity.

Sixth, saltwater is slightly more dense than fresh, so that rather than mixing uniformly, heavier ocean water tends to slide northward beneath a surface layer of freshwater flowing south. Thus, the dynamic of this estuary's complex salinity includes both horizontal gradients and vertical strata.

And seventh, there is the Coriolis effect, whereby Earth's rotation causes objects in its Northern Hemisphere that are moving toward or away from the equator to be deflected to the right. Thus, saltwater moving northward up the Bay veers right toward the Eastern Shore, and freshwater moving southward drifts to the right or western shore. Where the waters are in layers, the more dense saltwater is slightly more affected by this dynamic than the fresh. The result is that the salinity on the Eastern Shore is consistently higher than at a point of equal latitude on the western side. This east/west differential below Smith Island is compounded by the fresh influx from the major rivers Potomac, Rappahannock, York, and James, all entering from the west, producing a counterclockwise motion so that fresh water disproportionately exits the Bay near Cape Henry on the western shore, saltwater enters near Cape Charles on the Eastern Shore.

The variance within each of the above seven factors complicates enormously the manner in which salty and fresh water mix in the Bay, and hence the salinity at a certain location at a certain time. And why does this matter for Tylerton? Its economic mother lode over the last century has increasingly been the blue crab, a critter which thrives within an optimal salinity window offered only by an estuary. Salinity is a major reason why the environs of Smith Island have been the "sweet spot" for blue crabs, particularly soft shells, on the Atlantic coast.

The salinity around Smith has been roughly estimated at 15–18 ppt—the same as human tears, someone has opined, but that is an average built on dramatically different combinations of the above variables. Needless to say, the critters thriving on their ideal salinity window need to move smartly if, indeed, mobility is available to them. It is crabs and finfish who thus "play" the estuary's salinity gradient. While sedentary critters such as clams and oysters have nutrients brought to them by the oscillating tide, they cannot alter their salinity environment and often suffer as a result.

C. Bludgeoning the Bay

That the Chesapeake is an estuary, replete with a host of delicate, nuanced, and fragile variables optimally in equilibrium, is a major reason why it is so vulnerable to destabilization. It is far too finely tuned an instrument to be managed with a hammer!

The list of present threats to this equipoise is long and troubling. One might begin by noting that the Bay's landmass container has lost nearly half of its 95 percent forestation since European settlers first arrived.

The near denudation of Smith Island—in the seventeenth century called "Isle of Broken Woodlands" by colony leaders in St. Mary's City—is much more the result of humans than encroaching salinity. Forests moderate flooding through absorption and evaporation, buffer erosion through their clutching root systems, and, particularly in riparian areas, help to trap and retain pollutants.

The deforestation of the Bay's perimeters has been largely the price of development, as the expansive coastline including the tidewater tributaries has enabled a major part of the watershed's inhabitants and many industries to be located near water. The Bay's watershed population increased 34 percent between the 1970 and 2000 censuses, totaling about seventeen million at the time of this writing and increasing at about one hundred thousand persons a year. During this thirty-year interval, the average size of household decreased while lot size and use of lawn fertilizer increased; these changes have only compounded the pressure on this ecosystem which, while adaptable and indeed resilient, is not immune to destabilization.

But the list of anthropogenic challenges to this estuary goes on and on:

- High runoff of nutrients containing nitrogen, much of it originating from farming operations in Pennsylvania, triggers algae bloom that clouds the water, reduces photosynthesis, and undermines submersed aquatic vegetation that provides cover and food for critters. In recent decades, this has resulted in "dead zones" where few flora or fauna are found.
- Delmarva's economic dependency on the poultry industry has made both the private and public sectors reluctant to make hard decisions that could reduce runoff from manure.
- The relatively modest width and, in particular, depth of the estuary mean a lower volume of water, which translates into dissolved oxygen deficiency (especially in summer), higher pollutant ratios, and greater vulnerability to destabilization by hurricanes.
- While gains have been made in the legal curtailment of wetlands destruction by developers, these are often offset by illegal or unregulated projects. In addition, sea level rise predictions threaten thousands of acres of wetlands in the next several decades.

- Despite improvement in recent decades in the sewage treatment plants of larger cities, many smaller communities and manufacturing plants, together with air pollution, continue to add to the nitrogen content of the Bay.

- The Bay's biosphere remains scarred by the rapacious harvest of oysters more than a century ago and, to a lesser extent, of waterfowl. Neither has returned to more than token fractions of former levels.

- And infestation by the parasites Dermo and MX continues to plague efforts to bring back *Crassostrea virginica*, the American oyster.

Although the coalescing of will in the 1970s to save the Bay resulted in significant strides regarding waste dumping by recreational boats, the metallic residue of heavy industry in Baltimore's harbor and channel, and treatment of waste in some of the major cities, during the subsequent thirty years science has shown that the wound has yet additional causes and is more serious than anyone had thought.

D. The Chesapeake as Endangered Species

Since we opened the Inn in 1997, the criteria for the estuary's health have expanded even as the good fight has been waged, and it is currently unclear whether overall progress is being made. Absolutely every aspect of life on Smith Island depends on at least the partial success of the campaign to save the Bay. While the Chesapeake is a marvelous little pocket sea, an inimitable, prolific, and gorgeous estuarine hybrid neither fish nor fowl, it is now, alas, *itself* a one-of-a-kind endangered species. And if this one dies, there will be no bringing it back, for this particular critter has but one habitat.

4. The Biospherical Place

The tale comprising the first three chapters of Part II—the cosmological, geological, and estuarial emergence of the place that is Tylerton—contains the astonishing and the sublime. The unfolding of this place is both a richly orchestrated symphonic work and a suspenseful drama, seemingly punctuated by episodic cosmic crapshoots.

But arguably, all of this pales before the showcase of the Bay and its sphere of *life* located where the lithosphere, hydrosphere, and atmosphere intersect. On the blue planet sparkling uniquely with teeming life, the Chesapeake is one of the brightest jewels. For example, the prodigious output of estuarine flora in a salt marsh wetland is up to fifteen tons of organic material per acre per year, outstripping by multiples most other ecosystems. Nearly half of this is circulated by the tide.

Much the same can be said of the fauna, most memorably in the astonishing accounts of the past—whether Capt'n John Smith's 1608 notation of fish so plentiful that his crew members attempted (unsuccessfully) to catch them with frying pans; the bounty of oysters in the late nineteenth century such that one could walk across Crisfield's harbor on the decks of her thousand working schooners and skipjacks without getting damp; or early twentieth-century descriptions of migratory waterfowl darkening the noon sky or rafting in flotillas measured in miles. If life is the rolling crest of the unfolding of the cosmos, then this Bay arguably is the dance, the gala, the exuberant bacchanalia, the Dionysian orgy.

This said, an irony immediately presents: because of the strictures presented by salinity in particular, the number of species in a particular zone of the Bay, whether flora or fauna, is relatively few. Stated otherwise, those species able to tolerate the heat of a particular gradient of the Bay's kitchen often have few competitors, and thus prosper.

A. Tylerton's Flora

The Riparian Gradient Before the Inn

My initial, and perhaps richest, botanical experience on Tylerton was to learn about the flora stairway rising out of Tyler's Crick twenty-five feet in front of the Inn. At the bottom of this gradient, below mean low tide, was the submersed aquatic vegetation (SAV): widgeon grass and eelgrass. Below mean high tide grew first the tall saltmarsh cordgrass (*Spartina alterniflora*) and, slightly higher, its cousin the saltmeadow hay (*Spartina patens*).

Before the Army Corps constructed a bulkhead in 2001–2002 from the back harbor to Drum Point with riprap continuing all the way to Merlin Gut, the ten-to-fifteen-foot margin between the lane that runs before the Inn and the Bay water had been covered with the *alterniflora,* bathed twice daily by the tides. Sharryl and I were delighted that the engineered permeability of the bulkhead allowed this beautiful stand to reestablish itself in the low swale after project completion. (I might add that I threatened civil disobedience in the final August of our decade by standing in front of a Somerset County tractor mower which had already cut down part of our swale.)

Moving farther up the bank, but still below the spring tide at full or new moon, were the sea lavender and edible glassvort, and then black needlerush. And finally, above the spring tide line, I learned to identify the wax myrtle, marsh elder, seaside goldenrod, and, at the top of the incline at about two feet elevation, the woody groundsel tree, a bush which can exceed ten feet in height. Each October I would look with pleasure across the way at the groundsels' lines of filmy white blossoms accenting each copse of trees.

In our opening season, Sharryl and I had brought in scores of marsh hibiscus from a nursery specializing in saline-tolerant plants, only to see nearly all of them succumb to that very salt. The coming of the bulkhead provided the hibiscus with just the margin they needed, and they have since been glorious!

The Vegetation Behind the Inn

Along our lot's nearly 135 feet of frontage on the Bay, none of it higher than two feet above sea level, the one additional species was the common reed (*Phragmites australis*). This exotic, invasive, and tenacious stowaway is thought to have arrived from the Orient. In the swale I eradicated it on a very personal basis, one plant at a time, in favor of the *alterniflora*, but behind the lane it swept all before it, rising to a height above ten feet in places, nearly eliminating all competition but the groundsel.

The previous owners had planted a number of trees in this front part of our lot, but all had succumbed to the salt several years after we opened. With the exception of the marsh hibiscus, every plant that Sharryl lovingly nurtured throughout our decade—including perennials such as crepe myrtle, dogwood, clematis, honeysuckle, trumpet vine, and wisteria—required containers elevated above the tide.

Although much of the rear portion of our lot, extending back 425 feet from the water, was also nearly homogeneous *Phragmites* sprinkled with groundsel, a very different pattern had unfolded along our northern boundary, the village side. Some decades before, the spoils from Army Corps dredging of Smith Island's navigational channels had been deposited there. Over the years, the salinity had been leached from the material as it settled to an elevation but one foot higher than before, just enough to allow the trees seeded by birds a slight advantage over the salt. Today a half dozen mature loblolly pines (up to thirty feet) are joined by several dozen smaller red cedars interspersed with groundsel and, alas, poison ivy. Undoubtedly aided now by the bulkhead, all of these dominate that margin of the tree-challenged environs, a testimonial to the delicacy of vegetative gradients in the salt marsh. The area behind our lot and extending to the Back Cove is of slightly lower elevation, on the other hand, and is nearly homogenous with the two species of *Spartina*.

The Greening Beyond

The nearby land masses, both a quarter mile away across Tyler's Crick to the west and perhaps a half mile away into Virginia to the south, as well as the other two directions, are nearly uninterrupted *Spartina alterniflora*, the classic staple of near–sea level wetlands so critical to the Bay's health. The only other vegetation which snags the eye in any of the four directions are scattered hammocks, remnants of either pre–twentieth-century settlements whose large trees had the rootage to survive rising sea level or more recent dredge spoil. The combination of 1933's dike-ravaging hurricane, rising sea level, and growing pressure from labor-intensive crabbing have eliminated virtually all gardening on Tylerton at present. Guests, however, are able to see and sometimes savor fruit from small trees along the village lanes—apple, pear, cherry, pomegranate, and fig. Some locals still go after the tender wild asparagus ("goin' spárgusin'") on ditch banks in spring.

And then there was the spooky, botanically haunting incident that I remember from a stellar night in late August 2000. Sharryl and I were returning to Tylerton from Crisfield after attending a Miss Crustacean contest—yes, indeed!—with the parents of a Tylerton contestant. The prop action of our workboat agitated what was most likely blooming phytoplankton (algae) to produce a dazzling display of bioluminescence all the way across the dark Tangier Sound. I had occasionally seen this phenomenon in the crests of waves coming at the Inn on moonless nights, but this looked like thousands of buckets of light flowing out from beneath the stern of the speeding boat. The sight was luminous, but I, planted at the stern, kept thinking *numinous* was an apt descriptor as well.

Of my five senses, it is the olfactory that first arrives home as I mount the Bay Bridge near Annapolis, driving eastward. Not to be confused with the pure saltiness on the nearby Atlantic coast, this scent melds salinity with a vague bio-detritus, a mustiness born of generations and tons of vegetation breaking down in the fructive alchemy of the wetland's mud. Here on Tylerton, an "upland" islet surrounded by the 90 percent of Smith Island that is salt marsh, which is in turn encompassed by the Bay—here the houses smell of marsh, the lanes smell of it, it rolls in as I enter my balconied perch to survey the new dawn. The scent assures me that I am here and not elsewhere. The major criterion making possible this scent, of course, is biodegradability, the death of flora, but I love the scent nevertheless. I fully expect it to exercise stowaway privileges with me when I move away. That said, I am resigned that my olfactory life will then become quite tame.

B. Tylerton's Fauna

Unlike the birds and aquatic creatures, Tylerton's terrestial fauna, like the flora saline-tolerant, and prolific, are few of species. Invertebrates include the marsh mosquito, deerfly, and greenhead fly; the "marsh" preceding each of their names a reminder of widespread adaptation to both the isle's salinity and skewed biosphere. Marsh periwinkles (snails) can form a line across the *Spartina* that they ride up and down in unison with the tide; surprised fiddler crabs by the teeming scores can sometimes be glimpsed briefly. The most illustrious crustacean, of course, is the blue crab (*Callinectes sapidus*, or "beautiful swimmer") upon which nearly all of Tylerton's present economy rests. The terrapin is present, as are a few snake species (black, water, garter) representing the reptilians, but there are simply no amphibians to be tormented in this brackish inferno.

Fauna with Two

Birds are an entirely different matter, and a listing of those identified by innkeepers and guests from the Inn porch or Green House tucked back among the loblollies is an index of their bounty. Gulls, whether herring, laughing, or the resident bully great black-backed, perch on piles just beyond the dock nearly year-round. They serve as the Inn's weather vanes, always pointing into the wind. Both Forster's and Caspian terns, shrill in voice, angular in profile, and forked of tail, can be seen in the summer, as well as the occasional oystercatcher. The appearance nearly year-round of herons—whether the gun-metal little blue, the green, the black-crowned night, the yellow-crowned night, the tri-colored, or of course the majestic great blue—always constitutes an event, as does that of egrets, both great and snowy. The habitat of the brown pelican, earlier ravaged by DDT, was just brushing as far north as Smith when we began visiting in 1992; a decade later New Jersey guests reported them there and I would count as many as thirty-seven perching simultaneously in front of the Inn. Jessica Powers (188) wrote, "That God made birds is surely in His favor," a sentiment with which I and many of our guests concur.

During a winter season of this writing, we repeatedly had a dozen or so Canada geese feeding in the shallows just beyond our bulkhead with small numbers of ducks (mallard, black, or redhead) in addition to some brant geese mixed in. I never did see large numbers of duck-like waterfowl during this decade, with the small buffleheads the most numerous, but occasionally one could also pick out the merganser (red-breasted or hooded), green-winged teal, old-squaw, wigeon, canvasback, pintail, or lesser scaup, among others.

Phalanxes of tundra swans, occasionally sprinkled with mute swans later in the decade, would arrive in November near the remnant sandbar of Cheeseman Island just into Virginia, departing in early March. Big Alan Smith, consummate waterman and hunter for sixty of his seventy-two years, narrowly escaped injury as we began our last season when an offended mute swan—the more exotic, invasive, aggressive, large (forty pounds), and stunningly beautiful of the two species—flew in from rear starboard and barely missed him as it self-immolated into his speeding skiff.

Some of my most emotional biospheric experiences occurred while watching from my balconied perch as thousands of tundras, their layover ended, prepared to depart as the ides of March approached. Perhaps thirty-six hours of crescendoing hubbub, a prolonged consolidating and coiling ritual of ascent, and then, as if a string snapped, centrifugal force catapulting them out over the village and into the perilous journey north to the Bering Sea. While marveling at their courage and homing faculty, I have been seduced by their haunting calls emitted through impossibly extended necks. And I have repeatedly cried "Look!" to Sharryl, tears streaming down my face, as I was out standing in my wetlands bidding them farewell. Given the greviously wounded condition of our planet, swans, what they do and what they are, seem almost too good to be true.

There are other birds to be seen from the Inn porch: the ever-distraught and disheveled kingfisher, cautious bitterns, coarsely brazen fish crows, pigeons, the Ichabodian glossy ibis, and the double-crested cormorant, whose numbers swell in the autumn when one might see a hundred at a time flying feverishly from one place or another in long black lines. In addition, there are the barn (shanty) swallows, the insectivorous purple martin, the ruby-throated hummingbird, finches (house and gold), song sparrow, barred owl, and, infrequently, the northern cardinal. One accomplished birder guest left the house a list of fifty-four species identified in but a single weekend.

One can see at least four resident raptor species on or above Smith Island, all thriving in the aftermath of the DDT debacle. Sassafras Hammock, perhaps a half mile in front of the Inn, has a bald eagle pair whose massive nest I monitor in the winter via binoculars from my perch, and in the summer from my skiff. Guests guided through the Martin National Wildlife Refuge—the northeastern third of Smith

Island—have reported as many as forty osprey (or fish hawk) pairs; one osprey would often retrieve rockfish remains on the fly from the water in front of the porch after I had departed my filleting station on the Inn's dock. And the peregrine falcons re-introduced to the refuge in the 1990s are stealth assassins, taking care of themselves as well. Late in the decade, I began adding the turkey vulture, occasionally detected soaring high above Tylerton, to this raptor list.

Fauna in Blue

The region's pre-Columbian denizens called it the Chesapeake or "Great Shellfish Bay," and that is above all else what it has remained for those deriving livelihood from it. In the mid-nineteenth century, when the Smith Island economy shifted precipitously from agriculture to seafood, the lode to be mined was the American oyster (*Crassostrea virginica*). Crisfield, built metaphorically on its plentitude and literally on its shells, became the oyster capital of the world, and both the prosperity and population of Smith Island rose sharply as well. Pursued as if limitless in a raucous and unbridled environment, the oyster harvest represents the region's most egregious and rapacious abuse of nature. The boom crested in the 1880s, but was declining by the early twentieth century, a descent that continues into the present.

The blue crab (*Callinectes sapidus*) was waiting in the wings when oysterers began to need additional income. Across much of the twentieth century many watermen actually had two harvest seasons: crabs in the heat, oysters in the cold. They applied their ingenuity and imaginations as well as their backs to the task of catching the combative critters with the use of various devices and stratagems. Arguably the biggest breakthrough for Tylerton was the honing of the process whereby the crab, monitored in floats until molting and then transported quickly as soft shells to urban markets, could be sold for multiples of the price of a hard shell. Across the twentieth century, in times that were ebb and those that were flow, the principal distinctive of Tylerton crabbing was the scrapin', peelerin', and sheddin' of the labor-intensive soft shell regimen. When I first visited in 1992 I was told that fully half of the soft shells on the planet were shed within fifteen miles of Tylerton! Neither soft shelling nor crabbing in general ever made people rich as the oyster briefly had. But for a century crabbing, particularly soft shells, sustained a culture, leaving an indelible imprint upon its economy, work ethic, diet, lore, bouquet, and beauty contests.

Only a handful of Tylerton's men were still oystering during our decade. This was a graying cohort, with nostalgia seemingly the realm's principal remuneration. Clamming, involving several different species, was even farther into its anecdotage:

the last Smith Island waterman still on the water with his boat outfitted for drudgin' clams packed it in around the time that we opened the Inn.

The waters around Smith Island contain abundant aquatic critters *sans* shell. Sharryl and I began visiting the island shortly after the moratorium on harvesting the rockfish (a.k.a. striped bass) ended in the early 1990s, with the taking of the fish in subsequent years tightly regulated. The species' rebound since then has been slowed by Virginia's commercial harvesting of Menhaden, the Rock's principal food. Nevertheless, I remember an October evening at the confluence of three dredged channels by Tylerton's County Dock, where for a quarter hour as many as a dozen rockfish were noisily breaking the water each second.

We operated, involuntarily as it turned out, the Inn of Silent Music as a "Bed & Breakfast & Dinner," since there were no sit-down dinner options elsewhere in the village. After our initial season of serving primarily Atlantic croaker (hardhead), dinner at the Inn has featured rockfish up to every other evening, if the catch supported this (generally alternated with soft shell crab).

Red drum, oyster toadfish, blowfish, spotted sea trout, and the occasional bluefish are also taken in Tylerton's waters from time to time. The cownose rays can be plentiful in the summer, playing havoc with anglers' rigs, as are several species of nettles and jellyfish that threaten exposed skin of swimmer and waterman alike. A season with a meager crab harvest might find a waterman or two also harvesting blowfish, or perhaps seeking to ensnare American eel on their way to the Sargosso Sea.

In their peregrinations about the Bay, watermen report sightings of larger marine species as well: a pod of arcing bottlenose dolphins, an occasional sandbar shark, the odd seal in Tyler's Ditch near the village. Capt'n Larry Laird, who may have crossed Tangier Sound more than thirty thousand times in his nearly twenty-five years with the *Captain Jason II*, has seen more than most: numerous whales, particularly during a season in the nineties, and porpoises, on one occasion numbering as many as a hundred. When I mentioned the name "Chessie" he smiled mischievously, wanting me to know that while he knew that sea cows/manatee had visited the Bay, he didn't buy the Loch Ness monster stuff.

Fauna with Four

The only small number of surviving mammalian species on Smith Island is attributable to both the salinity strictures (directly and indirectly via flora) and the isle's isolation. There is the muskrat, still occasionally trapped for fur and liable to grace the table of a rural Delmarva church dinner. The invasive nutria, a serious erosion agent in nearby Blackwater National Wildlife Refuge, was occasionally trapped on Smith

Island in earlier decades but is not present now. From time to time, I have seen river otters cavorting on the bulkhead cap in front of the Inn or in the water just beyond; one spring during our decade a few were trapped for their fur. Common mice and rats also may be encountered, particularly during cold weather and/or high tides. Watermen see red fox from time to time—one reported he had trapped perhaps twenty-five across his life, but I have not sighted one. Despite parts of Smith Island being used to graze cattle from its initial European patent in 1665 until early in the twentieth century, the encroaching salinity appeared to make the environment increasingly inhospitable, even more so for horses.

Tylerton's fauna file also includes its famous cats. When Sharryl and I first arrived rumor had it that the cats—pets, intermediates, and ferals—outnumbered *Homo sapiens* three to one. That changed after a vigorous spaying/neutering project mid-decade in which Sharryl played a role. The domesticated dogs of Tylerton, mostly labs, Chesapeake retrievers, and miscellaneous charity projects, are quintessentially seen serving as bow ornaments on workboats or golf cart passengers being promenaded in the lanes by their handlers.

The absence of large wild mammals today in and around Tylerton calls for a historical comment. Near the end of the last ice age, the heavily forested Chesapeake watershed was inhabited by mammalian megafauna. Some are now extinct, such as the American mammoth and mastodon, as well as the giant beaver, musk ox, and short-faced bear. Caribou, bison, and elk were driven far to the west and north. Only the white-tailed deer, beaver, and black bear remain in the watershed today. Although I know of no megafauna remains found on Smith Island, the low sea level during the last ice age means that some of them certainly could have been in the vicinity. There is controversy as to whether the relatively rapid disappearance of the megafauna, perhaps within only five hundred years, should be attributed primarily to the prowess of recently arrived Clovis hunters, the pathogens of them or their dogs, shifts in climate, or all of the above.

C. Flora, Fauna, and Islands

Late in our decade I found myself musing about the huge role islands have played in making the case for a developmental understanding of life, both flora and fauna. Granted, this usually involved islands far more remote and isolated than my own—the likes of Madagascar, the East Indies' Moluccas, or the Galápagos, for example. Yet their extraordinary varieties of unique forms had been raising hard questions long before Charles Darwin (1809–1882) dropped his *The Origin of Species* on the world in 1859. The Crick was an appropriate location for me to ponder this contribution of places of the isle sort.

In conclusion to this biospheric section, I cite again the paradox of the Bay. On the one hand, the salinity spectrum means that somewhere in the Bay there are niches for a great variety of critters, with as many as 3,600 identified and named species of flora and fauna presently dwelling in the basin at least part of the year. At this macro-level, the Bay is thus a wild profusion, a lavish and extravagant display of plenitude very hard to match in any other part of the world. On the other hand, the number of species at a particular niche or rung of that salinity ladder tends to be few, even as their fruitfulness is prolific. This bio-showcase, called "Great Shellfish Bay" by its pre-Columbian denizens, has repeatedly reduced me to awe.

5. The Historical Place

The biases of our public education system might well result in most Americans correlating the history of human habitation in the Chesapeake basin with the founding of Jamestown in May of 1607. In reality, human artifacts discovered in the watershed have been dated from at least forty times the age of the Jamestown site.

A. The Amerindian Cultures

American Aborigines: The Conventional Wisdom

The question regarding the first humans living in the Americas has generated lively debate. The working hypothesis since about 1930 had been that the initial human migration to the Americas was of Asians from eastern Siberia into first North and then Central and South America as the last ice age was waning, perhaps 11,500 years ago. A relatively brief time window made such a passage both possible and datable—framed first by the disappearing Beringia land bridge (now drowned as the Bering Strait), and second by an emerging corridor to the south in the receding glacier just east of the Rocky Mountains.

The signature artifact of this influx is the distinctively elongated, fluted stone projectile point called "Clovis" after the New Mexico site where they were first discovered, a find subsequently repeated in many sites across much of our continent. Clovisoid peoples would have found their way fairly rapidly to the mid-Atlantic region, where their points have been found in various Chesapeake basin sites, including Smith Island.

The Probability of Pre-Clovis Peoples

But across the past twenty years, the Clovis hypothesis has increasingly been found wanting, this because of archaeological finds suggesting both earlier dates and greater variety among human remains and artifacts. Sites on both American continents have been dated via various means to thirty thousand years ago and possibly more. Furthermore, linguistic analysis as well as comparisons of skulls, artifacts, and general cultural practices have pointed toward much greater diversity among the peoples and cultures represented, itself an argument for earlier or multiple origins, or both. In just the last decade, DNA analysis has made major strides in the study and differentiation of human remains, and it promises to play a huge role in the future.

While nearly all archaeologists continue to hold that there was a major influx about 11,500 years ago represented by the term Clovis, the evidence increasingly supports the hypothesis that some humans were already here to greet them. Some argue that Beringia was crossed as much as twenty thousand years ago, with southward land movement stalled until the interglacial corridor opened much later. During this interim, smaller groups might have braved the exposed western continental shelf or the Pacific itself, leaving footprints on neither, thus bypassing the glacier.

Other scholars suspect that contributing to the settlement of the southern continent there was a pre-Clovis Polynesian influx, these also arriving via sea, followed much later by their movement into the northern continent following the receding of the glaciers. Attempts in the last decade to verify a non-Asian component in a multiple origins mix, including efforts to identify the Kennewick Man discovered in Washington State in 1996 as in some sense "European," have found less support. A component in the excitement of the last two decades has been growing conversation among professional archaeologists, paleoanthropologists, and keepers of the myths of living Amerindian tribes.

Peopling the Chesapeake Basin

Evidence of pre-Clovis peoples in the Chesapeake region has come from several sites: Cactus Hill on Virginia's Nottoway River, fifty miles west of Norfolk; the Barton Site in the Potomac floodplain near Cumberland, Maryland; and possibly the Paw Paw Cove sites on Tilghman Island, fifty miles north of Smith Island.

The Cactus Hill site is located but ten miles south of what is *now* the watershed of the James (and the Chesapeake). Beneath a Clovis stratum containing the distinctive points dating to eleven thousand years ago, a level as much as five or six thousand years older has been uncovered. It includes both butchering and hide-processing artifacts, together with flora remains. The earlier level thus dates from the plateauing rather than receding of the last ice age. An index of the current fluidity in the dating of human arrival in the Americas was the discovery in late 2004 of stone artifacts on the Topper Site along the Savannah River in South Carolina, said to go back as far as fifty thousand years.

Dating the first human residents in what is now the Chesapeake region to as far back as merely sixteen thousand years carries far-reaching implications. First, the last ice age was at its maximum extension to the south, well into Pennsylvania, and the warming temperatures triggering the rapid retreat of the ice cap, and an interglacial corridor, had not yet begun. With so much seawater tied up in the ice cap, the mid-Atlantic coastline would have been more than a hundred feet *below* the continental shelf. The river system draining the area, the trunk of which was the proto-Susquehanna, emptied over the shelf nearly one hundred miles east-southeast of what is now Norfolk.

Second, we must concede that nearly all archaeological traces of such early inhabitants on the floor of that fertile valley are forever lost, covered first from the north with sediment as the system drained the melting ice cap, and then from the south as the valley was subsequently drowned by the ocean. The same would be true of such early traces of human settlements on the continental shelf outside the Delmarva Peninsula. All of this heightens the urgency for more archaeological work on the remaining Chesapeake islands before they too are lost. Assuming that the Bay reached its present configuration only three thousand years ago, this means that only a small portion of Native American history before contact with Europeans was lived out on sites currently accessible.

Thus, when I want to ask these earliest of my kin in this place whether they loved the Bay as I do, I need to remember that for perhaps 85 percent of the period between their arrival and the present, the Bay simply did not exist as we know it.

The Clovis Period

Across the last century, archaeology has provided a sketch of the Clovis culture in what is now the Bay basin, dating back as early as 11,500 years ago. They were seasonally nomadic hunter/gatherers living in small groups, united by kinship. The necessity of mobility would have shaped their social structure, tools, weapons, and shelters. They depended extensively on hunted animals for both food and clothing, and may have employed fire as well as domesticated dogs in their hunting. There are some indications of the importing of materials and ideas from peoples outside the region. A number of the region's megafauna also became extinct during this period, a development to which the people may have at least contributed. The Clovis people were concentrated in river valleys for reasons of water, game, fishing, transport, and security. Human gravitation toward water, it seems, has been present from the outset.

The many thousands of projectile points found on Smith Island and its eroded shoulder shoals have included more than a few of the distinctive Clovis type. Alan Smith, Tylerton's patriarch of "proggers"—artifact-seekers who walk the shoreline in knee-boots with a walking stick after a storm—reports having found twenty-five to thirty Clovis points during his lifetime, some of these in his crab scrape. While such artifacts may have circulated via trade, possibly for long periods and distances if well-made, the sheer number on Smith constitutes a strong argument that Clovis folk were here at least ten thousand years ago, a time when what are now the islands were the tops of a range of hills running north to south in the alluvial valley on the fertile continental shelf.

The Archaic Period

The millennia between about ten thousand and three thousand years ago are called the Archaic period, an era of constant human adaptation to the emerging Bay as it was crafted by the various dynamics of the receding glacier. Climate grew warmer and forestation gradually shifted from pine and spruce, similar to a Canadian forest today, to oak and maple, with new food plants emerging. Both the flow rate and size of rivers draining the meltwater were growing. The early Archaic period (10,000–7,000 years ago) saw the area's inhabitants living in somewhat larger communities than earlier, and more closely tethered to specific locations, even while remaining seasonally nomadic. Notches appeared on now-smaller projectile points to affix them more firmly to shafts. Frances Dize alludes to projectile points and other artifacts in addition to oyster middens discovered in Smith Island Amerindian sites, the oldest of these dating to this Archaic period.

The middle Archaic period (to 5,000 years ago) introduced so-called "banner stones" used as counterweights on spears; increasingly specialized tools such as axes, adzes, and net-sinkers made from rocks are also found. The late Archaic period (to 3,000 years ago) reveals food storage pits and the first soapstone vessels as the yet-larger and less-mobile communities sought to address growing food needs. Garbage pits filled with animal bones, oyster shell middens, hearths, and other food-related artifacts also date from this period. The absence of surviving human remains throughout the Archaic period has limited archeological efforts to reconstruct how life was lived at that time.

The Woodland Period

The Woodland period (3,000–500 years ago) concluded with initial contact with Europeans. This period saw continuation of the trajectory toward larger communities and smaller distances for seasonal travel. The Bay had reached its present configuration by the beginning of this period, and together with its tributaries would increasingly render possible a stable economic and nutritional life. Now a blossoming estuary, the Bay burgeoned with waterfowl, fish, mollusks, and crustaceans, as humans ever more cunningly positioned themselves atop its food chain.

In the early Woodland Period (3,000–2,300 years ago) there appeared a variety of crude fired ceramic pots, copper beads, and projectile points evidencing expanding patterns of trade. The emergence of yet more containers during this period reflected food storage innovations by an increasingly sedentary and numerous population. The middle Woodland period (2,300–1,000 years ago) found yet more pottery innovations as well as other uses of clay, again distinctive projectile points, and yet more far-flung trade linkages. The first clear evidence of cultural distinctives between Amerindian groups, particularly between those on the upland Piedmont and those on the coastal plain, dates from this period.

The final period before European contact—the late Woodland (1,000–500 years ago)—saw hunting and gathering in the Chesapeake basin giving way yet more to agriculture. Domesticated crops such as beans, squash, maize, and tobacco were introduced to support larger and more sedentary populations. This necessitated greater clearing of forests which were taller and far more pervasive than today. In addition to numerous innovations in ensnaring birds and fish, the bow and arrow using small triangular points—of which many thousands have been found on Smith—first appeared here, with vast implications for both hunting and intertribal conflict.

Yet more social, political, and economic consolidation is signed with the initial appearance of permanent year-round settlements, sometimes palisaded. In contrast to earlier patterns of exposure or cremation, the first ossuaries date from this period, also reflecting yet more sedentary settlements. Much change during the late Woodland period evidences influence from outside the Chesapeake basin, as both transportation and communication played increasing roles.

B. The Period of "Initial Contact"

Countering the myth that the mid-Atlantic area at contact was sparsely populated with small nomadic clans who left minimal marks on the topography, the culture encountered by European explorers and settlers around 1500 was relatively populous, sedentary, prosperous, and *visible*.

Chesapeake Cultures Encountered by Europeans

At the dawn of European incursion, the Chesapeake basin was the site of an impressive system of governance, consisting of several political networks. Leadership, formerly based on consensus and wisdom-bearers, had increasingly come to be rooted in authoritarian power, within a more stratified society able to pass on power to successors. The best example was in the lower Bay's tidewater area, extending from the lower Eastern Shore to the Piedmont, where an empire of several dozen tribes led by chiefs was under the sway of the Powhatan, the "paramount" or emperor.

A second lesser block existed in the Potomac watershed, with the Piscataway chief being the paramount. And a third block, in the central portion of the Eastern Shore, was populated by the Nanticoke ("Tidewater People") confederation or chiefdom, whose various tribes included the Choptank, Wicomico, Manokin, Pocomoke, and Annemessex. The Nanticoke tribe proper was located on the river retaining that name, its mouth but fifteen miles north-northeast of what would be called Smith Island.

All three blocks were bound by related Algonquian dialects, ethnicity, and defensive alliances, with the Nanticoke block paying tribute to the Powhatan paramount. It has been argued that surplus flowing out of economic prosperity, which made possible higher and higher tribute, combined with external threat, most notably from the Iroquois to the north, accounted for this concentration of power in the southern tidewater area. It was the center of this formidable block that the founders of Virginia's Jamestown colony encountered in 1607.

The Algonquian had interesting neighbors. Aside from the Lënape (Delaware) confederation extending north from central Delaware into eastern Pennsylvania, the above blocks were bounded to the west of the Piedmont and throughout the watershed of the Susquehanna River basin to the north by Iroquoian-speaking tribes. Most feared were the Susquehannock—judged both formidable and numerous in Capt'n Smith's report of his 1608 encounter with them at the mouth of their river—who presented a real or rumored threat on both sides of the Bay. The Susquehannock had centuries earlier rejected invitations to join the Five Nations League farther north, and were at the time of the founding of the Virginia and Maryland colonies implacable enemies of that Iroquois block.

In contrast to the Susquehannock, who became extinct in 1763—from warfare, disease, and, finally, massacre—the League, adding a sixth nation in 1720, survived and in the twenty-first century maintains a vital communitarian life. Some historians contend that this Iroquois League (a.k.a. the Six Nation Alliance or Haudenosaunee), with its democratic, egalitarian, and peaceful institutions predating European contact by centuries, would in time make an impact on both the U.S. Constitution and the women's suffrage movement.

Contact: a Cosmological Collision

What can be said about the worldview of Chesapeake Amerindians prior to contact? Despite the variety of their cultures and paucity of written sources, the benefits of several generalizations appear greater than the hazards. First, virtually all tribes in the region worshiped a Great Spirit, often encountered via secondary spiritual entities more directly involved in people's ordinary lives. Second, most tribes had orally transmitted accounts of the creation of the world and of themselves. Third, there was an afterlife characterized by an abundance of that experienced to be good in the present. Fourth, communitarian life included significant personal liberty and only limited social stratification. And fifth, the Amerindian worldview tended to see "all that is" as part of an encompassing whole of being.

The post-Enlightment bifurcations of Europe—whether between humans and their natural environment, the human fauna and the nonhuman, the animate and inanimate, the profane and the sacred, the natural and the supernatural, the material and the spiritual, this life and the next—all were, for the first Americans, of an alien cosmology.

It might be argued that degrees of continuity existed between Amerindian religion and European Christianity on each of the first three points above, giving rise to syncretistic conversions among the indigenes of varying ratios of the two belief systems. But on the fourth and, particularly, fifth points, there was major discontinuity.

Further complicating the Amerindians' efforts to understand the settlers was the discrepancy between the latter's professed faith and their behavior, between their arrival in the name of Christ and either their highly stratified communities (ranging from privileged gentry to indentured servants and slaves) or their frequent brutalizing of locals, for example. Many Amerindians, whether converts or no, found much of this appalling—indeed, evidence of savagery.

The fear of guns, horses, and germs might force apparent conversion and external compliance, especially when the alternative was quick or protracted death. But the heart would not thus be won, particularly on points four and five. And in that refusal, whether conversion or no, was often sheltered a resistance, the power and impact of which Amerindian scholarship today is just beginning to awaken. The so-called "contact" was in fact a seismic collision of cosmologies in the most comprehensive sense of that term, the fallout of which continues to rain down upon us, in no spheres more obviously than those of ecology and social stratification.

The Fate of the Bay's Amerindians

A concluding word about the fate of the Chesapeake's indigenous peoples before moving into the European portion of the history of the Bay and Smith Island. Estimates of the Amerindian population around the Bay's perimeter at the time of European contact range as high as thirty thousand, with the extensive watershed inhabited by as many as one hundred thousand. By the 1660s, the decade when European settlement of Smith Island began, warfare, murder, alcohol, slave-catching, unrelenting socioeconomic disruption, dislocation to the west and north, and especially European diseases such as smallpox may have reduced these populations to only 10 percent of those figures.

The Nanticoke tribe remained a sociocultural entity well after other federation members were in free-fall. Estimated by Capt'n Smith in 1608 to number about 2,200 and judged militarily formidable, they would retain a measure of cohesion in the face of increasing influx of English settlers after 1660. Consequently they were feared by Maryland's colonial government as potential allies of the powerful Iroquois to the north. In an effort to secure the northern boundary of the territory to the east of the Bay, St. Mary's City initiated a series of treaties with the Nanticoke tribe, thereby acknowledging their strength.

Nevertheless, the fate confronting the Nanticoke was merely delayed rather than different in kind. Despite vigorous Nanticoke resistance to settler encroachment, the last third of the seventeenth century found them increasingly sequestered around the fork of Marshyhope Creek and their river near the Maryland/Delaware border, perhaps forty miles north-northeast of Smith Island. In 1704 the Maryland government, now in Annapolis, created the Chiconi Reserve near that location, further throttling the Nanticoke way of life and triggering demographic hemorrhaging to the west and north.

Words of a Nanticoke warrior to the Maryland House of Delegates in the mid-nineteenth century speak poignantly for the entire post-contact period:

> We are driven back until we can retreat no further. Our hatchets are broken.
> Our bows are snapped. Our fires are nearly gone out. A little longer and the
> white man will cease to pursue us, for we shall cease to exist.

In light of this catastrophic decline, it seems improbable that Smith Island's colonists ever had significant contact with Amerindians on the island, except for the few families, such as the Messicks, who sought to assimilate. By the 1660s when the island was first settled by Europeans, the smaller tribes across Tangier Sound to the east were ceasing to exist.

C. The European Cultures

Latins Explore Bahia de Santa Maria

The Chesapeake received disproportionate attention from early European explorers, just as it would in the wars to follow. An Italian in the employ of England's Henry VII, Giovanni Caboto (1450–1528)—John Cabot to us—sailed from Baffin Island to Maryland in 1498, although he did not come ashore.

In the spring of 1524, another Italian, Giovanni da Verrazano (1485–1528), sailed his ship *Dauphine* from the Carolinas' Cape Fear to Newfoundland, probing for a passage to China. Some crew members came ashore for three days somewhere on Delmarva, probably near Assateague, Maryland, an area Verrazano called "Arcadia." This constituted the region's first documented "contact." In a letter dated July 8,

1524, to King Francis I of France, under whose flag he sailed, Verrazano described various aspects of the indigenous culture in "Arcadia," in addition to the crew's abduction of an eight-year-old boy to be returned to France. The modern bridge that now connects Assateague Island with the mainland forty miles northeast of Crisfield, like that joining Staten Island and Brooklyn in New York City, is named after Verrazano.

In 1561, Pedro de Menendez de Aviles, sailing north from Spanish Florida, arrived at the mouth of the Chesapeake which he named *Bahia de Santa Maria*. (A map of the Bay with the same title is credited to Diego Gutierrez the following year, 1562.) Here too, an Indian youth was enticed or abducted: one Paquiquino, the seventeen-year-old son of a chief, to be exhibited, trained, and catecheticized in Spain (by Dominicans), and later Mexico (by Jesuits), as translator and wedge into the Powhatan culture. Paquiquino, now Don Luis, was not returned to *Ajacán* (as the Spanish called what would be Virginia) until 1570 as part of a missionary settlement of eight Jesuits on the York under the leadership of Fr. Juan Bautista de Segura.

However, as relations between the Jesuit priests and the Powhatan, particularly their shaman, deteriorated, Don Luis reverted to his native identity. This was a frequent pattern in such cases, probably having to do with his observations of Spanish treatment of Indians elsewhere. On February 9, 1571, a company of warriors, probably including Paquiquino, attacked the Jesuit settlement, massacring all of the priests. Later that year, Menendez de Aviles returned to the *Bahia* to discover *Ajacán* in ruins. A battle ensued, culminating with the hanging of eight Powhatan warriors from the rigging of the ship while their companions watched from the shore. The demise of *Ajacán* effectively ended the Spanish dream of annexing the Chesapeake into Spanish Florida, although Vincente Gonzales would sail to the head of the Bay in the armada year of 1588.

The British Settle the Bay Basin

The British establishment of the Jamestown colony in 1607 was preceded by several other British efforts in the Bay in which Sir Walter Raleigh had a hand. All were failures. The 1585–1590 Roanoke colony, including a group of settlers left there in 1587 when their ship's crew refused to transport them to the Chesapeake as planned, disappeared. Some contend that Roanoke's "lost" colonists migrated north, where they were either massacred or absorbed by the Powhatan. Then in 1603, captains Bartholomew Gilbert and Samuel Mace were each dispatched by Raleigh to establish colonies inside the Bay. Bartholomew probably failed to find the Bay and, together with several of his men, was killed by locals, likely in the Delaware Bay. Mace seems to have entered the Chesapeake, but no colony materialized.

In May of 1607, a group of 108 colonists under a charter to the Virginia Company established the Jamestown colony sixty miles up the Powhatan River. They were immediately beset by a range of threats to their very existence: sloth and ineptitude among the cohort's gentry, vulnerability to attack from both Powhatan warriors and Spanish ships, lack of food and fresh water, and disease. In the autumn of 1608, Capt'n John Smith (1580–1631), one of the original council members, would be given major powers, which many credit as having saved the colony from Roanoke's fate.

Capt'n John Smith in the Neighborhood

Before assuming this responsibility and amid the ferment precipitating it, however, Smith initiated two explorations of the estuary—he called it a "faire bay"—in a thirty-foot open vessel he called the *Discovery Barge*. He sought gold, a northwest passage, and trade possibilities with Indians. Departing Jamestown on June 2, 1608, Smith was in command of an ill-conceived crew of fourteen gentry, soldiers, and physician Walter Russels. They sailed up the eastern coast of the Chesapeake, making amiable contact with the Accomac tribe.

Continuing north, Capt'n Smith noted in his journal "many Iles in the midst of the bay," but efforts to make landfall there were thwarted by a squall. The map emerging from Smith's explorations shows a string of islands, including Watts, extending south from what is now the Crisfield area, and a second larger strand including Tangier and Smith that hangs below what is now the Blackwater Wildlife Refuge. It is not certain which archipelago he references in this citation, or which of these islands was approached.

Smith's journal continues:

> The next day searching those inhabitable Iles (which we called Russels Iles)
> to provide fresh water, the defect whereof forced us to follow the next East-
> erne channell, which brought us to the river Wighcocomoco [Pocomoke] . . .

There they were aided by the locals in searching for fresh water. Hugging the main as they sailed yet farther north, the craft was driven by a second storm on the northern "Russels Iles" (Bloodsworth?) when its foremast was lost. Following repairs, Smith's party returned to explore the Kuskarawaok (Nanticoke) River, although historians disagree whether they reached Broad Creek inside what is now Delaware. Smith lauded the Nanticokes, shorter and darker than the Accomacs, as "a great nation" and formidable as an opponent. Still in search of fresh water, Smith's party then traversed "Limbo" (now Hooper Strait below the Blackwater), crossed the Bay, and anchored under what we know as the Calvert Cliffs on the western shore. After proceeding north to the Patapsco River and then exploring the Potomac at some length, the party returned to Jamestown on July 21.

On the second voyage between July 24 and September 7, the course Capt'n Smith charted to the top of the Bay and back remained near the Susquehanna channel to the west of the Russels and included the exploration of many tributaries to points west approaching the Piedmont. All told, Smith mapped out nearly 200 Amerindian villages in his two excursions, sailing around 2,500 miles, and inadvertently providing a fascinating glimpse of indigenous life just before the region would be forever changed by the surge of settlers.

The Founding of Terra Mariae

The Maryland colony (named Terra Mariae in its charter after Henrietta Maria, consort of ill-fated Charles I) was formally established on March 25, 1634. A company perhaps exceeding two hundred on the ships Ark and Dove made landfall on what they called St. Clement's Island in the Potomac (meaning "where goods are brought in") in the territory of the Piscataway. The party included Governor Leonard Calvert (1606–1647), Jesuit fathers Andrew White (1579–1656) and John Altham, two lay brothers, and both Protestant and Roman Catholic settlers. The site selected for the initial settlement, and the colony's capital until 1689, was nearer the mouth of the Potomac on a tributary and site subsequently called St. Mary's.

The Maryland colony was no stranger to conflict in its early years, much of it with the Virginia colony: first with William Claiborne's effort to extend Virginia jurisdiction to Kent Island well north of St. Mary's, second with Protestant refugees from Virginia's Episcopalian establishment over issues of power-sharing.

But the major problems of Maryland's religiously heterogeneous colony were the ripples of British divisions that began in 1642 with the civil war between King Charles I and the Puritan forces under Cromwell. On the one hand, the fledgling colony's origins and the Act of Toleration (1649) served to draw uneasy Puritan, Presbyterian, and Quaker dissenters from Virginia as well as from England. On the other hand, the colony retained a proprietary government under Lord Baltimore, even while reacting to the latest waves from London. This delicate house of cards collapsed abruptly in 1689 in the aftermath of the Glorious Revolution in England and the ascension of William and Mary to the throne: the colonial proprietorship of Lord Baltimore fell, the capital transferred to the Puritan stronghold which would be called Annapolis, and the Act of Toleration was replaced by laws rendering illegal public Roman Catholic worship. And so the unique saga of the Maryland colony moved into a very different chapter.

Formative developments in the south of Maryland's Eastern Shore took place during this 1634–1689 "Lord Baltimore" period. In 1666, an Order in Council in St. Mary's established Somerset County ("Old Somersett" or "Somerset main"). It originally including all territory between the Nanticoke River and the Atlantic (including present Wicomico and Worcester counties), which until then the Council had officially called "The Eastern Shore." And it was thus that the island that would become Smith became part of Somerset County.

The St. Mary's Council had shielded this area from settlement during the previous thirty years to ensure a free hand to lucrative fur trading, particularly beaver. The argument has been made that this reprieve provided some area Amerindians an additional generation to accommodate and assimilate before the rush of land-grabbing settlers set in, thus precluding their complete disappearance as occurred in most other parts of the Bay basin.

First Colonists on Smith Island

The initial European owner of land on our island was apparently Robert Cager of St. Mary's. In 1665 he was granted a patent for two hundred acres south of what is now called the Kedges (a corruption of "Cager") Strait along the north side of Smith. Content to put cattle ashore and digging cow holes to collect sweet water—one such indentation survives in a backyard across from the Tylerton church—Cager died shortly thereafter, having never himself resided on his property.

It was not long until Smith Island, situated between the Maryland and Virginia colonies, became involved in a major boundary dispute. Shortly after Cager's patent, one Henry Smith (no relation to Capt'n John), an unsavory bigamist on the lam from Virginia's Eastern Shore seeking to reinvent himself, was awarded a patent for one thousand acres in the southern part of the island for having brought twenty indentured servants to the Virginia colony.

About the same time, Lord Baltimore granted to a Colonel William Stevens a similar patent of 1,000 acres in the central part of the island that Stevens would call, in honor of his wife, Elizabeth née Pitt, Pittcraft. That term, morphing into "Pitchcroft" by the twentieth century, was long associated with the portion of this patent on the southwest edge of the village of North End marked by a stately building. Spanning the years from its antecedent structures early in the eighteenth century to its destruction by fire on November 1, 1986, that structure, the island's oldest, would variously serve as a plantation house, boarding house, and restaurant.

The line separating the patents of Smith and Stevens was the Calvert-Scarborough Agreement of 1668 between the two colonies. Where exactly this boundary sundered

Smith Island would be a matter of contention right through the Civil War until 1877! For now conflict was deferred, however, when in 1679 Henry Smith came into possession of Steven's one thousand acres as well, thus owning virtually all of the island below the waterway called the Big Thorofare. The document of this transaction, referring to the changing hands of several houses in addition to orchards, gardens, pastures, and "wayes," placed William and Elizabeth Stevens at the very beginning of European settler life on the isle.

Both Henry Smith, who would never reside on the island, and Stevens would in time help to establish Old Somersett as well as their own prosperity on the mainland. Both would also be representatives in Lord Baltimore's general assembly in St. Mary's. Although our island had earlier been called one of the Russels Iles as well as "Isle of Broken Woodlands" by the St. Mary's people, it was for the scoundrel Henry Smith that it would be known.

My sketch of Tylerton's subsequent history might best be constructed by braiding the results of my 1996 research on the ownership history of the Inn's plot of land with information gleaned from various sources on the unfolding of Smith Island's religious piety and institutions.

On August 8, 1693, our island's namesake, Henry Smith, depleted of funds, sold off two hundred of his two thousand acres to one John Tyler, a resident of Smith Island before 1688, for nine thousand pounds of tobacco. The deed for this sale, "part thereof being in Virginia & part in Maryland," included " . . . houses, yards, gardens, orchards, meadows, marshes, feeding pastures, fishing places . . . ." It is this Tyler family—grandson Butler in particular—that gives its name to the village of Tylerton, on the edge of which the Inn stands today.

Another early resident, John Evans, had by 1685 already purchased from Smith a two-hundred-acre parcel called Dogwood Ridge, although from the central Pittcraft portion. Each having roots on Smith Island going back at least to the 1680s, the Tyler and Evans families thus were the earliest of those whose names have been carried uninterruptedly to the present.

The argument has been made that religious dissenters were among the early settlers of Smith Island: Quakers and Puritans from the Virginia colony, where Anglicanism was established, and Protestants of any kind from the fledgling Roman Catholic entity across the Bay in St. Mary's, all joining yet other settlers from both Old Somersett and Accomack counties on the Eastern Shore. While some dissenters were probably so drawn, it is noteworthy that there is no evidence of organized congregations of any hue on Smith Island before the Methodist revival broke out in 1807, when the population was but one hundred people. If religious dissent were a motivation among Smith's seventeenth-century settlers, they were seemingly more intent on escaping others' strictures than establishing their own.

Joshua Thomas and Wesleyan Revivalism

A priceless glimpse into the Smith Island religious situation from the late eighteenth century is Adam Wallace's *The Parson of the Islands*. This is a biography, published in 1861, of Joshua Thomas (1776–1853), a waterman from nearby Potato Neck on Somerset main. Following a decade-long spiritual search for a conversion experience, and having "made up my mind to have it in the Methodist way," Thomas came to faith in the early autumn of 1807 at the Annemessex camp meeting, near where Old St. Peter's Methodist Church building remains just outside Crisfield to this day. He would become the evangelist for and embodiment of the coming of Wesleyanism to the entire archipelago. Indeed, Joshua Thomas was arguably the person most responsible for shaping what the isles Smith, Tangier, and Deal are to this day.

While there were no houses of worship on Smith before the first revival-spawned structure in 1809—a simple private home—biographer Wallace makes clear that at least some of the islanders "were all attached by early predilection" to the "Old Church" (Episcopal). The nearest Episcopal parish at the time was on Somerset main.

Joshua Thomas, never more than marginally literate even though he tried to use the *Book of Common Prayer* as encouraged by an Episcopal minister "who occasionally visited the Islands," marveled before his conversion at those able to "pray without a book, or preach without a sermon." He would later recall that his marriage to Rachel Evans (in 1799, probably on Smith) was solemnized by one John Evans, "probably a clergyman of . . . the 'old church,'" after which the couple resided in Horse Hammock, southeast of what is now Tylerton.

The Episcopalian *Book of Common Prayer*, of course, presupposed literacy, a condition that excluded many islanders. That they gave themselves in large numbers to the new piety centering in experiential conversion, extemporaneous preaching, and "shoutin'" enthusiasm—Wallace on several occasions calls it "experimental religion"—is thus not so surprising.

The revivalism dating to 1807 gave rise to the formation of a so-called Methodist Society and then a congregation meeting in a purchased private home just southwest of North End in an area called Old Orchard or Kizzie's, near the grand Pittcraft house. (It is interesting to note that the Inn of Silent Music's smallest and most economical room was called "Orchard Ridge," another name for Old Orchard.) This meetinghouse was supplanted in 1855 as village population approached three hundred, and then again in 1866, by ever-larger structures as the island population burgeoned following the Civil War.

One can speculate whether the same illiteracy that was a barrier to Episcopal worship may also have tempered a kind of biblicism among islanders; it is reported, for example, that it was not until the mid-nineteenth century that some Smith Islanders owned their own Bibles.

Shortly after 1840, a seismic economic shift took hold on Smith Island. Agriculture was supplanted by the harvesting of the sea, particularly oysters, as the dominant occupation. A comparison of the federal censes of 1840 and 1860 reveals that a large majority of the men shifted from declaring "farmer" as their livelihood to "captain."

Returning to the history of the land on which the Inn is situated: in May of 1855, Thomas Bradshaw, Sr., purchased from the Tyler family two acres near the southern part ("down below") of the region called Drum Point (later Tylerton). Bradshaw's forebears had originally come to Smith Island in the eighteenth century,

After Bradshaw died in 1885—the population of Smith Island had by then rapidly inflated to about five hundred—the lot on which the Inn is now located was purchased by Capt'n John Cooper and Miss Manie (Evans) Marshall. The first Marshalls had come to Smith Island in 1828 from Saxis Island in Accomack County just below the state line, and their family name would constitute, at the time of this writing, about half of Tylerton's population. In 1913, just after the demographic highwater mark of Smith Island—the 1910 national census counted 805 persons—the Marshalls sold the lot to their son, Capt'n Howard Wesley (1890–1967) and his wife, Miss Venie (Evans) (d. 1970), even as the oyster boom was waning. Capt'n Howard had a good net fishing season, and the couple constructed the major wing of what is now the Inn around 1914.

One Congregation or Three?

A far-reaching decision was made by Smith Island's faith community in the late nineteenth century. With population swelling toward its 1910 crest and the third structure on Old Orchard already crowded and worn, and with the inauguration of the annual camp meeting in North End in 1887 drawing both from other islands and the central periphery of the Bay, it was determined that three new dispersed meetinghouses be constructed. As such, the years 1893–1896 saw the raising of houses of worship in North End ("Corinth") serving that part of the island; Rhodes Point ("Calvary") in the southwest; and Oak Hammock or The Pines ("Union"), including the small settlements of Longbranch, Johntown, and Hootenville in addition to Drum Point (Tylerton).

The Corinth structure in North End was replaced by a new and larger one in 1934. Only three years later, however, a fire that jeopardized the entire village destroyed it, together with parsonage as well as camp meeting tabernacle and cabins. The present Corinth meetinghouse was built in 1938. In 1921, the Calvary congregation in Rhodes Point built a new sanctuary, with the older structure becoming a community center that is utilized as such to this day.

In 1928 the Union building, having been constructed close to the ground on relatively low elevation just west of The Pines, was disassembled and rebuilt on a larger scale adjacent to the Tyler family cemetery in the middle of Drum Point/Tylerton on a loftier elevation of 4.5 feet. The imposing Tylerton church building remains the center of the village. Thus, each of the three meetinghouses built in the 1890s—the faithful of which in Methodist parlance came collectively to be called the "Smith Island charge"—has been replaced by a new and larger structure.

The argument has been made that the decision to build houses of worship in each of the isle's "parts," to use the local term—rather than one large, centrally located edifice—exacerbated and indeed rendered permanent the community's trifurcation, as dispersed farmers-turned-watermen continued to move to hamlets at higher elevations. In contrast to Tangier Island with its single settlement, the argument goes, the convenience of access in the late nineteenth century has become pressure upon all institutions in the early twenty-first.

For example, Tom Horton writes in his memoir that Tylerton had 153 inhabitants in 1980. That would mean that the population of 58 in 2005, but twenty-five years later, was 38 percent of that 1980 figure, a decline which threatens most village institutions, although to differing degrees. Conversely, it could be argued that Smith's population was already significantly trifurcated before the 1890s decision, and would only become more so, given rising sea level, limited upland, and beginning in 1949, electrification that would round up the last stragglers. Tylerton, of course, had the additional challenge of being separated by water from the land mass of the other two villages, and the cost for it would have been most dear had the 1890s decision gone the other way. My own opinion is that this village in particular would not have survived in any recognizable form without the church, both people and building, at its center.

6. The Meteorological Place

The term "climate" has to do with generalizations about weather, or the meteorological, over three to five decades or longer. Thus, while the meteorological can be understood only against the background of the climatological, meteorology in its aggregate determines the latter. It is self-evident that the geological history of the area which is now the Bay watershed has had a profound climatological component. As indicated earlier, the repeated oscillation over the past several million years between ice age and interglacial period, a critical aspect of "paleoclimate," was triggered by varied combinations of shifts in Earth's axial tilt, a wobble in that axial rotation, and fluctuations between the elliptical and circular in the planet's orbit itself. Each variable had major climate implications, the constantly changing combinations among them only generating greater climate extremes.

The Bay as we know it, clearly in the debt of climate, is but a brief and sweet dalliance in geological time. While climate seemingly called nearly all the shots at the beginning of this affair, it will be joined by sizable anthropogenic factors in saying *adiós*.

A fascinating example of an isle phenomenon that is both climatological and meteorological is the Bay/Delmarva temperature differential. The water has a much greater heat capacity than land, so the Bay itself gains or loses heat less rapidly than its surrounding land. While in the springtime Tylerton's daytime temperature lags below that of Salisbury, on the mainland some thirty-five miles to the northeast, it may be well above Salisbury's temperature that night. The reverse is the case in the autumn. I have logged a Salisbury/Tylerton differential during spring or fall as large as twenty-two degrees! In the summer, our high temperatures may be six degrees lower than the mainland, and yet further cooled by stiffer breezes; in winter, we might be nearly that many degrees warmer on cold days or nights. The differentials are greatest at the temperature extremes.

Incidentally, the different cooling rates of land and water can also generate island breezes or calms around dawn and dusk that augment larger air movement patterns. In short, Tylerton's location, surrounded by water and yet, across the Bay and Tangier Sound, by land as well, delivers comfort via both moderated temperatures and more frequent breezes. And the context for all of this is the Chesapeake basin, one of the most volatile and mercurial meteorological regions of the country—with its bull's-eye being Tylerton! While all locations are said to be created equal regarding weather, some, apparently, are more equal than others.

A. The Fifth Horseman of the Apocalypse

It can safely be said that Sharryl and I each experienced weather on Smith Island—what William Rodgers in his 1979 article called a "Wet and Windy Kingdom"—somewhat differently. With Sharryl, a native Californian, we are talking here primarily about wind. No, *Wind*: a persona with a proper name. She, forty-seven years a denizen of California's central valley, where fronts take four sleepy days to amble through, was ill-prepared for his antics. An ordinarily peaceful person, Sharryl would in time be branding Wind as predator, excoriating him with maledictions. He would buffet her blossoms, litter her frontage, scramble the formats of her life, put the screws to her resolve. No, when resorting to Holy Writ, she was *not* liable to intone, "from the treasuries YHWH sends forth the wind" (Ps 135:7).

Who other than Wind could have bludgeoned Sharryl into reducing her beautiful long blond hair to a minimalist and pragmatic crop only weeks after the Inn's opening? Who but he could have bullied her into taking both notice and pleasure in the brief transitional interlude between a blow from the south and one from the north? She had two four-letter words our first five years—"Tide" and "Wind." Enter the bulkhead in 2002, and she was left, well, mostly, with one: Wind. Sharryl had *five* Horsemen of the Apocalypse, and sometimes at night, the house shaking, we had *ménage à trois*!

My own experience was different. With the exception of days hot, humid, still, and seasoned with no-see-ums, I found most of Tylerton's weather interesting. And while in the early years I would occasionally apologize to guests for rain or snow or even wind, the *hubris* of it all put a stop to that. I was particularly seduced by the fierce opera of storm: the pungent ozone, the shades of colors for which "yellow," "green," "violet," or "indigo" were the least inadequate words I knew, the churning vortex amid which gulls played the wind, the suddenness with which the rain itself exploded, cold, stinging, and *horizontal*. Ah, the splendid wildness, the *violence* of it all!

And then, amid the din of thunder directly above, there were those sometimes nearly constant lightning strikes knifing down into the Bay: great tree trunks of ice blue, self-immolating fire. I loved to stay outside until the very last moment, and beyond, in the thrall of both terror and beatitude, as that squall line, having rolled out of the Potomac and crossed first the Bay and then Hog Neck, was now racing across the Crick's open water. Sharryl was usually behind me somewhere, trying, ever in the name of love, to coax me to shelter and safety. Finding myself finally on the porch, I was seldom dry or unhappy. Fear of lightning? Of course! I, a Minnesotan of yore, should have known better, for more than once a waterman hollered me off the dock as I gazed up in wonder.

But, you see, I liked Wind that way, spirited, decidedly *whatever* and with an attitude, occasionally in my face and sticking it in my ear, and just often enough for me never to forget what he could become: *treacherous!* Capt'n John Smith logged three violent storms during the first week of his exploration of the Chesapeake in June of 1608 . . . must have been a calm year. For the full decade, I was grateful that I had not been exiled to Santa Barbara—rumored seasonless meteorological bliss, not unlike the image of heaven in American culture. No, give me the Chesapeake *anytime!* But yes, Wind did bring stresses to our union; he would come between us.

While the weather could be delicate and nuanced, occasionally even inert as in what the locals call "slick cam" ("calm"), on Tylerton it was much more frequently swaggering and overwhelming—indeed, into serious domination. Nor was I surprised when, having stumbled upon the pieces of two millstones in a backyard on Marshall Street, I subsequently learned that Tylerton, on the site of what would be the school no less, had once had one of the few windmill-driven gristmills in Maryland. Guests, having survived leaning into Wind at forty-five degrees and groping for handholds, might be found in the shelter of the Inn parlor speculating about a wind farm as the isle's economic salvation. Earlier the land, now the sea, tomorrow the sky: why not?

On an early December night, with a nor'easter clawing at the eves, I might intone my house litany for Sharryl: "This old house took Agnes' best shots in '72; she survived Hazel's 120-mile-per-hour winds in '54; she triumphed over the August of '33 mother of all storms; and she'll still be here in the morning!"

"LeRoy, we were moving!" a guest might calmly report in the morning, over a baked frittata with artichoke hearts. Early on, I recall trying to repair our third-floor commode, only to trace the swirling of water in the bowl to the moving house, not a leak! I might enter the kitchen during a March blow to hear Sharryl wistfully musing: "And here I thought we were living in the American *South*," as if wind was a Yankee affliction! One morning, the two of us had just completed prayers on the third floor and were indulging in a leisurely five minutes together before breakfast, when a hefty spike above the common thirty-five mile from north-northwest did a real number on the opposite side of the Inn. Sharryl cried out, as one having received an epiphany: "LeRoy, we live in the Hebrides! We live in the *Outer* Hebrides!"

B. The Innkeepers and the Sound

I must concede that my bravado regarding eventful weather subsided somewhat whenever I faced a rough ferry crossing, sometimes to the extent of transforming the passage into a prayer tutorial. During the off-season, the Sunday morning decision as to whether to attend Mass in Salisbury was often a hard call. The *Capt'n Jason II,* the forty-five-foot nonvehicular ferry serving Tylerton, could roll, particularly if Wind was coming in anywhere near ninety degrees. Marge Laird—she didn't love her ferry captain mate primarily for his profession!—and I would periodically tease each other about the Sound Survivors Anonymous group we were going to found.

In the early years, Sharryl's strategy in rough seas was to cling to me, sometimes leaving lacerations on my back. However, with time she adopted a mind-over-matter M.O. of withdrawing deep into a safety within herself, off in a corner, legs splayed and braced. My own means of coping consisted of remaining upright, eyes affixed to the heaving horizon, hand ensnarled in a rope tethered to the ceiling, body flexing so as to remain vertical, mostly.

The stories of two treacherous crossings in particular linger, the first being one we never even made. It was a stormy April Friday in 1997, our final visit to Tylerton before moving there, when Sharryl simply could not compel herself to board the 5:00 PM ferry in Crisfield. She froze in the car parked twenty feet from the vessel.

After a night in a motel on the main, we passed some time before the 12:30 PM ferry in a nearby antique store. Imprudently mentioning her previous day's experience to the Delmarvan proprietor, Sharryl was bludgeoned with this: "Well, I wouldn't cross that sound today on anything smaller than a battleship!" Trying to get on the ferry again an hour later, during which time first the preacher and then a scout troop boarded, was, well, *déjà vu.* We drove back to D.C. aware that our decision to become nautical islanders was not off to an auspicious beginning. It needs to be said that that kind of immobilization by fear would never happen again to Sharryl, not in ten years.

The second story about a treacherous crossing of the Sound is about one we actually made. But, alas! I could never include it in my Tylertales to guests lest they remain our guests *in perpetua!*

It was a January dusk in 2002. Sharryl and I were returning to Tylerton after two months of travel and family. The Bay Bridge crossing had served to warn us about both Wind and the size of seas, and by the time we embarked from Crisfield's dock, a full blizzard had set in. Sharryl and I assumed our respective survival postures, noting the only other passenger to be a North End woman. Recumbent on the bench, she helpfully volunteered that she would be taking Imodium if it got bad.

We were scarcely cast off before she commenced popping pills. As the pounding from the seas grew, each blow was matched, antiphonally, by a bleating animal sound from the supine one. As we cleared the lee of Janes Island a mile out of Crisfield and began absorbing the full brunt out of the northwest, it was apparent that, between the driving snow and seas breaking over the bow, Capt'n Larry had zero visibility and was navigating solely by instruments. Particularly disconcerting was the sound of the craft's "wheel" spinning wildly whenever the seas heaved the stern up out of the water.

Ordinarily skillfully evasive of rogue waves and tender of heart regarding tenderfeet in his care, Capt'n Larry never saw this one coming. What he would later estimate as a ten-foot sea hit us from starboard over Puppy Hole. This clinched the experience as my most terrifying ever, two Middle East wars and 1981 Guatemala notwithstanding. My wheels flew south, my hand still entangled above, as we labored beneath the rogue's glacial green mass only to plunge into the trough behind it, the big John Deere marine engine below sounding like it had departed its mounts. Sharryl had gone far, far away. The psalter's line, "though I walk through the valley of the shadow of death" (Ps 23:4), seemed neither melodramatic nor hyperbolic.

The rest of the voyage to the relative shelter of Smith's Big Thorofare was strangely anticlimactic. While I had indeed feared for my life, I was now wondering both whether the Imodium supply would hold out and whether the patient could survive the cure. All of which begs the question: without the intermittent rush of those passages across the Sound, would not life lived anywhere else be blasé?

C. And Then There Were Hurricanes

Coming as Sharryl and I had from the centers of countries—Fresno, California and Minnesota, USA, respectively—the generations had atrophied our instincts for evacuation. The first time around—Felix, Saffir-Simpson Category 4, during a renovation respite in August 1995—it wasn't pretty between the innkeepers as we moved into the "watch" phase. The last departing ferry canceled as Felix quickened and we barely managed a hitch on Rhodes Point's *Miss Maxine,* a forty-five-foot workboat with a tiny triangular cabin in the bow. The passenger manifest for that space: seven (mostly) wide-bodies, two Lab dogs (one lacking sight), two cats (including our non-pacifist Gustav), and the fetid amalgam of the anxiety of all of the above. I remember Tangier Sound during that passage: glacial green, the mechanics of wind and tide giving it an emulsoidal appearance, as if it were being boiled down below.

Three years later a powerful Coast Guard craft took off with just the three of us and a seasonal neighbor as Bonnie, Category 2, bore down on the Bay. Upon reaching Crisfield, we stopped at our bank and Sharryl went in to get some cash. The teller looked at her check and volunteered: "My son is with the Guard here and I just heard him radio in the message, 'Comin' in with three persons and one animal.' Must be you." So much for the anonymity of remoteness!

Next it was Floyd (Category 2, September 1999). The night before we evacuated, I visited the homes of three trusted village couples for counsel. All would stay, I unhelpfully learned, the men to be with their boats, the women with their men. Included in my survey was Capt'n Charlie Marsh, Tylerton's last true oysterman, with his seventy-foot *Rebecca Forbush* buyboat tied up—appropriately—below the cemetery. Now *Rebecca* had long ceased being a young lady, and for some years Capt'n Charlie had devoted his anecdotage, ultimately unsuccessfully, to her complete makeover. I once heard another waterman say—Capt'n Charlie had just left the store—he wouldn't go to North End on her!

Anyway, as I left Capt'n Charlie that day, he kindly proffered: "Now if you decide to stay and she gets real bad, you and Miss Sharryl are welcome to join me and Frances down in her hold, and we'll ride 'er out together." Judging from how often she reminisced about it, I do not think Sharryl ever quite forgave Capt'n Charlie this expression of Christian hospitality. Having learned a bit by now, Sharryl and I evacuated in an orderly manner from Floyd, using the ferry. Almost exactly three years later, September 17, 2003, the two of us did the same before Dame Isabel who will, together with Floyd, resurface later in this narrative.

A concluding storm note: on our very final weekend as innkeepers, Labor Day of 2006, the eye of tropical storm Ernesto, flirting with hurricane status, passed just west of us, generating tidal surges that approached those of Isabel. This gale, for which there was minimal warning and zilch evacuation talk, rang out our decade-long production with cymbals. I, sick in bed on the third floor at the time, thus did not hear Sharryl's cry, "Hey, it's up to Frank's neck!" as she surveyed our thirty-inch-tall statue of Francis of Assisi on the back patio through the kitchen window. Nor did I witness two game guests, clutching each other for support in the churning waist-deep water, using one dishtowel to tether the kayak poised to float away *over* the bulkhead in front of the Inn, another to secure the handcart to the piles of our dock. Neither of us was surprised that, just three days before we closed our final season, the weather managed to get in one more good lick. It was the decade's most traumatic storm for which we did not evacuate.

I concede that when it comes to the weather portion of silent music, I prefer the scale and power of a Mahler symphony to the *adagio* in a cello sonata. Yes, I thrill before nature big, rambunctious, and grandiose. But expressions of the more subdued pole were also part of living in Tylerton, as in this journal excerpt:

> *It is just now dawn. The rain falling through the night has been intercepted*
> *by the falling thermometer. The entire marsh has been transformed into a*

carpet of crystal the imagination could scarcely have conjured up. I open the oratory window just as a soft breeze triggers a pervasive metallic cascade, and then all returns to a chilled silence. In the still air, the mournful call of the foghorn at the jetty on the Bayside outside of North End reaches me, and then all is still again. It is a scene for both eye and ear before which words hesitate, then, finally, recuse themselves.

7. The Disappearing Place

From the outset of our experience in Tylerton in October 1992, Smith Island's vulnerability to the Bay was at least an implicit constant in many, perhaps most, conversations with its citizens. The most obvious catastrophic threat to the island would be a major hurricane, a Category 4 or 5 coming straight in between "Hank and Chuck." On the morning of September 17, 2003, all but a dozen Tylertonians evacuated before Isabel, wondering whether she would be the game-closer. Fortunately, during the next thirty-six hours, Isabel drifted westward and weakened slightly. But Sharryl and I have lived here fully aware that there are storms out there that could disappear not only the Inn but the entire *island*. Given the accumulative water-related fatigue in the village, merely being brushed by another big storm might be the death knell.

A. Jeopardy I: Erosion, Drowning, Subsidence

The more incremental threats, in contrast to the catastrophic ones, are three, their effects deeply interrelated and compoundable. *Erosion*, the first, is the horizontal encroachment and gouging away of the island by heavy seas. While estimates of Smith's actual acreage loss to erosion since Capt'n John Smith sailed by do not suggest imminent demise, more foreboding is the fact that as much as 90 percent of the isle's footprint is now near or at sea level. In short, the footprint will soon reach a tipping point, resulting in far more change in the present century than in the last.

That the sub-isle Tylerton is located near the center of the larger Smith Island complex and thus shielded by low barrier landmasses from all directions except south-southeast—whence Isabel blew in—has limited its erosion losses. The new bulkhead across the northern and western sides of Tylerton, completed in May 2002 by the Army Corps of Engineers, has further lessened, at least for the short term, that threat to the village and Inn frontage. In contrast, some headlands on Smith's perimeter have been known to erode as much as eight feet a year, particularly where the configuration was spit-like and the elevation minimal.

A second incremental threat is sea level rise, resulting in *drowning*, the term for occasions when parts of the island are submerged at flood tide. Before the bulkhead, the frontage of the Inn property (two feet above sea level) was intermittently flooded, particularly in March/April and October/November. The spirits of the villagers were invariably dampened when this pattern continued for several days. The bulkhead significantly reduced such "nuisance flooding," but the infrequent extra-high tide will still enter the village from the exposed back or around or through the bulkhead, reminding all that sea level rise is the unacknowledged elephant in the room, with no solution in sight. In addition to the relentless pressure exerted by rising sea level, there are the increasingly erratic weather patterns associated with global warming, about which Sharryl and I mused more and more as our decade wound down.

The major cause of sea-level rise is the accelerating rate of glacial ice cap melting, with secondary causes including both thermal expansion of seawater and the breaking off of portions of the polar ice sheet. The common cause is rising global tempera-ture, about one degree Fahrenheit across the twentieth century. And the cause of that warming appears to be some combination of macroclimate cycles and anthropogenic factors. I have lived on Tylerton this decade, increasing convinced that the govern-ment's failure to confront the latter portion of this causation is a crass bartering of the future of our children and grandchildren for economic gain. In addition to being anti-family, such a failure is an immoral act of cowardice.

The third component of the incremental threat is *subsidence*, the slow sinking of the floor of the Bay, including its islands. The causation here is complex, probably including both tectonic and sediment-weight components, in addition to the western shore cities' heavy withdrawal of water from the aquifers far below. This is the com-ponent of the three most difficult to measure, and in Tylerton it is not as serious as over the unstable bolide crater, the rim of which is less than twenty-five miles to the south. Still, subsidence remains very real, again with no solution in sight.

The rate of change of the combined vertical variables—sea level rise and sub-sidence—has accelerated during the last third of the twentieth century. This is most disturbing, with combined change projections for the twenty-first century exceeding three feet—roughly the estimated total change that occurred during the four centuries since John Smith's explorations in 1608. During our first half decade, drowning from high tides was the most immediate headache. The bulkhead mitigated that problem sig-nificantly, while of course doing nothing regarding the macro issue of sea-level rise.

Given Tylerton's highest elevation of less than five feet (the church and softball field), we can project that, all other things being equal, Tylerton might cease to be sometime after the mid-twenty-first century, perhaps preceded by Rhodes Point and followed by North End. To Tylertonians, like the residents of thousands of the planet's other coastal communities, sea-level rise is no hypothesis: it is a very concrete and nonabstract matter. That the causes of this change are rarely discussed by watermen says more about their politics or sense of powerlessness than about what they see plainly with their own eyes.

In late autumn of our first season, I hitched a ride with Pulitzer-winner Stan Grossfeld of the *Boston Globe* to explore Holland Island, one of John Smith's Russel

Iles, a dozen miles to the north. Home to as many as three hundred waterfolk in 1900, Holland shortly thereafter lost its protective bayside land barrier to a storm, allowing seas access to the interior ridge. The island was totally depopulated by 1918. Following our explorations of the isle's two remaining cemeteries, its single surviving house, and a small beach replete with shards of glass and pottery of another time, I returned home soberly aware that I had been afforded a glimpse into Tylerton's future.

B. Jeopardy II: Globalism, Demography, Development

But the longer I lived in Tylerton, the more apparent it became that the threats to her existence were not restricted to developments on the land/sea interface. The question whether the scarcity of crabs at a given time was attributable to annual fluctuations or more ominous parallels to the oyster tragedy was never far away, particularly in our concluding years. A major complicating factor during that period was the massive influx of foreign crab, undercutting the market and seducing the clientele that had always prized Smith Island's product as absolutely top-quality. Globalism is very real, and shockingly near, in Tylerton!

Demographic changes mirror these uncertainties as many youth opt for the mainland's goodies like salary, benefits, and pension, in addition to diversions. For the relatively few choosing to remain, land appreciation has often placed home ownership out of reach, while tempting older residents to accept buy-out offers by seasonal folk. In both cases it is the indigenous population that wanes. Some watermen have speculated, tongue only partly in cheek, about what would disappear last: the crabs, the watermen, or space in Tylerton's nearly full cemetery.

However, beginning around 2003, the uncertain future of Smith took on an additional overlay. With dwindling amounts of Chesapeake frontage remaining, development arrived to Crisfield, and with a rush. Hundreds of condominium units sprang up along the water the following year, with many more to come. All this occurred amid continuing deliberations regarding a vehicular ferry from Reedville on Virginia's Northern Neck to Crisfield, passing just below Smith Island.

When Crisfield's boom began, its municipal leadership failed to drive hard bargains with developers in the interests of the town's collective well-being, especially its long-term citizens. Owners of major Crisfield frontage institutions cashed out in the face of offers that would have been laughable but several years before. The collapse of the housing market beginning in 2006, coming hard on the heels of this boom, leaves the configuration of Crisfield's future wildly uncertain, with Tylertonians also waiting for the other shoe to drop.

During our first six seasons, I would often muse with guests regarding an envisioned development project in the early 1980s near North End. Championed by mainlander Clifton S. Justice, longtime friend of and landowner on Smith, the multifaceted plan included a marina, condominium complex, golf course, and airstrip. These came bundled with incorporation of each of the three villages and a vehicular road and bridge, bringing moneyed visitors to Tylerton. My comment to guests: that fork in the road—saving the island by transmogrifying it into a spot of mainland squared—had been seriously weighed back then, was rejected by islanders for many reasons, and was now dead.

Alas, my death announcement was premature. That the waterman population will continue to wane while the seasonal mainlanders wax now seems inevitable. The question is whether the latter will be drawn by respect for what Tylerton has been, largely the case to date, or whether they will simply create another resort community. One local, married to a waterman who is probably ontologically unable to live on the main, seemed resigned: "Well, we're stayin' . . . s'pose we'll just be takin' care of rich peoples' houses when we get old."

C. The Bay as Daylily

Geologically speaking, Tylerton's story is a sedimentary rather than igneous one, an oscillating spot of tenuous space and time in the thrall of megaforces continental, planetary, and even cosmic. A day lily both improbable and serendipitous, Tylerton has "transitory" written all over her. And this fragility, this "one brief shining moment" quality in a sea of temporality and mortality, characterizes the culture as much as it does the natural environment.

It is hard to dodge the conclusion that this endangered species, a culture both hauntingly beautiful and prophetically provocative, has extinction in its future. But if so, how will that happen? Who will be present at the wake? Will there be singing and dancing in celebration of this flower in time? Or will the isle's way have long since mutated in the face of the dominant culture, so that the one who bloomed and the one consigned to "pushing up daisies" are no longer one and the same? Such questions are part of the uncertainty of a tale not yet fully told.

One motivation for this work is my desire to capture some of the inimitable substance of what I, but one admirer, have experienced Tylerton's environs and culture to be, before—one way or another—it becomes the disappeared place.

PART III
THE MEANING OF PLACE

There was much more to the hold Tylerton was fixing on me than can be accounted for by the research and reflection giving rise to Part II of this book. From our first visit to Smith Island in 1992, I felt a lure, a haunting seductiveness, about the place. It was as if I was being worked by some primeval siren, one whose lilting music I "heard" deeper down in me than either my mind or senses. Early on, my self-understanding as a "romantic" seemed to account for all of this attraction.

While during the ensuing decade reality would inexorably, and not always painlessly, wean me of much of that isle romanticism, Tylerton would not thereby be reduced to just another geographical location with GPS coordinates. Rather, around mid-decade, I became aware of the setting's powerful spiritual effect upon me, of the way it was improbably becoming a player in my life of faith.

I did not come to Tylerton uninitiated to the interface of geography and faith. After all, I had lived in none less than Jerusalem—*Sheikh Jarrah* in East Jerusalem—for five years, 1971–1976. I had been affiliated with the Mennonite Central Committee, a relief, development, and peace agency with projects among Palestinians. Backed up against the slashing scar of no-man's land harking back to the Arab/Israeli war in 1948 and Jerusalem's divided status during the subsequent nineteen years, our family's house as a perch was scarcely believable, starting with backyard Jordanian military fortifications.

From our balcony, I would watch the panorama of the Jewish Orthodox *Mea Shearim* neighborhood beyond the scar recline into the dusk of *Shabbat*. At first I would be awakened from sleep by the Moslem *muazzen*'s call to prayer, when first a black thread could be distinguished from a white. And our family was but a drive of minutes from the incense-soddened recesses of the Church of the Holy Sepulcher in the Old City and the adjacent Lutheran Church of the Redeemer where we worshipped.

Jerusalem is *el Quds* in Arabic, meaning "the Holy," and sacred it is to each of the three Abrahamic faiths. Innumerable forays into that city were given larger context by my excursions throughout Palestine and Israel in addition to intermittent visits to Jordan, Syria, Lebanon, Cyprus, and Egypt (including Sinai, with Nikos Kazantzakis' *Report to Greco* in hand). All imprinted irrevocably upon me that in each of these three related faith traditions, events of transcending import had transpired *in particular places.* At that stage of my journey, it was largely this tether to formative historical faith events that rendered a place spiritually special.

I certainly did not come to Tylerton expecting that I would ever use its name and Jerusalem in the same sentence, certainly not one about the geography/spirituality interface. After all, I knew of no towering religious events that had transpired here on this dot in the Chesapeake. Oh, I found the faith component of the waterman saga to be both fascinating and instructive, and from the first visit, I mused about how such a topographically challenged setting could yet be so mysteriously fetching.

But I did not choose Tylerton for reasons like one might choose Jerusalem or Assisi, Medjugorje or Gethsemane Abbey. Perhaps that is the point: I did not choose Tylerton. Rather, in retrospect, it seemingly chose me, and apprenticed me in the truth that the "holy" can be *now* and *here* and *random*, not just of the historically tethered variety. Tylerton would offer the gift of an external environment within which, and in partnership with, an internal journey could flower. Describing that kind of "spiritually evocative landscape," one not better but different from the historical sort, is the challenge I address in this chapter.

Ironies and incongruities abound in this geography/spirituality odd couple that became so prominent in my Tylerton decade. One is that the setting itself is least likely to be chosen, like the stripling David summoned from his flocks by Samuel only after all Jesse's studs had been found wanting (1 Sm 16). When Sanford Alwine introduced to me that notion of "spiritually evocative landscapes" early in our decade, he itemized three criteria: flowing water, the long vista, and mountains. While Tylerton arguably has two of these, that third one raises difficulties: its "mud hill" of dredge spoils from the excavated harbor, representing the village's peak elevation of nearly five feet, severely taxed both the imagination and aesthetic sensibilities. Mount Carmel or Sinai or Athos, the mud hill wasn't. This would be a bit of an ugly duckling story.

I found this incongruity—the least likely being chosen—built into the isle's ubiquitous "backwards talk." I discovered early on that the phrase "Ain't she *ugly!*" whether about boat, woman, or stark islescape, was, with the proper intonation, one I never quite mastered, actually lofty compliment!

There was a second irony in Tylerton's hook that was becoming set within my spirit. Jerusalem notwithstanding, I had moved to the isle in 1997 without any geography being home. What had contributed to this? The Minnesota farm I departed at age eighteen had contained multiple places, narratives, and meanings, but I would never live there again. Working across the following three decades in Mennonite church institutions as student, peace/justice activist, pastor, and professor had me traveling far and wide. Burying my second parent in 1996 severed my last familial link with the place of my birth. And I continued to nurture a wanderlust that had me living in more than a score of dwellings since college. All of this left me essentially a man without a place, one for whom places had become almost interchangeable.

Sharryl and my conversations in Tylerton about cremation following our eventual deaths had been fueled in part by each of us being among the un-placed. I had inhabited many places, toured many more, even fallen in love with one here and there, smitten, flirting mindlessly with "'til death do us part" thoughts, but I had always moved on. I was clearly not the protagonist in Pat Conroy's *Prince of Tides*, who begins his book with this: "My wound is geography. It was also my anchorage, my port of call." What in the Benedictine tradition is the vow of stability, in the institution of marriage monogamous fidelity, I had not entered into regarding place: I was a vagabond, place-promiscuous. All of this was about to change . . . well, for a decade.

A third incongruity in Tylerton's draw upon my spirit was the deep tension regarding place that exists within the Christian tradition itself. On the one hand (as I will elaborate upon later), Christianity in its Scriptures and tradition is place-specific: events—*seismic events*—unfolded in spaces that one mostly can find on a map and identify with GPS. Crowning the biblical narrative of the One encountering humanity in time and space for Christians is the birth of the Anointed, a birth at a particular time in a particular space. Place matters in the Christian faith!

And yet, there has always been for Christians a placelessness as well, for the One cannot be located in or confined to a particular location. There is a beautiful metaphor for this in the book of Exodus: instructions for the crafting of the ark of the covenant of YHWH at Mount Sinai included four gold rings designed to receive poles: *the ark was portable, ambulatory* (Ex 25:12–15). Thus that faith community was, not unlike my own, a pilgrim people for whom the "road" is home, the "journey" stability, and "flux" the constant.

Philip Sheldrake, in his *Spaces for the Sacred,* writes about the "perpetual departure" that is a basic feature of both the Scriptures and the Christian tradition, particularly monasticism. In short, while space/place matters, no one place can trump the journey, remove the transiency intrinsic to who the pilgrim is, or contain the One.

And finally, the argument has been made that rooting down in a place—*any* place rather than a particular one, any place rather than *the* place, to know that one place very well, entering into a kind vow of stability in relation to it—is the portal beyond which stretches an entirely new plane regarding place. A good example is anthropologist Richard Nelson's haunting love story, *The Island Within*. In his Preface he writes that the isle of his heart, which he protectively leaves unidentified, is special because of "the love and respect . . . [with] which its bounty is received," not because of how it presents itself to the sensorium. Places like persons, he argues, bury themselves in the heart; that is why they are loved, not because of this or that trait.

I both understand and empathize with Nelson's argument. Indeed, I have wondered whether its implicit truth—that having really loved one place well, *any* place, can take one beyond homelessness or living life out of a suitcase—may yet be part of the legacy Tylerton gives to me, long after I no longer reside here. His book seems a testimonial that what counts is to choose, focus on, give one's self to, and come to know intimately a place, not whether its face and charms are superior to all others.

Yet, Nelson's argument is not my own. Tylerton is a very particular place, an inimitable one, both the fact and specific content of whose dissimilitude seduced me off the scale of my previous experience. Yet the twist is that the features about her that drew me were so perversely improbable and had never drawn me before.

8. Place as Contested Construct

Some have argued that there are places, whether on land or sea, that intrinsically engage and impact the visitor's interior life: the desert renders one ascetic, the sunset aesthetic, the sea perhaps melancholy or awed. Were this so, one could reinvent oneself on demand, and with precision, merely by relocating to the appropriate place, a result some jet-setters perhaps pursue. The self in such a view is essentially plastic, being determined by the latest geography at hand.

The basic problem here, in addition to a vastly inadequate view of the self, is that not all, or even most, mountain denizens are noble, wilderness inhabitants contemplative, or dwellers under the night sky humble, for example. Human interaction with the natural environment is far more complex and interesting than such geographical determinism. A more encompassing understanding of the link between the internal journey and the external environs is needed.

A. Toward a Definition of "Place"

Belden Lane, in *The Solace of Fierce Landscapes,* writes of "place" as the product of interaction between a geographical space and the human imagination. What the place is experienced to be—and, indeed *is*—grows out of this interface.

A "Place" Is Not Merely a "Space"

The word "space" is used here as a physical expanse or extension over a surface or in a three-dimensional area. A particular space can be demarcated with GPS coordinates; it has or is location. In contrast, "place" is such a space which, in addition, has been encountered by human interiority. A place, in contrast to a space, is an object/subject collaboration. In this sense, a groundsel tree crashing to the ground in a storm on South Marsh—Smith's adjacent isle to the north, uninhabited and lacking more than minimal evidence of historic human culture—makes neither sound nor progression from space to place.

Place in this sense is more than space, more than a latitude-longitude location, larger than something filmed or digitized or pinpointed by GPS. It is rather something constructed or crafted, a kind of artistic synthesis or "construct," one at least slightly different for each visitor, visit, or locale. Whatever one's view of the origin of the cosmos, we mortals do also create. Indeed, argues Lane, we create place. The term "place," already employed in parts I and II, now takes on this more nuanced usage as something artistically crafted, not merely located or measured. Stated otherwise, while the terms "space" and "place" are both nouns, place is also something becoming, something happening!

A metaphor of this collaboration, one suggested by my pedagogue spouse, might be that of the reader bringing "pre-text"—background knowledge and perspective, including both personal and cultural context—to the "page" to produce "text." Amid the receiving of the objective data on the page, the reader is interpretively shaping it in terms of who she is and what she subjectively brings to it. The experience of reading, centering in this confluence of object and subject, is a "construct."

Stated otherwise, a construct is the fruit of union between something *out there* (in this case, a mid-Bay location) and something *in here* (the subjectivity of this *fúrr-ner*). But this fruit can be much more than mere progeny: it can emerge out of an affair moving through stages of acquaintance, familiarity, and passionate intimacy. Indeed, it can be a lovechild issuing out of the relationship between a space and one increasingly desiring to enter deeply into it. The birthed child, while indebted to both "parents," is clone of neither, but rather a collaborative creation of and beyond both, an entity increasingly having a life of its own. Some writers employ the term "topophilia" for this amorous relationship which people and spaces generate together.

Place as Troika: Space, Cultural Memory, Visitor

A contribution of the British writer Philip Sheldrake, as highlighted in the subtitle of his *Spaces for the Sacred: Place, Memory, and Identity*, is to emphasize a third component of place: memory. Space has become place for Sheldrake in part because it has been able to evoke remembrance of the collective dreams, narratives, emotions, and cosmologies of those of yore who have embraced that place. Rather than merely binary in structure, the place construct is a *troika*: space, human imagination, and cultural memory.

Place is most powerful when space encounters human interiority amid the murmuring recollections of others for whom this place has been their own. Indeed, rather than seemingly having been thrown together, the three are increasingly seen to possess some mysterious ontological affinity. This threefold understanding of place (space, the visitor's imagination, evoked historic memory), a sturdy three-legged stool, is adhered to throughout the remainder of this book. The power of place is always shaped by the extent to which the visitor engaging the space is drawn into what has previously been experienced there.

While enriching the working definition of place operative here, however, Sheldrake's third leg also complicates the task. His emphasis proscribes private snuggling of space and self; it means that a place cannot be known ahistorically, apart from its evoked memory and narratives. In part for this reason, parts II

("The Place"), III ("The Meaning of Place") and IV ("Receiving the Stranger Without: Hospitality") of this work have distinct historical components. In its own way, Part VI makes this point even more strongly. To love a particular place is to open oneself to the love legacy left by others in earlier times.

But more difficult questions follow: in the messiness of history, whose memory gets evoked? Of the evoked memories, to whose do we listen? What are the criteria for that decision? What is the responsibility of the visitor to space where, among various re-callable sagas, it is the accounts of those who won the battles that are actually recalled?

In the remainder of this chapter, I comment first on some of the implications of such a construct approach for understanding the past four hundred years of Bay history. Second, I employ that same approach to the dialogue between the differing dreams that Sharryl and I brought to the table, out of which emerged a construct vi-sion of the Inn of Silent Music.

B. The Bay's History of Contested Constructs

A single location is frequently an ingredient in several different constructs, each cre-ating a different place, with tension the result. The question of what shall be the definitive construct generates conflict. Jerusalem is arguably the clearest example: an urban location and population, definable by map coordinates, interpreted pro-foundly differently by each of the three Abrahamic faiths (among others), each in turn containing a spectrum of competing political and ideological perspectives. The result is that Jerusalem is essentially three constructs, *three places.* Twentieth-century conflicts in South Africa, the Balkans, the Punjab, the area between the Jordan Valley and the Mediterranean, Northern Ireland, or around the very notion of a Kurdistan can also be understood as part of a much longer history of contested and contesting constructs.

The Clash of Amerindian and European Constructs

Across its post-contact history, the Bay has been a repeated target for contesting con-structs. The first European visitors encountered a paradigm, seemingly supported by all of the basin's residents, quite contrary to their own. The ancestral rivers and the Chesapeake ("great sea of shellfish") itself were a center around which Amerindian cultures had emerged and now thrived. The Bay provided transport, a source for much of their food and materials for clothing and shelter, and included vistaed living sites offering a measure of security, to say nothing of delight.

Beyond this, however, the various tribes shared to a remarkable extent a sense of the Bay, themselves, and all else of their existence as part of a whole, a seamless material world imbued with spiritual realities. The Amerindian thus lived in the watershed as partner, collaborator, and constituent, rather than as dominator and subduer of nature. With the possible exception of hastening megafauna extinction by the Clovis hunters and some deforestation by late woodland practitioners of agriculture, the interaction of the Bay's pre-Columbian tribes with their natural environment left the Bay's watershed as whole and healthy as they found it. Viewing themselves as an integral part of nature, they generally sought the common good of that whole by seeking to live in harmony with the other components.

In contrast, the Europeans' initial explorations of the basin packed a radically different pre-text. Nature, particularly New World nature, was wildly unbridled and ripe for subjugation and domestication. When early explorers came up empty with the first tier of prizes—gold and direct passage to the Orient's spice isles—they moved to plan B, and beyond: extraction of commodities such as furs; planting of crops such as tobacco that accelerated deforestation and were harmful to soil and water alike; and formation of settlements to reinforce geopolitical power. Indigenes were subjugated as slaves by the Spanish or became candidates for proselytization or exile by most other Europeans, including the English. Europeans later exploited forests for agriculture and rivers for the power that manufacturing required.

All of these European values, poured into the crafting of place, were both possible and inevitable, driven by the underlying assumption that the European's role in relation to nature was one of subduer and dominator. Or, as one still occasionally hears plainspoken in Tylerton, "it was put here by the Creator for us to take." To European settlers, what humans shared with the rest of nature was less important than what was different about them.

The paradigms of the indigenes and the Europeans, each containing radically differing pre-texts, and thus texts, collided head-on in the Bay region. In the 160 years following initial contact, the Amerindian population was decimated, with the culture of numerous tribes disappearing completely. Two constructs and two cosmologies jousted. But one, in addition to its metallurgical skills, armor, gunpowder, horses, geopolitical power, and natural immunity to its own diseases, promoted its cause with a religion-fueled militancy. For the majority of Amerindian individuals as well as tribes, the contest between their constructs of the Bay and those of the newcomers, was, to cite contemporary Thomas Hobbes, "nasty, brutal, and short."

Construct Conflict in Three Wars

It is interesting to note that construct conflict would remain a central theme in the involvement of the Bay in the young nation's three major wars during its first ninety years: the Revolutionary War (1775–1783), the War of 1812 (1812–1815), and the Civil War (1861–1865). In each of these, control of the Bay was mightily contested, both with ships and with constructs.

The Revolutionary War was fought over the issue whether the Bay and the colonies surrounding it up and down the coast would remain England's exploitable asset or become an independent nation. The outcome of efforts by the British and American navies (the latter supported by the French) to control the Chesapeake would play a huge role in the war's decisive battle, which occurred in the autumn of 1781 at Yorktown on the York River, just off the lower Bay.

In the War of 1812, the construct conflict remaining much the same, British forces passed just west of Smith Island on their way to the Patuxent and the August 14, 1814, burning of Washington, D.C. Exactly one month later, the attack by the British fleet on Fort McHenry in Baltimore was launched from Tangier Island, part of the "Russels Iles" seven miles south of Smith, again passing just to the west on its way north to that fateful battle.

One could argue that both sides in all three conflicts were primarily motivated by the geostrategic value of the Bay. But it was particularly in the Civil War—a conflict that would split Smith Island fields, families, and hearts—that two competing visions collided as to what this place called the Chesapeake would be. For blacks on Smith—and there were small numbers of both slaves and free before 1860—the magnitude of this collision of constructs cannot be exaggerated. A large portion of the Union forces that would eventually take Richmond on the James on the way to Appomattox in April of 1865 came down the Potomac, turning to starboard within sight of our island.

That war, together with the continuing loss of farmland to rising sea level and the 1866 opening of the railroad head in Somerset County's port of Somers Cove (now Crisfield), hastened the transformation of Smith Islanders from reapers of the land to harvesters of the sea.

Construct Conflict Today

This legacy of contested constructs involving Tylerton is not likely to change in the early twenty-first century. The newest confrontation on the block during our decade is between the traditional *waterman vision* (more attention to this later in the chapter), and the *development vision* that is presently transforming Crisfield and that may spread to Smith Island. Allowing only loosely regulated development and the market to make a wide range of judgments that have profound ethical and ecological consequences and defining "good" primarily in terms of wealth generation are major reasons why the Bay today is on the ropes, fighting valiantly for its life.

Relatively new actors in the construct conflict are mainlanders who have bought waterman houses on Tylerton for seasonal or vacation use. The bulk of them have come because they value the local culture and seek to absorb some of its pace, peace, pristinity, and price. They—we—have also surely changed Tylerton, generally with sensitivity and restrained self-interest. In fact, we relatively benevolent interlopers will be important players in the future of the community, intermediate construct-ors who are seeking to conserve amid change.

The marsh, tidal passages, peerless horizon, and teeming biosphere—these are among nature's given. Many other ingredients of each competing construct are what we humans bring to the table and then fight over.

C. Our Complementary Spousal Constructs

So what did Sharryl and I each bring that contributed to the place this islescape would become for us? What predispositions did we pack that would influence what we would see, and to what we would give our passions?

Sharryl's Vision for the Inn

Sharryl's earlier life in central California was graced with an extended family cabin near Santa Cruz with its redwoods and coastal beaches; later there was a second home as well in Yosemite in the high Sierras. In both of these, among other spaces, her crafting of place had included the enhancing of its beauty. And it was to this challenge of transforming deficient spaces into something beautiful that she gave herself throughout our decade on the Crick.

Outside the Inn, this impulse could have taken her in various directions, but she chose gardening. Or perhaps, again, it chose her. In a saline environment that precluded trees, vegetables, and most flowers planted in the ground, and where the word "lawn" sometimes warranted quotation marks, she made our wetlands bloom with flowers *ex nihilo* throughout the major portion of our decade's seasons. This required many halved whiskey barrels, fabricated flower boxes, and elevated pots, to say nothing of bags and bags of dirt—more about them later—all providing me with an important supportive role in her construct. Some of our guests would be reticent to leave the comfort of the screened porch when the surrounding petunias, marigolds, day lilies, lantana, gladiolas, clematis, coleus, crape myrtle, morning glory, trumpet vine, and marsh hibiscus were in their glory.

Inside, the analogue of rogues Salinity, Tide, and Wind, was the dark paneling that Tylerton must have purchased en masse at some fire sale in 1963. It was, shall

I say, ubiquitous. And melancholic, our building was, with furnishings to match. So Sharryl had her challenge of deficient spaces, her sow's ear candidate for silk purse-hood. With no guidebook at hand, she was both condemned and freed to find her own way to make it sing. And sing it would!

But created beauty must finally be shared, the singing requires an audience, and Sharryl had several, the first our guests. Whether with the wisteria covering the deck off the kitchen, the deep yellow decor of the Sassafras Hammock room which the sun would ignite daily as it rose out of the loblollies, or simple ingredients beguiled into German apple puffed pancakes, the highest reward for Sharryl was guests made joyful. This love for the conspiracy of eye, hand, and imagination sustained her through both the thirty months of renovation and the ten years of one guest after another, through the dinner or room preparation, even when she ran on fumes.

The other audience to whom Sharryl brought joy was the citizens of Tylerton, who one way or another were seduced by her alchemy. They might be cruising past the Inn in golf carts as dinner approached, commenting on the scents wafting from the kitchen (often in their inimitable—"that dinner ain't no good!") or on the beauty of her flowers, set off by the marshglow just before Sol retired for the night.

Much earlier, Sharryl and I had recreationally visited potential B&B properties, including some at the end of the Bay's innumerable necks, several with no community and scarcely any neighbors. In contrast, Sharryl loved the fact that our Inn was at the edge of a hamlet: out off to itself, yet only a three-minute bike ride from the social frenzy in Tylerton's tiny store or tinier post office. Her reclusive potential was never fully developed, her favorite apparel never the hair shirt. In short, Sharryl loved the place first and last; she never stopped loving it more than any of its possible esoteric meanings; and that love was returned in bounty by guests and Tylertonians alike.

My Vision for the Inn

On the other hand, there was the pre-text that I brought to the Inn project. As starters, I, like "isle groupies" sprinkled among our guests over the years, had had this thing about islands. During the Middle East years, my work had given me several opportunities to explore Cyprus, both before and after the Turkish invasion in July 1974. Having dated but one island, I was forever smitten. Granted, part of my seduction was by whatever isle was the setting of my most recent venture into the writings of Kazantzakis. Amid my political alienation at the time, I dreamed vacuously of moving my family to the Greek isle of Hydra in the Saronic Gulf after leaving Jerusalem.

I thus brought to Tylerton a decades-long hankering for, among other things, islands' sea vistas; for the microcosmic quality vis-à-vis planet Earth of all aspects of island life; and for the isle uniqueness of travel and provisioning logistics, culture, self-understanding. Interestingly, neither the boating life nor either fishing or gunning had ever been on my serious wish list, although I was fascinated by the waterman culture made up of those doing this much the time.

What both Sharryl and I brought to this setting was a scintillating excitement: could we really pull off this B&B thing? Family and friends seemed to fret about early-onset dementia. And my Washington dentist—whose home was on Kent Island, opposite Annapolis—lectured me on the inhospitableness of watermen toward out-siders, doing so while he had my mouth clamped open, leaving me uncharacteristically bereft of words. Yes, following seven plus splendid years on Dupont Circle, an Inn on Tylerton was an even bigger challenge, and that for us was both draw and pre-text.

But for me there was more. Amid the frenzied life deep inside the beltway, I had become aware of a hunger to unclutter my life, to make in my midfifties some seri-ous choices about what mattered a lot and what less so. I wanted to live slower and better, read more and listen more to classical music, spare my sensorium some of the blizzard of advertising, build with Sharryl what would be our first real home together, pray and marvel more and more deeply. I knew myself too well to think that all this would unfold automatically or even readily on an island—after all, I was bringing *myself* along! But I had longed for a more supportive environment for these growing edges, and Tylerton seemed promising.

My bringing of the decluttering criterion to the emerging construct for the Inn ran counter to some of Sharryl's instincts, and in the hard-nosed negotiations in the years following, I lost more than I won in that tussle, fortunately for our guests. But on the personal level, the impulse for a simpler, slower, and deeper life was right there for me, both when we began and as we approached our decade's end.

One insight upon which Sharryl and I agreed was that, for better or for worse, tourism would increasingly be a resource for the modest redistribution of wealth, whether at the local or international level. If one's locale was relatively poor yet at-tractive in some sense—this being the case with Tylerton in relation to the profes-sional classes of the nearby mainland cities—there was leveling to be had, local benefit to be gained. This dynamic became increasingly clear to both of us across the decade.

This leveling never took place without a price, namely that urban visitors in-variably altered the social entity they came to visit. But we thought that, for various reasons, Tylerton was managing that price better than, for example, either North End or nearby Tangier Island.

In retrospect, my decluttering thing was what might be called "entry-level detachment." Not reactionary Luddism, not Gnostic rejection of the material world in favor of an ethereal one, not primarily a countercultural reaction to the prevalent "consumolatry" (although some of the latter was in me). Rather, what I wanted with whatever years I was given was to clear away some of the mediocre, the good, and perhaps even the better, so as to make room for the gift of the best.

Deep beneath my consciousness and intellectual machinations there was simple desire, a hunger for the Center, for the One beneath and beyond this and that. And for that direction, Tylerton proved itself to be journey-friendly. Alas, in contrast to my mate, as the decade unfolded, I just might have come to love the place's meaning even more than the place itself.

The Construct Jousting that became the Inn

The objective material of our place construct in Tylerton was fairly straightforward. The main part of the building we purchased in January 1995 was a two-and-a-half story "Maryland House," with an attic gable midway along one side facing a few degrees south of due west. I ascertained that the first European owner of land that included this site (a Smith) had sold it to the second owner (a Tyler) in 1693. But I unearthed no evidence of a building on the location until about 1914, when the youthful Capt'n Howard Wesley and Miss Venie (née Evans) Marshall capped a fruitful net-fishing season by building a house that would become the Inn about 83 years later.

Sometime in the 1930s a rear wing was added. Formerly a small two-story house that Capt'n Alonzo and Miss Lola Hoffman had abandoned to rising sea level half a mile away in the tiny settlement of Hootenville, it was floated in on a scow and attached. The total square footage, including the third-floor innkeepers' quarters completed after our second season, approached two thousand square feet, but only if the spacious screened porch that a Tylerton craftsman built for us before we opened was factored in.

The building was about twenty-five feet from Tyler's "Crick." This is not a creek as most would visualize it, but a quarter-mile-wide, very shallow tidal passage between the several nearly flat islets that comprise Smith Island. (I use "the Crick" throughout this book as shorthand for the Inn and its immediate environs.) The Inn site had nearly 135 feet of "crick frontage," and extended back about 425 feet.

In my orientation pitch to new guests, I often spit out the fact that the elevation around the building was an even two feet above sea level. (I would sometimes wonder whether the guests were suddenly less sure that they had placed themselves in responsible hands for their stay.)

I indicated that Sharryl and I each brought a pre-text to this Inn text, and thus two constructs that we sought to bring into closer proximity throughout the renovation period. What exactly did we want our *niche*, our nonnegotiable criterion for a B&B, to be?

My part gravitated toward integrating hospitality and spirituality, but this was a hypothesis in quest of a model. The overtly *Christian* B&Bs we had visited, actually or virtually, were primarily evangelical efforts whose brochures might highlight no-alcohol policies. On the other hand, Roman Catholic houses of hospitality were generally affiliated with religious orders and not pitching the B&B crowd. I never did find a clear existent model. Rich and extended conversation over brunch in July 1995 with friends Teri and Bill Hocking was but one of the many settings in which I in particular was seeking to sketch out such a model.

Naming the Inn

In the end, we followed Sharryl's wisdom by entering the B&B mainstream, but with a name that would hopefully connote our spirituality interests to at least some guests. I had hopes that, in time, the name and its elicited responses would provide additional direction in the courtship between our two constructs.

The August vacation that Sharryl and I had spent in 1994 in the cottage adjacent to what would become the Inn had been an idyllic experience. Repeatedly during the subsequent renovation period, Sharryl and I would return to that month as if to extract the full measure of its elixir. We realized that the natural environment had had a marked impact on us: slowing our urban rhythms, initiating us into silence, generating within us harmony being played out without, and eliciting within us awe and gratitude and joy. And there were yeasty questions to be explored: could not the very presentation of an inn in this place nudge interested guests in the direction of some of the experiences we ourselves had enjoyed that month? Were there not people out there desiring a similar respite? If we built such an inn, would they not indeed come? And was there a name for the inn that would hint of such an alternative vision?

Hoping that niche would follow name, I argued strongly, and successfully, against the likes of "Swan Fall Inn" or "The Inn on Tyler Crick" in favor of "Inn of Silent Music." My case for this name is a window into what I brought to both my own Inn construct and the negotiated result that would perhaps look, taste, and feel more like the other innkeeper. I had first encountered the term *silent music* in the poem "The Spiritual Canticle," written by the sixteenth-century Spanish Discalced Carmelite mystic and poet John of the Cross (1542–91), while imprisoned in Toledo in 1577–78.

Following is a translation from the Spanish of stanzas 14 and 15 of this poem by Fr. Kieran Kavanaugh, OCD:

My Beloved, the mountains,
and lonely wooded valleys,
strange islands,
and resounding rivers,
the whistling of love-stirring breezes,

the tranquil night
at the time of the rising dawn,
silent music,
sounding solitude,
the supper that refreshes, and deepens love.

During the years following his escape from prison, John of the Cross would be prevailed upon to write extended commentaries on much of his poetry. He would write the following, probably in 1584, regarding the audio image of "silent music":

> [T]he [person] becomes aware of Wisdom's wonderful harmony and sequence in the variety of her creatures and works. Each of them is endowed with a certain likeness of God and in its own way gives voice to what God is in it. So creatures will be for the [person] a harmonious symphony of sublime music surpassing all concerts and melodies of the world. She calls this music "silent" because it is tranquil and quiet knowledge, without the sound of voices. And thus there is in it the sweetness of music and the quietude of silence. Accordingly, she says that her Beloved is silent music because in him she knows and enjoys this symphony of spiritual music. . . . a symphony of love, . . . In this same way the [person] perceives in that tranquil wisdom that all creatures, higher and lower ones alike, according to what each in itself has received from God, raise their voice in testimony to what God is. She beholds that each in its own way, bearing God within itself according to its capacity, magnifies God. And thus all these voices form one voice of music praising the grandeur, wisdom, and wonderful knowledge of God.

And so it would be the Inn of Silent Music, a place awash in a grand symphony of love to which each represented creature, according to its capacity, contributed its notes by virtue of its very existence. The fact that the name was, at some levels, a kind of faith wine poured into entrepreneurial wineskins, precluded the absence of tension. Several articles during the decade explored this spirituality component of our construct, including one in the *Washington Post*. The pieces were largely benign, generating but a single piece of hate mail.

Tylertonians seemed puzzled by our handle, and a family member thought it sounded too "New Age," but it was the shingle we hung out for (in the words of our brochure), "An Inn with a difference in a place with a difference." The name would, in time, be shown to serve equally well each of the construct contestants in our hair shirt/satin sheets *affaire de coeur*.

9. Place as Shaper of Culture and Narrative

Place is crafted amid the interplay between a space and what the visitor brings to it. But that process is further enriched in a space populated by people of a relatively long-term and cohesive culture. The collective life and memory of such a group are themselves a complex of constructs crafted across the generations in a process not unlike that of the visitor coming to the space. And that complex of constructs continues to shape the very population having given rise to it. In fact, space, resident culture as embodiment of historic memory, and visitor are all affecting one another. "Place" comes to life amid this trialectic, even as each of the other two parties is changed.

This chapter focuses on one facet of this dynamic: how Tylerton's culture has been shaped across the last nearly 350 years by the given of its natural environment. Stated as a question, what has being islanders contributed to the villagers' self-understanding and identity during that history?

It goes without saying that the villagers' own construct of place had a profound impact on that process for Sharryl and me. This was partly the result of the way they accepted us, rather than holding us off, as my toothdrawer had warned. That we, urban and educated Roman Catholics with profoundly different life experiences, were taken in by this community—and that I in particular was entrusted with a teaching ministry in their congregation—would enrich our experience here beyond measure. While Adam Wallace, biographer of the islands' revered revivalist Joshua Thomas in his *Parson of the Islands*, was not above turning a phrase like "the withering blight of popery," I would never hear anything of the sort in our decade.

While we would in some respects ever remain foreigners—our degree of alienness seemed to vary from subject to subject, from villager to villager—both Sharryl and I came to experience the Tylertonians' embrace of us as more than we could ever have hoped for. I was granted an "honorary captainship" at the May 7, 2000 Blessing of the Boats, because we too were recognized as making our living from the water. Furthermore, many of our guests have also had sufficient interaction with villagers for their own isle constructs to be shaped by more than merely the Inn's geography, accommodations, and cuisine.

So, again, how are the culture and narrative of Tylerton place-tethered, perhaps in a way distantly analogous to Jerusalem, my previous geographical significant other? A comprehensive response to this question is itself a book-length study calling for the skills of sociologist, geographer, anthropologist, and perhaps shaman, most of which I do not possess. Rather, the method I use here is that of glimpses—a perfect seven of them—of ways in which more overtly *faith-related* aspects of Tylerton's history and culture are shaped by its citizens' experience of place, isle-place.

A. The Stunning Immediacy of Nature

Outside the tiny grid of buildings that is home to Tylerton's fifty-eight year-round residents (as of 2006) and the similarly minuscule skylines of neighboring Rhodes Point and North End, virtually everything accessible to the sensorium here is nature, whether big sky or vast salt marsh or enveloping Bay or the ceaseless cries of seabirds or the marsh's olfactory bar code. And aside from tiny artifacts of civilization dotting the distant horizons—angular smudges of Crisfield's new condos floating nearly ten miles away on the eastern horizon, the Smith Point Light splitting the upland of Virginia's Northern Neck to the west-southwest, the defiant water tower of neighboring Tangier Island seven miles due south, the ghostly mirage of occasional container vessels en route to or from Baltimore, the odd aircraft or satellite in the night sky—everything beyond the island accessible to the senses is nature.

Furthermore, nearly all of life, especially for the watermen and their children crossing water to school, unfolds in this natural world. A waterman may run his working boat east into Tangier Sound before first light six days a week for most of seven months of the year, and what he sees out there as sunrise approaches severely taxes language.

Early on, Sharryl and I were out there with Dwight Marshall, then in his late forties, on his *Miss Marshall* before dawn, when I asked if he ever tired of seeing what was before us. He delayed his unadorned "no" long enough to study my face, seemingly puzzled one would pose such a question.

Thursday night's sunset might surface in Sunday morning's "class meeting," a testimonial service harking back to Smith's Wesleyan origins. "Breezin' up!" "Ain't she purdie!" "Speaks of rain!" and "Gittin' *nasty!*" are more than information bytes. They are greetings one receives in the hamlet's narrow lanes, the functional equivalent of "how ya doin'?" The response to a question about *anything* is liable to begin with a qualifying clause projecting tomorrow's weather, especially the wind, which, with co-regent tide, rules. The life of the waterman is simply *sodden* with nature. Regarding matters of land and sea, he is ambidextrous; the lot of them, in the words of Adam Wallace, are "an amphibious race."

The Symbiosis of Waterman and Nature

The immediacy of nature that colors both the waterman's psyche and the culture at large is best showcased in story. The village's culture is a narrative one, *oral* narrative insofar as stories reside chiefly in memory, both individual and collective, rather than in books. An evening in the Drum Point Market, the village's tiny general store and luncheonette, listening to the men yarnin', is replete with tales in nature settings: the return of the migrating fish hawk within a day or two of St. Patty's Day, the scent of watermelon indicating the presence of a shark, the little black flies as harbingers of weather change, the encounter with the day's unruly squall, recitals of past brushes with death on the Bay, the unusual critter turning up in the crab scrape.

It would be impossible to exaggerate the pervasiveness of such nature tales or the cunning with which the watermen read nature's book. In the store one winter night, I listened as Alan Smith, with tears on his cheeks, employed Holy Writ (Dt 32:11, Ex 19:4) to relive his experience having watched a bald eagle teaching its young to fly.

These seamen have retained a solidarity—indeed, symbiosis—with nature that repeatedly has had me thinking of the Amerindian living in the Chesapeake basin five hundred or five thousand years ago. But rather than more analysis, better here to re-spin a couple of yarns, each involving the osprey (fish hawk). . . .

Welcoming Back the Fish Hawk

Fish hawk. The words were spreading up the nave during Miss Stella's organ prelude as the Tylerton congregation awaited the arrival of Rev. Rick Edmund ("the preacher") on the crab boat *Patti Ann,* in his Sunday morning circuit among Smith Island's three congregations. I turned, catching the eye of Missy, three pews back: "Yup, Ronnie saw a fish hawk coming back from Rhodes Point!" she exulted.

The hubbub about what mainlanders call an osprey subsided as first the choir and then the pastor processed, but then resumed briefly as one of his first announcements was that on this, the vernal equinox, the first fish hawk had finally been seen. It was only at about this time that Capt'n Ronnie Corbin, having safely conveyed the pastor, himself entered the sanctuary to find that everyone there already knew his good news. Three or four days late the fish hawk was, her appointment being St. Patty's Day. But the cosmos hadn't thrown a sprocket after all, spring had indeed arrived, and all was well on Tylerton!

Tell me: about what other place in the cosmos might the above paragraphs have been written?

Waterman Encounters Fish Hawk

And then, occasionally, it all goes far deeper. An example involves, again, Dwight Marshall, arguably the village's consummate waterman: a man of few words, facile mind, gruff exterior including arresting ice-blue eyes passed on to his four adult children, and an expansive heart. In the Sunday morning "class meeting"—nearly 150 years ago Adam Wallace called them "experience meetings"—he told a story about his father, Russell.

The senior Marshall had a heart attack in 1975 while in his skiff just off Peach Orchard Point, perhaps a mile into the Commonwealth below the Inn. Marshall had managed to make his way back to the county dock, where he was found unconscious, and died later that night in the Crisfield hospital. Over the following decades, Dwight conceded, he had found himself giving a wide berth to Peach Orchard Point.

However, now he was relating how he recently had found himself in his boat in that vicinity, when he thought he detected movement on the shore out of the corner of his eye. Looking more closely, he saw that a fish hawk, ever on the prey, had gotten itself caught inside an abandoned crabbing bank trap near the shoreline. Recognizing that the raptor would starve to death if not freed, Dwight located his heaviest gloves, maneuvered his craft as close as possible, and gingerly reached inside the bank trap. The bird, improbably docile, allowed him to draw it out and then loft it up into the sky and freedom. Dwight described how it flew a large circle above him, as if signing gratitude, and then climbed up and away.

"Suddenly," Dwight told the hushed class meeting, struggling to find the words, "the fish hawk was my father's spirit ascending up to God, and I was able to let Dad go and be at peace." I would later have to corral Dwight to get the end of his story, because I had long since gone to tears. For while I shared Dwight's problem—my father died when I was thirty-one—I had not been favored with such an apotheosis. Even now, I suspect that the story as here told is colored as much by how I heard it as by what he actually said.

Only later did I become aware of a second tier of response to Dwight's story: amazement. His tale is not the sort likely to be overheard at the office water cooler; in fact, it is the kind of thing I might rather have expected from a Nanticoke warrior of yore. Beyond that, I marveled at Dwight's compassion for the fish hawk's predicament and certain fate, at the implicit sense of solidarity with this beautiful critter, at the courage summoned in the face of the danger this powerful raptor represented in close quarters (four pounds of muscled talons), and at his trusting of his own impulse to compassion.

Above all, however, I was astonished by the way a highly improbable encounter in the natural world had become a profound spiritual tutorial regarding one of a man's principal passages: letting go of a deceased and beloved father. Only a people living with nature in their faces could have generated such a narrative. Through my tears, both then and now, I know that its truth is near the center of the Tylerton I came to know and would always love.

Gender and the Relationship with Nature

A qualification, however. The gender specificity that is characteristic of nearly all Tylerton culture pertains here as well. All the men have varying degrees of intuitive knowledge of, and affinity for, the natural environment. Otherwise, they would not be here. Those not so equipped live on Delmarva.

In contrast, many women, with several exceptions, seem to be tethered to the isle primarily because their men are, and they seem to possess a lesser link with nature than the males. Indeed, there are women who fear the rough passage across the sometimes turbulent Sound, whose anxiety for their men's safety is seldom far away, and even a few who view nature almost as predator. In the larger Bay environment in which some seem willing to kill for frontage, one Tylertonian sequestered on its Back Street expressed gratitude that she could not see the hated water from a single one of her windows!

On the other hand, I know four or five women who might read a magazine straight through a rough crossing which had me praying "Out of the depths" (Ps 130:1). My point is that *whatever* their disposition toward the natural environment, the isle women, with several exceptions, had not been socialized to read its message and inhale its ambience as had the men. Later in this chapter I will discuss a beautiful quality shared by most of the women precisely because they have not been socialized as Lone Rangers out on the Bay.

B. The Sensate Life

Tylerton is a community in which the people's interior bias for the particular over the universal is supplied with raw materials by the enormously rich organic world around them. Each—the people's preference for the concrete over the abstract, and the sensual fecundity of the environs—seems to spark and amplify the other.

"Herring Hucksters" are Nominalists?!

For example, only a *fŭrr-ner* would have entitled a chapter "The *Meaning* of Place"! Ask Tylertonians—"herring hucksters" is an old nickname for them used by the "cheese eaters" of Rhodes Point and the "bean snuckers" of North End—about the meaning or significance, the implications or ramifications, of this or that, and what you get is either a tsunami of specifics or a yarn that is really a bail (read *pail*) of detail crafted as a tale. In terms of the medieval scholasticism debate regarding the reality of particulars or universals, Tylertonians, at least Monday through Saturday, are nominalists (or, of more recent vintage, logical positivists). Only physical particulars actually exist; universals, abstractions, and generalizations are merely tetherless clouds, *sans* utility, floating high above. Abstractions, *a la* horses, do not thrive here on Tylerton, and they never did: life is in the ordinary particulars rather than the grand generalizations. Why, while I'm still asleep these men are gulping down specificity with their scrapple before hitting the water!

I call it a "sensorium" culture, a way of life in which the gorgeously visible is actually seen, the understated audibly heard, the tactile really felt, the arresting aroma actually inhaled, the succulent really tasted and then devoured. An evening visit to the Women's Crab Picking Co-op in summer matches the men's circle in the Market in winter: the sensate life rather than an ideational or abstract one, a utopian or extrapolated one. Oh, there can be the occasional wild ejaculation from the store's liars' benches about *all* Democrats, *all* Muslims, or *all* women, but these often politically incorrect haymakers only confirm the rule.

An Olfactory Sampler

Since my memory (if not my present faculties) has a sense port of choice, the olfactory, allow me to play some tapes related to this sense, that of the neglected and occasionally dishonored proboscis. As indicated earlier, the *terra firma* of Tylerton's olfactory symphony is the salt marsh air, an odor a local might term "clean," something else by some *fŭrr-ners*.

Odors are difficult to describe, but this one, a smell on the road to becoming a scent or even fragrance, is briny to the point of slightly musty. The odor is pungent enough to clear the sinuses, whether literal or metaphorical. After I had lived in Tylerton for some years, the scent had become second nature to me so that I could detect its *absence* elsewhere more readily than its presence here.

And playing above the salty air is a bevy of other smells, odors, scents, and fragrances. The recurrence of any of these can transport me instantly back to Tylerton from wherever else I may be:

- the lovingly nurtured marigolds in Ruth Evans' garden;
- the tincture of ozone under the violet, violent dome as the big June thunderstorm gathers itself to strike;
- the airborne detritus of the menhaden processing plant in Reedville on the Northern Neck of Virginia, having ridden the honing-in east-northeast breezes across the Bay's thirteen miles into Tylerton;
- the slightly putrid swampy odor on those few summer days when there is no wind and it is, as the islanders say, "slick cam";

- the lavish honeysuckle bookending the Inn's screened porch in June, seducing guests to linger;

- the vast amounts of crab imperial on the groaning tables in the church basement at an autumn community dinner;

- the price paid on clothes, hair, and body of having lingered too long in the friendly scented confines of the Co-op;

- the recalcitrant reminder on the hands after having filleted a bushel of hardheads.

The marsh surrounding Tylerton is an organic kingdom, and especially on a still day in fall, it can really smell that way. There are so many moments on Tylerton when life leads out with the organ of the nose.

Yet ... "This World Is Not My Home"

Finally, an irony on a place not a stranger to such. Despite the profound impact of the locale—the natural and the sensual, the historical and the cultural—upon the islanders' faith, the living out of that faith remains among many of Tylerton's faithful a preliminary bout to the main event: the next world. The gospel song, "This world is not my home, I'm just apassin' through," characterizes much Tylerton piety. Tears in the choir on a Sunday morning, sometimes copious, are far more likely to be shed amid songs about the "new heavens" than the "new earth" (2 Pt 3:13); about the next world removed from this one rather than this one healed, the garden of lion and lamb, the final domicile of the One. Totally embedded in the created world, the islanders are, nevertheless, seemingly *fúrr-ners* here.

Despite the immediacy of nature among islanders across the day, the season, and the life span, that nature does not seem to have a significant role in their understanding of the Greater Life. Souls are saved, not bodies; creation more escaped than restored. While my deepening appreciation for nature was indebted to water folk beyond any words I could find, reflection on the redeemed destiny of that nature from a Christian perspective—one of my growing edges during the decade—was for me a lonely journey. The ultimate future of that nature, the world in which their lives are so totally immersed, seemed to be a theme checked at the church door.

C. The Absence of Control

The shadow side of Tylerton's immersion in nature, accessed via the senses, is absence of control. Being in control is only a modern myth anyway, it seems to me—particularly after 9/11, the Asia tsunami of late 2004, and hurricanes Katrina and Rita the following August—but a myth easier to fall for while dashing between fabricated urban envelopes. Shedding that myth came early in our time on the Crick. This lack of control can touch isle life in many ways: fog or ice may delay the children's voyage to or from school; the doctor's appointment may need to be postponed; the hurricane may either terminate the crabbing season or gouge a ten-day bite out of it. The sudden squall may mean collecting the mail tomorrow instead of today, the ice that there's nothing there to collect.

Furthermore, the islanders often feel powerless as their micro is throttled by the macro of mainland institutions:

- Seafood harvest regulations hatched in distant offices by bureaucrats who may be in the thrall of special interests;
- The health of the Bay and the waterman hunter/gatherer livelihood dependent on the behavior of farmers in Pennsylvania's Lancaster County, sporting boat operators, poultry processors, recreational crabbers, and developers;
- The commitment to sound waste treatment policies on the part of distant municipalities;
- The vagaries of partisan politics making Byzantium seem fairly straightforward by comparison.

The *hubris* of the control freak takes a real beating here. In fact, this Smith Island setting might be the strongest argument in favor of context having an intrinsic and predictable impact on its human residents: I found living in Tylerton year-round to be inescapably *humbling*. The water folk don't use the word "contingency," but the notion that there is nothing, not even one's self, that needs necessarily *to be* rather than *not be*, is familiar to them.

"Keep Me Safe 'til the Storm Passes By"

This awareness of lack of control is at least as fully present in the consciousness of the women as the men. More than a few times in dangerous weather, have I heard women invoking the protection of "Jesus asleep in the *starn*"(Mk 4:38). Nor will I soon forget Dora Corbin, herself a fearful traveler on rough seas, her voice breaking at one of the village's Blessing of the Boats services on the CBF green, as she read the following:

> *Those who go down to the sea in ships,*
> *Who do business on great waters; . . .*
> *They rose up to the heavens,*
> *they went down to the depths;*

Their soul melted away in their misery.
They reeled and staggered like a drunken man,
And were at their wits' end. (Ps 107:23, 26–27)

And then there is what might be called the Tylerton theme song: "Keep Me Safe 'til the Storm Passes By." While I have heard the choir sing it on a Sunday morning, it is really the signature piece of the women of the Smith Island Crab Picking Co-Op, composed of both the blessed and the rest. Across our ten I repeatedly heard them sing it for guests in three-part harmony while tilting with steamed crustaceans (once dubbed by an exhausted picker as simply "damn orange").

This poignant song will nudge me toward tears: for a moment, I am waiting with each woman as her overdue navigator, or one of their sons, or a father, races to make safe harbor before the storm scatters all before it. No wonder it is said that the Bay's salinity approximates that of human tears.

But there also can be an upside to the lack of control. There might be a monster crab harvest, totally unanticipated by either watermen or bureaucrats in the Maryland Department of Natural Resources (DNR). Or that squall driving in toward the Inn's screened porch out of the Potomac River to the west at 6:00 PM might be succeeded by a glorious and tranquil dinner ambience but an hour later. Or the ubiquitous silt from the mauling by last autumn's hurricane can generate an unprecedented flower season, to say nothing of increasing the island's diminishing elevation ever so slightly. In short, to live on Tylerton is to be awash in the unforeseen, both ill and good. It is to be surprised more than in most other places, whether by dread or joy. The reckless have even ventured that it makes life *intrinsically* more interesting here.

Prayer Amid the Absence of Control

All of this powerfully affects the way in which faith is practiced and the manner in which Tylertonians experience the role of the Almighty in the world. The One may not be less relevant in a world of tight schedules, secure environments, and the latest generation of electro-gismos than on an island looking like the bull's eye on the Chesapeake storm target, but it sure can seem so. In the face of all of this absence of control, Tylerton's faithful pray to the One often, long, and *with specificity*: to create the crabs *ex nihilo*, to steer the hurricane away, to apply leverage with the U.S. Army Corps of Engineers, to resuscitate the oyster bounty of yore, to disappear the tumor or heal the heart valve, to stop the drug and alcohol use among the youth, to keep the village going.

Rather than a distant and murky principle, the One in Tylerton is experienced as near, immediate, and enmeshed in the particulars of life. Yes, life is indeed uncertain, but there is the rock of certainty amid that life, and the sense of dependency on this One is palpable. Hence, Hester Smith's prayer at the midweek Bible study in early 2004 after the Crick finally cleared following five weeks of being virtually ice-locked: "Thank you, Lord, that the overboard is water again."

D. The Disencumbered Life

There is no reason why a small island can't have automobiles, roads, franchised junk food, bars, cinemas, jobs with time clocks, malls, tattoo parlors, billboards, and Muzak. But the fact is that Tylerton has none of these, and none of many other things taken for granted on the mainland. Aside from the unforgiving ferry departure schedule or the more flexible approach to beginning church services, few time restraints are rigidly adhered to. Islanders are rarely seen dashing frenziedly around. Particularly in spring before the crab picking begins, threesomes of women can be seen taking the air together, passing before the Inn, either on foot or in golf carts, around sunset.

Speaking of which: these battery-operated vehicles, which came on strong following their introduction the decade before we arrived, are slow, quiet, open, and isle-friendly. Not even the two-golf-cart families disturb the tranquility unduly.

The Pedestrian Life

And then there is the sheer numbers thing. After all, just how frenetic, how frenzied, how frantic could fifty-eight folk be together? "What you have here is the pedestrian life," mused a retired music professor ensconced at the Inn; "Folks actually greet one another in the lanes rather than zipping around in hermetically sealed pods." Another guest boarded the departing ferry with furrowed brow: "I can't quite tell whether they're behind us . . . or ahead."

I must concede that Tylertonians, particularly the women, are not ideological or religious zealots for all aspects of the simple life, especially if they have the requisite economic resources. The suggestion that unbridled consumerism is placed in judgment by the Christian gospel is met with blank stares. Indeed, the village could nominate some very promising candidates for the "shop 'til you drop" lifetime achievement award.

While this innkeeper has occasionally been troubled by the choice of purchases by the parents of a family flirting with destitution, I try to understand how episodic generosity or self-massaging makes its case with the fiscal wolf already halfway in the door. In fact, many Tylertonians are incorrigible consumers, as evidenced by the ferry wallowing beneath the load of December Saturdays' Christmas purchases packed right up to the freeboard, or the number of electronic gismos in the typical kitchen. Nor is the reported palpable rush derived from the knickknack collectibles that fill some houses something that I understand. No, while E. F. Schumacher's 1973 classic *Small is Beautiful* might be mistaken for a volume on Tylerton—the village welcome sign sports the gospel song lyrics "Little is much if God is in it"—the book's dissection of unbridled consumerism has few voluntary disciples here.

Then again, it still makes a tremendous difference that all this stuff cannot be purchased on a whim at 5:50 PM at the nearby mall. This isle-based scaling back of opportunity, if not commitment, bundled with some discipline with the TV remote, means one can reduce being assaulted by pitches for things one doesn't yet know one simply can't live without. And in contrast to purchases made for inside the house, those destined for outside's harsh environment are usually made with an eye to utility and durability, rather than obsession or frivolity. Despite the fact that they work brutally hard more than two-thirds the year, particularly the women, there is a measure of tranquility, slowed pace, and sanity about Tylerton. My initial uncluttering desire had a different configuration and content from that of any local, but we share a common resultant benefit: greater opportunity for what matters more rather than less.

Tylerton a Federal Witness Protection Program?
Of course, a commitment to the disencumbered life can be sorely misunderstood, whether as Luddism, *hubris*, or rank stupidity. At least one other possibility—intrigue—emerged when a sleuthing guest inquired whether the entire isle's population had been stashed away out here in a federal witness protection program. "And the two of you too," he added, enormously pleased with his own wit.

E. Conflict, Privacy, and Mutual Assistance
How the villagers of Tylerton get along together is yet another example of the impact of island's place construct upon its culture. First, the darker side: Tylerton, neither Camelot nor the kingdom of God in full flower, is decidedly not exempt from its share of interpersonal conflict. Living as they do in each other's pockets, with some windows of adjacent homes scarcely ten feet apart, and with virtually no space to run away without going aquatic, they are to be congratulated for not periodically shooting each other.

Much Conflict Is Passive-Aggressive
That open flare-ups are rare, however, should not necessarily be equated with good conflict management skills. Sometimes it rather masks repression of anger, resulting

in silently ticking time bombs walking around. Only in my final year, for example, did I learn the particulars about a boundary dispute that had scarred a family and perplexed the village across an entire generation.

Options available to most mainlanders in conflict—like changing schedules, schools, congregations, friends, or even spouses—are not as available here. When all else fails, one simply leaves, or "de-isles." More than a few have done this over the generations, even though the stated reason might be too few crabs, too much government regulation, or economic opportunity on the main.

Because the holding cell to which conflict sentences them is both small and relatively escape-proof, there is a question running deep within the Tylerton collective subconscious: is the risk of confrontation, intervention, or initiative worth it? This query is simply part of the psyche of the culture. If an incident is interpreted as confirming that it is not worth the price, then yet more repression probably results.

While the village is seemingly tranquil most of the time, the subterranean and submerged feelings are cause for concern. I once overheard an adolescent guest at the Inn answer her mother's question about whether she would like to live in Tylerton: "But Mom, if I broke up with Donny here, I would have to see him every day!" Precisely. The islescape greatly narrows the choices available to conflicted neighbors: embracing the risks of initiative, or bolting. A third option, passive-aggressive behavior, is the one perhaps most frequently chosen. Sharryl and I, in our relationships with villagers, were not to remain unaffected by this aspect of the place.

One tactic amid conflict (thought by many to be less lethal than homicide) is gossip. With the VHF radio blaring in nearly every working boat and shanty (to say nothing of kitchen), the daily confabs in the post office and Drum Point Market, the ligature of the isle's size, and only so many things to be talked about, the typical villager knows everything that is going on and quite a bit that isn't. It would have been impossible for me to prepare myself for this feature. While it has a positive side—anyone met in the lanes is liable to volunteer the latest news—the pattern of carping against persons not present can also be terribly destructive. Some have given up and de-isled because of it. An octogenarian still there uses the device his daddy did: he carries the same pebble in his pocket every day, fingering it whenever tempted to talk behind another's back. The stone, rumored to be smooth, is not known to have a mate in the village.

The Privacy Issue

My initial visit to the church basement on a Wednesday morning, to consult with a Crisfield hospital team making their biweekly visit, was a clinic cubed. I watched with growing curiosity, and then dis-ease, as villagers ahead of me spoke plainly to the nurse practitioner about sensitive medical matters while the rest of us, separated by neither screens nor distance, sat nearby. My assumption that I needed minor medical help was steadily eroding. After receiving treatment I left, having learned that there was little reason for privacy—a signed confidentiality statement several years later notwithstanding!—when everybody knew everything about each other's health anyway.

Sequestered *intra*personal conflict on Tylerton can be no less complicated. One night early in our decade, Sharryl and I were riding our bikes through the soft, marsh-scented darkness beneath the velvet sky after having cleaned up the kitchen following dinner. It was just before the peeler run, a week when up to 30 percent of the year's crabbing income is won—or lost. As we rode onto the county dock, I noticed someone sitting in the shadows in an open freight vehicle near the tethered ferry. It was a waterman whom I enjoyed—from my balcony in the early light I'd often hear him before I would see him, eight-track of the Beatles turned up high—and I greeted him heartily. In the next instant I heard his slurred response, saw the empty six-pack on the seat beside him, and recalled that he had "tore up" his working boat's engine a couple days back.

I felt shameful, like a voyeur getting off on another's private misery. My friend had easy access to no bar where he could barter a few hours of amnesia. He might have preferred, but failed to find, a companion to split that six-pack. Home was probably off-limits for this activity. And, of course, the praxis of the pillars of his community was abstinence. Furthermore, there might have been some shame involved for my friend, for misfortune doesn't seem to adhere to an equal opportunity policy: often the bad things keep happening to the same people. Question: where does a Tylerton body go when a day is bad, and then promptly gets much worse? I have known several here who have needed to find an answer to that question but never did. On occasion, I was one of those.

Mutual Assistance

But on the brighter side, Tylerton *works* in part because there is an enormous amount of mutual assistance. The most obvious examples of this might be identified as Christian virtue, *a la* the memorable mutual aid of my rural Mennonite origins, and the examples abound involving the local congregation. For example, it has on at least two occasions sent checks of $5,000 each to Africa, the first one in the face of the massacre in Rwanda in spring of 1994. Similar generosity characterized responses to Hurricane Mitch (Honduras) in the autumn of 1998 and Hurricane Katrina in August 2005.

A quite different face of this virtue emerged in the congregation's class meeting on my first Mother's Day on Tylerton. It was perhaps only when the *third* person employed the plural in testimonial, when mothering by women who had not birthed them was lauded, that it occurred to me that this community unself-consciously practiced the truth of the African proverb, "It takes a whole village to raise a child."

Then there are the innumerable examples of mutual assistance extended by individuals living out their faith. Lindsey Bradshaw was one of twelve residents defying the mandatory evacuation—Tylerton's first—during Dame Isabel's visit on September 18, 2003. I think he did that primarily because of neighbors—two women with fully 175 hurricane seasons between them—who had determined that if it were their time to go, they'd pass "over home." Another example of sustained generosity was the aid rendered to us by Joan Corbin, our housekeeper, in her service, loyalty to, and advocacy for the Inn during the second half of our decade.

And finally, I cite yet again the words of Dwight Marshall, the congregation's lay leader early on, after our initial open house: "If you or Sharryl ever has trouble down here with a guest, call me and I'll have five watermen in this living room in five minutes!" I never needed to play that card, but did I ever enjoy telling some of our favorite and more rambunctious guests about the possibility!

Benevolent Burglars

Interestingly, some of the most memorable generosity Sharryl and I experienced on Tylerton was at the hands of unchurched men. For example, across the decade, I would repeatedly find in front of the Inn baskets of crabs, oysters, or finfish that neighbor Eddie Russ Smith—described to us by one Smith Island authority as "the most deconstructed person there could be"—had stealthily left. In the winter, what appeared *ex nihilo* might be venison or the occasional waterfowl, both dressed, and received with great joy.

Sometimes bounty appeared even more mysteriously. On a cold February morning in our last off-season, Sharryl and I, upon descending to the kitchen after morning prayers, came upon both a five-pound rockfish gracing our kitchen sink and a line of shy footprints to the never-locked door. On another morning, that sink produced a dressed goose. In the meals following both of these gifts, Sharryl and I discerned yet again that indeterminate legal status had no bearing on the succulence of the gift. Eddie Russ' final expression of generosity to us, a bag of oysters he had caught, was on the Crisfield dock after he had helped me unload our rolltop desk on moving day.

On one occasion, I needed help to retrieve a canoe that a guest had abandoned in Rhodes Point after panicking when it breezed up a tad. Christine and Eddie Russ' son

Daniel, still short of twenty, helped me. When I tried to pay him, he said: "Naw, that's what neighbors are for." I insisted; he prevailed. The thing is, I had heard that exact phrase from both his father and grandfather, Big Alan. It was a familial aphorism, but one actually lived out.

Another waterman, Danny Tyler, whose life has been harder than most, looked out for my skiff for several seasons when I still had it in the back harbor and sometimes lacked the sense to know when it was in harm's way. Watermen are rank softies when it comes to boats, and in my klutziness, I was repeatedly the beneficiary of Danny's largess.

Whence This Magnanimity?

So, what is the source of this pattern of mutual assistance, one lacking simplistic correlation with a particular generation or clan, to say nothing of social standing or religiosity? My two thoughts here are but the beginning of an answer.

First, few specialists live in Tylerton. Such could not be economically supported by fifty-eight souls, and importing such from the mainland is usually prohibitive. As a result, most Tylerton men are generalists, having passable skills in mechanics, carpentry, "'lectric," plumbing, and the like to keep their workboats, shanties, shedding floats, and residential systems going, after a fashion. I as innkeeper, for similar reasons, also found myself becoming a jack of many trades, master of few. The encountering of a problem by a waterman might thus result in a number of fellow generalists converging in a scrum of counsel, or at least company, a pattern that might be different were there more experts in residence.

Second, and more to the point, Tylertonians know well that their way of life has survived nearly 350 years by standing together, *particularly* under the gun of crisis. To a *fúrr-ner* like myself, their pattern of being galvanized by danger looks and feels almost *instinctive*. This applies to a workboat dead in the water needing a tow, a house threatened by the fire company's controlled burn that became otherwise, the failure of the water supply, or an approaching hurricane. One of the ironies is that their collective response, then, is not a product of networking or organization in any formal way, but rather something almost hormonal!

A gender distinction needs to be noted here. Tylerton's women can organize: Sharryl never would figure out how they could emerge from an *eat'n' meet'n'*—a tutorial in simultaneous oratory, a cacophonous din, a veritable Babel—with a strategy to attack a project, break it into components, delegate tasks, and get it done. And get it done they miraculously would.

But the men, alas, appeared to be ontologically unorganizable—like herding cats, as an exasperated bloke was heard to grouse. Generations of Lone Ranger formation on the bounding main—earlier in sail-driven skipjack oysterin' vessels with tiny crews living out there for a month at a time and more recently even more solitary in powered crabbing workboats, verbally mitigated only with CB radio first, and then VHF—have contributed profoundly to the independent socialization of Tylerton's males. And yet, alchemist Danger magically (albeit only temporarily) transforms them into fierce collaborationists!

The beneficiaries of this Tylertonian instinct for aiding others, much more than the darker side of conflict previously discussed, repeatedly included our guests and other visitors. I recall a rough and crowded ferry crossing from Crisfield that included several dozen middle-school children coming to the CBF facility on Tylerton. A slip of a girl was in the corner of the cabin, whimpering with terror, the chaperones preoccupied with her unruly peers. A waterman, he of the tore-up engine, slipped in beside her, cradled her in his arms, and held her for the duration: a beautiful triumph of compassion (with which he was familiar) over political correctness (with which he, fortunately, was not).

This collective instinct, likely born of necessity but reinforced by faith, tradition, and countless experiences, is today about as nonnegotiable a part of the islesphere as the tangy salt air sailing by at about thirty mile. Under the gun of danger, the collective instinct gets very, very real. I expect, in nearly all cases, that it would trump any simmering passive-aggressive patterns—albeit only temporarily, of course.

I concede that I never did reconcile these men's rugged individualism and seeming lethargy regarding the common good with how they self-sacrificially knit together when the crunch was on. This puzzlement is, of course, my problem much more than theirs. The fact that no part of Smith Island has ever had any kind of legally recognized government has placed the onus squarely on this virtue, which will always be a core part of my memory of these people.

Conflict and Mutual Assistance Lie Down Together

During a sixty-day period in the early autumn of 2005, the impulses toward both mutual assistance and conflict made a joint appearance. First the hamlet's water system, consisting of a single well, went down. Then the waste treatment system failed. It would become a near-perfect storm.

During the first crisis, lasting intermittently for several weeks, we literally issued plastic pails to our Inn guests upon arrival, each being invited to get brackish water from the "overboard" beyond the bulkhead to flush their commodes. During the second crisis, even more stringent policies were put in place. Aside from the scarcely believable upbeat response of our guests, embellished with sundry witticisms about hygiene and adventure tourism, the crises reminded all of us that the two impulses in point, conflict and mutual aid, were right there, side-by-side, just below the surface in the village. This insight came as a surprise to no one.

F. The Islanders' Perspective on the Mainland

Us Against the World

Islanders, not unlike residents of small communities in general, are inclined to see things through an "us against the rest" lens. Smith Island's inimitable brogue, the paucity of professional options, a gene pool *sans* deep end, lack of self-confidence among some of the youth, the horizon melding sea and sky—these are among the many factors that set apart and sequester. The Island's unique history, tradition, stories, and a "circling of the wagons" reflex growing out of repeated jeopardy also do the same.

There was a defect in my sampling of Tylertonians' attitudes about the main: the only ones I knew well were those who had decided to stay. I did not get to know many who had bailed out on the waterman life, relocating all the way to Crisfield or even distant Salisbury. Oh, I might see some of them hanging out at ferry departure time at the Crisfield wharf—dubbed the "depot" from railroad days, transplants looking wistfully after disappearing vessels before driving back to houses not yet fully homes. Yes, it is indeed harder to take the island out of the islander than vice versa. But my chief sample, one thus skewed statistically, was made up of the residue—the true grit—remaining, as, in the words of one waterman, "the story was playing out." This section is thus about that grit, not more generally folk with Island roots.

Many Tylertonians remaining—be they motivated primarily by courage, stubbornness, lethargy, fear, such qualities in a spouse, or any combination of the above—would nevertheless declare, at least in public, that their way of life is the best on the planet. Furthermore, the churchgoers would attribute their lot to the protective and generous hand of Providence.

The mainland culture, on the other hand, tended to be viewed as permissive and even decadent, and although it was making inroads on Smith—alcohol, drugs, domestic violence and fractures—the difference remained sizable, particularly on Tylerton. Located on an informally dry island in wet Somerset County, the Tylertonian congregants had long since determined the legal sale of booze to be an issue for which they would collectively go to the mat and, if need be, the wall. In this regard, they remained perhaps bloodied but unbowed as we boarded the ferry the final time.

Oogling the Main

At the same time, not surprisingly, there is a telling fascination with mainland culture. Most Tylerton homes have large-to-huge television sets hooked to cable or dish, and in many of them the set seems to be turned on during most waking hours, pouring in sense-candy from the dominant mainland culture. The faithful might justify having TVs by citing gospel programming, but there is a whole lot more spewage as well. I consider television one point at which the waterman culture evidences an undeveloped faculty of critical thinking.

I suspect there is an element of villager voyeurism here, with the tube providing a window for sneaking recurring looks at the bad and bawdy main. After all, is not the taboo alluring, the forbidden fetching, and the recurring experience of reminding one's self of what one is not titillating?

There is yet another delicious twist in Tylerton's "us against the world" thinking. While the dominant, mainland culture may be viewed by the faithful as hedonistic, with selected vices needing to be kept at bay by Tangier Sound's brackish buffer, that same culture is paradoxically viewed as part of a Christian nation, one founded on divine principles and bearing a destiny as chosen.

For example, Tylerton's faithful have little difficulty reconciling the village's proud history of support for the military with the Christian faith, because, in their minds, America is—or ought to be—a Christian nation. That this does not always fit together easily with the notion of Tylerton as a bastion of righteousness and light to a nation and its darkness is rarely discussed. Nor is the fact that support for the politics of the religious right in the present is viewed as fully compatible with an eschatology speaking much more of a "new heavens" than a "new earth" in the future.

The hazards of holding together such tensions are not, of course, peculiar to persons en-isled, but they do hint at aspects of the complex love/hate relationship these particular islanders have with the mainland culture.

The "Dionysian Exemption"

A final reflection on the tendency of many Tylertonians to set their world off against that on the main. The first-time visitor might identify this dichotomy as prudishness, a puritanical eschewing of the debauched dominant culture in favor of a severe spirit in shades of gray, especially among the more religious.

Don't go there! No, the Tylerton culture a restrained and gray place is not! Its center of gravity is lower than either head or heart! Solemn denunciations in class meeting of the spirit of the (mainland) times, expressions of gratitude to the One for having been able to remain *here*—these are decidedly not incompatible with a joviality and indigenous earthiness among locals which is immediately evident and occasionally scarcely believable.

Here lieth one of the conundrums I spent a full decade failing to unpack. It is as if Tylerton's culture contained a time-out option, a codicil of exception making provision for the coarse and outrageous, a Dionysian exemption condoning debauchery of table and language in a microcosm that is otherwise all work, serious inconvenience, and perpetual jeopardy. Indeed, a Shrove Tuesday card, playable any time in the year, for a community viewed by outsiders as in Lent. But, in contrast to any naughty import, this maintaining of room for the ribald and raunchy is totally homegrown and thus, apparently, acceptable. When this exemption is invoked, the atmosphere is suddenly filled with insider talk of multivalent hues, serious decibel ratings, and, in time, serious petting with the risqué, the lewd, the off-color. But, again, it is their own and thus in no respect "exotic," of *us* rather than of *them*, and thus seemingly safe from church condemnation.

Although ever a possibility, this "Dionysian exemption" is encountered most predictably at three annual occasions. There is Tylerton's Valentines Day party in the church basement. And then there are two events involving all three parts: the Waterman's Dinner in North End in November, and the rotating Ladies' Aid Christmas event in December (a photo of which made the front page of *The Washington Post* the month after our departure).

While each exemplifies well the exemption, the women's Christmas party—which I attended religiously, albeit only vicariously via Sharryl—is way over the top. The event begins upstairs in the sanctuary with prayers and a lay meditation on some aspect of our Lord's nativity, delivered with devotion, often tears. At the women's request, I sang in this module one year, after which I was summarily sent home—not because of my voice, but my gender. The group to the basement then descends, both literally and otherwise, for a night of food abuse—again the grousing men trot out *eat'n' meet'n'*—and uninhibited quasi-burlesque presentations around the theme, or so I infer, of "things we do when the boys ain't here." It can be slightly unbelievable to the uninitiated and initiated alike.

My point here is that suggesting an incongruity between such events—two of them in the church building no less, amid an island culture with a strong fundamentalist religious tradition—is itself something only a *fúrr-ner* like myself might do. The insiders, adept at diving on a dime into a sea of double entendre, are comfortable with all of the jokes, because the jokes are, after all, their own. In this sense, the entire Tylerton culture is an inside joke, one which the *fúrr-ner*, myself not excepted, never quite gets.

To me it might seem that the material of a women's Christmas event, but presented by a burlesque troupe from Wilmington on a one-night visit to the isle, would be pilloried, at least by the blessed. But that is probably a musing an outsider would be expected to dream up. It's ours, from and out of us, so it's okay. And besides, this carrying on—it's the way we've always done it *here!*

G. The Contours of the Village

Finally, how is the actual physical layout of the hamlet itself shaped by its unique natural environs? I'll pass on the temptation to parse what is cause, what effect—a complicated matter, given the nineteenth-century roles in Tylerton's "urban planning" of movements from agriculture to seafood and, later, from lower elevation to higher. The configuration of Tylerton, whether viewed aerially or from the watery approaches to the north, west, or southeast, is fascinating.

The Church as Axis Mundi

In my early visits to Tylerton I found myself thinking of a tiny medieval walled city. There is the surrounding water, serving as both moat and defining/defending wall in the face of the chaos and danger, with fields and pastures beyond. In the very center is the cathedral, the *Axis Mundi* ("Pole of the Earth"), that signs contact with the transcendent and brings focus, order, witness, and peace to all surrounding it. The *axis* in this case is an improbably imposing edifice with high, crenellated towers. Crowding the cathedral on three sides is the necropolis, a garden of memory where the dead and their stories live on.

There is an established religion in this realm, although the description of Tylerton's arrangement as a "theocracy" seems excessive. In the surrounding areas between cathedral and mote is the concentrated grid which brings to mind the psalmist's description of Jerusalem as "a city compacted together" (Ps 122:3). Within this tight weave are lodged the professions and guilds, institutions and homes, as well as several small plazas where citizens encounter each other in the course of the day. And dicing up this grid, this gestalt of Tylerton, are the narrow lanes, passages, and "wayes," all arguably more medieval than modern.

Tylerton: A Place of a Certain Sort

Tylerton's contours, sketched here as I see them, speak of a community with strong identity, a distinctive profile, even in comparison with the other two villages (Rhodes point and North End), or more distant kin like those on the nearby isles of Tangier or Deal. For better or for worse, Tylertonians are of a certain *sort*. At the center of this community, the core of its identity and stability and peace, is faith. Community life, including both work and play, revolves around that pole in an ordered manner. There is relative cohesion in the whole, and density rather than fragmentation prevails. The village is, yes, "compacted together."

Within this grid are the post office, fire company, picking house, the Inn, and the Drum Point Market, each serving both an economic and a social function. And to those beyond the pale, the church building's profile up there against the sky signs the presence of both the One and a living community of faith across the generations. I recall Lindsey Bradshaw, in class meeting, expressing gratitude for what was communicated by those towers, visible to voyagers from a large part of the central Bay.

I acknowledge that implicit in my medieval metaphor is a comparison of our village with Rhodes Point, a community of comparable population perhaps a half mile away. Rhodes Point, its handle rehabilitated from the earlier "Rogue's Point," is primarily a string of beads: a long road with water on one side becoming Sheep Pen Gut as it opens to the Bay, and on the other side houses, some inhabited, some otherwise. Rhodes Point seemingly has neither center nor compactness. That village has lost all of its institutions, save the struggling congregation. Not surprisingly, of the three communities, Rhodes Point seems most vulnerable, whether to the sea, emigration, or death-by-lethargy. In contrast, the heftier cultural and spiritual weightiness of Tylerton is partly caused by—and to a greater extent symbolized by—the ordered and centered grid of its layout. In short, this compacted configuration is part of what makes this space a place.

In conclusion, I have explored here seven selected aspects of the role of place construction in shaping the Tylerton culture. Another writer, or this one on another occasion, might have crafted an entirely different list. What probably would remain the same, however, would be the conclusion that the imprint of "isle-ness" on this people's collective psyche is difficult to exaggerate.

10. Place as Perch and Perspective

In contrast to the impact of watermen's perceptions of the mainland culture on their self-understanding, an island can also be a unique point from which one looks out at and seeks to understand that larger world. It may be particularly so for one like myself coming from the outside.

From our first visit to Tylerton in 1992, I was enamored of the microcosmic quality of the place. The issues it faced were analogous to those of both the American society and the planet—government, waste disposal, conflict management, religion's role in the public square, etc. But the reduced scale here sometimes afforded fresh perspective. All other things being equal (which they rarely are), it should, for example, be easier to define the common good with fifty-eight persons than over six billion; perhaps insight gained at the micro scale could be useful at the macro.

Indeed, trying to examine challenges facing the planet in terms of the Tylerton microcosm became a useful tool for me across the entire decade. David Quammen's *The Song of the Dodo: Island Biogeography in an Age of Extinctions* is an excellent example of this strategy. His thesis is that islands can be the canaries sent down into the mines, warning us that global behaviors point toward unsustainability or worse.

One of Sharryl and my inadvertent learnings made possible by our isled perch had to do with emerging technology. We would take extended off-season mainland junkets to visit family, a monastery, and other locales. These excursions included nearly all of our television viewing during the decade. We both would be taken aback by some shift in technology prevalence or usage during the previous year. These shifts included cellular phones, iPods, high-speed Internet service, SUV girth, hybrid autos, and the pharmaceuticalizing of advertising (cereals down, performance enhancers up). Our encounter with the incremental change of an entire year was compacted into the first few days of our off-season travel. We thus experienced more cultural shock in these thresholds than did our mainland family and friends, or our fellow islanders.

A. The Derivation of Isle as Perch

However, in addition to providing a micro model for the macro, the island can provide a perspective, a perch, a vantage point or listening post, from which one seeks to make sense of what is beyond. Such a function of place is not unique to islands, of course: every human being, as well as every social or political collective, constitutes one or a series of them. But such perches are typically embedded in that which they wish to understand, with clarity of vision often being the casualty.

Perch as Reduced Embeddedness

Thirty-five years ago in the Middle East, I learned that whether an armed man was a "terrorist" or "freedom fighter," a soldier whose uniform signed legitimacy or war criminal, depended extensively upon one factor: perspective. It was the unusual person in the Middle East in 1973 who could address that question without embeddedness dictating a simplistic answer, and that remains the case today.

The issue is one of distance, and with distance can come freedom, imagination, receptivity, and the possibility of the new. Being able to extricate oneself entirely from embeddedness is not allowed, for the observer always brings along her own self, her own subjectivity including constructs, to say nothing of lingering cultural predispositions. Mainland culture has made profound inroads into Tylerton—the two world wars and television are but the most obvious examples—so that purity of perch, which never did exist here, exists even less today. The dilemma is devilish: how can I have sufficient access to the culture beyond so as to reflect upon it, seek to understand it, but not so much as to be co-opted by it, most dangerously in ways of which I am not even aware? Still, I would argue that a perspective with less embeddedness is superior to one with more. Hence the following.

The distance that qualifies Tylerton as a promising perch for assessing the world beyond its horizons is of several sorts. The nearly ten miles of Tangier Sound separating Tylerton from the mainland port of Crisfield, a backwater (at least until recently) at the bottom of a sleepy Delmarva peninsula, all further buffered by Bay or ocean, is only the most obvious element of separation. This distance, spanned only via watercraft or aircraft—there are no plans for a causeway—will continue to be both real and telling.

Furthermore, despite suffering some erosion throughout the twentieth century, Tylerton culture remains very much a thing unto itself. This differential can translate into additional distance, allowing one better to see the ways in which the mainland is different. Hence, a visitor's reference in the Inn guest book to "your near–foreign country." It is the argument here that the pristinity, pace, and paucity of artificial sense stimuli in Tylerton augur well for it as perch from which to reflect on the larger culture and raise the neglected questions.

In his *Spaces for the Sacred,* Philip Sheldrake reminds those of us in faith communities of our indebtedness to *disempowered* or *boundary* persons, those compelled to think and pray and love outside the box. Examples might include Teresa of Jesus,

OCD (1515–1582) living her entire unbelievable life amid the Spanish inquisition, waiting for the other shoe to drop regarding her family's status of *conversos* ("converted Jews"); or persons like Julian of Norwich, John of the Cross, and John Bunyan, whose journey to the One unfolded amid literal sequesterment. (Incidentally, neither Sharryl nor I was above occasionally referring to isle life as incarceration, mostly in humor, occasionally not.)

While no disempowering experience births insight automatically or even usually, yet that very opportunity is always being offered. Our own routines can become ruts of mind, heart, and body, and it is these that most delimit us, rendering our interior lives predictable and *safe*. I found island living, beginning with the literal but extending far beyond, to be a marginated, constricted, restricted, and exiled life, and therein rested both its promise and peril as perspective and perch.

My interest in Tylerton as perch was seeded early by three groups of experiences, and I enumerate them here in reverse order of occurrence.

Books and Guests on Island Psychology

First, there were the books written about islands that Sharryl and I read during long winter evenings, particularly early in the decade, varied works involving varied genres about varied places. A partial list: William Cronin's *The Disappearing Islands of the Chesapeake*, Jon Gower's *An Island Called Smith,* David Guterson's *Snow Falling on Cedars*, Barry Lopez's *Arctic Dreams*, Wayne Johnston's *The Colony of Unrequited Dreams*, Alistair MacLeod's *Island: The Complete Stories*, Adam Nicolson's *Sea Room*, Richard Nelson's *The Island Within*, Annie Proulx's *The Shipping News*, Sue Monk Kidd's *The Mermaid Chair*, Linda Greenlaw's *The Lobster Chronicles*, Ernest Shackleton's *South: The Endurance Expedition*; David Shears' *Ocracoke*, Adam Wallace's *The Parson of the Islands*, the island studies in both Jared Diamond's *Collapse* and David Quammen's *The Reluctant Mr. Darwin*, Frances Dize's *Smith Island, Chesapeake Bay*, and of course, Tom Horton's *Island Out of Time*. In each of these diverse works, I was on the lookout—first subconsciously, later intentionally—for what seemed generalizable about the ways in which islanders saw the world from their inimitable context and vantage point.

Second, there were the Inn's occasional guests—"isle groupies," I called them—who brought experiential perspectives from residing on or visiting various islands. These included the likes of the Danish Faeroes in the North Atlantic or the Hebrides of Scotland or Bavaria's Lindau am Bodensee or Franz Josef Island above the Arctic Circle or Patmos off the coast of Turkey or La Maddalena twixt Sardinia and Corsica or St. Kitts, to name but a few cays.

Added to these were the yarnin' isle collectors in our own country, especially the eastern seaboard, a sampler of which might include Maine's Monhegan and Deer through isles Nantucket, Block, Long Beach, Assateague, Ocracoke and Harkers, Jekyll, and on to Key West. Sometimes under the rubric of "island psychology," these conversations were an intermittent feast that was forming within me the notion of isle as unique perch, especially for the outsider having taken refuge there.

"Notes From Out on the Edge"

Finally, during the thirty-month period when we were commuting from Washington, D.C., to renovate the building, a barrister friend from Holy Trinity Parish had made an interesting suggestion. Consider, he said, doing a series of reflective pieces—he suggested the audio medium—on how the world looked from Tylerton. "Notes from out on the edge," is how I remember his nudge. While initially intrigued, I demurred, finding the idea tempting albeit presumptuous. Yet I recall musing at that time about Paul Tillich's *On the Boundary*, a series of autobiographical essays on various themes, each written from the perspective of the hinterland between, and often beyond, contesting constructs. The present book in general, and this section "Place as Perch and Perspective" in particular, may be my belated acting upon my friend's counsel. And doing so may still not have completely avoided being presumptuous.

For the purposes of this study, my perch, both literal and metaphorical, was the modest two-person balcony I had constructed off our third-floor living quarters above the Inn back in the spring of 1998. From there—whether at dawn, when the menagerie of avian life was shaking off the night, or at sunset when the sky's beauty was so palpable that words stuck in the throat; whether with Shostakovich or in silence; whether nude under the Summer Triangle or bundled against the frigid and assaulting wind beneath the incendiary splendor of the Great Nebula in Orion—I would intermittently gaze out and up, seeking to drink deeply of this most wonderful cosmos and my place in it.

B. The Event of the Decade: A Lament

The decade bookended by 1997 and 2006 was one of the most eventful in recent United States history. These ten years included an impeachment; two few-holds-barred presidential elections; wars in Afghanistan, Iraq, and Lebanon; more of the seemingly interminable Palestinian-Israeli impasse; rampant AIDS as well as war-fueled famine in Africa, including genocide in Darfur; the great tsunami in Asia at the end of 2004; continued movement toward economic globalization and interdependency; and the 2005 visit to New Orleans and environs by siblings Katrina and Rita. Having decided at the outset to have no television in any part of the Inn, Sharryl and I nevertheless had remained informed, primarily via National Public Radio, the weekly edition of the *Washington Post*, and the *New York Times* online, in that order.

Being on Tylerton on 9/11

But the major event of the decade, one arguably rendered inevitable by what preceded, as well as altering all that would follow for the foreseeable future, was the 9/11 attacks in lower Manhattan, the Pentagon, and over Pennsylvania. This event was just short of the midpoint of our Tylerton decade.

Our only guests that ordinary September morn were two academics from Massachusetts. I had earlier seized the chance to make a day retreat in the Green House, a structure I had crafted for use by guests back among the cedars and loblolly pines on the slightly higher elevation behind the Inn, but realized midmorning that I had neglected to pack water. I entered the kitchen to find Sharryl and our guests silently huddled around the radio, tuned to NPR, just before the second tower went down in New York. That day's events and, to a greater extent, the response of our government to them, would change the United States, certainly for the remainder of my lifetime.

As the unspeakable unfolded that Tuesday, I found myself drawn between wildly conflicting sentiments. On the one hand, disbelief: our isle tranquility seemed light years from the horror. It would not be until the subsequent July 4, when thinking I glimpsed from our balcony the fireworks on the National Mall, that I wondered whether I would have been able to see the smoke above the Pentagon on 9/11. On the other hand, belief: as one who had earlier lived among Muslims, and had some knowledge of manipulation of their countries and resources both during and after the colonial period, I was not on that Tuesday among those paralyzed by incredulity or incomprehension. In fact, one of my first responses, shared only most discretely, was surprise that an attack on this scale had not taken place much earlier.

A Washington couple, he in the government, she the Red Cross, canceled their reservations for the nights of September 11 and 12, but in the remains of that season we received many new reservations. Thus, while having been spared the World Trade Center footage that the nation viewed again and again, our own isolation was mitigated via the eyes of guests, some of whom had been in the Pentagon or the Naval Annex or buildings adjacent to the World Trade Center that day. One guest had been physically injured; many were emotionally or spiritually exhausted; and all were profoundly needful of the tranquility and rest that Tylerton and the Inn offered. And it was in dialogue with these people that Sharryl and I tried to come to a better understanding of the enormity of what had transpired. No, it did seem absurd that

Tylerton had remained its largely pacific self, even as the Pentagon had been burning but eighty-five miles away as the peregrine falcon flies.

My Lamentation After 9/11

What follows might be likened to the contents of a narrow archaeological trench cut across my musings of the five years between 9/11 and the 2006 election. This sampling is in the interest of trying to make sense of the world from the pacific perch of this place. The trench here could have been dug in other times or places, thus addressing other issues. But I chose the one having to do with 9/11 because of the scale of the impact of both that day and of the weeks, months, and years that followed.

To repeat, the location of this exploratory dig is of my choosing, as is the decision to air its findings here. For purposes of this account, I am conceding the general accuracy of our government's account of that day, an assumption that I view as slowly decaying with time. I have phrased my musings as questions, both because that mode better suits my finite understanding and because the greater casualty in the post-9/11 period was not the right answers so much as the right questions.

- Why has neither the government nor more than a small minority of people of our country been willing to reflect on the profoundly spiritual critique of the hegemonic designs of American culture and policy central to the message of Osama bin Laden and Al-Qaeda in the months following 9/11?

- What was the unspoken rationale for my government's framing of its response to 9/11 in terms of war (albeit not formally declared)—a war the duration of which has now been projected to last an entire generation—rather than as a concerted international police effort, as was the case in Europe's response? What were the ideological agendas served, the benefits envisioned, in regard to both domestic and foreign policy, by the decision to "let slip the dogs of war," placing the American nation, culture, and prioritizing on a fear-lubricated war footing *in perpetua*?

- Will we the people continue to defer to a government intent on saddling our children and grandchildren with both the financial cost of its tragically misconceived military adventures and the casualty list of urgent domestic programs—for example, that regarding the natural environment—eclipsed by the largely undefined and unaccountable wielding of the National Security flag?

- Is it indeed surprising that my own government, *talking* Christian values while oxymoronically *walking* war, is perceived by many in other countries as *the* rogue state, one given to military adventurism, to repeated submission to Lord Molech's demands that his maw be fed with children (Lv 20:2–5)?

- Why does my government wrap its foreign policy in an alleged commitment to establish secular democracies, especially in areas where Islamic fundamentalism is on the ascent, while at home it adheres to a self-understanding as *Christian* nation, indeed, *Christian* empire, as envisioned by our own homegrown fundamentalist clerics? Why would the reasons that secular democracy was best for Iraq not apply at home as well?

- Why has the tragic irony of curtailing individual rights here at home since 9/11, in the interests of growing democracy and freedom worldwide, been given so little scrutiny and generated so little rage? Why do we continue to chant the "they hate us because we're free" mantra, designed to wrap our arrogant foreign policy, particularly in the Middle East, with virtue and block more serous inquiry, even as both Al-Qaeda recruiters and their potential recruits knowingly look on?

- And most importantly, is not the entire U.S. anti-terrorism effort condemned to chronic stalemate at best, the unspeakable at worst, if constructed around a void where the central question should be grappled with: *Why are we in the United States hated so in much of the Islamic world, and how have we contributed at the policy level to incubating and then igniting that hatred?* Do we not owe it to ourselves and our own survival to understand *why* 9/11 happened?

We may never abandon our manifest destiny mindset, now extrapolated to the entire planet and into space, with our economic and military manner of swaggering with impunity across Earth during much of the past half century, guided almost always by self-interest. But don't we owe it to ourselves and our children to be aware that it is precisely this reading of us by many Muslims that is central to the blows struck at the World Trade Center and Pentagon? Even if, *particularly* if, we agree on self-interest as the necessary core of U.S. foreign policy, can we afford not to face this question?

From the vantage point near the end of our Tylerton decade, I remain convinced that the U.S. impulse toward empire—the messianic *hubris* alternately advancing and holding through my lifetime but surging forward in response to 9/11—is emblematic of a national decline. The unsustainability of behaviors and policies in this mindset on myriad fronts in the post-9/11 period is a harbinger of the implosion awaiting us.

The signs are distressing: the relative disappearance of the poor from the domestic radar screen; the spin-sired gaggle of gimmicks rather than courageous decision-making regarding the shrinking supply behind the petroleum spigot; the criminal mortgaging of our children and grandchildren's fiscal future by so-called "pro-family" conservatives; and the cynical dismantling of generations of social and environmental policy anchored in a commitment to the common good.

Another sign of national decline is the unquestioning obeisance to an economic ideology, sometimes obscenely huckstered in Christian apparel, whose heart is quantitative greed, its eschaton gismo-city. And, perhaps most distressing of all: the fact that the facile treatment of the virtue truth, the spin shamelessly put on *everything*, has generated so little rage.

These, I believe, are among the late-term symptoms that are irreconcilable with the sustaining of our national culture. I grieve what my two grandchildren will have to endure when there could have been so much good that we passed on to them.

From my perch, I painfully lament the waning of the flower of this, my native land. Not the empire of self-righteous and near-blasphemous pontifications about ridding the world of evil, but the nation of many peoples having together generated a modest measure of wisdom and humble awareness of finitude across its more than two centuries of life, a precious learning now in jeopardy far more from within than without.

I remember telling a Canadian guest how I envied him, he living in a generally good and decent country: nothing more, nothing less. His is a country without messianic delusions or aspirations to hegemonic empire—just a simple country to which to belong and to love. It's a country where I could fly the flag, be a patriot—and, from time to time, even be real proud.

11. Place as Metaphor

In chapter 8 I raised this question: are there geographical spaces that intrinsically engage the visitor's interior life, nudging it in a certain direction? My response began with an implicit critique of the question for not acknowledging a subjective component, whether the interiority of the visitor, the collective memory of residents past, or both, in the understanding of place. The subsequent discussion of that subjective component centered on how it and the objective space interact, resulting in a "construct-ed" place. That discussion implied that humans function as co-creators in the transforming of a swatch of vertically challenged and salinity-laced space such as Tylerton into a powerful place.

We return here to the above question, now chastened: do certain topographies *predispose* visitors toward spiritual experiences, this apart from involvement of visitors' pre-texts and/or cultural memories? Are there qualities of some objective components of place, the spaces, which nudge them toward what Alwine called "spiritually evocative landscapes"? Or are all spaces created equal in regard to this potential?

Travelogues, for example, particularly those of pilgrims, often contain reports of certain spaces seemingly imbued with an intrinsic power of a figurative or analogical sort. Some have claimed the Himalayas as examples, others Mount Fuji. My candidate might be the Sinai, what Nikos Kazantzakis in his *Report to Greco* termed the "anvil of Jehovah." It is a space I experienced powerfully as One-haunted and indisputably a place.

But, it could be argued, did I not tramp Sinai in May of 1974 with the Hebrew Bible, a powerful collective memory overlay already filling my head and heart, a set of interior glasses unavoidably shading the simple objective space? And might not something analogous to this often be the case with pilgrims ascending the Himalayas or Mount Fuji?

My working hypothesis in what follows is that there are latent qualities in some spaces more than others that, when sparked by the subjectivity in the visitor, may become formative spiritual symbols, particularly when a powerful collective memory is also in play. This understanding would have the space contributing to the chemistry of, rather than simply determining, spiritual evocation. It would account for the fact that spiritual traditions and disciplines are both begun and sustained in some topographies more than in others.

Let us test this hypothesis with the category of spaces we call islands. Isles have contributed various metaphors to the common usage. One is that of a thing apart, unto itself, isolated from the rest, the very antithesis of the intrinsic interconnectedness of human life—thus, John Donne's "no man is an island." It is this isolation, flaunted as undauntedness, that had Oklahoma City bomber Timothy McVeigh quoting William Ernest Henley's "Invictus" as he went to his execution in 2001: "I am the master of my fate: I am the captain of my soul." While I have already noted that an isle's geographical separation is a fruitful metaphor for the lives of its denizens in general, that, for better or for worse, it connotes nonnegotiable solitudinal aspects of human existence, this quality was *not* central to "island" becoming a spiritually powerful symbol to me.

Rather, the first metaphorical quality that did engage my faith was not so much some aspect of isleness in general as it was a characteristic of this one, Tylerton, in particular. I discuss that quality below under the heading "The Island Salt Marsh as Apophatic Desert."

The second and more familiar isle-related metaphor, "The Sea as the Boundless One," focuses more on the Bay, the encircling aquatic context, than on the isle itself. Both metaphors are ambiguous in that that to which they point entails both promise and peril. The emphasis below in both cases is on the promise, although the darker side is never far away.

Again, as with the village/island Tylerton herself, I did not so much select these two metaphors—harsh and saline island *sans* makeup and unbridled sea often not on its best behavior—as they improbably selected me. Each helped me to identify and name budding shoots within me, even while generating more of the same.

Finally, in the course of my writing, two additional spiritual metaphors emerged from the islescape, each lobbying for inclusion here. One would surprise the other innkeeper: *Wind.* The Hebrew *ruah* can be translated as "wind," "breath," and/or "spirit." This delicious ambiguity is partly passed on to Christian scriptures via the Greek word *pneuma*, and it has enormous possibilities in the Tylerton environment!

Very promising as well is the image *Fire,* identified most immediately with both our solar system's star, nourisher of all known life, as well as the primeval Ignition out of which the cosmos has unfolded. In the faith tradition passed on to me there are innumerable examples of fire as image of the One's love—whether the psalmist's words "And there is nothing hidden from [Sun's] heat" (Ps 19:3–6), or the central thrust of John of the Cross' "The Living Flame of Love," or the words "That you may become the brother of God and learn to know the Christ of the burnt men" with which Thomas Merton (1915–1968) concluded his autobiographical *The Seven Storey Mountain.* Alas, both time and space restraints limit the exploration here to the first two images cited above, although that of Fire smolders until Part VI.

A. The Salt Marsh as Apophatic Desert

My initial take on Tylerton's isleography back in August 1992 is one that remains: its minimalism. Smith Island is beautiful, Tylerton particularly so, but it is not a voluptuous or lavish beauty, an over-the-top grandeur. Tylerton might be contrasted with certain heroic or majestic topographies—Yosemite Valley in California's Sierra Nevadas, for example, that Sharryl frequented across earlier decades of her life. Well, Yosemite Valley Tylerton is *not*, literally or metaphorically: the sheer scale and stunning majesty are simply not here. The place gets its hooks into you via understatement and quiet ambience rather than overpowering scale.

A Vertically Challenged Isle

An obvious difference between Tylerton and Yosemite is verticality. Tylerton and environs are vertically challenged—indeed, virtually nonvertical. Smith Island is only theoretically cubic! The highest Tylerton elevation, less than five feet, is either in front of the church entrance or the softball field where soil was deposited during the excavation of the back harbor. The highest point on all of Smith Island, just inches higher in the vicinity of the "over the hill" sector of North End, was one I never managed to identify for certain in our decade.

To look toward, or away from, Tylerton is to see overwhelmingly in but two dimensions: expansive breadth and great length. No "purple mountain majesty" verticalities here. As the *Capt'n Jason II* clears Janes Island out of Crisfield on the mainland and bends to due west, Smith Island, about eight miles farther across Tangier Sound, appears on the horizon as a faint, linear, and extremely low smudge. Halfway across the Sound, occasional clusters of trees called hammocks break the water's horizon line. (With the appetite for converting trees into boats, houses, and fuel, the seventeenth century handle, "Isle of Broken Woodlands," could not hold.)

If Tylerton were to supply imagery for the words of the prophet Habakkuk that "[YHWH] makes my feet to walk upon the heights" (Hb 3:19), perhaps we might conscript the angry thunderheads before a June storm, the high flight of Sassafras Hammock's nesting pair of bald eagles that I approach in my skiff, or the luminous lantern of Jupiter and his children.

Thus if Tylerton is *more*, one of my principal contentions, it is more *with less*. To be sure, this island, itself an argument that the horizontal can indeed stand alone, has its moments: from my third-floor perch I can see forever, the planet's curvature finally occluding more than obstructing topographical features. A tiny minority of guests might exclaim, "Oh, it's so flat, so boring!" Hmm. Perhaps boring like some people consider photographs in black and white boring, or the atonal "Suite for Piano" by Arnold Schoenberg (1874–1951). It all depends on who is looking or listening, and how.

Tylerton's stark and severe beauty often deposits me in a subdued mood. Sometimes this is laced with a quiet joy or an awareness of being favored, but *hubris* is rarely present. Tylerton's is a one-winged beauty, one slaked with delimitation and thus melancholy. It's a *humble* topography. When drinking it in from perch or porch, I am seldom haughty or lacking in respect.

A Florally Challenged Isle

In addition to lack of verticality, part of Tylerton's isleographical profile involves its flora and, indirectly, fauna. Enveloped in a sea of aquatic vegetation, Smith's "upland," the less than ten percent which is inhabitable/inhabited, is inexorably shrinking. The aberrational hammock marks an area once disturbed by either human habitation or deposited dredge spoils.

In between is a luxurious carpet of near-homogeneous *Spartin alterniflora,* which in the spring is a deep brown, with the green life beginning to thrust up from below. In the autumn, the season in which I now live my life, a thousand shades of brown, brass, copper, sienna, and gold are ignited by a marshian analogue to "alpenglow" at the dawn and dusk of the day. Appreciating such variegation from but one quadrant of the palette, one of the exquisite delights of Tylerton's water and marsh, was not unlike that of my youth, when negotiating a post-blizzard snowy expanse required distinguishing among endless nuances of white. (A poem I wrote in 1985 included these lines: "a glimpse of both infinite palette of white/and the consummate cunning of wind's sculpting hand.")

Even a stand of the exotic invader *Phragmites australis* (common reed) that forms a walled noose up to ten feet tall around the mowed "lawn" of the Inn can be exquisite, especially its pattern of uniformly plumed heads waving in lush synchronicity at sunset. Sometimes dismissed as a "swamp," a marsh—often amazingly uniform and sea-like under the "consummate cunning of wind's sculpting hand"—can be gorgeous. It is a severe beauty, however, one painted with reserve from a truncated palette, and for many an acquired taste. I acquired it.

All this minimalism reaches its zenith in winter. I arrived schooled in winter's denudation and the ubiquity of death from my Minnesota origins, but nothing has ever been as stark to me as Tylerton in January. The bludgeoning of marsh and hammocks by sleet and snow hardening the vistas; the stripping of the hamlet's trees, leaving it jarring to the eye and its imperfections writ more large; the occasional extremely low tides, abetted by northwest winds, draining much of the Crick except for the icing covering the mud: all this can extinguish any residual rumor of verticality.

The houses in winter are left on their own, their slab-like walls setting up there against the sky even less garnished than during the foliaged seasons of the year. In nearly half of our Smith Island winters, all the interior channels, together with external approaches, were frozen at least part of the time, with dock pilings a series of ice-ribbed and columned chronicles of the twice-daily tidal lifts and releases. Winter's ice can and often means sequesterment: from the larger world, often from the mainland, and occasionally from mail and even neighbor. Some would add: from one's senses.

Kataphatic and Apophatic

A distinction in the study of mysticism in various religious traditions between the Latin *via positiva* and the *via negativa* is instructive here. The *via positiva* is a way of using the trove of language to describe what something is; the *via negativa*, generally opted for in the face of the limitations of language and magnitude of the task at hand, describes primarily in terms of what is not. Although the former path is well traveled in popular religious worship and devotion, the latter is often utilized by mystics in the face of the harrowing challenge of finding serviceable language for the One.

A closely related distinction, again from the mystical tradition, is between kataphatic (Greek for "with images") and apophatic ("without images"). The term "kataphatic" is often employed when the luxuriant powers of language and nature seem to offer promise in the face of the representational task at hand. "Apophatic," in contrast, is chosen when language, in over its head, is thought to communicate best while either remaining mute or employing images that disclaim or even self-immolate before the enormity of the task. The apophatic would include what Paul Tillich called the "self-negating symbol," one that undercuts the possibility of its abuse as an absolute.

The kataphatic seeks to respond to the challenge to represent what is. The apophatic is, at least in part, a protest against the possibility of representing more than remotely what is. The apophatic is thus a kind of nakedness of eye, mind, imagination, and tool chest before the mystery, a paucity of content and method. Furthermore, the apophatic is ever-vigilant, lest representation of the unrepresentable, description of the indescribable, enclose or supplant and thus corrupt and render idolatrous that which is ultimately mystery.

In contrast to the kataphatic, the apophatic's commitment is, above all else, to acknowledge and worship the mystery rather than describe, to say nothing of "solving" it. The apophatic (or aniconic) holds out the possibility that, in a culture of sensorium overload and verbiage such as our own—one in which everything is reduced to what can be imagined or reasoned in the mind and represented to the eye, ear, or intellect—the absence of all of these may itself be the vehicle for conveying the greatest meaning of all. In short, when dealing with levels of reality that matter the most, less might actually mean more.

Tylerton and Environs as Apophatópia

The present study, with its central interest in *topos* (Greek for "place") and a particular place called Tylerton, one which rides in on all five senses—and by extrapolation, all places and all things as "spiritually evocative"—is, at first take, kataphatic. There is much about it which can be represented with images, described with words.

And yet, already in the first half of our decade, I began to suspect that Tylerton, both its culture but particularly its isleography, was also, perhaps primarily, an apophatic phenomenon: that its *more* somehow resided in its *less*-ness. Unlike the mainland culture—where more/faster/bigger/ higher are mindlessly prized, where more is packaged as more while often actually being less, where the good life for many focuses upon the deprivation of deprivation—here the isleography nudged me in a different direction. And as the many facets of that islescape and culture became increasingly translucent or diaphanous to me, as the absence of embellishment aided me in seeing through and down into, awareness of that apophatic quality grew. Tylerton: severe, stark, lean: an apophatic place, an *apophatópia*.

The setting's soft starkness amazingly approximated the pre-text I had packed in of Tylerton becoming a penitential place, one somehow ever, at least partially, in Lent. If Yosemite was a place brushed out lavishly and sumptuously, an analogue of the Dionysian pole of life, perhaps Tylerton's was fast and hair shirt, inviting one to detachment, sobriety, centering, and awareness of mortality. Although Tylerton during that decade came to be my isle Bali, the source of unending and exquisite pleasure to the entire sensorium as well as intellect and imagination, it was, I now know, Bali in winter, Bali in Lent. Tylerton had no *ordinary* time, to employ a liturgical term. The understated colors, the modest vegetation, the squashed horizon, the salinity strictures, and the minimalism all signed that here it was always a penitential season, always *extraordinary* time.

An interesting part of the deprivation ambience that Tylerton and environs gradually came to represent involved, of all things, the Eucharist, or lack of it. My greatest uneasiness in the initial stages of the Inn project proved to be well-founded: should we as a Roman Catholic Christians freely choose to remove ourselves from the opportunity of regular Mass attendance, especially the Eucharist?

Our decision in late 1994 to purchase property had followed serious work on my part with my spiritual director, Fr. Kieran Kavanaugh, OCD. I recall one of our sessions being couched in the imagery of the dream of Pharaoh interpreted by Joseph (Gn 41): the contrasting of the feast of our (literally) seven liturgically fat years in Washington, where daily Mass was an option, with perhaps seven lean years on Tylerton.

Our commitment to live among and worship regularly with Tylerton's Methodists as siblings in Christ would prove to be one of the most rewarding aspects of the entire venture—but that was *despite* major faith differences that, at times, tended to center in the Lord's Table. The United Methodist communion and Roman Catholic Eucharist are less equivalent than meets the eye, or palate. In our third-floor dedicated prayer space at the Inn, the perpetually empty chalice represented what I came to call my Eucharist of Desire. I imbibed repeatedly of that void across those ten, believing that, when opportunity or virtue is elusive, the very desire for the same is yet somehow honored. That decade of longing for the body and blood of Christ came to represent yet another aspect of the minimalism and deprivation that were Tylerton. Ours became an apophatic chalice.

Tylerton as Desert

So, for what were my penitential environs of Tylerton becoming a metaphor? Interestingly enough, *desert*—an improbable one, given all the water around, whether Bay, ocean, or rainfall. Tylerton: a wet and wild . . . *desert*?

The desert or wilderness, an image running through the histories of all three Abrahamic traditions, is the space which via construct becomes the place of detachment, divestiture, and stripping down; the place of separation from all merit, prized pious notions, and practices; the place of danger and vulnerability to demons within and without. The desert is a setting where all that one brings and is gets exposed, sifted, weighed, and found wanting. It is the place of silence, solitude, scarcity, and self-forgetfulness. It is the place of emptiness and abandonment that is both the edge and beyond the edge. It is the place, ironically dismissed as "godforsaken," to which men and women have long retired in both fear and hope of being found by the One.

In the categories of an early Christian hymn (Phil 2:5–11), the desert beckons to the pilgrim "clutching" (v. 6) this or that, inviting that one to "pour herself out" (the verb in verse 7 is a derivative of *kenosis*) as did the Christ. Elsewhere Paul employs different imagery to make the same point: "though the Christ was rich, yet for your sake He became poor" (2 Cor 8:9).

Belden Lane speaks of life in the desert as "an exercise in deconstruction." John of the Cross has his own serrated term in his discussion of the "Dark Night": in the desert all that obstructs the pilgrim's radical freedom to choose union with the One who is Love must be "annihilated." The desert is nothing less than the arena of annihilation. What Barry Lopez writes in *Arctic Dreams* applies here as well: "You must come . . . with no intention of discovery." In the desert, even outcome-expectation is casualty.

Desert in the Hebrew and Christian Scriptures

In the Hebrew Scriptures, Sinai, both mountain and desert, is the crucible where the Hebrews receive *Torah* (Law), a gift gestalt for holy and wholesome life. It is where they, formerly a gaggle of tribes, become a people, their transition from slavery to deliverance rendered irreversible. It is where their very identity is forged with the result that they would always be understood in terms of a relationship, a covenant. It is where they take the formative step toward living in relation to and becoming dependent upon YHWH ("I AM WHO AM"—Ex 3:14).

Every subsequent testing of the Hebrew people at the edge is seen in terms of the imprinted image of Sinai's wilderness, where the trustworthiness of this YHWH proved to be a matter of life and death. The towering figure of the prophet Elijah would forever be associated with this same topography (called Mt. Horeb in 1 Kings 19) and what transpired there, part of the reason for his stature among each of the Abrahamics.

In the Christian scriptures, it is the Gospel of Mark in particular, beginning with the preaching of repentance by John the Baptist in the wilderness, that continues this theme. Jesus, immediately upon being baptized, is "driven"—indeed, "propelled"—into the wilderness (Mk 1:12). The deprivation and temptations he suffers there are harbingers of the cross, as are the One's nourishment and faithfulness of the resurrection. Later, when Saul, arch-persecutor of followers of this Jesus, is confronted near Damascus and converted by the risen Christ, he retreats for an indeterminate time to "Arabia" (Gal 1:17). While scholars dispute this location, it was undoubtedly a place of desolation, depletion, and transformation for the one who would emerge as Saint Paul.

Desert in Christian Monastic Literature

The role of desert in the history of Christian spirituality is an enormous subject that only can be touched upon here. Beginning in the mid-third century, a pattern of retreat to the Egyptian desert unfolded, involving first isolated hermits like Sts. Paul and

Anthony, and then communities such as that of St. Pachomius. In the fourth century, this pattern extended to Syria and Palestine (probably including Mount Carmel), as persecuted Christianity became first tolerated and then grew to be the established religion of the Roman Empire. These changes, associated with the reign and legacy of Emperor Constantine, constituted grave compromises of the gospel for many who chose to vote with their feet and move to and beyond the pale.

My own visits to Coptic Orthodox monasteries—Wadi el Natrun northwest of Cairo (fourth century) in 1983, the communities of Sts. Paul and Anthony in the eastern Egyptian desert near the Red Sea (late third-century sites) in 1988—were important in igniting the desert image in my faith journey.

This rich desert motif was brought to the West, where St. Benedict (c. 480–547) and the rule bearing his name would shape most monastic life in the Latin or Roman Catholic tradition. The European topography and the Benedictine vow of stability would together serve to render *desert* an increasingly metaphorical reality—an *inner desert*. However, the initiative of sixth-century Irish monk St. Columba (521–97) to establish the monastery Iona on an island off the coast of Scotland is but one example of the impulse to keep alive the literal wilderness as the optimal setting for spiritual warfare and journey.

Any of several monastic traditions could exemplify the role of image of desert or wilderness in the journey to the One. But it is my own contemplative Carmelite order that I cite here.

The Carmelites probably began within the small Christian enclave, including Mount Carmel and the present day Israeli cities of Haifa and Acre, resulting from the negotiated standoff between Richard the Lionheart and Saladin in the Third Crusade (1191). On the southwestern flank of Mount Carmel a group of Latin hermits—likely a mix of pilgrims and former crusaders, Latin in rite and predominantly lay—joined themselves to the numinous legacy of the place. Cultic artifacts Latin, Byzantine, Hebrew, and pagan—including bodily remains both *Homo sapien* and Neanderthal, some as much as 150,000 years old—have been uncovered on Mount Carmel. Regarding both duration in time, and the rich diversity of hominids so drawn, this site has few rivals on the planet.

The thirteenth-century jeopardy of the Christian enclave before the Muslim armies—the Carmelites remaining would be massacred in 1291—saw Carmelite hermits fleeing to western Europe, where in time they became both urban and mendicant. It was there, a full century later, that the order generated a "founding myth" crediting their origins to Elijah, the eighth-century BCE prophet who had confronted the prophets of Ba'al (1 Kgs 18) on that very Mount. That image, both eremitical and prophetic, would continue to haunt them: it proved easier to remove them from the wilderness than to remove the wilderness from them.

Prominent in both the writings and biography of the Discalced Carmelite John of the Cross is the theme of fierce landscapes as context for the work of both stripping away (active) and having stripped away (receptive) to make room for the One who is Love. Three centuries later, during the last eighteen months of her life, Therese of Lisieux, OCD (1873–1897), she of the "little way," experienced a kind of metaphorical desert in which she underwent what she understood to be final severe preparations for the Greater Life.

In more recent years this desert image has turned up in various provinces of both Carmelite orders, Ancient Rite and Discalced (Reformed), around the world. For example, the remote West Virginia hermitage maintained for extended silent retreats by the Discalced friars of my own order's Washington Province is simply called their "desert."

I have hurriedly summarized here how the stories of both ancient Israel and Christianity have included a special role for the desert or wilderness as context for encounter with the One. And were we to explore the third of the Abrahamics— Islam, with both its historical taproot and contemporary center being in Arabia—the trajectory would probably be in the same direction. The desert, both as topography and metaphor, continues to be present in the memory of each of the three faiths. It has left its grain on the imagination, the pre-text, of many Abrahamic descendants, as witnessed to by my own experience on the Crick.

My Personal Grace

What an irony, albeit a joyous one! After a life of insatiably devouring experiences— of seemingly being driven by the old Schlitz ad that "you only go around once," as I packed yet more into my repository of less-than-thoroughly-lived life—that I should inadvertently blunder into self-sequesterment on the proverbial "desert" isle, having bound myself to geographical stability and self-delimitation for a full decade!

What a grace that I was caused to slow down enough—partly for reasons of age, health, and exhaustion, as well as longing—to begin more seriously to pray, be attentive, listen, love, *marvel*. Oh, the world I had earlier experienced had been lush and beautiful, as were its people, ideas, and arts. But in self-sequesterment emerged the gift to savor, to relish, and to exult.

Thirty years ago I would not have tolerated this isle's sequesterment, this cloister, nor would its urgency have been what it was now. In the *kairos*—a New Testament word contrasted with *chronos* and translated as "the fullness" or "ripeness" of time—I landed on this wet and wild space, whose rich emptiness seemingly matched my fill of wide roads more traveled. The Crick became a place where the call to spiritual leanness could be more serious entertained; where I could grow into prayer outside the box; where the iconoclastic One could continue to bang away at my obstructing images, pre-occupations, and affections; and where I could settle into listening to the silent music.

Jessica Powers beautifully captures this apophatic impulse in several of her po-ems. Two years before she entered the cloister in 1941, she was already leaning to-ward that threshold in her "Place of Ruin" (75):

> *There must be some house from which even a poet*
> *would hide her frightened face,*
> *where God, grown weary of the brush of beauty,*
> *has used the burning pencil of His grace.*
> *O come and take my hand, you whom I love,*
> *and let us find that place.*

In her "Not Garden Any More" (18), penned in 1949, the apophatic has already deeply marked her:

> *God is not garden any more, to satiate the senses*
> *with the luxuriance of full exotic wilderness.*
> *Now multiple is magnified to less.*
> *God has become as desert now, a vast unknown Sahara*
> *voicing its desert cry . . . .*
> *I write anathema on pool, on streams of racing water.*
> *I bid the shoot, the leaf, the bloom no longer to intrude.*

A Monastic Camp Follower

Perhaps this is the point to acknowledge the obvious: I have been something of a mo-nastic camp follower, a religious life groupie, through much of my adult life. Married not once but twice, the father of three children and twice a grandparent, one who can quickly tire of the precincts of religiosity and yearn for something quite differ-ent, whether concert hall or bar or open vista, I nevertheless have had a strange and improbable forty-year affair of the heart with religious life. I concede infatuation has been a factor: I have looked longingly from afar while exempted by my choices from having to pay the cost. Having said that, I find monasticism profoundly relevant to my ordinary lay life.

I was first infected by several days at New Melleray of Our Lady Trappist monastery near Dubuque in late 1968 as part of a graduate studies term project on the Rule of St. Benedict at the University of Iowa. The making of promises "for the rest of my life" as a Discalced Carmelite secular nearly thirty years later was thus both the end and the beginning of a joyful journey. Given Jane Marie Thibault's reference to aging as life's "natural monastery," a theme I explore in Part V, my enigmatic and perhaps perverse attraction to religious life will remain with me for the duration.

When Sharryl and I are in choir, chanting the Psalter with the Trappists at Mepkin Trappist Abbey in South Carolina as we have done for a week each of four off-seasons during our decade, I am repeatedly filled with amazement that, in this world as presently constituted, there would continue to be communities that do and *are* this! Monastic communities are, in regard to so many issues (not the least of which is response to war and militarism), a call back to greater faithfulness, to what I term the "minority report" of my own Roman Catholic tradition.

It is in religious life, the principal custodians of this "minority report," that the "hard sayings" of Jesus are more likely to be embraced, rather than exiled to the safe past, future, or elite. Here the call to "have no other gods before me" (Ex 20:3) may be understood as at least as relevant as it was three millennia ago. Here weapons are checked at the door in the name of the nonviolent Christ. Indeed, it might well be that central to the urgency I found within me to bring to words my decade in Tylerton was the fact that I had experienced it *to be a monastery*.

So these have been my insights of a harsh and vertically challenged isle as metaphor for desert, a natural environment whose barrenness has been experienced by me and more than a few guests as a promising environment for the journey to the One.

The One as Desert

However, in the Christian tradition, *desert* has also served as an image to represent none other than that One: hidden, incomprehensible, undomesticated, mysterious, the One encountered yet never possessed or controlled. "God as desert" is a formulation that Belden Lane contends might first have been explicitly brought to words in the sixth-century Syrian monk Pseudo-Dionysius and that is then radically developed by the Dominican Meister Eckhart (c. 1260–c. 1328). "God as desert" is to be responded to, wrestled with *a la* Jacob (Gn 32:24–32), and loved apart from either attributes or consolations (goodies).

My own musings about this more lofty meaning of "desert," as a metaphor not merely for the *environment* of the journey but also for its very *Destination*, were fanned into life quite late in this writing project, and await another occasion for their development.

B. The Sea as the Boundless One

A Minnesotan who had experienced numerous of that state's many more than ten thousand lakes, I was a college student before I encountered an actual sea—the Pacific. A beautiful day a dozen years later, spent with my family at the United Nations Club outside Gaza City with the Mediterranean working me, also snags in my memory. Several years later, during the golden autumn preceding the horror of Lebanon's civil war, we would periodically stroll the Corniche atop Beirut's cliffs, the Mediterranean pounding the rocks below, Gibraltar far out to sea beneath the horizon.

An overcast afternoon with heavy surf rolling in on the beach at California's Carmel in 1978 found me first conscious that in the sea there was that below, deep down below, the aesthetic that was beckoning me. In the subsequent decades, the sea would increasingly possess a compelling spiritual power, and, in retrospect, that power was part of what lured me to the Crick.

As with all symbols for the One, my experience of the sea surrounding Tylerton offered kataphatic symbols *first*. Granted, the Bay is but a pocket ocean, its "Chesapeake chop" a function of shallowness in contrast to massive Atlantic's swells over the depths. But as our storm experiences grew in the early years—whether in winter transits to and from Crisfield, as new and nervous homeowners precariously perched but two feet above sea level, or amid our first evacuation during the renovation period—the relentless and powerful qualities of the sea hinted of spiritual qualities. I became increasingly aware that experiencing the scale, power, and majesty of the sea was providing me with images of the One.

Yet with time, the sea, as with the salt marsh, waxed increasingly apophatic, increasingly exposing the poverty of image or language, the metaphor whose meaning was its incomprehensibility, its off-the-scaleness, even as traces of the kataphatic remained. Whether in its volatility and uncontrollability, its relentless and inimitable qualities, the sea was becoming a metaphor for the One who could be neither depicted nor denied. Precisely what does a body do with the heaving sea? In addressing the One in prayer, I found myself groping for handles, words like Engulfer and Courser, Deluger and Surger, Torrent and Tsunami, Inundator and Slaker—"You who are thirsty, come to the water!" (Is 55:1).

Embracing the sea as an apophatic image of the One became for me an acknowledgment that both description and control were illusory, and that my barque was indeed infinitely dwarfed by the One upon whom I was sailing my life. The sheer scale of the sea rendered any analogy impossible: to say that the One is like the sea is to propose an image for that which cannot be represented, one which connotes awe and reverence vastly more than similitude. By mid-decade, I was thinking that nothing in creation had gathered together the immensity, uncontrollability, awesomeness, abyss, and stark inadequacy of human language regarding the One as had the sea. That judgment too would require emendation before the decade was out.

The One as Abyss

An aspect of the metaphor of sea that throws wide open rather than enclosing and defining is that of *depth* or *abyss*. Granted, the Atlantic beyond the continental shelf nudges one more forcefully in that direction than can our oft-shoaled Bay. Nevertheless, take a January passage from Crisfield to Tylerton over "Puppy Hole," where depths of eighty-five feet and northwest winds of thirty-five miles per hour are intermittently "buryin' the bow" in the icy green seas. Mix in awareness of the February 1951 death of Waverly Evans' twin, Weldon, captain of the *Melrose*, to starboard. Recall the March 2005 disappearance of both Tangier waterman James Crockett and his working boat, the *Eldora C*, to port. Consider these things, and you have a reasonable facsimile of ocean. One could say that what Tylerton lacks in elevation is more than offset by the abyss component, the negative verticality—the depth and danger of its brackish environs.

Abyss hints of that far below the sensorium, below the understanding, beneath the consciousness: that which the early twentieth-century German theologian Rudolf Otto called the *mysterium tremendum*. "The One as Abyss" is not to be found at the end of a rational argument for the existence of the One by dusty deists or their twenty-first century advocates of intelligent design, both seeking to *prove* the existence of the unprovable.

Like the Psalter's "Deep calls to deep at the sound of Your waterfalls; All Your breakers and Your waves have rolled over me" (Ps 42:7), it is the person opening herself to the mystery—awe-full, fearsome, indescribable, yet luring and undeniable—of the One. The Abyss: while it generates fear within us, we also do not seem to be able to let it alone. Jessica Powers queries: "Have you seen water ever that got tangled / with light and came alive and was divine?" (141)

Paralleling a shift from the image of acting upon the Other (active) to that of being acted upon *by* that Other (receptive), the images of the divine across my adult life had gradually been moving from those of the One residing within me to those of the One within whom I reside. The sea is obviously a promising example of the latter. I remember shouting out "Yes!" within myself during our pilgrimage to the city and convent of Catherine of Siena (1347–80) in Advent of 2001, upon coming across the image of the One in her sometimes wild *The Dialogue*: "Sea Pacific" (*mare pacifica*).

The Sea in the Hebrew and Christian Scriptures

For the student of Hebrew scriptures, the sea is forever that over which the divine Spirit brooded at the beginning of the creation of the cosmos (Gn 1:2). In fact, the sea in the Hebrew text continues to be a fearful place of chaos and peril, its depths the dwelling place of the mythical monster Leviathan (Is 27:1) and the dragon Rahab (Jb 26:12). It is the site of YHWH's deliverance of Israel from the Egyptians, an event recited recurringly in subsequent periods, such as in Habakkuk 3:15: "You trampled on the sea with Your horses, on the surge of many waters."

In other Hebrew texts where the sea and YHWH appear together—whether in the book of Jonah or Psalms—it is generally to show YHWH's preeminence, not for the sea to serve as metaphor for deity. For example: "More . . . than the mighty breakers of the sea, You, O LORD, are mighty on high" (Ps 93:4). A partial exception may be the Messianic promise: "For the earth will be full of the knowledge of YHWH as the waters cover the sea" (Is 11:9).

This chaotic and perilous thrust of the sea image does not change substantively in the Christian scriptures, where it can be the arena for attributing the power of the One to Jesus: "Who then is this, that even the wind and the sea obey Him?" (Mk 4:41). In chapter 13 of the Apocalypse, the sea is that from which emerges the beast, archenemy of the Lamb, so that with the emergence of " . . . a new heaven and a new earth . . . there is no longer any sea" (Apoc 21:1). In the fourth gospel, the image of Jesus as *living water* (Jn 4:7–26), one with strong baptismal overtones, stands in sharp contrast to the sea as realm of chaos.

The Sea in Christian Monastic Literature

Mysticism scholar Bernard McGinn uses the term "adjunct" to describe both desert and sea imagery for the One in medieval spirituality when compared, for example, with the erotic language of the Song of Songs. Of the two, he finds the oceanic to have a much smaller role than the desert. Nevertheless, despite the generally negative use of this image in Scripture, noteworthy practitioners in the medieval period have used the sea as a metaphor for the One.

McGinn identifies the Greek monk Evagrius Ponticus (c. 344–399) as the first Christian whose writings contain positive sea imagery for the One. By contrast, in the Latin West the pejorative use of this imagery is still present in Augustine (354–430) and Gregory the Great (c. 540–604), with a shift credited to John

Scotus Eriugena ("Irish born," c. 810–c. 877) whose writings contained phrases such as "the sea of infinite goodness" and "the Ocean of Divinity." (The Latin Eriugena was most unusual in being fluent in Greek, and he was influenced by Evagrius.) McGinn cites as well Richard of Saint Victor (d. 1173), who wrote of the "flowing wave of divinity and overflowing of love," as among the practitioners of oceanic imagery for the One.

McGinn contends that various of the Beguines, medieval lay female communities that did not have vows, added to this rehabilitation of the image of the sea. Most notable is the thirteenth-century Hadewijch of Brabant, whose images of the One involve whirlpools and violence. For example: "He is outside of all, for he rests in nothing other than the tempestuous nature of his own profusely overflowing flood, that overflows everywhere and everything." In his employing of images for the One such as "a flowing, ebbing sea," "a fathomless whirlpool of simplicity," and "the wild waves of the sea," the Flemish priest Jan van Ruysbroeck (1293–1381) might have been evidencing influence from these Beguines whom he read. McGinn speculates whether oceanic and watery abyss symbols are not more developed by the (female) Beguines in contrast to desert symbols for the One being more common among learned (male) priests.

Catherine of Siena repeatedly has the One speaking in the first person, inviting the soul to immerse itself in this "Sea Pacific" (*mare pacifica*) as a fish swims in the ocean. This One Catherine addresses as follows: "Thou . . . art a deep sea, into which the deeper I enter the more I find, and the more I find the more I seek; for the soul cannot be satiated in Thy abyss."

John of the Cross, in his culminating *Living Flame of Love,* powerfully combines the images of fire and the sea:

> [S]eemingly there flow seas of living fire within the [person], reaching to the heights and depths of the earthly and heavenly spheres, imbuing all with love. It seems to the [person] that the entire universe is a sea of love in which it is engulfed, for conscious of the living point or center of love within itself, the [person] is unable to catch sight of the boundaries of this love.

Jessica Powers, whose poem "The Place of Waters" (71) may well be inspired by St. Catherine's *mare pacifica*, requested before her death in 1988 that an envisioned publication of the definitive collection of her work culminate with her "Doxology" (191). These are the final lines:

> *And lo, myself am the abode*
> *Of Love, the third of the Triune,*
> *the primal surge and sweep of God*
> *and my eternal claimant soon!*
> *Praise to the Father and the Son*
> *and to the Spirit! May I be,*
> *O Water, Wave and Tide in One,*
> *Thine animate doxology.*

I wrote portions of this book during winter stints in Edisto Beach, South Carolina, and Ocean City, Maryland, both islands with oceanic vistas to the east. On both occasions, we had more experience with Hadewijch's image of "the tempestuous nature of his own profusely overflowing flood" than with Catherine's *mare pacifica!* But that the employing of the image of the sea for the One has connotations both comforting and disturbing is most instructive. For example, for many of the faithful, Hadewijch's imagery hints of the One's propensity for surging across barriers, transgressing ecclesial routines, ever breaking into the "other": people of color, AIDS sufferers, Iraqi insurgents, the biosphere in general, the entire cosmos. In this respect, her images can be decidedly discomforting to the comfortable.

Finally, my Tylerton experience of integrating the desert and sea images for the One was influenced by the interpretation of 1 Kings 17:2–7 central to the Carmelite "founding myth." The prophet Elijah is dispatched by YHWH to the wilderness east of River Jordan. With "brook" read as "torrent," which the wadi's lazy stream can seasonally become, and the consonants of the place's name, *Cherith*, as tantalizingly close to the Latin *Caritas* (charity), the prophet Elijah's persona in early Carmelite collective memory was of one miraculously sustained and formed in a wilderness deprivation by the One who is a Torrent of Love. Thus, this text would have paradigmatic stature throughout the more than eight-hundred-year history of the Carmelite saga, including this secular member of that tradition.

12. Place as Sacrament

A. Place in the Biblical Tradition

Within the worlds of both the Hebrew and Christian scriptures is a plethora of places. Biblical faith, whether in the initial or subsequent testament, is witness to the astonishing news that the One encounters humankind in both time and space, two familiar strictures of creaturely life. Geography was thus an integral part of the faith story of both ancient Israel and the community which hailed Jesus of Nazareth as Messiah.

Place in the Hebrew Scriptures

Many of these spaces have come to be saturated with meaning by what transpired there: Hebron with Abraham, the friend of YHWH; Bethel with Jacob's encounter with YHWH; Egypt with slavery; the Sea of Reeds with Israel's deliverance; Sinai with *Torah* and peoplehood formation; Jericho with the triumph of YHWH, Israel's King; Bethlehem with the Davidic dynasty and destiny; and Jerusalem with both the Hebrews' loftiest glory and their most ignominious calamity. Thus have these spaces become places.

Yet unlike mythical sites, all of these places had location before they had meaning, and most of those locations remain known today. For example, the Taggart fortress, dating back to the League of Nations' British Mandate for Palestine (1922–1948), was the place where, in the 1970s, I would intermittently meet with Israeli military representatives regarding our society's projects among West Bank Palestinians. It was located in no less than Beit El (*Bethel* in Hebrew), site of Jacob's encounters with YHWH (Gn 28:10–22; 35:1–7), but twelve miles north of Jerusalem.

Biblical Judaism was place-specific in the sense that salvation history was hooked deeply into salvation geography, the narrative into the natural world. All of this was in sharp contrast to Hellenistic religion, for example, with its antithesis between the realms of spirit and material, precluding the taking with equal seriousness of either geographical place or historical time.

Place in the Christian Scriptures

Much of the Christian scriptures is profoundly Jewish in its reporting of events repeatedly tethered to specific places. Place remains primarily geographical, and only secondarily mythical. Thus, Bethlehem, Egypt, Nazareth, the Sea of Galilee, Bethany, Jerusalem, the Mount of Olives, and Calvary, as well as Antioch, Corinth, Ephesus, and Rome each came to have deep meaning, but meaning attached in most cases to a location known both before and since.

The great events of the New Testament story, the fulcrum of history for the Christian faithful, involved specific geographical places, many of which I personally have walked, studied, and continue to savor. (On two different off-seasons during our decade, my purchase of air tickets to take Sharryl for her first visit to Jerusalem, my "other city," foundered in the face of the violence in that region; the task remains to be realized.)

And despite the fact that the major expansion of Christianity by the end of the first century was out of the Hebraic into the Hellenistic culture, "the Way" (as Acts 9:2 describes the nascent movement) remained profoundly Jewish in its declaration that the mighty acts of the One had unfolded in geography that is firmly lodged in both memory and map. The One was not encountered primarily in ethereal precincts high in the mythological air or in esoteric mysteries accessible but to the elite. No, the One self-disclosed in and through the same beloved creation this very One had brought into being. Place specificity was no embarrassment to those of the Way, although a darker side of this valuing of place would be manifested a millennium later in the Crusades (1096 ff.).

B. Place and the Incarnation

For Christians, all of the above are both exemplified and culminated in the story of Jesus the Christ, beginning with the birth accounts in Matthew and Luke. Researcher Luke's effort to pinpoint both the time—the initial census during Quirinius' governorship of Syria—and space—Bethlehem of Judea, the city of David—is arresting in its precision (Lk 2:1–7). Is it any wonder that the one place in the profession of the *Credo* where the faithful bow is at these words: "by the power of the Holy Spirit he was born of the Virgin Mary, and became man"?

The eternal Word (*logos*) of the One, not confined to the finite strictures of *time* and *space*, indeed the very Creator of these and all else, is set forth in the prologue of John's gospel as having embraced ligature to both! The enfleshed Word of God, present before the beginning, through whom all that is has being (Jn 1:1–14); the Living Bread of Life who feeds the five thousand (John 6); he in whom all that is consists, according to Paul (Col 1:17); that person was born in an animal shelter in an insignificant village, a runt among towns (Mi 5:2), interestingly called *Beth-lechem* ("House of Bread").

This Anointed One, confessed by his followers as the hinge of human history, is tethered to most improbable space, one transformed for the duration into place, a wondrous place. Thus, the Roman Catholic Christmas Vigil is summed up with these words: "This night in the Word become flesh is earth joined to heaven." And that earth, indeed the entire cosmos being the space so embraced, is never the same again. No wonder that Palestrina's *Alma redemptoris mater* includes the lines "O thou who begot thy holy creator, while all creation marveled"! No wonder that at that same Vigil we sing together, "heaven *and nature* sing"!

All Creation Rendered Holy

It is impossible to overstate the implications for the creation, for the natural environment, of belief in the One's identification/solidarity with it (literally, "tabernacling" in John 1:14) in a specific time and place. In contrast to Greek religions, with their ambivalence about the material, the stuff of creation (beginning within the body of Mary) in Christian scriptures on the Incarnation ("Enfleshment") is shown to be the hut or habitat of the One.

The implications of this faith affirmation reverberate: all the creation extending from infant and stable in that particular place to the farthest galaxies is honored, blessed, and forever embraced as precious. The entire cosmos, lovingly ignited into being, patiently unfolded and nurtured into plush plentitude, and ever wooed forward with loving care, is in Bethlehem shown to be the beloved of the Lover. Nature thus becomes forever the arena of epiphany, the showcase, the manifestation, the exposition of the love of the One. In the Incarnation all that is in all of its physicality and materiality is thus rendered holy, the Hellenistic deriding of materiality in favor of spirit forever rejected.

Thus Thomas Merton could write:

> We do not dare to believe or trust the incredible truth that [the One] could live in us, and live there out of choice. But indeed we exist solely for this to be the place he has chosen for his presence, his manifestation in the world.

The time-and-space specificity of Bethlehem is the Creator's *re*-affirmation: all of the cosmos, already repeatedly declared "good" (Gn 1), is precious and holy. In the Anointed One is the cosmic scale of the Love Project laid bare. Rather than diminishing human materiality in favor of some spiritual level of existence, the Gospel writers go out of their way to emphasize that the Risen Christ, rather than a noncorporeal ghost, is the resounding triumph of the One's embrace of humanity.

Saint Paul takes the argument a large step further by claiming that the risen Christ is first fruits of a far more vast human resurrection and glorification (1 Cor 15:20-23). The Epistle of James appears to view the One's redemption of humans as the first fruits of a yet wider harvest among the One's creatures (Jas 1:18). Finally, in his letter to the Romans, Paul unequivocally links the salvation of humans through Jesus the Christ with the healing and consummation of the larger creation (Rom 8:18–25). Indeed, Paul argues here that the entire creation, amid groanings and suffering, awaits with eagerness the salvation it will *share* with the human family. In short, in the resurrection accounts of the Christ is prefigured the destiny of the entire cosmos!

In the third century, the mercurial Origen (185–232) would laud this universal destiny with the word *apokatástasis* ("restoration") and prayerfully contemplate the possibility, as would others from Gregory of Nyssa (fourth century) to Karl Rahner, SJ (twentieth), that this healing be comprehensive, all-inclusive. The doctrinal controversies in the fourth and fifth centuries would forever settle the issue for people of the Way: the stuff of the One's creation is both the raw material for and the arena of that One's self-disclosure and triumph, and it should be stewarded accordingly. The implications of all of this for both how we think about and care for the natural world simply do not quit!

Incarnation as Kataphatic

The notion of Incarnation has a kataphatic aura about it. The invisible (and unknowable) One, desiring intimacy with the creation in which offered love is reciprocated, "pitches a tent" (Jn 1:14) of identification and solidarity with the physical and material creation in a space called Bethlehem.

This initiative by the One, going by the name of the Christ (Anointed One), is, in the words of Paul, the "icon of the invisible God" (Col 1:15; 2 Cor 4:4) prefigured in the transfiguration accounts in the gospels (Mk 9:1–13; Mt 17:1–13). The fourth Gospel thus has Jesus saying, "The one who has seen me has seen the Father" (Jn 14:9).

In the Christian tradition, the coming of the One in a manner so as to be heard with ears, seen by eyes, and grasped by hands (1 Jn 1:1), would appear to be that One's accommodation to our propensity toward what the sensorium and the intellect can receive, that which is locatable in space/place as well as time. Thus that the human tendency to function at the level of what we can encounter with our senses and/ or mind is not only known to the One, but has been accommodated to, by the One.

In short, the Incarnation is the One's Word (*logos*) "spoken" in the creation's language, in our humanese brogue. All of this so far, not unlike this study's focus on place, is boilerplate, albeit paradigmatic, *kataphatica*: the Infinite encountered via the ordinary stuff of the creation.

Incarnation as Apophatic

But there is more: the deeper meaning of the Incarnation remains dark and luminous mystery, the Mystery of the One. The kataphatic, having run its caretaking course, delivers the pilgrim back where (s)he began, before the invisible, unfathomable, and unnameable One. The kataphatic, far from "solving" the One via analogies drawn from the cosmos, can but offer direction, nudges, hints, toward the One of whose works Paul writes that "eye has not seen, ear has not heard, nor has it so much as entered into the human imagination . . ." (1 Cor 2:9).

In terms of my focus here, the theme of Incarnation, with its specificity of place, time, the sensorium, and the intellect/imagination, ultimately delivers us into the arms of the One who is Source, End, and Darkness: YHWH. The kataphatic, the enfleshment of the One in the stuff of the creation, is tutor and guide, not destination: beyond all images, representations, and analogies is the darkness of the apophatic. The creation's destiny is the One who is Mystery and before whom everything that is, in the words of the psalmist, can but cry "Glory!" (Ps 29:9).

C. Place and the Sacraments of the Church

The foundation for the sacraments in the Roman Catholic tradition is the Incarnation of the One in the Christ. In Bethlehem, the finite, the creaturely, was shown to have been fitted out with the capacity to receive the infinite, the Creator; the human receptive of the divine (*finitum capax infiniti*).

Despite having assumed their present sevenfold form quite late, the sacraments are a kind of derivative tier, a second level of expressions, of Immanuel ("God with us"), a name given to the infant Jesus (Mt 1:23; Is 7:10–16). The seven sacraments are signs of the gracing presence/activity of the One, mediated via the stuff of the creation, whether water, wine and bread, oils, committed love, or covenanted vocation. The sacraments are kataphatic (imaged)—at least at first take—extensions in our world of the presence of the risen Christ, extrapolations of the One, who perhaps not so much *came to* Bethlehem as there showcased having never been away!

The following is but a partial inventory of the marvelous sensuality of the sacraments: the auditory, visual, and tactile in baptism; the olfactory, auditory, and tactile in both confirmation and anointing; the visual and auditory in holy orders; the auditory, visual, and tactile in reconciliation; and in marriage, the five-fold flush of the sensory spectrum, and beyond. And the sacramental summit of Eucharist: Immanuel in time and space, the One's great embrace, the divine table with its shocking invitation to ingest the living One! What image, what setting, what activity could more powerfully convey the artful invitation of the One's hospitality than a table spread for all, for the uni-verse? It was an insight not lost on this hospitalier as he set tables on the porch of the Inn!

The message of the Incarnation—that the One, rather than disdaining the natural world has not despaired of it, has self-embedded in it, and cannot be separated from it—is thus secondarily played out in the seven sacraments. The divine embrace of the created cosmos of time and space, duration and place, a theme present throughout the Hebrew Bible as well as both scriptures and tradition of the Christian churches, is exemplified and amplified in these Sacraments. And in each experience of the sacraments the recipient is, in effect, being drawn near by the One's question: will you allow Me *here, now*, to dilate your heart (Ps 119:32) to receive Me yet more fully?

Despite the fact that our Tylerton location severely limited our access to the sacraments during our decade, each reception of the Eucharist in particular, whether actual or of desire, was a powerful reminder of this divine embrace that has made all the difference. That the sacraments played such an important role in my emerging awareness of the natural world as *chosen,* during a period when I did not have ready access to them, is one of numinous ironies of this decade.

D. This Place as Sacramental

The Cosmos as Sacrament

In the Roman Catholic tradition, the One's "settling in" in the place called Bethlehem, and being self-availing to us via sacraments, opens floodgates to an understanding of the entire cosmos as visited, wooed, inhabited, and embraced. This opening, most obvious and explicit in the doctrine of the Incarnation and, derivatively, the sacraments, is thus but the beginning. *Capax Dei*—a hunger, and capacity, for the One: an infant and, by extrapolation, the stuff of sacrament, and beyond, the entire cosmos, gifted with the capability of receiving and mediating the One. The seven sacraments are thus a kind of way station, a halfway house, nudging us from the incarnational truth of Immanuel ("God with us") to its unbounded implications for every corner of the cosmos, whether marshglow, periwinkle, solstice, or that glimpsed via the Hubble of the infancy of all that is.

It is a challenge larger than this life to embrace the meaning of the Incarnation for all that is, for nothing less than the cosmos itself. The extrapolation from Incarnation to the sacraments is but the iceberg's tip, for all that has being is now proclaimed to be prized, chosen—indeed, *inhabited for the duration* by the One.

The self-accounting natural world—that consisting of merely what the sensorium can receive, scientific instruments measure, and the intellect reflect upon—simply does not exist. Indeed, it never did, for the Creator and Incarnator have been shown to be one and the same. That natural world has been lovingly stalked by the

One. It is a world that is, in the words of novelist Flannery O'Connor (1925–1964), "Christ-haunted." In Bethlehem, the One's disposition toward the created cosmos has been irrevocably laid bare. All of the cosmos, created as good, is honored, becoming candidate for sacramentally mediating the love of the permanent Resident Lover.

Tylerton as Translucent

What happened to me in Tylerton—what is central to this book—is that the incalculable implications of Incarnation for EVERYTHING were slowly sinking in. As the decade progressed, I increasingly experienced my natural as well as cultural environments to be translucent and diaphanous to their deep-down depth, indeed, luminous of the inhabiting One. The words of Gerard Manley Hopkins, "the world is charged with the grandeur of God, It will flame out, like shining from shook foil," came, at least at times, to be as self-evident as the igniting of the eastern hemisphere by Sir Sol rising out of Tangier Sound to the east.

Sometimes the awareness, palpable in the chest, of our isleography as *decisively* visited and embraced, was triggered by something minute: the precise tide level, reported by a guest over dinner, at which all the periwinkle snails attached to the stalks of *Spartina alterniflora*; the appearance each September of the tiny yet brilliant blooms of the seaside goldenrod; the specter-like puffball clusters of the groundsel tree decorating the skirts of distant hammocks the following month; the *adagio* tempo of a great blue heron's flight to its appointed perch at the end of our dock.

Sometimes the scale was larger, as with a thunderstorm front steaming majestically across the sky, its bow as sharp as a knife-drawn line, or the overture petticoats of pirouetting Hurricane Isabel, or the numinous November arrival of the tundra swans from the Arctic Circle.

Sometimes the awe was triggered by a waterman's comment presupposing a oneness with nature alien to modernity, or the slapping *pak, pak* cadence of waves against the bulkhead as I surrendered to sleep, or the unabashed delight of two brand-new parents as they showed us their little Faith.

But the increasingly powerful experience of my environment was not only amazement and awe, marveling and internal high-fiving. Increasingly it also was awareness of the One whose intentions—whose disposition toward the cosmos, including the entire biosphere and every critter, every single person—had been laid bare in Bethlehem. In the stable-born; in the teachings, life-style, and death-style of Jesus the Christ; in the sacraments was the One whose brooding presence was becoming increasingly self-evident to me in this particular place. Rather than an esoteric exercise in Aristotelian metaphysics, the doctrine of the "real presence" reflected two millennia of joyful efforts in the Christian tradition to point to, name, laud, and adore the Whirlwind. And I, here, *here,* came to believe more fiercely still.

Experiencing on the Crick the real presence of the One became a part of many days. Here more than ever before I experienced the Incarnator to be brooding upon the face of the waters, glimpsed in the lavish biosphere, mediated via sunsets of nameless hues or the attentive care of neighbor. And no longer only aesthetic rush, but being seized by the cascading and reverberating truth of Immanuel, God with us. Jessica Powers' "The Place of Splendor" (123) points toward this experience of the One in the many:

> *The soul grows clear*
> *when senses fuse: sight, touch and sound are one*
> *with savor and scent, and all to splendor run.*

Ah yes, and all that is to splendor runs. My own shorthand for all of this is that this place, the Crick, became for me, at least episodically, sacramental—indeed, a sacrament of the One.

One of the implications of the experiencing of place and its components as sacramental is that the natural world is translucent to the One, simply by being what it was unfolded to be. Nature can become sacramental not only by being historically linked to a revelatory encounter *but by simply being what it is.*

When the psalmist sings, "Let everything that has breath praise YHWH" (Ps 150:6), he is implicitly including the crab, cormorant, and clapper rail, each offering its praise simply by its inimitable existence. Understanding place and all of its components as sacramental bestows upon all critters, and beyond, a dignity as intricate miracles transparent to the One rather than mere fodder for consumption or development.

The linking of belief in the One with how one experiences one's environment, particularly the natural one, has a long and varied history. For example, deists of the seventeenth and eighteenth centuries extrapolated from the complex and multifaceted watch to the watchmaker, from the many of the natural world to the One who is deity.

My experience has seemingly moved in the *reverse* direction, from the One to the many. That is, during this decade I increasingly came to see and recognize in my natural and cultural surroundings the One who has encountered me in biblical text, Christian tradition, and Eucharistic table, whose disposition and loving trustworthiness I know primarily through the person born in Bethlehem.

Mine was not a journey of reason and intellect nearly as much as one of desire and love. As Thomas Merton wrote, "when the mind admits that [the One] is too great for our knowledge, love replies: 'I know Him.'" Indeed, many of my days began with a step onto the balcony, a survey of the beauty before me, and the prayer rising within: *Oh*, I recognize You! Such moments of coherence are among the principal fruits of being open to a decade-long commitment of stability to a particular place, and thus coming to love both it and its meaning.

As with space, the sacramental has profound implications for how we experience time, especially the future. The Eucharist in particular is harbinger, inkling, foretaste, indeed, promise, of a "new heavens and new earth" (2 Pt 3:13) yet to come. It is remarkable that each of the synoptic accounts of the Last Supper has Jesus telling his companions that he would not again share table with them until the full flower of the One's Reigning (Mt 26:29; Mk 14:25; Lk 22:18).

Paul's parallel account also faces the future: "For as often as you eat this bread and drink this cup, you proclaim the Lord's death *until he comes*" (1 Cor 11:26, EA). The sacramental thus both points and prods toward the culmination of the One's restorative project, *apokatástasis*, the healing of the creation, both our human brokenness and that of the entire cosmos.

The Crick as Commission

I learned more deeply on the Crick that to view that place as sacrament carried profound implications both ethical and prophetic:

Ethically: I am called to allow my care for sibling Earth to be shaped by its having been declared precious in the enfleshment of the Christ. I am also called to fuel this stewardship by the hope that its destiny of wholeness in the One's embrace is as certain as is our own. Chapters 15 in Part IV ("Hospitality as Pilot Project") and 31 in Part VI ("Prayers Offered Out of the End: Consummation") develop further how the sacramental vision faces the future.

Prophetically: I, together with all persons and communities of faith in the Anointed One, am called to be a sign of contradiction to our culture's propensity to view sibling Earth as the granary servicing the maw of our consumerism, that beast with a self-destructive eating disorder.

John of the Cross on Being Freed to Love the Creation

In conclusion, none more than a Discalced Carmelite should be as wary of the hazards of rhapsodizing a mere aesthetic of nature into what purports to satisfy the longing of the human heart. The book of Wisdom in the Apocrypha speaks sympathetically of those "distracted by what they see, because the things seen are fair" (Ws 13:7), a temptation to which all are susceptible.

On this score, the legacy of John of the Cross is uncompromising, shorthanded by his *Nada, Nada, Nada* (No! No! No!) mantra warning against identification of the One with this or that. He insists on the primacy of hunger for the One of consolations, rather than the consolations of the One. Nothing, whether nature in all its fairness or our precious pious notions and images, can be equated with or be allowed to distract us from the One. The hunger of the human heart, we belatedly discover, is not for this or that, but for this One, the Lover. All else, including nature, religion, spirituality, and devotions, must be held conditionally, as mere preparer of the way for that Lover.

In *The Dark Night*, John wrote that some, having long been climbing the ascent of stripping down and sorting out false deities, are inexorably drawn by the One into that night where there is, finally, only the self and that One. But now, supplanting all that was stripped away, is the reality that it is the Lover who is doing the climbing. Such is not an encounter for the timid, nor does John counsel running after such nakedness and solitude. If and when this desert emerges, it will have been lovingly given by the One, a gift crafted to purify, pare, and further prepare.

Interestingly enough, I have read few writers with a zest for the created world, for the beauty of nature, the arts, and, in particular, human love, like the friar John of the Cross. Adamantly refusing to countenance the usurpation of the Creator by the creation, he was thereby freed to love that creation passionately for what it is, *no more and certainly no less*. This is one of the delicious tensions in the heart of John's vocation, one to which I have repeatedly repaired for direction during my own habitation in the world of Tylerton—which, to use one of its citizens' pet phrases, is also so "very, very *fahr* (fair)."

PART IV
RECEIVING THE STRANGER WITHOUT:
HOSPITALITY

"All guests who present themselves are to be welcomed as Christ."
—Rule of St. Benedict

And now to the matter of innkeeping itself. Our shift in late 1989 from teaching at the graduate level toward hospitality certainly seemed to have its random aspects. Planning to wed in early 1990 and eschewing a commuter marriage, Sharryl (head of the graduate department of teacher education at Fresno Pacific University in central California) and I (teaching ethics and theology at the Associated Mennonite Biblical Seminary in Elkhart, Indiana) chose to open our professional lives beyond familiar educational confines.

With this widening, we encountered possibilities that would have us actually working together. Let it be said here that in the seventeen years following, we would often laugh, and occasionally weep, at the extent to which innkeeping would fulfill that aspiration!

In January of 1990 we assumed a shared position as co-managers of Davis House, an international guesthouse operated by the American Friends Service Committee, a Quaker peace and justice organization, in the Dupont Circle neighborhood of northwest Washington, D.C. Here we cut our teeth on marriage, urban life, Roman Catholic identity, and hospitality.

The innkeeping option was not as arbitrary as meets the eye, however, particularly for me. I had long found the theme of "hospitality" a very promising theological one in speaking about the disposition of the One in both Hebrew and Christian scriptures. My earlier formation as a young Mennonite pastor had been deeply influenced by Henri Nouwen's *Reaching Out*, including his section on hospitality as a life stance. Furthermore, hospitality had been a helpful theme in working with a range of relational issues involving race, gender, sexual orientation, otherwise-ablement, and one's relationship with one's self in my ethics classes. Indeed, I had become quite accomplished in *talking* about hospitality.

Now we were opting for a professional role in which what I had formerly talked about would need to be transformed in very explicit and concrete ways. It would be a choice that would alter the rest of my life. Hospitality would provide a livelihood, a context for worldwide travel, a growing circle of fascinating friendships, an exquisite window on the human predicament, a repeated shattering of boundaries, a love affair stretched between first a city and then a marsh and its inhabitants, an unfolding relationship with my co-innkeeper, deeper self-understanding, and a deeper conviction regarding the One as Hospitalier of the cosmos. Our two houses of hospitality would become laboratories for both theological reflection and, more importantly, prayer. Across the following seventeen years, what began as a profession would become a calling—or, in Roman Catholic parlance, a "vocation."

13. Hospitality Among the Abrahamics

Each of the three Abrahamic faith traditions—Judaism, Christianity, and Islam—has contributed to shaping my understanding of hospitality, although in wildly varied ways. In the case of Judaism, I have been shaped principally by the Hebrew Bible and its powerful hospitality mandate rooted in the actions of *YHWH Sabaoth* ("Lord of hosts"). Regarding Christianity, I have been formed as a participant within that faith family, first Mennonite and then Roman Catholic, including both its scriptures (rooted in the Hebrew Bible) and tradition. As to Islam, the influence here has been the least theological and, in some respects, most graphic. This schooling occurred at the hands of Palestinian Muslims to whom I in my early thirties, together with my family, appeared, literally, as strangers at their gate.

A. Hospitality in the Hebrew Bible

The defining event for the peoplehood formation of the ancient Hebrews was the Exodus (their deliverance from slavery in Egypt) coupled with Mount Sinai, where they received the *Torah* (the Law, a configuration for wholeness and life rooted in covenant). Both components of this paradigmatic event were gifts from YHWH, gifts revisited for direction in scores of texts in the Hebrew Bible across the next millennium and beyond.

Entering into their peoplehood formation as a beleaguered, ragtag collection of clans and tribes, the Hebrews emerged from this formative period on the road to becoming a nation, one forever marked by an inimitable relationship initiated by this One.

YHWH as the Great Hospitalier

Although the Exodus / Sinai event sheds light on virtually every aspect of the Hebrews' subsequent history, I focus here upon hospitality. In a part of the world and era of history when one's identity and safety were entirely lodged in social solidarity with his or her clan or tribe, the thirteenth-century BCE Hebrews in Egypt had neither. Bereft of shielding, whether customary or legal, they were at the mercy of their oppressors. They were, as various translations have it, strangers, aliens, sojourners, slaves.

To this jeopardy, YHWH responded out of compassionate love, championing and liberating them, and then safely ensconcing them in *Torah,* land, and culture. In short, the Hebrews were the recipients of the *hospitality* of YHWH, and this divine initiative would be repeatedly recited as the paradigm for their own reception of others.

This central linkage for the understanding of hospitality in the Hebrew Bible is exemplified in words like the following: "[YHWH] executes justice for the orphan and the widow, and shows His love for the alien . . . . So show your love for the alien, for you were aliens in the land of Egypt" (Dt 10:18-19). This is a powerful example of Hebrew ethics derived from the mighty acts of YHWH—in this case, reception of the alien (as well as orphan and widow).

The Israelites were to extend hospitality to the stranger at their gate, as they themselves had once received the same from their Deliverer. The Hebrew prophets in particular would not allow their hearers to forget that response to the vulnerable aliens among them was to be viewed through the lens of their own such state back in Egypt.

Hebrew social legislation appears to recognize a variety of situations calling for hospitality. On the one hand, the *temporary* alien visitor depended primarily on the hospitality of the host family. How the hosts followed through on this major responsibility can be glimpsed in innumerable encounters in the Hebrew text, many of them revolving around the sharing of table—note Abraham and Sarah's reception of the three visitors (Gn 18:1-15). The role of food is prominent in Hebrew hospitality, as it had been in the Passover feast commemorating YHWH's deliverance of them from Egypt.

The *resident* aliens, on the other hand, lacking such advocates, were highly vulnerable, and were thus more directly addressed by the Hebrew legal structure, even while the citizenry had to remain wary of those who meant them harm. The fact that more than a few such aliens entering Hebrew society would become full citizens and play important roles in the subsequent narrative suggests that hospitality was both urgently needed and widely practiced. Each such account was a milestone on the road to the exilic Isaiah's vision of the Hebrews as a "light to the nations" (Is 42:6, 49:6, 51:4, 60:1-3), one joyfully celebrating the hospitable disposition of YHWH toward *all* the peoples of Earth.

The Ruth Story as Paradigm

The inimitable book of Ruth offers a window into several dimensions of this hospitality theme. After the death of her husband, the Moabitess Ruth (daughter-in-law of the Hebrew Naomi) determined to leave her own people, among whom she and her mother-in-law had lived, and affix herself to Naomi's society and deity. Upon their return to Naomi's ancestral home in Bethlehem following a famine, Ruth's social status as member of a people perennially at war with the Hebrews was that of alien subject to the vagaries of custom and conduct.

The text artfully hints at how first Naomi and then Boaz (a member of Naomi's deceased husband's clan) sought to shield her from exploitation and support her livelihood in the vulnerable role of young and widowed resident alien. Boaz's motivation waxes less and less disinterested, and in time the two are joined and have a son, Obed, who would come to be the grandfather of King David. The Davidic dynasty would forever be chronicled as having come through a young Moabitess stranger at the gate, a tale recapitulating the hospitality of YHWH centuries before in Egypt.

In short, the contribution of Judaism, elder of the Abrahamic faiths, to its two siblings regarding the stranger, is powerful: the very meaning of human "hospitality" is shaped by the acts of the One who beckons, welcomes, embraces, nurtures, and creates a place for the other. YHWH is the first and the last of the great hospitaliers.

B. Hospitality in the Christian Tradition

Hospitality in the New Testament

On the theme of hospitality, as with so many others, the Christian scriptures are built firmly on their Hebrew foundations. Conspicuous in the Gospels' early chapters— including Matthew's genealogy (Mt 1:1–17), which specifically names Ruth, Boaz and Obed among the progenitors of the Messiah—is the inauspicious birth of Jesus in a cattle shelter, because of hospitality denied the holy family at an inn (Lk 2:1–7).

The reverberations of this birth immediately go transnational, with the inclusion in the narrative of the Magi from the East, to say nothing of the flight into Egypt where the holy family is dependent on the largess of strangers (Mt 2:13–23). The irony of having received hospitality from Egyptians, citizens of the very land where YHWH's paradigmatic acts of hospitality had first unfolded, was surely not lost on the boy as he listened to his parents' stories while growing up after the family returned to Nazareth.

Matthew—A theme in Matthew having strong hospitality overtones appears in 25:31–46. Here, Jesus teaches that upon his return as king at the end of the age, he will judge each individual based on that person's response to having found him hungry, thirsty, a stranger, naked, sick, or imprisoned. To those protesting that they had never so received Jesus, he counters: "Truly I say to you, to the extent that you did it for one of these least brothers or sisters of mine, you did it for me" (v. 40).

Jesus is saying that we encounter the One in the person hungry, thirsty, etc. Stated otherwise: when deciding how to respond to the stranger in need, one is determining one's response to Christ, who is Immanuel.

Luke—But it is Luke's gospel that most intentionally sketches the extent to which the public ministry of Jesus embraces strangers, those lacking social and/or legal cover. Luke's genealogy of Jesus via Joseph (3:23–38), unlike Matthew's, goes back to Adam, focusing on the universal rather than merely Jewish scope of the hospitality initiative.

That Jesus' initial public appearance in Nazareth ended with designs on his life was triggered in part by his reminder that it was to a pagan Sidonian widow, not a Jew, to whom the prophet Elijah went during the great famine of his time (Lk 4:14–30; 1 Kgs 17:8-24). Jesus healed untouchable lepers (5:12–16; 17:11–19); the servant of a Roman centurion who might have been what Luke in his book of Acts would later call a "God-fearer" (7:1–10); and a pagan demoniac (8:26–39). He also fraternized with the hated tax-collecting collaborator Zaccheus (19:1–10).

Luke has Jesus receiving and extending forgiveness to a public woman in the context of the Pharisee Simon's dinner, an account fairly bristling with hospitality issues (7:36–50). When Jesus, in the aftermath of declaring the Great Commandment (10:25–28), is pressed as to "Who is my neighbor?" Luke has him telling the parable in which the exemplar of hospitality is a hated Samaritan (vv. 30–37). And Luke repeatedly has Jesus healing the infirmed on the Sabbath (6:6–11, 13:10–17, 14:1–6).

Luke, not surprisingly, also has unique words directed to women as Jesus makes his way to Golgotha (23:27–31), as well as following the resurrection (24:10–11). This overview of Luke's treatment of Jesus in relation to the strangers at the gate of his time focuses on his associations and miracles. But a survey of his teachings, whether in Luke or the other three Gospels, would have come to a similar conclusion: Jesus of Nazareth, he of whom it would be said "He is risen!" was the human embodiment of divine hospitality paradigmatically modeled in Exodus.

Luke's Acts of the Apostles is a sequential prying open of the early church's understanding of the hospitality implications of the Christ event. The vision of Cornelius (Acts 10), an officer in the Roman army that had executed Jesus, and the council in Jerusalem (Acts 15), sparing Gentile converts to the Way becoming Jews first, were important steps in laying bare the scale of divine hospitality.

Paul—The initial Pauline modus operandi for spreading the Way into first the northeastern Mediterranean and then southern Europe began with the often small communities of the Jewish diaspora. Many of these included Gentile recipients of hospitality, whether full proselytes or the more conflicted "God-fearers" (Acts 10:2; 13:16), both of whom might in time be Christian bridges to their populations of origin. It remains arguably the greatest tragedy of the Christian movement that its begrudging response to the universal scope of the One's hospitality came at the terrible price of alienation from the very community whose formative deliverance by that One had first showcased that vision.

The core of both Hebrew and Christian scriptures' contribution to the theme of hospitality has much less to do with etiquette of accommodation or table than with, first, formative acts in history by the One, and then the behavioral implications of these acts for those identifying with the One's communities. In both Hebrew and Christian scriptures, there is a theological density to the theme of hospitality that alters all it touches. Indeed, that theme is a very promising one for setting forth YHWH's redemptive project central to both testaments.

Hospitality in the Subsequent Tradition

Nevertheless, in the unfolding Christian tradition, the biblical vision of hospitality would also have concrete implications for what would become, two millennia later, the B&B genre. Jerome (ca. 340—ca. 420), upon arrival in Bethlehem near the end of the fourth century and resuming his Vulgate translation of scripture, established a free hospice for pilgrims. He did so lest it ever again be said that Mary, the Mother of God, needed to take quarters in a stable!

In western or Latin Christianity it was monasticism, with the resources of its microcosmic society, that would render hospitality most literal and concrete— particularly the Benedictine tradition. Its *Rule*, attributed to the Umbrian Benedict (c. 480–547), contained an entire chapter (#53) entitled "The Reception of Guests." It begins: "All guests who present themselves are to be welcomed as Christ, for he himself will say: "I was a stranger and you welcomed me" (Mt 25:35).

Guests, especially the poor and pilgrims, were to be received in humility, with every kindness shown to them, including the abbot's washing of their hands and feet. Two brothers were to be responsible for the kitchen of the guests—"and monasteries are never without them"—while a third, a wise man, was to attend to their accommo-dations. The monastery being a boundary community—between society and the wil-derness, as well as between the secular and transcendent worlds—guests were viewed as pilgrims to this hinterland, and the guesthouse as nothing less than holy ground.

In the winter of 1979, I made a two-week retreat on the third floor of the guesthouse at the Abbey of Gethsemani near Bardstown in northern Kentucky. My window over-looked the grave of Father Luis (Thomas Merton). It was during that stay that the words "All guests . . . are to be welcomed as Christ" first—and permanently—snagged me.

Since my initiation to monastic hospitality at New Melleray near Dubuque, Iowa in late 1968, I had recurrently returned to such communities as a guest. During the first half of the 1970s, these visits included, among others, the Greek Orthodox monasteries of St. George in Wadi Qelt, St. Catherine's (occupied Palestine and Sinai, respectively), and Ayia Napa (Cyprus) as well as the Latin Visitation Convent in Ein Kerem and the Trappists in Latrun (both in Israel). In more recent decades, Sharryl and I were the recipients of monastic hospitality at Trappist/Cistercian communities in South Carolina, Georgia, and Colorado. In addition, we took accommodations in

Dominican, Brigittine, Franciscan, and Carmelite monasteries during pilgrimages to Italy and Spain in 2001 and 2005, respectively.

So, have these communities in our experience met the Benedictine criterion of welcoming us as Christ? Yes, for the most part. It has not hurt that we have always wanted to worship with our hosts, an experience which invariably draws us in. Or that I possess an incorrigibly historical nose, so that I smell the hard bread at break-fast in the refectory and am in the Coptic orthodox Monastery of St. Anthony in the Egyptian desert; inhale the incense in the nave, and am transported to the dim recess-es of the Armenian Orthodox Convent of Saint James in Jerusalem's Old City; sense the sweet fragrance of the chalice's contents, and am atop the Benedictine Monte Cassino, a site I have never even visited!

But more substantively, Sharryl and I have repeatedly felt unconditionally re-ceived in monastic communities. Having gone to the trouble of coming—Woody Allen said that "Eighty percent of success is showing up"—seems to qualify us to be their guests. Aside from a few self-evident rules, one's stay is self-guided.

The monastery's guest master or mistress is nearly always patient and nonjudgmen-tal, never hovering, and predictably in the lean mode of the long-distance runner. It is assumed that one has come for one's own reasons, these known but to the One and per-haps to the guest. This frees the hosts to get out of the way rather than micromanage.

However brief and superficial it may be, Sharryl and I have always embraced as our own the very short geographical tether which is part of monastic life, accepted this tiny time and space gestalt as that within which life will unfold during whatever the duration of our stay. These acts seem to be preparation for the dispositions of waiting and receptivity, apart from which a monastery might as well be a motel.

At its best, monastic hospitality, never understood as ancillary or treated as an interruption, is practiced as expressive of the community's faith in the Christ. The monk is formed to live in the moment. It is thus not inconceivable that the task at hand be carried out *ad majorem Dei gloriam* ("for the greater glory of God"), the Jesuit motto attributed to St. Ignatius. Whether it be accompanied by the banging of pots and pans in the kitchen, the coaxing of a cantankerous commode, or the rubrics of Lauds whispered yet one more time to arrivees both uninitiated and tardy, all of this might well be equivalent to receiving the guest as Christ. And with time, I discovered that none of this was irrelevant to hospitality at the Inn of Silent Music on the Crick.

Hospitality as Prophetic, Even Seditious

But sometimes receiving the stranger can be seditious and downright dangerous. In 1986, I was leading an annual retreat in El Salvador for Mennonite Central Committee personnel gathered from throughout Central America. In an informal setting, one young woman recounted the experience of a fellow *gringa*, "Alexandra." The latter had been on a rural bus in El Salvador that had been pulled over at a military checkpoint. It was not uncommon in those dangerous years for such checks to result in persons being led away, never to re-emerge.

As the passengers stood against the outside of the bus, being interrogated one-by-one at gunpoint, an older woman next to Alexandra was pulled out for more intense questioning. Suddenly the interrogator turned, addressing Alexandra: "Do you know this woman?" "Yes," she responded evenly, "she is my friend." The soldier held her eyes, momentarily skewered on indecision, then shrugged and moved on. Soon the bus, all of its passengers safely back in their seats, resumed its journey.

The older woman, a fearfully vulnerable stranger at the gate within her own country, had been in need of hospitality, and its extension had not been thwarted by the fact that Alexandra had never seen her before in her life.

C. Hospitality Received from Palestinian Muslims

In contrast to Judaism, whose sacred scriptures have been my lifelong companion, and Christianity, which I came to know from inside its communities, my experience of Muslim hospitality was as a vulnerable resident alien outside their gate. The majority of persons with whom I worked as the *muhdir* (director) of the Mennonite Central Committee's educational, development, and peace/justice projects during the years 1971–1976 were Palestinian Muslims. What I experienced there was not only off my hospitality scale: it *recreated* that scale.

The early 1970s, two *Intifada*s and several wars ago, was a situation in the Palestine/Israel theatre quite different from the one at this writing in 2007. While the same land and sovereignty issues existed then, the tactics of both the Palestinian resistance organizations and the occupying Israeli army had yet to pass through the bloody flash points that we have watched in subsequent decades. Perhaps most obviously, the Palestinian resistance to foreign occupation then had a secular identity rather than one which included *Hamas*.

I, a scruffy, bearded American, who looked unnervingly Israeli, traveled freely. With or without a translator, I moved among Palestinian villages and refugee camps, being repeatedly showered with warmth and kindness, Turkish coffee and cigarettes, ah, and especially, food. While the fact that I was the *muhdir* (with resources to be jockeyed for) did complicate things, I regularly experienced the hospitable thrust of Palestinians' common phrase *beitna beitkum*: "our house is your house."

Whether in urban East Jerusalem or the remote village of Surif just inside the Green Line (the pre-1967 Israel-Jordan border) southwest of Bethlehem, where our family lived one summer; whether among devout staff persons or displaced Palestinians in the Hashemite Kingdom east of the Jordan River, which I periodically visited: despite being under the gun of a foreign occupier, there was among these Muslims an extraordinary *culture of hospitality* of which I and my family were beneficiaries.

Hands-On Hospitality

More than thirty years later, the memories encompassing the full sensorium remain pungent:

- The scent of orange blossoms: our host in Jericho, eight hundred feet below sea level and warm at midday in the late winter, had moved the family table into an adjacent grove on the occasion of welcoming the Friesen family to their unique part of Palestine.

- The sight of a vertical stack of beautiful brown eyes through a kitchen door, ajar: the *mukhtar*, traditional leader of the village of Surif, on various occasions arranged to receive my family on an Islamic feast day. We were ushered into a room covered with the family's mattresses where we sat cross-legged on the floor. The fare was *mansif*, a dish of rice, lamb, and pine nuts with hot liquid yogurt poured over it. We and the *mukhtar* ate with our hands from a common tray as large as a truck tire in the middle of the floor. I would always eat well, in part because my hands are large. On each occasion, the host's children, sometimes joined by their mother, would watch from the kitchen in hope that some of the lamb, rumored to be the family's meat ration for the month, would be left when we departed. We tried not to disappoint them.

- The sound of a gurgling water pipe: a "hubble-bubble," as this curious contraption is called, would always mysteriously appear at the conclusion of a meal in one home after we had retired to the sun porch for fruit, Turkish coffee, and languid conversation. In contrast to the fact that the device invariably left me with a headache, the warmth of that family and their home is not forgotten.

- The metallic taste of shame: we as a family were guests of a Muslim family in *El Khalil*. This city's name, called Hebron by Israelis, means "the friend (of Allah)" and refers to Abraham (2 Chr 20:7). On this occasion I recall ignorantly informing my host that I was on a diet and would eat only fruit. His face clouded and he responded simply: "You can diet tomorrow."

- The tactility of the hostess' hug: seven years after leaving the region, I returned as part of a study group. With no advance notice I, with a colleague in tow, appeared at the door of the Palestinian woman who had cooked the noon meal for our family for several years in Jerusalem. What she, with her husband's help, created *ex nihilo* will always remain my concrete embodiment of the Levantine feast! And provide a harbinger for the *celestial* one! As we hugged farewell after several hours and made our reluctant departure, I ached both for joy and overindulgence.

The Feast: A Mosque in Time

Like the other two Abrahamic traditions in that bloodied and beautiful land, a Muslim holy day is not a holiday but a *feast*, a point in time analogous to mere space qualitatively transformed into place. Such a day is a "mosque in time," for not all time is created equal! In my experience, nobody does it better than Muslims. For a rural American youth for whom food in his community of origin had functioned largely in terms of utility, my experience of Muslim hospitality at table would in some sense ruin me for life. I would forever after approach table as potentially holy ground and that which transpired around it as translucent to life's deepest meaning and destiny.

And I muse over the ironic possibility that, in retrospect, Muslims' extension of hospitality to me was part of my preparation for the centrality of both the eucharistic table in my present life and the image of celestial banquet for the One's consummation of all that is. I know that experience with Muslims informed the serving and busing I did at daily breakfast and dinner on the porch of the Inn, even while reinforcing my resolve, particularly after 9/11, *never* to condone the maligning or stereotyping of these, my Abrahamic kin.

I believe that the hospitality Muslims extended to my family and me back in the 1970s was the closest living thing I would ever know to that practiced in the world of both the Hebrew Bible and the world of Jesus of Nazareth. It has remained a very high bar by which to assess myself and what passes for hospitality in both our Inn and our national culture. Neither the decades nor 9/11 has soiled this precious gift an iota.

Finally, there is surely a tragic irony in the fact that the enormously rich traditions of hospitality embodied by the sibling Abrahamics has often found each withholding that gift from the others. And as a follower of the Christ whose open arms, both across his life and on the cross, extend embrace to all, I live convinced that across the last 1,500 years it has been my own of these three families most responsible for this tragedy. I acknowledge, grieve for, and lament all that is irretrievably lost, even as I remind myself that this tale too is not yet fully told.

14. Hospitality as "Profession" and "Vocation"

A literary device I employ repeatedly in this work is identifying both the distinction and relation between two or more levels of reality. One of a more surface nature—not to be confused with superficial—is accessible via the sensorium and intellect. The other is a deeper reality, accessible via faculties less traveled. It is a distinction in life between the apparent or manifest and the implicit or depth, between the boundary and the center.

In Parts II and III, I explored this mystery-laden dynamic in the islescape on and surrounding Tylerton. But it works as well in discussions of the Tylerton culture, including the life of faith, as well as in the notion of an external place in which an internal journey unfolds. In this part, I bring that same distinction to bear on the endeavor of innkeeping.

So what is this distinction between the manifest and the implicit levels of reality when it comes to innkeeping? The terms that I have found most helpful are "profession" for the explicit or manifest, "vocation" for the implicit or depth.

A. Innkeeping as Profession

Innkeeping as profession is a way of receiving overnight guests in exchange for the remuneration needed for a livelihood. This profession involves, like any other, both measurable threshold qualifications to be met and a job description to be fulfilled. We commonly call it one's "job," the labor one generates.

In *The Solace of Fierce Landscapes,* Belden Lane calls this level of reality his "cover," the way in which he makes a social claim on respectability and dutifulness. In a society whose obituaries are often litanies of professional achievements, such a cover is widely equated with personal worth: one is "successful" and has lived well, if one is professionally accomplished. In the view of many, one *is* what one *does*.

Innkeeping Skills—Especially on an Island

In the "hospitality industry"—an inevitable term in today's environment, in which everything from news to climate to ethics can be preceded by the word "business"—there is definable content in operating a B&B. It involves skills in visioning, finance, supervision, promotion, writing, logistics, integration, conflict management, culinary arts in breakfast preparation, and communication. In a small operation such as our own—just three or four guest rooms with the owner-innkeepers in residence—other necessary skills include property procurement, interior decoration, and systems maintenance.

In addition, given our unusual location and setting, there is the necessity of skills in provisioning across nearly ten miles of water plus twenty-five more of mainland to major outlets, as well as the meeting of all requirements and inspections of a holder of a restaurant license in the state of Maryland. The bar is further raised in an establishment such as our own that, in addition to the full gourmet breakfast for which B&Bs are renowned, is committed to serving nightly dinners of "fresh, locally caught seafood," a feature presupposing working relationships and frequent communication with local watermen. As purveyors of fine food we learned much about both the demanding culinary expectations and gastronomical idiosyncrasies of our predominantly upper-middle-class guests.

Further, given the conservative nature of the villagers' culture and that a prerequisite of the Inn's success was the maintaining of their good will, I sought to remain attentive to how guests and locals were getting on together, yet without becoming obtrusive or patronizing.

In a setting in which e-communication was our economic lifeline and the dial-up telephone cables were in saline environs whether under land or sea, divining powers into those mysteries was necessary as well. Beyond the self-evident need for highly tuned organizational skills, hospitaliers must have the capacity to respond to a surprising range of requests, dilemmas, and crises extemporaneously, wisely, and unflappably. "If it can happen, it will" certainly applies to innkeeping. We learned to maintain a demeanor of affability and approachability, even while remaining alert to anything, including medical emergencies. Being able to walk on water would have been a plus, especially in the high tide months of March/April and October/November.

An atypical crisis—could they be otherwise?—merits re-telling here. For its spring week of revival meetings, and occasionally during the August camp meeting in North End as well, the Tylerton congregation would arrange for guest evangelists to receive room and board at the Inn. One of the more youthful, and corpulent, preachers, having toiled long and hard the night before, slept through breakfast only to find himself trapped in his second-floor bathroom by a failed lock following his shower. Time passed as our troubleshooting dialogue at sill-level kept coming up empty, and I began to fear that I would need to shatter the door to get him to the church on time later in the day.

Finally, the bathroom window being near the angle where the Inn's rear wing was joined, I succeeded in carefully lobbing him tools across the window-to-window hypotenuse, tools he deftly caught and then used to remove the hinge pins. Like some rosy and glistening suma wrestler, the be-toweled exhorter emerged, still fairly charitable. I later heard from several that he had had to struggle hard to reach serious territory in his sermon that evening.

And finally, the profession of innkeeping, particularly one on the intimate scale of the Inn of Silent Music, means having people around, people in your own home, all of the time. And that is but a skeletal outline of the innkeeper's professional profile.

Adventure Tourism—from the Innkeepers' Perspective

Combinations of elements from the preceding lists are legion. Consider:

- Meal preparation for the vegan family, including three finicky young children, with a five-day reservation, and the chef sworn never to repeat an entrée;
- Romancing a reluctant commode, the clock ticking, while guests are briefly tethered to the porch for dessert;
- Conveying calm and reassuring strength during a power failure, isle-wide sewer crisis, or thunderstorm replete with lightning bolts cleaving the Crick in front of the Inn;
- Seeking to notice and engage individuals neglected in the conversational dynamics across the tables at dinner;
- Deliberating over just how to offer a more substantial chair imported from the kitchen to the 450-pound guest currently occupying the entire love seat;
- Delicately shoehorning overly adventurous guests broad-of-beam into narrow-of-beam canoes;
- Rescuing with my skiff a kayaker who failed to monitor that ominous cloud bank to the northwest;
- Responding to the same perfectly reasonable question, but for the 5,037th time;
- Gently humoring the guest whose first question off the ferry is "What's to do 'round here anyway?"
- And, most *teég-iously* (as pronounced on Tylerton), hearing my own baritone roll out those stories yet again, while noting Sharryl again escaping the room in a spell of feigned coughing.

The Inn's daily routine varies little, the schedule virtual clockwork each day. Yet contingencies of weather, the varied interests and idiosyncrasies of guests, and the innkeepers' quality of sleep the previous night, among other things, can introduce enormous variety within that given.

The fact that the Inn of Silent Music, rather than on the way to somewhere else, is a destination; that the facilities, including common areas, are of modest size; that virtually all guests share both breakfast and dinner hours on the porch; that the Inn's nature and context draw gregarious guests, and has innkeepers similarly inclined—all makes our establishment more communal and intimate than most B&Bs.

One consequence is that chemistry among the guests is unusually important, and it is an issue of which the innkeepers are always conscious. Trying at the dock, upon the arrival of guests, to get a preliminary take on that chemistry, yet always remaining open for surprise and emendation, is an important competency for this innkeeper.

Thus readeth the job description for innkeeper of a bed and breakfast—especially one on a remote island. It goes without saying that none of our previous employment had demanded such a range of professional skills.

B. Innkeeping as Vocation

In contrast to profession, the term "vocation" has a very different ring. Vocation refers not so much to what you are remunerated for as what you are *really* in it for. More often than with profession, vocation has to do with what Paul Tillich called one's "ultimate concern" in contrast to all else, which is penultimate at best. Vocation, in contrast to profession and job, involves what *really* matters—that which is your passion, what you might gladly do for nothing were your remunerative needs otherwise supplied. Particularly in Roman Catholic circles, whether for religious, clergy, or laity, vocation also hints of "calling," a word connoting both values and transcendence.

So, in contrast to my profession, what has been the content of my vocation at the Inn of Silent Music? What makes me raise my fist and cry out "*Yes!*" at the end of a day, even though it is August, the heat has been oppressive, we are exhausted, and our November closing for the season seems three years away?

Enjoying People Is Nonnegotiable

My response to that query begins with people. So that you can understand from whence I come, let me say that I am an introvert, a Myers-Briggs INFJ, in many ways intensely private, somewhat shy, and, unfortunately, not immune to judging, whether others or myself. I nevertheless am repeatedly sparked, occasionally ignited, by people. Enjoying people is, in my judgment, nonnegotiable in this trade that for me is also a vocation.

Sharryl and I intermittently hear idle and mostly harmless chatter from guests who are flirting with opening a B&B. But as the reasons tumble out in the course of a meal, the motivation might include wanting to live in a scenic geography, already possessing the perfect house or furniture, being an accomplished chef, wanting to do something less intense in retirement (!), and so forth. Such conversations rarely include "I thrive on having different total strangers in my own home twenty-four hours a day, and meeting their needs!" And therein lies the difference.

In my Carmelite fraternity, we speak of the essential social, communitarian, and interpersonal fruits of the life of contemplative prayer to which our founder Teresa de Jesús repeatedly alluded in her writings. I always think first—well, second—of my vocation as innkeeper.

Yet it is that very situation of having guests in an intimate setting nearly all the time that has, much more often than not, been deeply rewarding for me. It is 5:40 PM, and I am pushing my luggage cart toward Tylerton's county dock as the ferry completes its U-turn and is secured. This is where I personally receive all our guests. It is August (still), the Inn's last empty night was seven weeks ago, and since saying goodbye to six guests only two hours before, I have unsuccessfully napped, reaching for the energy to do it all over again.

As I round the corner, I have little difficulty distinguishing the new six-pack, strangers with whom I will spend the next forty-eight hours of my life in close quarters. We introduce ourselves, transfer luggage to the pushcart, and walk to the village map, painted on the cinder block wall of the pump house, where I launch into the orientation, paragraphs I have delivered more than a thousand times. Perhaps thirty minutes later, after walking the winding path through the village to the Inn and settling the six in their rooms, I might pause and realize again: *Hey, I really do enjoy this stuff!*

So what happened in that thirty minutes that moved me from trudging weariness to satisfaction?

Granted, at times I run on adrenaline, particularly if words are involved. I have been accused of being a wordsmith. A family member was more blunt, once calling me an "inveterate BSer," and one who never saw an audience I didn't like.

I do acknowledge as a component in my innkeeping identity a kind of troubadour role, whose discretely creative enhancement of the oral traditions of Inn and village mitigates boredom in their repetition. In contrast to Sharryl, a disciple of the exact-reproduction-of-ancient-texts school, I have gravitated across this decade toward the embellishment-in-the-interest-of-survival school. As advocates for these two schools, the two of us have our disputations, and I am periodically skewered with "*What* were you saying out there!?"

Thus, I was instantly alert when, six weeks from the end of our tenure, Sharryl posed one of her questions to which only she, of course, has the answer: "Do you know why this has worked?" I eagerly leaned forward. "Because we have a cook . . . and we have a storyteller." I was radiant in the face of such affirmation!

But there is much more happening than mere narrative enhancement to get me through the evening. Granted, the daily schedule and routine are patterned, the geography the same, the guests' questions paralyzingly predictable—but the people themselves are different. And *vive la différence!* The age range of our guests has been from infancy (we received younger children the first half-decade) to about ninety—with the average slightly above the midpoint. So our guests are people with rich life stories and experiences, folk who often have done very interesting things, some of whom are well down the road toward distinguishing what really matters.

A good part of a typical forty-eight-hour visit is spent on the porch fronting the Tyler Crick arm of the Bay, being massaged by the water, or in the coziness of our kitchen if the weather is inclement. This is a promising interval for getting to know at least some of these folk, no less if the ambience is lubricated by their packed-in spirits.

A Journey in Place: The Diversity of Our Guests
Perhaps the most literal meaning of the subtitle of this memoir, "A Journey in Place," references how Sharryl and I have crisscrossed the planet via our guests. In addition to nearly all states east of the Mississippi and half the rest, including Hawaii, guests have come from nearly a dozen countries in the European Union as well as Russia, Kazakhstan, Israel, Japan, Canada, Kenya, New Zealand, Australia, Iran, India, and Brazil, among others. Thus, the unlikely, even inconceivable, would become commonplace on Tylerton. Not bad for a place hard to get to from there.

A retired Sikh general in the Indian army, grandly turbaned, was approached on the waye called Bugeye by a waterman's grandson: "Sir, are you Aladdin?" I, one whose dress code in high season virtually always includes a sweat band, will never forget when this same refined gentleman, with a twinkle in his eyes, later inquired of me: "Now, professor"—I had always addressed him dutifully as "General"—"this cloth piece around your head: what religious significance might it have?"

I remember a morning that began with a call from The Hague, followed by one from Chad in central Africa. The Brits, especially those from Cornwall, Devon, or Wales from which most of the isle's families hail, are always welcomed with an extra bit of warmth. Tylertonians could never quite figure out why all of these exotic people would spend good cash money to come to their island.

The inimitability of each person, the seemingly infinite variety of journeys and passions and sensitivities, professional/vocational identities—and yes, idiosyncrasies, proclivities, compulsions, foul habits, and occasionally worse—maketh not for the boring life. My previous professional career rarely had me experience, so frequently, simultaneous exhaustion and exhilaration, such an improbable pairing! I mean, how and where else might I have heard a Washington bar pianist tell me that I, pushing my luggage cart, reminded him of seventeenth-century Brother Lawrence of the Resurrection, OCD, banging away in the monastery kitchen as he, to employ the book title for which he is known, "practiced the presence of God"?

Among our delightful guests was a couple from the Netherlands. Serendipitously he volunteered that he, his Christian name "Titus," was nephew and namesake of the Carmelite priest Titus Brandsma, OCarm murdered in the Nazi death camp's hospital at Dachau in July of 1942. In response to my probing, the couple, neither Roman Catholic, spoke of their experience as guests at the 1985 Vatican beatification of their uncle, and mused about prospects for his eventual canonization. Making the encounter doubly precious was the fact that, in addition to he being a Carmelite, Fr. Titus' family is Frisian, from the Friesland district of my own origins in the northern Netherlands.

One could not always predict how the distant origins of a given guest might play out in their experience in the Inn. The U.S. ambassador to a central African country, together with his spouse, also in the diplomatic corps, were with us on their second visit when Big Harvey Corbin dropped off a covered basket of critters in front of the Inn. The ambassador sought out Sharryl, informing her that a man had brought her something, and had asked that he both tell her what it was and what she should do with it. "But I understood *neither!*" he confessed lamely. Sharryl, enjoying the moment a bit too much, exclaimed: "And you *thought* you had left a third-world country where people speak a language you can't understand!"

A portion of our guests, surely many more than chose to self-disclose to us, came to the isle and Inn because of special needs: persons facing surgery or terminal illness; the woman with deteriorating multiple sclerosis who came each of our first five seasons before it was no longer possible; the television anchor being stalked via cell phone; the couple, grieving the death of an infant son, given a gift certificate on the anniversary of that tragedy by loving friends; the cancellation by a couple—it would have been their fifth visit—followed weeks later with news of her death; two different inspiring couples during our swansong months, the male in one case descending inexorably into Alzheimer's, the other severely bludgeoned by a stroke, each gently cared for by the woman with whom he had shared love for a half century. Others came with the intention of addressing some major decision. Many more were surely nudged toward the same by the ambience, especially the tranquility and the water.

Sweet Love at the Inn

One stereotypically attired motorcycling couple informed us via email a year after their memorable visit that the Drum Point bed had been formally awarded their "conception tour" prize; an evidentiary photograph of their son, Silas Emmanuel, was enclosed. And, of course, there have been across the decade more than a few engagement occasions and honeymooners as well as hundreds of birthdays and anniversaries at the Inn, each received with a special dessert and (audible) musical serenade.

Early on, we had an elopement party consisting of the couple and six friends (one the photographer) that constituted a shot across the bow regarding the totally unexpected. The bride, having spent the preceding night with her beloved in Black Walnut Point room, declared unequivocally after breakfast that he dare not look upon her again until the ceremony. This triggered a series of hilarious stratagems including my transporting the two to the North End-bound boat on the Tylerton church limo (a golf cart). He compliantly faced forward at my side; she, raincoat over long wedding dress, resolutely occupied the second seat facing the rear.

After being duly solemnized by the island's Methodist pastor in North End and "riced" by Tylerton's women, for whom the entire occasion was a kick, the wedding party retired to the Inn and celebrated into the night. Our third floor was already completed and we slept soundly! The best man gave the couple a gift certificate for exactly one year later at which time they appeared bearing photographs of a baby conceived on the eve of their nuptials, or so we divined.

Speaking of love and sex, there is, of course, a whole lot of both in an inn, and we witnessed many hints of it, some of it new wine, some more vintage. I could not avoid noticing eyes sparkle as lovers spoke, touches and gestures of affection, honor, and respect. We witnessed with joy some for whom the marital bond seemed to open up the entire world, rather than sequestering or tethering.

On occasion, we would see eyes seemingly drawing the beloved toward the staircase as the evening wore on. And on occasion, I heard cries of ecstasy through the walls as I descended from the third floor at 6:00 AM to introduce the new day with my stout coffee. We were pleased that our rooms were the locus for much love and lovemaking, and thus I was generally patient when periodically reblocking the bed in Drum Point, it of the sloping floor.

Of course, there also were dilemmas, such as the tearful call from a distressed (former?) spouse of one who had checked in with another. Or the person, formerly at the Inn for a full week with spouse, both of whom we got to know quite well, seeking to make a reservation with another not long thereafter, only to find no room in the Inn. But then, is not love far too splendrous a thing not to be misused?

Feedback from Guests

Throughout our decade, we kept both a guest book in the front hall and a file of thank-you notes received from guests after their departures. A gleaning of these near the end of the decade revealed numerous pieces of poetry, various watercolors or sketches, embroidery, calligraphy, repeated use of musical imagery ("symphony," "vespers," "Here I could actually hear the spaces between the notes!" etc.).

Some of these comments even made it into our advertising: for example, "We loved your near foreign country!" Two months into our decade, one guest, a single parent of three, mailed us this quote from *The Problem of Pain* by C. S. Lewis (1898–1963): "Our Father refreshes us on the journey with some pleasant inns, but will not encourage us to mistake them for home."

We received a CD of an original musical composition (and accompanying sketches) by a guest who, together with his wife, visited the Inn six times. One movement consisted of his antiphonal recorder responses to songbird calls he had earlier taped in the Green House. An Australian composer of classical music used his laptop to give us a porch preview of his work, which would premiere in his home city of Adelaide but three weeks later. His words on parting were that there would surely be forthcoming a composition entitled "The Inn of Silent Music."

Among the guests expressing envy at the way of life we had carved out was a cheeky young thing who wrote, "That's how we want to be when we get old." We also received far more invitations to visit guests' homes or use their vacation houses than we could ever accept in several lifetimes.

Across the decade, we had perhaps forty journalist parties coming to write on some aspect of the island's culture or jeopardy. In addition to occasionally providing complimentary accommodations, I would often aid with their itineraries, arranging for them to sit down with villagers or go out on the water with a waterman.

While our personal experience with most journalists was very positive, and their visits often generated important publicity for the islanders' issues and the Inn, there were also writers whose M.O. left us uneasy, sometimes even more so when their efforts met the light of publication. In retrospect, I might have been more proactive with those writers who sought to get the gist of Tylerton during an overnight visit.

The Inn also drew an interesting array of different clergy who, generally speaking, seemed to thrive on the silence and solitude, and were enjoyed and found stimulating by this hospitalier. Yes, there was even some shoptalk. Perhaps half of these came as a result of gift certificates purchased by their sensitive congregations or parishes.

Most mainline Protestant denominations were represented, in addition to Roman Catholics. One corpulent cleric, whom the kitchen staff respectfully designated as "The

Eater," established consumption records which no subsequent guest would seriously challenge. A special time was had with a Roman Catholic seminarian who made his obligatory week retreat with us immediately before his ordination, one of numerous guests who did yoga on our dock at dawn. There was also the female circle of nine who, having bought the house for a weekend, is remembered in the hamlet for, among other things, their daily ceremony on the dock welcoming Sol.

Most of our feedback consisted of simple heartfelt letters or emails of gratitude and appreciation, often testifying to some edge of themselves beyond which they had been mysteriously drawn during their stay on Tylerton. And scores and scores of them, many more than I could have anticipated on the basis of conversations, offered some kind of benediction upon the house, the two of us, and the future chapters of our journey together. As our decade was concluding, I was more convinced than ever of the urgent need for alternative inns where guests can revel in qualities of life so often in short supply in cities—silence, solitude, and serenity.

But in addition to the guests themselves, the list of the "good stuff" for which professional innkeeping is "cover" includes more. Most obviously, innkeeping allowed me to live the best years of my life in this beautiful and extraordinary place among the villagers of Tylerton! It provided Sharryl and me with a setting in which to work together much of the time, be our own employers, and continue to work away at shaping life in the direction of the dreams growing out of our faith.

How Do Profession and Vocation Connect?

So what was our relationship between these two levels of innkeeping, between the purveying of hospitality as a profession and as a vocation? The possible options are fascinating. I shall skip over those unfortunates for whom there is only job or profession; also those for whom all is vocation. For many there is some ratio of both. One might experience the two oscillatorily—as in tolerating a mindless job to enable travel in Provence each summer—or interdependently—as in remaining in a supervisor-poisoned work situation to enable better education for one's children.

There are those for whom the "cover" becomes nothing more than a "front," those for whom "going through the paces" to attain what they really want raise issues of integrity. Sharryl and I know of an innkeeper who opened an establishment while having only marginal interest in receiving guests; his passion was raising goats in general, and perfecting cheese from their milk in particular. We never booked. Not dissimilar was the large and elegant Victorian inn on Delmarva where Sharryl and I spent a night. Everything—facilities, amenities, food—was splendid, but the manager appeared to view any inter-human contact as an interruption of what she was really there to do. We never re-booked.

And then, at the other extreme, are those for whom the profession—perhaps involuntarily joined, subsequently endured, or even despised—was mysteriously transformed into vocation. There are some (many would call them saints) for whom the brutal hand that life has dealt them did not deter their growth into a life of depth and luminosity precisely amid that hand. Some such have taken quarters with us at the Inn, and, to borrow the memorable words of Thomas Merton, "There is no way of telling [them] that they are all walking around shining like the sun."

There are also the fortunate who are granted the gift of profession and vocation being significantly overlapping or even nearly coterminous, while yet remaining distinguishable. Sharryl and I are among these more of the time than not.

For me, part of this overlap is because of what I might call innkeeping's element of "in-structured irrelevance," a measured thumbing of the nose at utility, at least some of the time, in favor of the serendipitous, the lure of the translucent, the haunting sliding around beneath the ordinary. The Inn operation's flex allowed that conversation to be extended, that moment to be nurtured and prolonged, that humming of, yes, the One to be savored in the silence and the emptiness. There is a breathtaking freedom that blossoms once one has made his peace with the reality that the heart of the vocation consists of its interruptions. Indeed, the vocation of innkeeping might be hinted at by an interpretation, one quite different than her own, of the title of the beautiful book by Etty Hillesum (1914–1943): *An Interrupted Life*.

Belden Lane discusses the relationship between profession and vocation in a way that resonates deeply with my experience on the Crick. Rather than identical or antiphonal or mutually exclusive, he writes of work as "sliding [around] under" the surface of job. The two dimensions exist in a paradoxical relationship, with one encountering the "Snow Leopard," his image for the Ultimate, as in the case of joy, amid the penultimate, inadvertently and indirectly.

There is thus no bypassing of the prosaic while, in Lane's words, "peering under the edges of the ordinary." Never available on demand, the transcendent hinted at by vocation is occasioned within the immanent, under the tangible, amid what Brother Lawrence did with pots and pans in the kitchen. The ultimate hinted at and acknowledged in vocation is encountered not by demanding or even seeking it, but via and as the fruit of disciplined engagement in the profession.

As with the relationship between surface and depth in any context, whether regarding isleography, cuisine, friendship, the art of innkeeping, a marriage, or the night sky, one needs to be absorbed with loving attention in the first to have opportunity to encounter the second. One whose anchor regarding everything is Bethlehem must always remain alert in and to the ordinary and commonplace.

Returning to the Dostoyevsky quote introducing Part II of this work, the meaning and depth of the place can only be discovered if one has first loved attentively the place itself. Sharryl, patient with my efforts to push out farther the strictures on vocation even as she is insistent upon professional attentiveness to detail, couldn't have said it better!

A late evening in our final June found Sharryl and me, as usual, in the kitchen cleaning up and preparing the table for breakfast. Suddenly Esther, a guest, friend, and former colleague at Davis House, walked in and simply began reading from Henri Nouwen's *The Wounded Healer*:

> The [innkeeper] who has come to terms with his own loneliness and is at home in his own house is a host who offers hospitality to his guests. He gives them a friendly space, where they may feel free to come and go, to be close and distant, to rest and to play, to talk and to be silent, to eat and to fast. The paradox indeed is that hospitality asks for the creation of an empty space where the guest can find his own soul.

C. Narratives of Vocation Emerging from Profession

Story might well be the best medium for conveying the subtle relationship between profession and vocation, of the way in which the latter can emerge out of, and then blossom far beyond, the former. Without diminishing the importance of those who came simply to get away, my memory lingers on four very different stories of persons with whom it all became much more rich.

Remembering Baxter

The first involves two sisters in their fifties—"Wanda" and "Dina"—who brought their husbands for the weekend. Since they had arranged to go out with near-octogenarian Waverly Evans on an excursion around the island, I chose during breakfast to brief them a bit about this salty waterman friend. Standing beside their table for four, I concluded my sketch by telling about the death by drowning of Wave's twin brother Weldon, while oystering back in February of 1951.

As my story unfolded, I first noticed Wanda becoming tearful and then Dina suddenly bolting from the table. Uncertain what was transpiring, I hastened to finish the story with the words to me of the twins' mother, Ma Ginny, since deceased, to the effect that she had tried for almost fifty years not to think about that terrible day.

After a time of silence, Wanda asked me through her tears, "Are you sentient?" "No," I replied, still puzzled. She then told me that the four of them had come to Tylerton and the Inn because it was the tenth anniversary of the death of Dina's son, "Baxter." He had been killed accidentally at the age of nineteen at a party by a youth horsing around with a loaded gun. She continued that, while her sister had survived the decade primarily because she had channeled her grief into the formation of survivor groups, she continued to fear that Baxter would simply be forgotten. Dina silently returned to the table about this time and the conversation awkwardly stumbled elsewhere.

That evening, I placed flowers on the table where the four were seated, and told them that they were in memory of the life of Baxter. The remainder of their visit, not least the long hugs at the dock, was filled with more warmth and empathy than I have words. "No [one] is an island"—John Donne's words—least of all me, and sometimes it is compassion which both calls us and actually contributes to our interconnectedness in the *kairos*, that New Testament word meaning "enriched" or "ripe" time. In contrast to my profession, my vocation gives me a great deal of direction regarding that virtue.

"Just once . . .": A Prayer

A second story involves a guest from Louisiana, her name a casualty of my memory, on a hot, still night near the summer solstice. Insects were smacking the screen, fireflies amorously igniting along the edge of the marsh. A collage of pastels and charcoals lingered above Rhodes Point on the northwest horizon, below which our star was already well on its way toward the new day. The other guests having retired, just she and her husband, joined by the innkeepers, sat on the silent porch.

Suddenly, out of nowhere in the gloaming, she blurted out: "I wish that once— once would be enough!—I wish that once I could experience God in an unmistakable way." The porch reverted to silence. But within my solitude, questions were crowding in, rhetorical questions: who of us, whether of the blessed or the rest, believer or otherwise, has not raised such a cry, or at least felt the tug to do so? Who has not in some way yearned at the center for the satisfaction of that hunger for which there may be no words? Who has not panted for the more that might not even have a name? I glanced at the marsh to our left, but there were no water bushes burning along the water, nothing more than the fireflies. Yet I knew it was holy ground (Ex 3:1–9).

Part of my vocation is both to recognize such moments, and to value them as precious. At its best, vocation—whatever the professional cover—positions one for fleeting contact with mystery, with alignments of thought and feeling serendipitous, with the permeable membrane between the ordinary or commonplace and extraordinary or transcendent. It is in one's vocation that this membrane is most porous. And the more I experienced that vocation, the greater the sense of unity, of wholeness, of a macro perspective far more expansive than my own.

A Lofty Bed in Anecdotage

The third story came to us via a letter from a middle-aged couple who had spent a weekend at the Inn six months earlier. They informed us that the man's aged father, who had accompanied them, had since passed away. They described his downward spiral in the months before the earlier visit, how they had planned the venture, his last excursion, in the hope that it would bring him joy. They thanked us unabashedly for making possible his visit and offering their father one final occasion of joy and vitality before his time was full.

In the blur of many faces, Sharryl and I were not even sure who this threesome even was. That is, until they mentioned the bed. The couple had reserved Sassafras Hammock for their father: located on the first floor, it is the most accessible of our three. But the bed, once common and generic, had emerged from Sharryl's machinations both beautiful and with an elevation rivaling that of Tylerton itself. But alas, it had been too high for the aged man to mount! (Sharryl and I had been through all this once before when, Mennonite driver in tow, a retired nonagenarian psychiatrist— Sharryl and I called her "Miss Daisy"—had required some cinderblock steps and my nightly assistance, replete with much mutual witticism and laughter, to get into that very bed.)

Now again the innkeepers caucused. I then reconstructed the crude steps, allowing the father to sleep *on top* of the bed. Now again there was much laughter: the high tide got in there, as did the rumored personal flotation devices in the pillows; also the case for developing pole-vaulting or rappelling skills in one's anecdotage.

So the gentleman had slept very well in that lofty bed, the letter informed us, enjoyed it all thoroughly, and had been as alive as they had seen him in months. The next morning, in contrast to his pattern of "endless months of sleeping his days away," he had appeared at breakfast rested and lively. The entire weekend had meant more to the father than he could have expressed to us, or that they could express in their letter six months later. The letter concluded: "[Father] loved the food, your stories, and your hospitality—and he was truly taken with the simple beauty of the place."

I have worked as a pastor, an international aid worker, and as a teacher of theology and ethics—all, together with my present work, enveloped in and fueled by a single vocation. But as Sharryl and I felt the sting of tears while reading this letter, I couldn't think of anything I had ever done that beat being a hospitalier!

When Hospitality Becomes Sacrament

A final story involves a thirties-something couple who had been at the Inn on several previous occasions. Accompanied now by another couple, of whom the woman was a physician, they had arrived safely Friday afternoon as the remains of Ivan, the strongest hurricane of the 2004 season, were spinning up the East Coast.

On Saturday afternoon, the edge of the system having arrived and the afternoon ferry run cancelled, there came an emergency call to the effect that the father of "Christine," who had a seven-year chronic health condition, had veered into crisis and was near death. Ivan's lingering ill behavior augured against a chartered return to the main, so plans were resignedly made by the foursome, our sole guests that night, to delay departure until the 7:00 AM ferry. Oh yes, and the date of that Saturday was September 18, the first anniversary of Isabel.

The hours ushered in by the onset of dusk were memorable. Much was going on within Christine: perhaps guilt at not being at her father's side, anxiety for her mother in that her father had long since decided to live out his life at home, struggling faith in the One laced with doubt and anger. A person in her thirties losing her father and not being at his side is a story I knew only too well.

Sharryl and/or I—I have no recollection where dinner preparation and serving were shoehorned in—were simply available to Christine and her husband, seeking to support and reassure. Midevening, the heavy overcast lifted slightly just above the western horizon out over the Bay and the Potomac to reveal a stunning crimson strip of post-sunset sky. As the six of us stood, mute, on the porch, Christine suddenly seized upon the sight as apotheosis and omen that she would yet make it to her father's side.

The four of them, Christine still anxious, indeed left on the 7:00 AM ferry for the very rough crossing. Four hours later—the entire Tylerton congregation praying for the family—Christine's father went to his Maker. She later informed us by letter that the four of them had arrived at his side but an hour before he passed, and that he had died peacefully. She described how her physician friend, having never previously met her father, had continued the competent and loving bedside manner we had witnessed the previous day.

Christine's gratitude to Sharryl and me for our meager offerings was palpable. Perhaps more than any other experience in our decade, our modest efforts on behalf of her and her husband were both offered and received as nothing less than sacramental.

15. Hospitality as Pilot Project

As a point on the human life span, September's run may be as good as it gets.

On the one hand—the past—one has lived long enough to know that experience is an unrelenting pedagogue, tempering both the easy optimism of youth as well as those ethereal dreams in midpassage of changing the world single-handedly or amid one's remnant cohort. In addition, by September, one should also have learned that there is a mysterious "predicament" (to employ Walker Percy's term) plaguing both the human family and the uni-verse in general, a cosmic conundrum evidenced by dissonance and conflict often being more prominent than harmony and peace. Furthermore, the Reigning of the One in full flower, various proposed Camelots notwithstanding, is surely not yet. And by September one has also had ample time to accumulate a long list of fraudulent slakers of the human thirst.

On the other hand—the future—despite the fact that not all bodily and mental powers remain fully intact, never again to be frittered away or taken for granted, there are yet, hopefully, good years remaining to savor and grow into the bit of wisdom one inadvertently discovers one has been given. Indeed, from September's perch, the best may indeed be . . . *now*.

So what does one who is singing September's song do with what is seen, both behind and ahead? One can, for example, snort the amber fire of cynicism; call down maledictions upon the darkness; drop out and pour another, thus buffering both the disappointments and the hopes. Or one can open an inn.

A. The Inn as a "Colony of the Future"

Yes, one can open an inn, metaphorically or literally—an operation embodying what is hoped for, rather than merely what is. In both my Mennonite forebears—most notably my former colleague, theologian John Howard Yoder—and the Roman Catholic monastic tradition, I have witnessed faith and hope embodied in alternative social configurations which are prophetically powerful. In these two traditions, among others, we who are followers of the self-pouring-out (Phil 2:7) and nonviolent Christ, are called to construct and embody alternative social models of what can be, shall be, but is not fully yet. In short, living *as if* the lion and the lamb is *now*.

Sharryl, a superb shaper of pedagogues, had long sought to ignite in the imaginations of her student teachers a vision for the classroom as both an urgent and a promising setting for the same: teaching *as if* every child mattered, teaching *as if* one need not be imprisoned by fear.

The Inn as Pocket Garden

If the option of pulling off planetary behavioral modification "is not allowed," to borrow C. S. Lewis' phrase, and the Reigning in its fullness is not ours to engineer, then perhaps one can plant a pocket garden, a microcosm of a future sure to be, although not yet—a patch of the transformed future in the contorted present.

A pocket garden displays what generally could be but is not, not everywhere: a cube of space which, in its understated suggestiveness, can alter all around it. Such a pilot project can be powerful, indeed seditious, for it places in question the non-negotiable "givens" of what is thought to be possible. It scrambles and opens up the categories and images allowed to circumscribe the entire conversation.

To live *as if* the future "new creation" (2 Cor 5:17, Gal 6:15) were already operative in the present is one of the ways in which St. Paul in particular depicts the significance of the crucified and risen Christ for those of the Way. Part of the malady of our society and world, both so grotesquely twisted as to press severely our hope, is a crisis of imagination, of the capacity to be, dream, and build *alternatively*. At its very best, the faith community can be the nurturer of an alternative imagination, that of none less than the One.

The Inn of Silent Music did not begin as such a "colony of the future," or pilot project, at least not consciously. But it was, episodically, lurching in that direction by the end of the decade.

Monasticism as an "As If" Social Alternative

Of course, the social pilot project is no newcomer to people of faith. It has almost always been a part of the Christian landscape, particularly since the fourth century, during which the church moved from persecuted to tolerated to officially favored status in the Roman Empire. That fateful inversion—forever a warning that more might really be much less, the taking up of the sword spiritually suicidal—drove yet more uneasy Christians to the deserts and, in the West, to monastic communities. Whatever else the early Benedictines were, they constituted a social pilot project, a minor report alternative to the official major report, an exercise of fresh and fearless imagination fueled by the gospel.

In such monastic communities, at least in many periods down to the present, the sword was checked at the door, a measure of egalitarianism prevailed, the hard sayings of Jesus were embraced, and prayers that "Your Reigning come . . . on Earth as it is in Heaven" (Mt 6:10) were raised seven times daily. This monastic tradition arguably saved Christianity after the implosion of the baptized armed might of Rome.

Lest I be misunderstood, I view monasticism and similar pilot projects as profoundly relevant *socially* as well as spiritually in our present situation, and I predict their resurgence as the wheels of our unsustainable culture begin coming off. In our era of oxymorons and breathtaking rationalizations—"just preemptive war," for example!—such communities also contribute mightily to the saving of truth as a moral value. As Etty Hillesum wrote in *An Interrupted Life* before disappearing into the maw of the Holocaust in 1943, "there is only one way of preparing the new age, by living it even now."

The Transient Inn as Socially Significant?!

But, pray tell, what hath alternative social reality to do with an inn, a "community" such as ours where there is no "stability," where the average duration of stay across the decade fluctuated somewhere between two and three days? What's the point of a pocket garden fleshing out an alternative to the larger society, when the time involved is only a weekend? Are not the residents of an inn at a given time but random pieces in an momentary and artificial bucket, one thrown together for as many reasons as there are persons, one possessing but the single commonality of everyone having come to get away from everybody else, including each other (and life's hard questions)?

Actually, the idea of "inn as alternative social reality" is not as zany as it sounds, at least not in a certain sort of inn. The Inn's residents share an additional commonality of all having distanced themselves from their mostly urban and professionally intense lives, and have thus perhaps freed themselves to smell the roses and give themselves to themes and activities for which there is ordinarily not time. And, as the decade unfolded, I wondered increasingly whether our Inn environment did not sign "safe" to many of our guests.

Furthermore, unlike most other houses of hospitality, our Inn is a destination: Tylerton is not on the way to any other place! People come to Tylerton to be on Tylerton, an island a bit more than a quarter mile long. They come to the Inn and end up being inside or near the building a good portion of their stay. Of course, the new dock is available for lounging, sunbathing, or launching aquatic excursions. And the Green House back in the loblollies is there for those finding the porch too frenetic, the passing working boat and golf cart traffic entirely too stressful!

But much of the time, six or seven guests and their two hosts are inside or near the well-porched Inn. An inimitable chemistry, unique as a fingerprint or DNA, invariably emerges among the eight or so of us. The major components of this chemistry are the guests themselves, their personalities, and their choices: whether they sequester themselves in their rooms; whether they warm to one another at table;

whether they bundle into shared excursions to the Market for lunch or Wave's tour of the Martin Wildlife Refuge.

While excessive alcohol bodes ill, moderate amounts and the sharing thereof invariably ease the chemistry. Political discussions are generally on the downside, but religion, surprisingly, can often be positive. In short, we have noted with interest that most people wanting to "get away" nevertheless enjoy a fair amount of social interaction at the Inn. Very interesting things can happen among the members of such an Inn-tethered, forty-eight-hour pod of persons. Like a gaggle of Agatha Christie's murder suspects sequestered in the Oriental Express, we are all stuck with each other, and often that is much more gift than burden.

Stated otherwise, the Inn is a small, brief, and transient village. The size makes possible a level of informality, care, and attention; it also allows for crash socialization, essential within the narrow timeframe. The porch's proximity to the massaging water is a huge plus.

Over time, the amalgam of these moments begins to emerge as a kind of culture, a base from which the particularity of every day is fleshed out. This inimitable culture, so nebulous and yet so desired by both innkeepers and guests in their respective ways, is part of the genius of the bed and breakfast. It is what guests write about in the guest book upon departing or communicate to us via email after returning to their homes. And when that culture is good, it is very, very good!

Stated theologically, the argument here is that innkeeping understood as vocation has an eschatological ("viewed from the end") aspect. The values of an inn operation can take their cues from the One's Reigning as showcased in the Christ which, while not yet fully unfolded, has indeed been inaugurated. Hospitality so understood as pilot project, while minuscule and never flirting with the threshold into the unflawed, can yet be an embodiment in the present of the cosmos' revolutionary future. The people of the Way are called to follow after the Christ in being part of the One's future now, in the present.

B. The Traits of a Hospitality Out of the Future

So what did we as innkeepers seek to contribute to this episodic, turnstile community, this temporary pocket garden? And what did we try to plant as a demonstration plot of what could grow, and become?

Respect: *Imago Dei*

First and foundationally, Sharryl and I sought to respect our guests—their persons, stories, and needs. As starters, I sought to respect why they had come. I viewed as almost sacred the implicit contract Sharryl and I had with them: they were reimbursing us for a unit of private space and time in which to rest, recreate, and be taken care of. If you came, whoever you were, you merited such respect, period.

On numerous occasions, this respect caused me to swallow a witty rejoinder or worse, particularly when table talk waxed political, because that was not part of what we had contracted together. With one or two memorable exceptions, it was only when another guest was being treated unfairly that I might intervene, and then gently and understatedly. But the sanctity of this respect remains central to my vision of hospitality: our guests had not contracted to be enlightened by me!

But the respect thing needs to go deeper. My defining Christian narrative contends that each person has indescribable value—each is, in a word, precious. This, above all else, is because she bears the *Imago Dei*, the image of the One. That folks of the Way confess that the One came embodied in the Christ is part of the reason why St. Benedict in his *Rule* wrote the words "All guests . . . are to be welcomed as Christ."

This level of respect runs much deeper than that involving the implicit contract the innkeeper has with the guest, and it is more difficult as well. It is not exaggeration to say that, intermittently across that decade, I would return to the kitchen after a difficult or unpleasant contact with a guest on the porch—it would often transpire around meals—muttering something like "Wow, but do we have a Christ out there tonight!" or "I'm having trouble with Immanuel at the north table!" or "O you of Nazareth: in what guise will you yet knock on the door of this Inn?!"

I did not always pull it off, but, with Sharryl's help, I rarely forgot that honoring the guest as a precious bearer of the image of the One—this despite however unpleasant they might be—was that to which my vocation unequivocally called me.

Inclusion: Color

Another value Sharryl and I brought to this "fluid community out of the future" was inclusiveness. I found it very satisfying, for example, to welcome to the Inn people of color, and I wished that this could have happened much more frequently than it did.

On an island . . .

- where slaves were once bought, sold, and worked;
- where pre–Civil-War national census-takers might record the numbers, genders, and ages of slaves, but usually not their names;
- where the 1844 split between the northern and southern portions of the Methodist Church over the slavery issue sent ripples through the faith communities throughout the Russels Iles;

- where three black deck hands on a skipjack moored in Tylerton's harbor were drowned in the early twentieth century when the barrel into which they had crawled rolled into the water;
- where under cover of darkness a gallows was assembled in 1906 for the "legal" hanging of a convicted black man, thereby eluding the mob waiting on Somerset main to lynch him;

on such an island, it is good for the Inn to receive blacks.

Even during the eighteen months when a seasonal owner from Princess Anne flew a confederate flag on his Tylerton shanty platform in the face of every incoming guest (and ethnically diverse Chesapeake Bay Foundation student group), it was important to receive all strangers of color. And it was important for the villagers as well.

Inclusion: Sexual Orientation

Furthermore, Sharryl and I, as we had in the Dupont Circle neighborhood of Washington, also sought to extend Inn hospitality to persons of homosexual orientation. We found that, with both other guests and villagers, lesbian couples encountered less scrutiny than did gay male couples, but we welcomed both.

We deliberately passed on both gay-friendly and gay-hostile web listings for the same reason that we had opted not to advertise ourselves as a Christian house: we coveted the spacious and spicy spectrum of all bearers of the *Imago Dei,* rather than the less interesting and authentic issue-driven selections. We wanted our house to model life together a bit more like we believe it should be lived, and someday shall be lived.

Early in our decade, I used an invitation to speak in Tylerton's Sunday evening service to outline Sharryl and my commitment to receive all comers, including those of gay and lesbian orientation. Our position and practice were not the easiest portion of the Inn for the village to stomach, but it was the right thing to do.

Inclusion: Class

An aspect of our commitment to inclusiveness that I found particularly interesting, and occasionally disconcerting, involved social class.

On the one hand, blue-collar guests, a relatively small minority, seemed decidedly less comfortable in the Inn and Tylerton than did their white-collar counterparts. Perhaps the village's modest standard of living, and occasional glimpses of almost literal hand-to-mouth existence, came too close to their own origins, or even their present. Blue-collar folk are, after all, less likely to employ words like "quaint" or "romantic" in such a setting than are those a couple of generations away from manual labor.

Near the beginning of our decade, two of our most dissatisfied parties were composed of working folk who came to check out then-inexpensive real estate. I overheard one couple arguing, with the woman hissing: "But you promised there would be a mall!"

Professional folk simply seemed more at home with the porch scene, whether at or between meals, with or without innkeeper(s): occasional serious discussion of issues, often leisured bantering, the dialogical life more often than not.

I was reminded as an innkeeper that, although I came from poor farming stock, I had experienced little sustained contact with blue-collar people in the forty years following, and sometimes, yes, found it more demanding to receive them as Christ. That this was so, even while I was living amid blue-collar villagers with whom I experienced strong identification, was an irony not lost on me. Of course, that might have been different had our waterman neighbors, some of them dear friends, also been our customers. . . .

On the other hand, although the Inn certainly was not a high-end operation, we did receive numerous relatively wealthy guests, many of them prosperous movers and shakers in their professions, others retired and into globetrotting or yacht-envy, grandparenting or volunteering. Despite occasional exceptions like the man of sour and racist disposition (called "Mr. Grumpy" by another guest) who burst into the kitchen upon being served dinner declaring that he "hated fish," my general experience with people of means proved to be a surprisingly positive one. I repeatedly found individuals of real substance among them. Many, whether retired or in the professions, could be predicted to thrive on the intellectually stimulating porch culture. Many often were experienced in marveling, and they were not infrequently insightful, often both wise and compassionate, as to what was at stake in the challenges facing Tylerton.

While members of this established group were not liable to be caught in the *Phragmites,* in *flagrante delicto*, as was one of our youthful pairs stumbled upon near the waste treatment plant, there were occasions of snooty name- or place-dropping. I recall two former strangers going on and on over eight-layer cake with lemon curd filling about how they had unknowingly been together on Bimini or the Riviera the previous spring.

Yet I found many of this stratum to be persons of deep and active faith, which more than infrequently had sought altruistic forms of expression in, for example, volunteering, sacrificial grandchildren care, and spiritual disciplines. I was intermittently chastened by the conscientization many of them embodied.

Innkeepers, having laid out the pocket garden and planted the values of acceptance, respect, kindness, conversation, and peace—and then nurtured them at times more faithfully than others—are themselves changed, profoundly, by that very experience. But how could it be otherwise? As in any community, pilot or otherwise, the option of receiving much more than one gives is always there, and I think I consistently received more.

My encounter with people of means was a stretching one that confronted me with my own provinciality at points. The experience has impressed upon me how firmly middle-class I am, what with background in academics and the church. And how during my adult life I had not had much more contact with the wealthy than with the working poor. Even now, I muse about whether I too readily equate the urbane and refined fruits of accidents of birth with character.

Inclusion: Persons Perceived as Arab or Muslim

There was another component of our commitment to inclusiveness—one, however, unforeseen when we opened in 1997. Especially after September 2001, Sharryl and I delighted in receiving persons who were Arab and/or Muslim, as well as the improbable list of those who reported being mistaken as such, some under bizarre or frightening circumstances. Muslim guests were not numerous, but often being connoisseurs of hospitality themselves, they usually responded to our own, and conscientized me to what they faced here in my own country. Some of their accounts left me deeply pained. It became a point of honor for me that such persons come to know there was indeed room for them in the Inn—at least in ours.

C. The Military: My Special Challenge

And finally, on the matter of inclusion, there was the military. The principal feeder region for the Inn being Washington, D.C., and northern Virginia, we had many guests who were military personnel, consultants, or contractors. This posed a special challenge for this otherwise usually inclusive innkeeper.

Growing into a Peace/Justice Vocation

Throughout my adult life, part of my Christian vocation has included pacifism, a commitment much more demanding and difficult than its alternatives—as well it should be. The roots for this stance center in the teachings, character, and cosmic significance of Jesus, the Christ. I believe that he calls all of his followers to configure our values, choices, and allegiances to the Reigning of the One, a vision best set forth in the Sermon on the Mount (Mt 5-7). I judge the authority of this Christ, designated by the Apostle Paul as the "icon of the invisible One" (Col 1:15), to supercede all others. I seek to become a

Christian peace/justicemaker despite the fact that both my intra- and interpersonal lives have often been characterized by the absence of *salaam/shalom*.

My Mennonite identity, particularly the years working in its church institutions, nurtured this commitment to the way of the nonviolent Christ. During my five-year assignment in Palestine, for example, I devoted considerable time and energy to facilitating interaction between pockets of Palestinians and Israelis more interested in dialogue and justice than violence. And my academic responsibilities at the Associated Mennonite Biblical Seminary in Indiana during the 1980s included oversight of a graduate program in peace/justice studies, as well as offering some of its courses.

Simultaneously, I was being increasingly shaped as well by the rich "minority report" in the Roman Catholic tradition, the alternative peace and justice vision, kept alive and deepened across a millennium-and-a-half most visibly in monasticism, and expanded in the twentieth century in Catholic social teaching. Indeed, most of the peace/justicemaker models in my middle years were Roman Catholic, persons like Dorothy Day, Thomas Merton, Franz Jägersätter, and Oscar Romero, as well as organizations such as the Catholic Worker and *Pax Christi*.

But formative as well were four occasions, first in the Middle East (East Jerusalem in 1973, Beirut in 1975), later in Central America (1981 and 1986), when I experienced war up close. In both regions, I witnessed brutal abuse of the disempowered, in each case facilitated significantly by the alliance of my own government with the principal oppressor. Indeed, between 1958 when I began an ultimately futile effort to obtain a conscientious objector classification with the Selective Service, and 1991 when I became Catholic, my contacts with the military and its apologists were primarily adversarial and impersonal.

However, upon entering the Roman Catholic Church in Holy Trinity Parish in Washington, D.C., Sharryl and I found ourselves worshipping regularly with siblings in Christ, some becoming personal friends, who were lifers in the Pentagon or CIA. It was a stretching time, one preparational for what was to follow at the Inn.

I pray daily, beseeching the One to, in the words of the hymn, "Cure thy children's warring madness." Both my experience and study of history, to say nothing of the teachings of Jesus the Christ, leave me little grounds for trusting the solutions huckstered by the slick ad-men and spin-doctors of war. War promises; war lies.

My government currently has our military striding about the planet, sowing the seeds of democracy with guns. The deathly fruit of this tragic oxymoron is the principal content of our headlines. But I do not accept the dream-deserted darkness, the despair-spawned military adventurism, not finally. I believe that the *cosmic* designs of the One, as laid bare in the Christ—I call it the Love Project—shall prevail. The word *cosmic* is carefully chosen, for the scale of that One's dream of "new heavens and a new earth" (Is 65:17-25 and 66:22; 2 Pt 3:13; Apoc 21:1) is infinitely larger than my or anyone else's personal salvation. Now, in my September anecdotage, I believe in the Love Project more fiercely than ever, particularly when the darkness presses in.

All of which is preface to acknowledging that I probably felt least comfortable with the slice of the Inn's guests who identified themselves with the military, particularly during the pre-9/11 half of our decade.

9/11 as Compassion Tutorial

In the autumn following September 11, 2001, our Inn hosted a series of guests who had been close to the horror of that Tuesday morning. On September 30, for example, one who had been trampled in a stairwell amid the panic in the Navy Annex, the building just under American Airlines flight 77 before it struck the Pentagon—yet obliged to remain at her work station nearly around the clock for the following ten days—was brought to the Inn by two friends for the healing of body and spirit.

Later that fall, our guests included various couples getting away together just before one of them left for Afghanistan. Sharryl and my non-video experience of the twin towers and Pentagon events via National Public Radio and the *New York Times* on the web was rendered more personal amid hushed conversations at table or on porch. Even as my vague suspicions emerged, and were then realized, that the central questions posed by that catastrophe—"How could the United States be so hated?" and "How had our policies contributed to that hatred?"—would be largely dismissed as unpatriotic by politicians and media alike, I was being drawn farther and deeper into a solidarity of grieving and compassion in interaction with these guests.

In retrospect, I think I was "woodshedded" by interaction with guests identified with military in the aftermath of 9/11. I was forced to allow them to become persons to me, rather than mere representatives of a mindset I do not share. More specifically, I recognized that in my stereotyping I was violating the very love and acknowledgement of personhood central to the Love Project to which I claimed allegiance. My small steps into more truthful self-knowledge emerged out of the day-to-dayness of my profession. For example, a career submarine officer and I discovered that we both loved the music of Jean Sibelius. He requested having his CD of Sibelius' symphonies #3 and #4 played that evening during dinner, and then simply gave me the CD as we headed down to the dock and his departure.

Enter the Admiral

And then there was the admiral. For all I know, dozens of them may have visited the Inn. We operated primarily on first-name basis from reservation through departure, and respected the need of most guests to block out their work. The hypothesis that the Crick draws more admirals than generals, more submariners than aviators, is arguable. Anyway, we did have at least one.

Amid the hum of porch conversation on an October afternoon in 2001, I thought I heard from one woman at the north table the words "Where is the admiral?" Attention on the porch immediately converged and a question was asked. She proceeded to describe Department of Defense efforts to locate her husband by telephone the morning of September 11. He, in his fifties, trim in his beige shorts and still tanned from the last summer of our national innocence, sat relaxed and quiet beside her. Someone asked about that day and, a tad shyly, the admiral revealed that he was also a yarner.

He had been at an early morning meeting in Chantilly, Virginia, out near Dulles International, when initial news from New York had him in his staff car, trying to return to the Pentagon. With neither traffic nor cell phones operating, the admiral instructed his driver to turn into a strip mall and find a land-line phone. The manager of a mattress emporium, seeing the admiral's navy dress whites and being a patriot, said "Yes, sir!" And there, ensconced atop a firm queen-size, the admiral began to learn about the fate of his staff and the beginning of the new era. Unlike the mood that Tuesday, his tale now was told with a self-depreciating and understated humor.

I came to like the admiral during our forty-eight hours together. He had little pretension and no interest in trading on his status. His curiosity about our Tylerton cosmos matched mine about his, and he had a fetching lightness about him, despite the grimness of the times. And, as their departure approached, I wanted him to know something of how I had received him within myself. It wasn't nearly so much something he needed to hear, as something I needed to say.

What I told him was preserved that night in my journal:

> ["Bob"], I am a Christian pacifist. I have never been able to get past Jesus on that score. This means, among other things, that you and I have often been on opposite sides on some of the great issues of our generation. It also means that I have had little contact with admirals . . . and most of that adversarial. Thus it is important to me to tell you that I have really enjoyed having you and your wife as guests this weekend. I have appreciated your spirit and the thoughtfulness with which you have talked about both your career and life journey. Thank you for all of this.

The admiral responded graciously, and then, together with his wife, boarded yet another vessel.

In conclusion, we innkeepers prayerfully laid out, in our own foibled way, a pocket garden, a patch of the "peaceable kingdom" sure to be, and cultivated there the values of acceptance, respect, inclusion, compassion, and love—flowers not everywhere grown, but believed to be destined one day to fill the cosmos "as the waters cover the sea" (Hb 2:14). We were ourselves changed, profoundly, not least in our self-knowledge. But again, how could it really have been otherwise?

16. Hospitality as Generosity Rising

The reader will recall the chapter 8 discussion of the construct jousting between the two innkeepers, a tussle referred to as the hair shirt/satin sheets affair. This chapter, drafted near the end of our decade, is my re-visit to that matter which now takes the form of a question: how was it that the *feast* of hospitality repeatedly broke through the *fast* at the Inn?

A. An Inn on the Lean Side

From the beginning of the rooting of our B&B fantasizing on Tylerton back in August of 1994, Sharryl and I had the general sense that our project, like both its natural and cultural surroundings, would be on the modest side. As the thirty months of renovation unscrolled, the decision to offer dinner reluctantly made, and the reality of actual operation set in, that expectation increasingly took on specificity.

Lean of Frame

The qualities of the building at the time of purchase were on the plain side: paneling throughout; in the center a middle-aged settling; average-sized rooms *sans* fireplaces, jacuzzis, and balconies; a single primitive bathroom hidden under the stairway; and nary a tree visible from the front windows or door. It was a sow's ear, the structure of which could be reinvented only so far in the direction of a silk purse; high-end potential it would forever lack. I kept trying to think up euphemisms for adventure tourism.

Furthermore, the innkeepers, one more than the other, sought throughout the renovation to keep the operation low-budget. We did all the work ourselves, except for what neither of us felt competent to tackle: additional bathrooms, the front porch, new plumbing, and electrical updating.

We largely gleaned furnishings from Washington's Georgetown flea market (right after Sunday Mass at Holy Trinity), transported incrementally across thirty months and the Bay Bridge to Maryland's Eastern Shore atop our Toyota Corolla, and refurbished on Tylerton. That the rooms may have undergone a Cinderella transformation was the fruit of hundreds of hours of grazing by Sharryl in fabric outlets, roadside sales, and third-tier antique shops.

In addition, discouraged by zoning restrictions from adding rooms to the existing building footprint, we also chose not to build cottages on the adjacent lot we purchased after our initial season to protect our north flank. We preferred the small scale of the operation, the mom-and-pop character of it. We enjoyed doing most of the operational work ourselves, and had only one local part-time staff person, this across the last five seasons of the decade.

Lean of Income

We opened the Inn, with only one of four rooms having a private bath, with the rates set at $65-$95/room with dinner at $12/person. The move at mid-decade to reduce from four to three rooms, each now with private bath, allowed us to increase rates so as to hold the income relatively stable. We finished the decade with rates at $105-$125/room, dinner at $20/person.

Although our first year had us receiving guests eleven of the twelve months, we had evolved into an eight-month season by mid-decade with late May through Labor Day weekend framing the head of the season. The two shoulders had lighter census figures with weather being a factor the farther one moved either way from mid-July. Thus our high season and that of the crabbers coincided almost exactly: like most watermen, we had to make the bulk of our annual income in four months when we could expect the Inn to be at near capacity.

The income potential of this package is decidedly finite. Given the Inn's size, our commitment to fair rates (keeping in mind each guest's $20/person ferry fare at decade's end), the impact on the season's shoulders of inconsistency in both weather and ferry service (exacerbated in 2005–2006 by rising fuel prices and declining isle population), our income possibilities had a ceiling. Although we had gross income of over $60,000 in half our ten seasons, even our best year, 2003, still had us just missing $70,000. Our biggest month was August of 2005 when we grossed $13,000, more than 90 percent of what was theoretically possible.

Granted, there were tax benefits from living in the same building as our business, we had no daily transportation costs, and the length of season allowed the innkeepers to indulge themselves in some other interests (such as writing this book). But we were going to become wealthy only very slowly.

Lean of Provisions

Even before we knew that we would also be serving dinner, Sharryl and I were confident that, given her gifts, food would be part of the forte of the Inn. However, this too would not come easily, and for reasons in addition to our income ceiling, we found food provisioning both costly and labor-intensive.

Both the size of the Drum Point Market and the differences between Sharryl and villagers' approaches to cooking meant that offerings there were relatively few, quite expensive, and not available in bulk. We worked hard at our commitment to spend half of our food budget in the village, most of that in the Market, but the remaining food purchases needed to be made on the mainland with all of its logistical challenges and labor intensity. The rates that local watermen charged us for fresh seafood were always reasonable, but the availability of rockfish was less reliable than crab, whether soft-shell or picked.

One of Sharryl's responses to these realities was that she derived a real kick from her biweekly standing in line and arm-wrestling for undelivered, damaged, or otherwise discounted food products in Pocomoke City's Sysco Restaurant Supply warehouse. She operated a mean cart in that melee, where mayhem might be around the next counter, forming some good friendships with Delmarva's culturally diverse restaurateurs in the process. I kept being amazed at how her spirits upon returning home were as if she had attended an athletic event.

It is never easy to generate a profit serving quality food, especially when you are volume-challenged as were we. When we opted for a restaurant license to avoid aborting the Inn, I suspected it would mean that our labor in preparing and serving dinner would be near gratis. That proved to be the case.

So far all is *fast*; where's the *feast*?

B. The Table: A Space Becoming a Place

Babette's Feast

In the February of our last off-season Sharryl and I had a night at the movies, courtesy of Netflix. We watched *Babette's Feast,* the 1987 cinematic rendering of Isak Dinesen's late-nineteenth-century story. It is the improbable tale about a *Parisienne*, chef in the finest restaurant in La Ville-Lumière, forced into political exile and somehow ending up on the stark coast of Denmark's Jutland region. This topography could be mistaken for that of Tylerton. Here she, Babette by name, is recipient of hospitality, given work as a cook, and lives among the elderly surviving members of a pietistic religious sect derived from Lutheranism. (It was not lost on me that Sharryl is descended from just such a sect, the *Svenska Missions-forbündet*, only in neighboring, but also Lutheran, Sweden.)

After some time, Babette receives word that she holds the winning lottery ticket she had purchased before her exile, and will be sent a considerable amount of money. For her own mysterious reasons she decides, with a co-conspirator, to devote the entire amount to a clandestinely prepared meal that her pious hospitaliers will never forget. Babette spares neither cost nor effort in securing the ingredients of what would have been her very best offering back in her Paris restaurant. The second half of the film is about the elaborate preparing and exquisite serving of that multi-course meal. Improbably lubricated by the finest wines Paris could send, the wizened cohort travels at table from silent tentativeness to unprecedentedly joyful celebration. At the end of the film one of the ancients is standing outside, looking into the night sky, and intoning, "Hallelujah!"

Although I had seen the movie shortly after its release, I came away now with this uncanny feeling that my co-innkeeper had been Babette herself: bringing pleasure to others via beautifully presented food, occasionally punctuated with surprise and the extra effort; employing round table as a setting for inviting persons out of what they had wanted to set aside when they arrived; and trusting the power of beauty in food, surroundings, and company to be its own lavish reward. This descendant of rapacious Vikings, Sharryl, carrying on like a hot-blooded *Parisienne*! She may not be French, but Sharryl was a whole lot more like Babette than those Scandinavians, perhaps her distant kin, to whom Dinesen's chef served the meal of their lives!

Generosity via the Lens of Kitchen

So how was the Inn of Silent Music a bit like Babette's Place? Or, to paraphrase Psalm 137:4, "How does one spread a lavish fare in a lean inn?" What about the Crick is equivalent to *escargot* for appetizer on the Jutland coast or the late appearance of the evening's finest wine at Cana (Jn 2:1–11)? While I might have responded to these questions in terms of the decorating and appointing of guests' rooms, Sharryl's literal willing that the Inn be enflowered, or our shared commitment to be available to guests as we sensed openness to this, my room of choice here remains the kitchen.

With few exceptions, Sharryl used only fresh and unprocessed ingredients, which meant that the tether linking them to sea or Delmarva produce fields was short. A pail of freshly caught rockfish, announced with a heads-up call from the water, would be placed on our dock every couple of days by Capt'n Waverly Evans. Sharryl would bundle her 2:00 PM stop at the post office, its entrance graced by Miss Pauline's blossoming pomegranate tree, with one at the shanty of Capt'n Billy or Little Harvey on alternate days for hand-picked soft-shell crabs caught that morning to be served for dinner. In the face of guests' compliments, I often heard her demur that with fresh vegetables not far from the Delmarva field, bread still hot from the oven, and seafood just out of the Bay, one couldn't go too far wrong.

The aesthetics of presentation mattered as well: every plate had to clear Sharryl's scrutiny before being released to me and then guests seated on the porch. She didn't always trust the help in this regard. *Never* was anything skimpily served; "just get by" was not in her lexicon. Although occasionally, when Sharryl was visibly exhausted, perhaps close to tears, I would appeal to her to cut this or that corner, she never listened to me. She was predictably fierce, occasionally insufferable, in this regard. Yet much of what I learned about how a table, a space, can become a place, one vital, joyful, even *holy*, I learned from her.

Sharryl always prepared food with an eye toward health issues, although she was not above some delicious dessert drift in this regard. Our desserts—whether fresh fruit, or baked crisps, crunches, or cobblers (which I chronically confused) punctually emerging from the oven as I began to clear the main course, or the eight-layer cakes delivered via golf cart by a village woman—invariably generated a festive atmosphere. It didn't hurt the ambience that a few of the famed Smith Island cakes achieved a verticality nearly equivalent to the elevation of the *terra afirma* beneath the Inn!

The Babette saga is a good setting in which to raise the issue of alcohol. Sometime before we opened, I had a conversation with Capt'n Romey who, together with Miss Nanny, had first hosted us strangers at their gate. "You know," he said, eyes sparkling, "if you ever tried to get a liquor license, we'd burn you down." It is amazing how such a sentence can focus one's attention!

Only mid-decade, after discovering that verbatim threat in Rev. W. P. Taylor's 1910 *A Brief History of Smith Island, Maryland,* did I realize it to be in Smith Island's public domain. While relieved that our context took the question whether alcohol out of our hands, I can envision how Sharryl might have incorporated wine into the generous fare of our table. Her work for the night completed, she never refused when guests pulled up a chair and offered to share their contraband—more often fine than not—with her. *Madam* Babette: holding court, bathed in adulation, sipping her triumph, radiance having displaced exhaustion.

The Model: The Lavish Generosity of the One

One Sunday we tweaked our dinner schedule so Sharryl could accept an invitation to speak in the evening service of the Tylerton congregation. She chose the theme "The Extravagance of God," based on the story of the marriage at Cana (Jn 2:1–11). There, in contrast to niggardly preparations resulting in the wine supply running out, the response of Jesus turning water into wine was one of lavishness, both quantitatively and qualitatively. The clueless wine steward thus compliments the groom for having held back the good stuff until the last. That story also communicates well the impulse that Sharryl repeatedly brought to all aspects of the Inn.

The definitive paradigm for lavish generosity for Sharryl and me is the divine one: it was to a common and nondescript village, a stable for animals, blue-collar shepherds no less, that the One came, and continues to come, thus forever elevating and celebrating the common and ordinary as precious. Notes in our guest book, hundreds of warm and joyful post-visit letters and emails, and, most concretely for me, the hugs at the departing ferry, testify that our efforts freely to share of ourselves, and in so doing emulate this definitive paradigm, were repeatedly well-received.

C. A Polyphony of Generosity

The Largess of Villagers

Whatever generosity we innkeepers sought to embody as well as practice, elevated occasionally by the extra effort on a special occasion, was serendipitously supplemented by that of villagers. To the expressions of "mutual assistance" explored in chapter 9, I add these additional examples of generosity:

- Waverly Evans' chartered excursions always lasted longer than touted, his fares always lower than that required by any standard of justice.
- Although their generosity was occasionally abused, the women in the crab-picking co-op were almost always engaging and congenial when our guests stopped to visit.
- Without exception, visitors to the church services on Sunday morning or evening or Wednesday night were warmly received, whatever their faith background or lack thereof.
- Far beyond the call of duty was Louise, fireperson and paramedic, who, tethered to the Drum Point Market's cash register, once sent Sharryl and a needful guest to the firehouse to rummage in the ambulance for a bandage.
- Woos (Willard), overhearing a guest being told that the Market was fresh out of sunscreen, ran to his shanty to get some for her.
- Guests who requested crab cakes at the Market, only to learn that the last one was just served, were astonished to see how a phone call could generate a tray of fresh ones in fifteen minutes.
- Guests were almost always warmly greeted and conversed with by Tylertonians, whether in the lanes or by our housekeeper in the Inn.
- Sharryl and I came to know exactly who among the Tylertonians had exhausted her/his conversational possibilities with the other fifty-seven, and thus was good for a lengthy exchange with an interested guest who constituted a fresh listen.

Another index of Tylertonian generosity was the offerings at the church, a matter alluded to earlier. In 2005, the congregation, consisting of about half of the fifty-eight year-round population and including a dozen retired persons with very limited and fixed incomes, contributed just under $75,000. The congregation's gifts that year to parties outside of Tylerton exceeded $13,600, including $5,000 in the aftermath of Katrina and Rita, $1,000 to survivors of the Asian tsunami the previous December, and $3,300 to several mainland food banks. The congregation also assisted in different degrees the other two congregations on Smith.

The fact that some *nonattendees,* both Tylertonians and seasonal, also contributed more than token amounts, hints at the central role of the church in a community lacking formal government. If it were a late May Sunday morning, and you were curious as to whether the crab "peeler run" had begun, you need only look at the Sunday School offering figures posted on the wall. On occasion I noted averages there above $100 per adult, and with the major morning worship offering yet to come!

In the face of pervasive patterns within Christian communities of practice falling short of profession, I was humbled by the fact that the generosity of the Tylerton congregation went many *more* places than did their theology: their largess traveled well beyond the salvation of souls.

The Largess of Guests

But I also must add that the generosity of guests themselves was widespread. In addition to other gifts already cited, literally dozens of books came to the Inn's many shelves from guests. In fact, guests' gifts or recommendations significantly shaped the extensive reading that we innkeepers did in our off-seasons. This included cookbooks that Sharryl sometimes received in trade, to say nothing of guests' recipes that sometimes made their way to the table.

Occasionally, guest generosity took the form of expert counsel proffered, as in the case of the Missouri corrections professional early on. For several days, he had been longingly monitoring from the dock my construction of the balcony, the "perch" of this book, when I resignedly broke my private space protocol and waved him up.

He immediately seized upon my major third-floor conundrum: how to pass from one half of the space to the other, the two halves cleaved by a transverse stairwell. Within fifteen minutes he had generated the solution, an improbable contraption which in time we would call the "drawbridge." Fortunately, its location outside the public portions of the Inn meant that it never had to face the gauntlet of building inspectors. Fascinating, though, that a corrections officer would know so much about drawbridges and moats. . . .

Actually, the most important gift that guests gave to the village was their informal advocacy on behalf of Tylertonians in their workplaces and social circles. One of my deepest satisfactions from the decade is that the Inn inadvertently transformed hundreds and hundreds of thoughtful and well-positioned professionals, many strategically embedded, into ambassadors for the people and culture of Tylerton. And that legacy lives on!

In conclusion, like the liturgical year, or the communitarian life of Tylerton, or simply living one's life, an inn is most richly experienced as an oscillation between the ordinary and the extraordinary, the common and the lavish, fast and feast. Life that is all fast, like that all feast, is neither: each requires the other for definition, separation, accentuation. This yeasty tension was nurtured and tweaked with intentionality in the Inn across our decade, and it has become a very important component of our understanding and practice of hospitality. Perhaps the short duration of our guests' stays, the finite time, was itself a "fast" component—the weekend, like the moment, was always fleeting, and our new friends, some of them quickly dear, would always go away—that always existed in tension with any "feast" component we offered. Actually, "fast" is too ascetic a word for our Inn's ordinary, "feast" too flamboyant for its extraordinary, but the use of the two marks a dialectic within which we sought to work and live.

And toward which pole might we have inadvertently tilted? In her 2001 articles on the Inn appearing in the prominent sailing periodical *Soundings*, Mary Drake opined thus: "The Inn of Silent Music's name reflects [Friesen's] less-is-more philosophy, though the ambience embodies more of Lindberg's desire to pamper than Friesen's leanings toward deprivation." Alas. . . .

17. Hospitality Toward You: European Spirits Past

When Sharryl and I first visited Tylerton in 1992, I was only vaguely aware that Smith Island had a rich history, one extending back to within a handful of decades of the founding of Jamestown in May 1607. I presumed that there had been Amerindians living in the Chesapeake basin long before, but I knew little of their history or culture. That a vast and varied stream of peoples had lived in this basin many millennia below the scrim of the present, and that they embodied questions of *hospitality* directed toward me: such matters were farthest from my mind.

However, as the years of our decade passed, I gradually became more aware of *you*—the vast and varied *you*—who lived here before me. In the categories of Philip Sheldrake's *Spaces for the Sacred,* this space belatedly became a richer place in part because of its power to connect me with the collective narratives, emotions, associations, and cosmologies of *your* lives here. And once I learned of you, you were here with me to stay.

Thus, in this chapter and that following, rather than writing *about* you, I will speak directly *to* you, the prior denizens here, personally, and invite my readers to listen in.

A. Learning to Become Aware of You

In the beginning, my interest was merely historical, and focused on you of the waterman culture including your forebears here across nearly 350 years. Early on I met some of you via Tom Horton's *An Island Out of Time* and the excellent genealogical work of New York Long Islander Gail Walczyk, herself of the Smith Island diaspora. And, of course, I encountered in day-to-day life on Tylerton your splendid residue, still living here with a measure of vitality and joy, and a vast repository of stories. As I became more familiar with your waterman tale, my circle of interest grew larger, reaching farther back in time.

Did You Love This Place As I Love It?

But during the second half of our decade who you were, all of you, slowly began to matter to me at a deeper level. How could I become intimately familiar with this place without opening myself to you: what you did, what you thought, how you felt, whom you worshipped? Sometimes I would be sitting in my perch with that breathtaking vista before me, and the questions would come knifing in like a storm front from the northwest: what were each, and all, of you *really* like? what were your hopes and dreams? how did you generate the courage to survive in this often-hostile topography, especially in winter? how did you view Earth? how did you hold it or, more accurately, how did you believe it to hold you? did you envision or long for a unity, a oneness, beneath all of the particulars, and what impact might this have had on your adventure of living?

Oh, I was aware of the danger in what I was doing, that I was putting my twenty-first-century questions in your mouths of other times. Conceding this, however, did not staunch the curiosity. Sitting in my perch, I might wonder whether you had had questions like mine long before me. From my relative safety I found myself experiencing shades of solidarity with what I thought you might have gone through: I marveled at your triumphs; I empathized with you in your tragedies and declines; I relished the Bay as I imagined you might have. And besides simply wanting to acknowledge that you had lived, that the joy and agony which have been my life might also have been a bit like yours, I found myself wanting to reach toward you, speak to you, finish some business with you.

Please: I held no séances, solicited no apparitions, consulted no mediums. Throughout the decade, my feet were solidly on the ground, less than *firma* though it be. And even though some departing guests have declared categorically that the Inn was haunted by the best of you, and I have wondered about that more than a few occasions myself, I remain noncommittal. The only kind of hauntedness about which I am certain is that of the One brooding, as in Genesis 1:2, over the face of the cosmos, including the Crick. Having said that, I do concede that here on the Crick I began to suspect that your presence once here means that, in some sense, you remain here still.

My Tylerton experience, together with being a Roman Catholic, with its doctrine of the Communion of Saints—a teaching that we in the present live with this "cloud of witnesses" from the past (Heb 12:1)—has nudged me toward an expanded practice of inclusion—not only across tables, streets, social barriers, and international boundaries, but also across generations and millennia, across the fissures between cultures and worldviews, even between this life and the greater one.

There is Room for You in the Inn!

I have begun to glimpse how my life has been slowly changing as I gain a greater awareness of you, when I begin each day silently acknowledging you as *presente*. I know now that the most important things are not cleaved apart by time or space. Tylerton, such a slip of a place and remote, shortened some distances, reversed a little bit some such separations of time and space, and I realized I could neither know nor love Tylerton apart from you. Yes, *that* is what I have been groping to say! At some level, we had access to each other, and there were things I wanted to tell, or ask of, you.

I might have written about my awareness of you in any of several ways. But in the end, the theme of hospitality, welcoming you from different layers of the mysterious past to the present and my time, to the Inn and my space, seemed most promising.

I know that in 2006 I stand on the shoulders of all who have gone before—not only you co-bearers of the *Imago Dei*, but all of you of the fauna, and before you as well. And I know that my life is diminished to the extent to which I live as if you had not. Indeed, I continue to grow into the awareness that I would not be had you of the past not have been. Thus, I wish both to acknowledge all of you and, yes, extend hospitality. During this decade, I have been discovering that all of you were strangers to me, that you were inexplicably out there, standing at my gate. And I have wanted to welcome you to our splendid time, to our modest yet beautiful space.

B. A Roll Call of Honor

Allow me to work backward from the present as I address first you who were participants in the cartography, exploration, and settlement of the Chesapeake basin by Europeans across roughly the last half millennium. I also recognize some nearer in time playing key roles in the building of communities on Smith Island. My greeting to you of European origin is both different and easier in the making than to the rest of you, African Americans and indigenes, whom I address in the next chapter.

Skilled and Courageous Latin Explorers

I recognize you who sailed to the Chesapeake region not long after the voyages of Columbus altered the worlds both old and new, especially Giovanni Caboto; Giovanni da Varrazano; Pedro de Menendez de Aviles, Father Juan Bautista de Segura, SJ, and the other seven Jesuit missioners in what you Spaniards called *Ajacán* (Virginia). Skilled and courageous explorers, southern Europeans, and presumably my Roman Catholic co-religionists, all: I acknowledge you and your cohorts as *presente*.

Capt'n John Smith and Crew

I recognize you, Capt'n John Smith, and your plucky crew, who came up what later would be named Tangier Sound in early June of 1608, landing briefly on our archipelago just north of here. Your exploration, splendidly documented in text and map, well assessed the grandeur of the Bay: "Heaven and earth never agreed better to frame a place of man's inhabitation." And in your inimitably cavalier and yet respectful manner, you provided us with an extraordinary glimpse of the indigenous populations whom you encountered. Capt'n Smith and crew: I salute you as *presente*.

Fr. Andrew White, SJ, and Companions

I recognize you, Father Andrew White, SJ, who, together with Governor Leonard Calvert and a company of colonists—the gentry Roman Catholic, the majority mostly Protestant commoners including many indentured servants, totaling perhaps two hundred—made landfall on what came to be called St. Clement's Island in the Potomac on the Feast of the Annunciation in 1634, establishing the Maryland colony.

You wrote at the time, Father, "This baye is the most delightful water I ever saw." Had you come today to what in your charter was called *Terra Mariae,* my binoculars and perch might have allowed me to witness your craft, the *Ark* and the *Dove*, as they negotiated the shoals off Virginia's Northern Neck and then bore to port up the Potomac.

I know something of your colony's historic albeit short-lived experiment with religious toleration. Auguring for a religiously heterogeneous society were both your relatively peaceful initiatives toward the Piscataway tribe of the area—enlightened by standards of that day, and of rich future portent—and the Act of Toleration (1649). I am proud, both of the dream that you pursued and our being able as Roman Catholics to follow you to this fair Bay. Father White and company: I salute you and your vision as *presente*.

First Colonists on "Isle of Broken Woodlands"

I acknowledge you initial colonists to arrive on Smith Island in the mid-1660s, many originally from the south of England—Cornwall, Devon, Dorset—or Wales. Some of you came via the Eastern Shore of the Virginia colony, others perhaps nervous Protestants from St. Mary's City in the fledgling Maryland colony.

"Isle of Broken Woodlands" was what some called your island, part of what John Smith had dubbed the "Russels Iles." But neither handle stuck, and you unfortunately ended up with the name of one Henry Smith, a lothario who never actually lived here. Anyway, you early arrivees on the part of the isle called Drum Point—first Evanses and Tylers and Smiths, later Bradshaws, Marshalls, Marshes, and, finally, Corbins—were a particularly hearty and courageous sort. As farmers, you tilled and harvested the rich upland. As sea level rose, another war erupted, and arrival of the railroad in Crisfield both invited and coerced adaptation, you shifted to harrowing the sea.

More than infrequently, I have found both who you were, and who you are, to be scarcely believable, your project a courageous, exemplary, and unparalleled one. Smith Islanders across nearly 350 years, including you, the beautiful true grit who remain: I humbly salute you, all of you, as *presente*.

All Who Went Down to the Sea in Ships

There are you, the untallied, who lost your lives in the seas surrounding Smith Island. Many of you died in war, whether Revolutionary, that of 1812, or Civil, during the repeated naval confrontations in the strategic Chesapeake.

There were you, as many as seventy British and colonial officers and sailors, who needlessly died in the Revolutionary War's last naval battle, fought in Kedges Straits, just north of Smith Island on November 30, 1782, thirteen months after the British surrender at Yorktown. There were you Brit sailors—not least you, General Robert Ross—who died in the standoff at Fort McHenry during the night of September 13, 1814. This attack was launched from Tangier Island, our neighbor but seven miles to the south, where the fleet had previously quartered. And at least one of you sons of England was returned to be buried near North End, where your grave, beneath the Union Jack, was faithfully tended for generations.

Know that it has been difficult for me to reconcile the tranquility here with the military violence of which all of you were a part.

Others of you were lost to the waters in time of peace, while pursuing your livelihood—most recently Tangierite James Crockett, somewhere southeast of Horse Hammock in a storm the afternoon of March 8, 2005. At Tylerton's annual Blessing of the Boats watermen solemnly recite the names of the nearly forty of you taken by the sea in our neighborhood since 1865, but there were undoubtedly many more before then. All of you who courageously "go down to the sea in ships" (Ps 107:23), whether in time of war or peace: I salute you as *presente*.

Joshua Thomas: "Parson of the Islands"

I affirm you, Joshua Thomas, waterman turned "exhorter" (lay preacher) and evangelist. You were tagged "Parson of the Islands" by the British officers with whom you built an amiable relationship during their 1814 military occupation of Tangier and control of Smith. Each isle gave you a bride and thus claimed you as its own.

These officers, just returned from leading part of the fleet up the Patuxent to torch Washington, inexplicably invited you to address their twelve thousand troops on Tangier and bless their naval attack on Fort McHenry and Baltimore the next day. Torn within your spirit, you would later recount that internal struggle, according to

Adam Wallace: "I did not like to refuse, and yet I was very unwilling to perform this duty. I thought and prayed over the matter, and *it came to me* that I must stand up for Jesus as a good soldier, in the fight of faith."

Never more than marginally literate, in the end you addressed that assembly with eloquence and power in the tradition of the prophet Jeremiah, as you would later report: "I told them of the great wickedness of war, and that God said, '*Thou shalt not kill!'* . . . it was given me from the Almighty that [you] *could not* take Baltimore, and *would not succeed in* [*your*] *expedition* . . . .*You cannot take it!*"

Parson Joshua Thomas, humble waterman yet fearless speaker of truth to power, you who triumphed over temptation to hide in pious platitudes when the hour called for prophetic courage: I confess that I am among the many inspired by and indebted to you, and I salute you as abundantly *presente*.

Capt'n Howard Wesley & Miss Venie (Evans) Marshall

I acknowledge the two of you responsible for the building of the home that would become the Inn of Silent Music "down below" on Tylerton: Capt'n Howard Wesley and Miss Venie (Evans) Marshall. In the home you built around 1914, and which you enlarged in the 1930s, you raised your seven children, six reaching adulthood. Here, for more than fifty years and for a time including three generations, you experienced much sorrow and much joy, something never far from me as I pause in the rooms.

After you, Capt'n Howard, a net fisherman, went to the One in what is now the Inn's living room on February 29, 1967, you, Miss Venie, moved to a smaller house inside the village, passing away on November 10, 1970. Please know that few visitors to the Inn have been as warmly welcomed and enjoyed by Sharryl and myself as your descendants, including three generations of them but six weeks before we closed, fine people seemingly pleased that good life continues to unfold here. Capt'n Howard and Miss Venie: I thank and salute you as *presente*.

Jennings Lee Evans: Waterman, Yarner, Keeper of the Memory

You alone, Jennings, of those here honored, carry on as part of the "true grit" still inhabiting Smith Island. Already sidelined off the water by health issues when I met you in 1994, you have poured your subsequent years into collecting and preserving the isle's fragile history, much of it oral.

Now well on the far side of seventy, you remain loquacious to a fault and possessor of a downright scary photographic memory. You are a crack genealogist, an islander equally at home singing in North End's church choir or being the MC at the less reverential annual Watermen's Dinner. An incorrigible yarner, you were surely born with a silver story in your mouth.

Your accomplishments have been legion:

- between your work with groups visiting the Smith Island cultural center and being a major source for virtually every book on the isle in the last quarter century, you have brought the island's story to literally many thousands.
- you have been part of a team which has accounted for nearly everyone in the Smith Island genealogical pool over the last nearly 350 years.

You, Jennings, more than anyone else are *the* consummate embodiment of the yarnin' waterman! You are, and will continue to be, *presente*.

18. Confession to You: Violated Spirits Past

My efforts to reach back to you not of European stock is more complicated. Some of you who walked on what now is Smith Island so long before me were dehumanized by slavery, then segregation, and lingering discrimination into the present. Others of you would be decimated by sword, European diseases, and treachery. And all at the hands of my European co-religionists, whether Roman Catholic, Anglican, or Protestant.

Living on Tylerton across this decade, and learning something of the Chesapeake story, forced me to ponder your experiences, increasingly inseparable from the places where you had them, and what they mean for me. And out of this have risen some questions which I have sought to articulate to myself:

- Do I, living in the present, have some responsibility in relation to you, both you who were here perhaps fifteen millennia ago, and you who were involuntarily brought here as chattel beginning nearly four hundred years ago?
- Can I, as a person of faith, ignore the fact that here in this alluvial valley, creased by the mighty Susquehanna long before it became "Great Shellfish Bay," there were you with whom I share the *Imago Dei?*
- How do I hold the fact that the building of what was first an English colony and then an independent nation was both literally and metaphorically on the backs of you, also co-bearers of the *Imago Dei*, brought here as cargo and property?

I give myself to a space, thus incrementally transforming it into a place, only to find it already inhabited by a host of you who in some sense are calling to me. How do I respond to you, strangers I am now finding at my gate? After initial perplexity, I have wanted to become acquainted, but do not quite know how. I have wanted to extend hospitality, my brothers and sisters, to welcome you into the Inn, but I do not quite know how.

Father Francis Kline, OCSO, abbot of the Trappist Mepkin Abbey where Sharryl and I spent a week during each of four off-seasons, and who went to the One the same week as we closed the Inn for the last time, writes:

> *The land on which we live . . . will grow quiet with its history, for good or for ill. But it will always remember what went on there. Anyone who chooses to live on the land, is invited to live with its history, in such a way as to expiate and redeem it.*

Kline writes from the experience of his Cistercian community on the Cooper just north of Charleston, South Carolina, also a tidewater space which became a place for the monks, in part because of evoked memories of first Amerindians and then black slaves, among others, for whom it once was home.

Kline's words address my conundrum: how can I extend hospitality to you strangers, both African Americans and Amerindians? My objective is not the excavating of the wasteland of treaty treacheries, or reparations, or assigning societal guilt. It is rather one person's effort to reach back across time and culture to those of you victimized by my sort—European stock, brandishing naked power in the name of the nonviolent Christ. I wish only to take a small step, in the words of the abbot, to "expiate and redeem"—to bring a modicum of peace to myself, and perhaps also to some of you from whom I am separated by death.

For me, the road to this peace is via confession. I volunteer to offer to the One prayers of acknowledgment and contrition on behalf of my people, who for personal gain, adventure, evangelistic zeal, or simply because we held the power, repeatedly crippled and/or destroyed your ways of life. I offer these prayers, neither certain about nor really interested in questions about the efficacy of such vicarious efforts; those questions I leave to others.

Rather, I offer these prayers simply because it is incumbent upon me to do so. However, before confession, allow me to summarize what my sort did to you, African Americans and Amerindians, in each case concluding with some questions for you.

A. To You: Spirits of Violated African Americans Past

The earlier historical sections in this work largely share a quality common to much historical writing about the Western Hemisphere: the saga of the Americas was begun, sustained, *and then told* by and through the perspectives of Europeans and their descendants. Such are the spoils and privileges of victory in war—the battles of conquest and/or enslavement, in this case. The choice and abiding prerogative of the winner is spinning the tale however he pleases.

We of privilege may be increasingly uncertain about the future, but we do own the past, and have rewarded ourselves by crafting its narrative from our perspective. Like place, it seems, history is crafted construct, its engine frequently conquest. In short, history is abducted, crafted, propagated, and, ultimately, recapitulated by the winners.

Thus, my understanding of history—of my hemisphere, to which a minimum of twelve million Africans were brought involuntarily, and my colony and then country, which received about 5 percent of that number—has required a lifetime of unlearning and relearning.

Your Arrival in My Neighborhood

My first glimpse of your role in Tylerton's story was during genealogical research of village families at the National Archives during our 1995–1997 renovation period. The conflict on Tylerton early in our decade regarding the flying of the Confederate flag further conscientized me to what you had endured here. Further, the first of you African slaves—"twenty and odd" in number—entered the colonies via English pirate ship in 1619, just across and down the Bay a bit from Tylerton. From my perch, I pondered how America's racism malignancy arguably began with importing the first black slaves nearly four hundred years ago into Virginia territory, at a site just beyond the reach of my eyes to the south.

Your story on Smith calls for some context regarding the Maryland colony, particularly the lower part of the Eastern Shore. Somerset County, from the Nanticoke to the Atlantic and to the northeast of Smith, was established in 1666; Dorchester County, between the Nanticoke and the Choptank to the north of Smith, was organized three years later. By the late 1600s, this sector was shifting its labor base from convicts and indentured servants to black slaves. An estimated one hundred thousand of you were brought to the Chesapeake basin during the eight decades from 1690 to 1770.

Some of you were free—those predating slavery, others via manumission—but your status deteriorated as you increasingly were seen as a threat to the institution of slavery. The pairing of your cohort, both slave and free, with a relatively large population of indentured servants, convicts, and their descendants made the lower Eastern Shore a volatile and violent place. (Note: Worchester County was carved out of Somerset in 1742, Wicomico County from parts of each in 1867.)

In the years just before the Civil War, a gradual decline in the census and economic value of slaves as Eastern Shore labor laid bare the extent to which the institution remained intact as a form of social control. Already in 1861, two years before the Emancipation Proclamation, President Lincoln placed Fort Upton, a Union garrison, in Salisbury in response to sympathies for the Confederacy and its "peculiar institution" of slavery. During the summer after the Proclamation—which did not apply to Maryland, a border state remaining in the Union—additional troops arrived seeking to entice you to rebel against your masters and join the Union army.

Lynchings on the Main

Lynchings in counties Somerset (seat: Princess Anne) and Wicomico (seat: Salisbury) in the late nineteenth and early twentieth centuries offer a glimpse of the horror that never was far from you. A partial list of those of you so murdered:

- You, Isaac Kemp, in Princess Anne in 1894;
- You, William Andrew, in Princess Anne in 1897;
- You, James Reed, in Crisfield in 1907;
- You, Matthew Williams, in Salisbury in 1931;
- You, Euel Lee (alias Orphan Jones), executed by the state of Maryland in 1933, in what would be called a "legal lynching";
- You, George Armwood, in Princess Anne in 1933.

The latter lynching—you had allegedly robbed an elderly white woman—took place in front of the Somerset County jail and courthouse at the hands of a mob of two thousand, and brought national scrutiny to the region's racism. This particular lynching and its repercussions exposed widespread complicity or acquiescence among local politicians, judges, law officers, and media leaders in Princess Anne and Salisbury. The mob's use of the epithets "Communists!" and "Reds!" to pillory all opposition was harbinger of things to come.

To this list some would add your name, George Scott "Kidd" Lee, secretly hanged on Smith Island in 1906. State authorities feared a lynching in Princess Anne, were either trial or execution to take place there, and so moved the trial to Baltimore and execution to Smith Island. Your story is told in greater detail later in this chapter.

The smoldering of these events in your collective memory contributed to an incendiary racial atmosphere that, in the 1960s, exploded in riots in Cambridge (seat of Dorchester County), including a memorable appearance there of H. Rap Brown in July 1967.

Blacks on Smith Island

Because Smith Island became a separate voting district only in 1860, the antebellum federal census records, which distinguished between free and slave blacks but often did not provide names of the latter, are of limited help. Other sources point to a small number of blacks on Smith before emancipation, some free, some slave. Historian Jennings Evans notes that several black farming families lived in present-day Martin Wildlife Refuge, the northeastern third of Smith, in the early 1800s, and that Maryland's first integrated school was established in that area by King Solomon Evans in the 1790s. In the 1860 census, six of you free blacks are listed by name, four being children.

Smith Island's mid-1800s transition from agriculture to harvesting the Bay resulted in a much larger need for labor, particularly on the hundreds of oystering schooners (and later, skipjacks) that worked the Bay from or near Crisfield.

That postbellum period was chaotic and frightening for you Delmarva residents, whether formerly free or slave, as you absorbed the widespread bitterness over the war's outcome. It grew apparent that the end of slavery would not soon mean equality for you. Thus, with the end of the Civil War, a number of you, some bringing families, found employment on Smith Island, where the environment seemed less hostile.

Why was the ethos different here? Smith lacked the earlier incendiary immigrant cocktail of convicts, indentured servants, enslaved blacks, and free blacks on Somerset main. Nor did Smith have the plantation scale of economy that characterized parts of lower Delmarva. The Methodist Church on the island was an additional, albeit cautious, restraint on racism. Smith only rarely harbored the deep-seated hatred that would plague parts of the southern Eastern Shore of Maryland into the mid-twentieth century and beyond. At the same time, we should not romanticize Smith Island as a postbellum haven for you, given that your alternative was one of the most virulent examples of the racist pathogen in America, Maryland's Somerset County.

This bump in your numbers on Smith Island is reflected in the 1870 federal census, which counted thirty-eight blacks. Jennings Evans notes you watermen living on the island with your families: Lewis Rogers, Ephrim Douglas, Edward Revell, John Wise, and Levin Boggers ("Boggs"). Most of you appear to have resided in either the Fogg's Point area up near Solomon's Lump lighthouse or on the northern shore of Big Thorofare, which cuts east-west through the island. The partially drowned remains of both areas are now in the Martin National Wildlife Refuge.

The 1880 census also includes you, Jett and Harriet Sutton, together with your two young daughters. Evans reports that you, Jett, born around 1856, were the sole survivor of a wrecked schooner found drifting in the Bay. You grew up in the home of a North End family and, after meeting Harriet in Crisfield, you as a family lived near North End until around 1899.

The number of you on Smith Island was tied to the oyster boom and thus fell precipitously as the rapacious harvest in the new century ate itself into a mere shadow of its former self. The 1920 national census lists but one of you on Smith Island.

Three Narratives

Against that background of violation of your people by my own, I want to tell three of your stories, each based upon research by Jennings Evans. First, Miriah Jacobs Parks, born sixty years before Emancipation. Second, George Scott "Kidd" Lee, born a generation after that event. And third, an account of three of you, resident aliens of Tylerton with names known but to God, also born well after Emancipation. My use of story is fitting because it is how your people have long communicated who you are.

Miriah Jacobs Parks—When you were born in the slave quarters on April 15, 1804, the name given you was Miriah Jacobs. Your family was owned by "King" Richard and Euphemy Evans on their fine two-hundred-acre plantation, King Richard's Garden, near Fogg's Point just below Kedges Strait on the north edge of Smith Island. Around the turn of the century the Garden was the scene of periodic balls and fiddled frolics at which a young fisherman dandy, Joshua Thomas by name, performed as the area's finest and most spirited dancer. More than a century later, you would remember those parties and the important people who passed through the Garden.

But times were changing with the Methodist Wesleyan revival sweeping the Chesapeake basin during the years between 1800 and 1830, stressing a personal conversion experience. This revivalism, which would profoundly imprint the Eastern Shore to this day, also spread to the islands.

You were a little child in 1808 when the same Joshua Thomas, now converted and a fledgling exhorter, showed up at the Garden for the first recorded religious meeting on Smith. What began as a prayer meeting was quite an occasion, with several, including your mistress, Miss Euphemy, coming under conviction, falling, and crying out for mercy in a manner not entirely unlike a Smith Island revival meeting today. The rich and powerful role of faith in the Smith Island saga for the following two centuries can be traced to that meeting in the home of your master and mistress.

You were but ten years old when the entire household received a big surprise: British Major-General Robert Ross, with the British Navy moored on Tangier, appeared on the wharf in front of the Garden with a cohort of officers, all of whom were invited to stay for dinner. Both you and your mother were part of the bustle to prepare the meal in the same room where first the frolics and later the revival preaching had transpired. You would later report that your task was to set out the teacups, and that General Ross asked for a refill.

None of you could have imagined that, only months later on September 13, 1814, Major-General Ross, leading the ground assault component of the attack on Fort McHenry, would fall to an American sniper before Baltimore in a battle that the household could actually hear from the Garden. Perhaps you later overheard that the British had been warned against initiating the attack by the same Joshua Thomas down on Tangier.

Miss Miriah, your master and mistress were good Christian folk, and you would unfailingly speak well of them throughout your very long life. Thus, you perhaps were not surprised that, when the King's health began to fail, he traveled to Princess Anne to draw up a will, stipulating that all of his older slaves be set free upon his death, the younger ones as each reached the age of thirty. This meant you would be freed in 1834.

But after the King's death on July 4, 1828, it somehow happened that you were sold to a mainland plantation, resulting in your freedom being delayed an additional thirty-one years. You would marry Richard Parks and raise a family in that interim, and then live out your life with your descendents in Crisfield, where you died in 1910 at age 106.

Miss Miriah, during your years at the Garden, you would have heard about the Christian gospel from Joshua Thomas and others. What did you think of that good news of liberty in Jesus the Christ that they preached? Did it sound like a message of deliverance to you and your family?

Despite the stipulation in your master's will that you be manumitted in 1834, your sale to a mainland plantation postponed that freedom until after the Civil War. Your children, like you and your husband Richard, were born into slavery. How could that sale, contravening the clear intent of your master's will, have taken place in a devout Christian family whom you would continue to hold in fond regard throughout your life?

Although there is not so much as a hint of it in the story we have of your life, did you struggle with bitterness in your heart toward those who contravened your master's will?

Miss Miriah: *Presente.*

George Scott "Kidd" Lee—In the predawn on July 26, 1906, you arrived at Smith Island on the large steam-powered *Governor McLane* for the purpose of being hanged. The site was the northern edge of today's Martin Wildlife Refuge, opposite Solomon's Lump Lighthouse, virtually atop the former sites of first King Richard's Garden and a subsequent scattering of black-owned homes. You and your captors, some thirty state and county officials, had sailed from Baltimore through the night on secret orders by Maryland Governor William Warfield. Having earlier intervened to change the venue of your trial—from Princess Anne to Baltimore—the governor now had done the same for your execution—from Princess Anne to Smith. The isle was in Somerset County, so the secret execution thus was legal.

You had been apprehended six weeks earlier at Cape Charles at the southern end of Virginia's Eastern Shore, the area of your origins, and confessed to raping two young women near Kingston on route #413 not far from Crisfield. Knowing you might be lynched if returned to the Somerset main, the authorities temporarily held you in Norfolk. Governor Warfield then intervened and you were transferred to Baltimore for a hastily arranged three-hour trial on July 5.

Among those at your execution were several North End crabbers, who stumbled upon the astonishing event. One, Capt'n Tobe Evans, later told the story within hearing of his grandson Jennings, whose written account is my source.

Capt'n Tobe described you as sitting on your coffin as your gallows from Towson prison was being assembled. A black clergyman, Rev. Samuel A. Ward, had been conscripted for the voyage, and he sat beside you, praying with and for you. The husband of Lillie Barnes, one of the women whom you had attacked, was also in the company. Having again made full confession of your crime, you asked Rev. Ward if you might have a word with Mr. Barnes. After he was called over, you reportedly said to him: "Mr. Barnes, I wants yo' forgiveness, 'fo' I die." Mr. Barnes responded, "I cannot forgive you for what you did to my wife and niece." You asked one last time, "Mr. Barnes, God forgives . . . can't you?" Barnes turned and walked away.

The ladder to the gallows being too short, and you being handcuffed, you were hauled by those cuffs onto the platform. That is where you are standing in a photograph that has survived: Rev. Ward to your left with upraised arm, praying to the One for the salvation of your soul, the hangman to your right with the waiting noose. This severe symmetry signs your life in the balance. At 8:25 AM that life was taken from you.

After you were pronounced dead by Dr. Harry M. Lankford of Princess Anne and placed in your coffin, your body was returned to the vessel. The cohort then sailed up the Wicomico to the Mount Vernon wharf, where an already angry crowd became more furious upon learning they had been deprived of their revenge. You were buried in Princess Anne, but the same Dr. Lankford was reported to have subsequently exhumed your body, severed your head, and displayed your skull on the desk of his office.

Mr. George, were you able to make your peace with your Maker, and yourself, in the face of the terrible crime that you forthrightly admitted committing?

The report has come down to us that in your last hours you requested forgiveness from the husband of one of your victims and declared that God forgives. May we assume that contrition and repentance, together with assurance of God's forgiveness, sustained you as you stood on the gallows waiting to die? May we further assume that you, like the thief on the cross (Lk 23:40–43), were received into paradise on that day, July 26, 1906?

And finally, Mr. George, if I may be so bold, have you, in the manner in which Jesus the Christ forgave both the howling mob confronting him and his official executioners, been able to forgive both of these? And perhaps even Dr. Lankford?

Mr. George: *Presente*.

Three Unnamed Sons of Africa—I acknowledge that I cannot even address you properly, for neither your names nor places of origin have survived in Tylerton's memory.

It was morning here on Drum Point (Tylerton) in about the year 1916, although there is uncertainty about the exact year, season, and day. Of about seventeen young and single black deckhands and handymen listed in the 1910 census as working out of the village, three of you were aboard a skipjack anchored in Tyler's Ditch, near the mouth of Merlin Gut off the north end of the village. Mooring of skipjacks that close in had become possible with the initial dredging of Smith's channels in 1913–1914.

One account has the bulk of the village at prayer nearby in the old church, located in a small community called The Pines. It would be about a dozen more years (1928) before this building would be disassembled and rebuilt at the end of the Tyler family cemetery in the center of Drum Point.

We do not know what triggered the tragedy of that morning. On the deck of the skipjack, laying on its side, was a large tank commonly used for collecting water from a roof. The three of you got into the tank. Were you just horsing around? Was it February, with you seeking shelter from the brutal wind and warmth from each other? In any event, your weight caused the tank to roll across the deck, through the railing, and into Tyler's Ditch, where all three of you drowned. The villagers were unable to save any of you.

Communication and transportation being what they were, efforts to find your next of kin were unsuccessful. If your names were even known to the villagers amid the shadowy, transient oystering culture, they were not recorded.

The home of Pearson Marshall, Capt'n Howard's younger brother, who lived but three houses north of what is now the Inn, was where watermen constructed your three pine coffins. After a funeral ceremony, burial took place not in the Tyler family cemetery, but on the near side of the recently depopulated Sassafras Hammock on Hog Neck. The hammock is easily visible from the porch of the Inn and the namesake of our room on the first floor. This same hammock had, in 1877, been designated as the official Smith Island marker for the long-contested Maryland/Virginia state boundary. In time, the rarely visited site of your interment succumbed to the wild flora and the ravages of shore erosion. The exact location of your graves was lost.

Before going to the One in 2003 at age ninety-two, Tylerton's Ma Margaret Marshall shared with me her recollections of your tragedy and subsequent burial on Sassafras Hammock when she was a small child.

Nearly eighty years after your deaths, in the spring of 1993, Jennings Evans and brother-in-law Alan Smith of Tylerton, together with Gail and Frank Walczyk, accidentally stumbled upon one of your graves when an extremely low tide exposed Shanks Creek shoals east of Hog Neck to their metal probes. With the aid of experts, they were able to confirm that these were indeed your remains.

At the annual Blessing of the Boats on April 29, 2001, the three of you were included for the first time in the dignified reading of a list of thirty-six persons known, through the sleuthing of Jennings Evans, to have been lost to the Smith Island waters. You were remembered in that worship service on the CBF green, even though your names were, as we acknowledged, "known but to God."

Young men, why were you on the skipjack deck that morning, while the villagers were in their homes or at the church scarcely one hundred yards away? Had you spent the night out there? What was life like for you when your vessel was in port?

While the record is scanty, there is every reason to think that your remains were treated with care and respect, and that you were given a Christian burial by the good people of Drum Point. At the same time, you were interred beyond the pale, where your graves would not be cared for or remembered, where your connection with the living would be precarious. How rested you three with this, you young men who had courageously gone down to the sea in ships?

Do you three know that you were remembered here on Tylerton about eighty-five years after your deaths, and that this community's prayers surrendered the three of you, together with the other thirty-three Smith Island victims of the sea, into the loving care of the One?

Three sons of Africa: you whose names YHWH has inscribed upon the hands (Is 49:16): *Presente.*

A Petition for Grace

In the augmented words of the penitential rite of the Roman Catholic Mass:

> *I confess to almighty God, and to you, my brothers and sisters of color past, including Miriah Jacobs Parks, George Scott "Kidd" Lee, and you three unknown African American sailors brave, that we Christians of European origin have sinned against you through our own fault: in our thoughts and in our words, in what we have done, and in what we have failed to do; and I ask blessed Mary, ever virgin, all the angels and saints, and you our brothers and sisters of color here acknowledged as presente, to pray for us to the Lord our God. Amen.*

B. To You: Spirits of Violated Amerindians Past

How I Came to Be More Aware of You

My first contact with you here on Tylerton, during an early visit, was via the artifact collection of Big Alan Smith, just up the lane. Talismans, ceremonial pipes, clay vessels, and an awesome array of projectile points were among thousands of items crafted by you and uncovered by Alan, either in his crabbing scrape or during his sixty years of progging, which he elevated to an art form. In time, Alan would respond to our guests' interest in your story by generously loaning the Inn a sampler case of projectile points, including a stunning Clovis.

A second piece of my introduction to you was via a mid-decade guest who was deeply involved in the legal struggle over Kennewick Man, whose remains had been found in 1996 along the Columbia River in east Washington State, dating to about nine thousand years ago. This guest could hardly contain himself when he saw the sampler, and after educating everyone at the Inn, he managed to arrange a conversation with Big Alan on the ferry trip back to the mainland.

And then, a mind-opening day for Sharryl and myself at the National Museum of the American Indian on Washington D.C.'s mall, not long after it opened in 2004, further informed and deepened my curiosity about how the Bay space had become place for you.

My initial interest was in you who populated the Chesapeake basin upon initial contact with European explorers in the 1500s. Offended by the violation of your way of life by these, my fellow Christian representatives of European culture, I found myself wondering how I could extend both confession and hospitality to you across the centuries.

But as our decade at the Inn unfolded, my interest was deepened yet further by several factors:

- Our culture's inexorable throttling of the Bay's vitality set me to wondering how you had stewarded its bounty.
- My country's initiation of yet another war, in Iraq, found me musing about how some—for example, you of the Haudenosaunee Alliance to the north, in your "Great Law of Peace"—had sought to craft justice between tribes, genders, and strata within your clans in a manner unparalleled in nearly all of Europe at the time of first contact.
- My society's mania for consumption had me musing about what constituted the truly good life for your people.
- My country's effort to export its religion of materialism to all nations and evangelize all peoples to our parochial groupthink found me wishing that you could send missionaries from your time and way to us in ours.
- My desire to learn about you was expanding to include learning *from* you, and this shift drew me further back into the centuries and millennia preceding your contact with my European folk.

I only gradually became more aware that you had long been here—on this spot of elevated sediment on the continental shelf called Tylerton, before there was a Bay and it became an island—at least on seasonal hunting forays.

- I learned that you had been here many millennia before the great civilizations of the Tigris-Euphrates and Nile valleys, to say nothing of those of Jerusalem, Athens, and Rome. In fact, during our decade on the Crick, archaeologists were considering whether your duration in the Americas extended back *multiples* of the twelve thousand years long accepted.

- I learned that around 1500 CE your Inca kin along the western slope of the Andes in South America built arguably the planet's geographically largest empire at the time. I learned that the Central American region called Mesoamerica had earlier generated cultures rivaling the complexity and richness of those in contemporary Europe.

- I learned that your numbers across the Americas upon first European contact likely were in the scores of millions, that they were almost always underestimated because decimation by disease preceded the conquerors' censuses.

- I learned that the notion that you lived so lightly on the land that your moccasined footprints barely betrayed your presence was a European myth betraying our ignorance and condescension. Indeed, throughout the Western hemisphere you had repeatedly joined forces with nature, using fire, agriculture-triggered clearing, irrigation, urban construction, and monument-building to transform portions of the landscape into what I would identify as a "collaborative construct."

- In short, I learned that most of what I had thought about you former denizens of the mid-Atlantic was based on ignorance—and that I had many questions for you.

Queries Directed to You

But before my questions, a reminder about who is the interrogator, and the one confessing. Regarding time: you violated spirits of Amerindians past, strangers at my gate, I live in the twenty-first century, not those of your lives. And regarding space: while the geography of my life has not been entirely different from your own, it carries for me massive cognitive and cultural differences from yourselves. In short, I know that my questions are couched in categories and culture of my context, not yours. Although my questions might thus seem alien, I simply cannot address you from outside that context. And ask them I must. This gulf between us helps explain our estrangement—I behind the gate, you before—and is goad for my extending hospitality to you.

221

So to my queries:

- How did you, of the Clovis period or times before or since, hold the experience of being alive as humans? How did responses of awe, contentment, fear, and being at home in the cosmos find expression in your lives? Can you receive, understand, and respond to my question?

- What sustained you and gave you hope in this demanding and often inhospitable natural environment where ocean jousted with continent, you ensconced between?

- Did you marvel at the swans' musical arrival, as our star declined and the nights waxed cold? And that luminous box kite of Orion in the southern sky on a still and frigid night as the year slowed to a halt and then began to retrace its steps? What about the wild beauty of a squall near the opposite on the year's ellipse? Tell me, my brother and sister, is the way I love this place, the way its beauty brings pain to my chest, tears to my eyes, and joy to my heart, similar to the way you loved it?

- Part of what I know about you is that, amid your experiencing of the many—animals, plants, minerals, the sea, the heavens, your clan, and yourselves—there was an impulse toward centering, toward encompassment and unity, toward the One both amid and beyond the many. So I ask: was that centering somehow enhanced by being in this place, especially as the Bay was slowly being born, in a way similar to how it has been for me?

- Is there a chance that the vast trove of narratives, talismans, rituals—and what we today call cosmologies, tools, and aids—with which you recited, remembered, and celebrated what I inquire about—is there a chance that they may yet be retrieved and serve to enrich the entire human family, including myself?

When we come to your initial contact with us Europeans half a millennium ago, my questions wax more specific and more troubled:

- Our European diseases, to which you had little or no immunity—smallpox in particular—preceded our Conquistadors, missioners, fur traders, and settlers. They decimated your communities across the watershed, continent, and hemisphere with local mortalities up to 95 percent, predetermining the outcome in the conflict of cultures. While our instrumentality in this catastrophe was not generally intentional, we were its agents and thus bear some responsibility. What do I do with this knowledge?

- From what indigenous cosmologies did your responses unfold to my fellow Roman Catholic explorers, followed by Anglicans and Protestants, nearly all of them seeking to subdue and break Earth, extract her treasure, tame her wildness, establish dominion over her, and invoke the One in the sanctioning of a stance of enmity with her? Those of you who survived the vanguard of diseases: what did you think of our savage deity, whose representatives offered you a choice between quick physical death via gunpowder, blade, and fire, or incremental cultural death via exile or assimilation?

- Spirited Assateague maiden, later described by Capt'n Verrazano as "very beautiful and very tall," you of the "great anger . . . [and] loud shrieks": how did you manage to escape the captain's cohort of twenty men when they discovered your hiding place, kidnapped the boy in your charge, and took him back to France aboard the *Dauphine* in spring 1524? What did you make of my Christian co-religionists who would steal a young child as if he were a beaver pelt?

- Paquiquino, seventeen-year-old son of a chief living on what would be named Virginia's York River: what all did you endure during that decade, beginning in 1561, in which you were taken from your people and reinvented as Spaniard, Roman Catholic, accomplice, and trophy in the royal court, bearing the name "Don Luis"? How was it that during those years you went about correlating the Christian God of love celebrated by St. John of the Cross (your contemporary, whom you conceivably might have bumped into in España) with the rigidly stratified, exceedingly violent, and gold-driven culture of both old and new Spain?

- Proud Nanticoke warriors, you among those hunting and fishing on the isles separating Bay and sound, you formidable ones snagging in the memory of Capt'n John Smith in June of 1608: what did you think of our Christian religion as the decimated remnants of your proud people were first sequestered by the Maryland Assembly in 1704 on the Chiconi reservation on your river, and subsequently driven farther and farther north and west so that some of you were in Ontario in the late 1700s, others in Oklahoma in the late 1800s?

- You Piscataway on the Potomac to our west, you who came to share my faith via the efforts of Father Andrew White after the founding of the Maryland colony in 1634: how did you reconcile your relatively peaceful traditional ways and new commitment to the Prince of Peace with the Glorious Revolution (1688), which rendered your nascent Catholic faith illegal, and with your very survival at risk, finally drove you to emigration and a fearful alliance with your longtime nemesis, the Iroquois to the north?

- Did any of you wonder whether it was you who should be sending missioners to us? Did you wonder whether the cleavages in our mental and cultural constructs, between ourselves and the rest of creation, between our indentured or enslaved and our free or privileged, between our bodies (which we could have now) and our souls (which we could have later), were ruinous to all concerned? Even as you were being proselytized, could you have done other than wonder whether we were the savages and you the bearers of a more humble, reverential, and sustainable way of life?

- And finally, were any of my European sort known to you who viewed you as they viewed themselves: bearers of the *Imago Dei*? I know of Frs. Bartolomé de Las Casas (West Indies and Mexico) and Antonio Valdivieso (Nicaragua), sixteenth-century Dominican bishops, who gave their lives because they saw you as brothers and sisters; and I know something of the integrity of Fr. Andrew White, SJ who would be returned to England in chains in 1645 by Puritan rebels. Were there others in the Chesapeake basin such as these, whether Roman Catholic, Anglican, or Protestant?

First sons and daughters of the mid-Atlantic continental shelf: *Presente*.

A Petition for Grace

Again, in the augmented words of the Roman Catholic penitential rite:

> *I confess to almighty God, and to you, my Amerindian brothers and sisters of all ages past, that we Christians of European origin have sinned against you through our own fault: in our thoughts and in our words, in what we have done, and in what we have failed to do; and I ask blessed Mary, ever virgin, all the angels and saints, and you our Amerindian brothers and sisters here acknowledged as presente, to pray for us to the Lord our God. Amen.*

I have sought here to confess to you, violated spirits past, both African American and Amerindian, the sins of my people against you. I aspire to be a proxy for my own kind who wronged you, often amid Christian trappings, but of whose efforts to "expiate and redeem," to employ Abbot Kline's words, I have no knowledge.

Only after writing the above prayer do I realize more fully that, in including the last line of my Church's rite in this situation, I was asking you whose origins are in Africa and America, respectively, as well as the total company of those who have lived and died in my own community of faith, to petition the One *on our behalf* that we be forgiven. This realization, that I am asking your aid in our being forgiven for wronging you, has left me both surprised and shaken.

Now, still later, it is clear that I *do* want to ask you, all of you, to help us in asking forgiveness. I *need* to ask your help. You see, this petition on our behalf is for grace, not justice.

PART V
RECEIVING THE STRANGER WITHIN:
HOSPITALIER SELF-CARE

Having explored the art of hospitality in terms of the biblical image of the "stranger at the gate," I turn now to the well-being of the innkeeper—the hospitalier—in terms of this same image. Now, however, that "stranger at the gate" is *within*, not without. The stranger is the one within who is fearful of being alone or being with others, the one lured by the painted face of false joys or the lies of frenetic activity, the one vulnerable to slow starvation on sense-candy or intellect-toys. This time, the stranger at the gate, weary of the road and seeking home, is I. Or, to change both metaphor and grammatical mode: how do I the hospitalier, a long-distance runner, tend to the persistent need for hydration?

I was not blindsided by the challenges our Inn project thrust before the well-being of its innkeepers! Sharryl and I had learned about this the hard way in our early years at Davis House in Washington. Newly married, needing quality time together amidst a bustling house containing minimum private space, lacking external support as newcomers to the Capital, and old enough to know better than to ignore issues of self-care, we found ourselves not always voluntarily on a fast learning curve. It was not always pretty. Over the years we would discover, anecdotally as well as via statistical studies, that we had company in the guild. An example would be a 2002 study of B&B owner/operators attending the bi-annual conference of the Professional Association of Innkeepers International (PAII) that showed them reporting the highest level of emotional exhaustion among eight industries surveyed.

Of the two of us, I had particularly good reason to be careful about the issue of self-care. I came to innkeeping in my fiftieth year, having burned out in two earlier professional settings, both of them interesting, challenging, value-laden, and omnivorous. In addition to offering resources, motivation, and vision, the church affiliation in both cases provided a big-time hazard: it is challenging to take seriously, and yet hold lightly, work understood to be that of the One. Many earnest clergy and lay ecclesial workers have foundered on this reef. Thus I came to Tylerton not only aware of professional sand traps but also of personal vulnerabilities. And I came wondering whether the major personal investiture by Sharryl and myself, at *all* levels of this project—in contrast to being employed by others at Davis House—would only make my susceptibilities greater on the Crick.

In Part V, I both sketch out and reflect upon my grappling with the self-care issue across our decade in Tylerton. Carried over from the previous part, in addition to the metaphor of the stranger at the gate, is the relationship between the explicit or apparent (profession) and the implicit or deep-downness (vocation), a pivotal distinction throughout this study. I had the opportunity to explore this distinction when I addressed the November 2004 annual meeting of the Maryland Bed and Breakfast Association on the theme of "Wholeness and the Innkeeper."

At the same time, the profession/vocation distinction should be held lightly: it is a tool aiding the understanding, not a mirror of such tidy compartments in reality. The vocational is more a spiritual deepening of the professional than its opposite. Nor is the sequence of profession-followed-by-vocation as sharp in our experience as here portrayed. Yet across our decade, the importance for me of the vocational, as fulfilling the professional and beyond, was growing ever larger.

The Christian tradition is unequivocal in valuing the self and the care warranted for its nourishment. Altruism, understood in some quarters as love for all *except* the self, to say nothing of self-depreciation, is not a Christian virtue. Foundational here is the implicit valuing of the self in the creation of humankind in the *Imago Dei* (Gn 1:26–27), and especially in the theme of the Incarnation. When pressed by a lawyer, "Teacher, what shall I do to inherit eternal life?" Jesus challenged him to answer his own question from his knowledge of Judaic law. Jesus affirmed the response the lawyer gave: love of God with one's entire being, love of neighbor *as the self is loved* (Lk 10:25–28).

Love of neighbor and self, properly understood, is not a choice: these cannot be decided between. None less than St. Paul, amid his extraordinary missionary work, acknowledges the need for personal discipline, lest having preached to others he himself be found to be disqualified (1 Cor 9:27). Below and beyond all of the lesser reasons for self-care, there is in the biblical tradition that valuation bestowed by the One who is both Creator and Incarnator. The towering irony is that the model for love of self, after God and as neighbor, is the Incarnated of whom St. Paul wrote that "he poured himself out" for others (Phil 2:7, Ps 22:14).

Finally, by way of introduction, three comments about the Old French word "hospitalier," employed occasionally earlier, but prominent in the title of Part V. First, I conscripted this term for the innkeeper in part because of its symmetry vis-à-vis "hospitality" in the title of Part IV. Second, "hospitalier" communicates the spiritual vocation element in innkeeping so important to me, particularly as embodied in both the sixteenth-century Spanish saint John of God (1495-1550), inspirer of the founding of the Brothers Hospitallers religious order, and the probably legendary Julian the Hospitaller, patron of innkeepers and travelers.

Third, I acknowledge the unfortunate downside of the term "hospitalier." Forms of the term are used for the Knights of St. John, a "military religious order" in Crusader Palestine. I lived a block from one of their descendant institutions in East Jerusalem. While I consider the notion of a "military religious order" oxymoronic, I have chosen to employ "hospitalier" here for the first two reasons cited.

19. The Anatomy of Depletion

While innkeepers occasionally have exhausting physical work, particularly under the gun of long holiday weekends or systems crises, the chief hazard of the profession is its *relentlessness:* the recurring routines and patterns result in weariness, psychic wear and tear, and a fatigue of chronic or low-grade nature. Few days in and of themselves totally wipe you out; rather you are always on duty, and the 24/7 pattern is going on and on and on. "Running on fumes" is one of my phrases for how it can be, come August; "depletion" is another. Here I explore first the more identifiable physical exhaustion; then those deeper and more elusive levels for which I use the word "spirit"; and finally, tongue only partially in cheek, the profile of an enigmatic disorder that might be diagnosed as either madness or splendor.

A. Depletion of Body

The thirty-month renovation of Capt'n Howard and Miss Venie's house required hard physical work toward the goal of receiving guests by the Memorial Day of 1997. We moderately altered the floor plan on each of the first two stories. Most of the floors themselves we stripped and refinished or, with the bulk of the first story, completely replaced. Most ceilings we replaced or repainted, and every square foot of the gloomy wall paneling received three or four coats of paint. We had decided that the labor involved in schlepping the requisite amount of drywall across the water would be prohibitive.

And then there were the doors, a seemingly endless succession of original four-paneled doors, each encrusted with a slightly different history of nearly a century of coloration fads, each showcasing a palette of sundry whites scattered among perhaps a clotted cream, a lurid orange, or an institutional green. I waxed relentless: I hacked and scraped each back toward beauty.

We Become a B&B . . . &D

The final stretch of our renovation timetable was complicated by our own delinquency. We served up to ourselves a wicked curve ball but four months before opening, when our plan for providing guests with dinner imploded. That plan, ill-conceived in retrospect, was to address Tylerton's paucity of sit-down dinner options by subcontracting that meal to a village woman, package it as Smith Island cuisine with ambience, have it served at the Inn, and leave some money in the village.

More careful research proved it unworkable, for two reasons: it was not cost-effective to place said woman on salary (in lieu of picking crab), this whether or not there were guests at the inn; furthermore, our movable-feast notion had little prospect of passing muster with the Somerset County Health Department to whom we were accountable. Thus, in the January before opening, we were eyeballing the possibility of the entire project going down if we were unable to generate a workable alternative. In the end, we hastily obtained a restaurant license and managed a dearly fought compromise with health authorities regarding the extent of commercial kitchen equipment. Wishing neither to ask our urban middle-class clientele to brown-bag it, nor abort the entire project, we were left with no choice but to become a Bed & Breakfast . . . & Dinner.

Sharryl's culinary skills had never been the issue. We just had not wanted to add the dinner component to our already heavy responsibilities. The added tasks of provisioning and preparing for dinner were the major reasons why the Inn we opened was much more work-intensive than the one of which we had dreamed. Food service is never profitable on the scale at which we offered it, but we accepted essentially working on it for nothing, because there was no other way to pursue our dream.

In retrospect, this final twist, like the rest of the renovation phase, was demanding yet not insurmountable. Adrenaline ran high, and the remaining forays to Tylerton, interspersed with the brainstorming of the intervening month in the city, were packed with efficient accomplishment.

Juggling Further Renovating and Guests
However, once past the midpoint of our first season, we began to address heavy projects that we had bumped down the list in the earlier drive to open on schedule. In fact, if our Tylerton decade beginning with the opening can be likened to running a one-mile track event, Sharryl and I, having completed our dreaming and training, came out of the starting blocks sprinting. I spent much of two months during the far shoulder of our first season under the Inn, removing decades of tidal debris, re-pointing brick piers, reinforcing support beams, building up the elevation with bags of soil toted in from Salisbury, pouring footings, and laying cinder block to enclose the underside of the building. Much of this was amphibious work lying prone in mud or water, during which my mind might drift between Fellini movies I had seen and Dostoyevsky's *Notes from Underground*.

We inaugurated December 1997 by purchasing the adjacent lot immediately to the north, toward Tylerton's center. We wanted to create a buffer against encroachment on that flank, plus purchase was the only means of getting our hands on a sixty-foot house trailer earlier left for dead on that property. Our guests' view from the commode of Black Walnut Point's bathroom was dominated by what we euphemistically called the "great yellow slug." I, assuming the role of "Shiva the Destroyer," was joined by Sharryl and Fred Marshall, a salvaging waterman in his anecdotage, in successfully disappearing that roadkill before the feast of the Nativity. Tasks with results in such high definition are most gratifying!

Immediately after returning from visiting our children over that feast, I began renovating the third floor as our personal quarters. During the first two months of our initial season, Sharryl and I had rotated at night among unrented rooms, a practice nothing less than incompatible with long-term psychic survival. However, all four rooms had been rented nearly all of that first August. This was good financially, but forced us to sleep in the living room for eight nights, in the home of a nearby seasonal couple at least that many more. That August was hard, both on our sleep and our relationship. Hence the urgency regarding our third-floor quarters was ratcheted up.

After clearing the unfinished third-floor attic of generations of debris and vermin detritus, I proceeded to open parts of its three walls. One was for the beams for and door to a balcony off the gable which I would build. The other two were for windows to the north and south. I erected scaffolding outside the windows, and at Sharryl's insistence, tied myself to the naked rafters inside while working outside in the Bay's raging January.

I had the windows and door in, the inactive chimneys truncated to the attic floor, and was beginning to frame inside, when I was diagnosed with walking double pneumonia and airlifted to Salisbury by emergency helicopter at the end of March 1998. Although Sharryl and I began to sleep on the third floor in June of that year—amid materials, machines, and sawdust—it was not until the end of that calendar year that our third-floor renovation was complete and our situation stabilized somewhat.

During our first two seasons, Sharryl's existing joint pain grew more serious. Walking became increasingly painful, and our plan of inhabiting the third-floor quarters seemed jeopardized. Her condition, subsequently diagnosed as rheumatoid arthritis, was greatly aided by medication that removed virtually all of her limitation. During my heavy projects beneath and above the Inn in the early years, Sharryl provided two meals daily for guests and mostly prepared our four rooms (we had a part-time village housekeeper only during our last five seasons). Since the Inn was open nearly year-round early on, although with inconsistent census, guests were intermittently in the Inn even as we worked on these major "off-season" projects.

Yet More Extracurricular Projects
There would be other projects that required exhausting physical work and for which I was primarily responsible. Most arduous was cleaning up after hurricanes,

particularly Floyd (1999) and Isabel (2003). Although Isabel was the much more destructive of the two, Floyd struck before the Corps of Engineers' bulkhead was constructed, meaning that the village's extensive dock and shanty detritus was driven deep against the *Phragmites* wall well into our property by the northwest winds at high tide. All of this wreckage had to be broken into manageable pieces and then moved by handcart at least a quarter mile to Tylerton's burning area, a disposal M.O. like that of all of my other projects.

A physically difficult project after the completion of the new bulkhead in 2002 was construction of our new dock and canoe/kayak launching ramp, a project for which I had expert help. Months before, I had the salt-treated planks delivered to the Crisfield wharf. From there, a young waterman and I brought them to Tylerton on his overloaded workboat, aptly named *Young Salty*. He was being coached by his father on the VHF through much of our passage as we nervously monitored the accumulation of water entering through the scuppers of our low rider. That passage, on a December day grey and melancholic, was probably my closest brush with being on a sinking vessel.

Enter the Issue of Pace

In retrospect, in those first years, Sharryl and I were steadily getting ourselves in trouble with the race: there might not be enough left for the third quarter mile, to say nothing of the fourth! While we would chat about the matter, neither of us was fully aware how hard we were pushing ourselves. At the same time, we might roll our eyes at each other when a guest would comment that he or she wanted to open a B&B after retirement from working!

Yet, even as I write this near the end of the decade, it is difficult to see how the urgency of those early projects could have been handled much differently. There were major tasks that simply had to be completed. Hired help was either unavailable or financially prohibitive on our budget. I tended to be headstrong about wanting to do the work myself, and the adrenaline pump was still operative. For me more than Sharryl, the energy level in the first five years—both that available and that expended—differed sharply from that in the second.

One of my questions when we weighed purchasing the property was whether the envisioned physical work, relentless but hopefully not too heavy, was compatible with my age (56–66 during the actual decade) and diagnosed, although largely asymptomatic, medical condition: cardiomyopathy. In retrospect, the chances I took with several of the projects were inadvisable. My chronic but not life-threatening medical issues would require more attention during our final year, reinforcing our earlier decision to stop at ten.

B. Depletion of Spirit

With the possible exception of our first two seasons, the primary exhaustion, for both Sharryl and me, was not physical but emotional/psychological. I should note here that, throughout the decade, I of the two innkeepers spent the greater time with guests: meeting at the dock and orienting all arrivees, and serving porch duty that included serving and busing the tables while Sharryl was in the kitchen preparing meals. Furthermore, I tended to hang out with guests more, occasionally to the neglect of tasks needing attention. It is interesting that I repeatedly chose more interaction with guests, even while more vulnerable than Sharryl to social fatigue.

People-Exhaustion

I submit that Sharryl and I were a strong team, together bringing a complementarity of gifts, mutual support, a survival instinct for bucking up when the other was down, and usually a solid pattern of consensual decision-making on the project. But sometimes our bad days coincided, and the ferry *still* had to be met, the dinner *still* prepared, the demanding guest *still* treated with, at minimum, civility.

Sharryl found that she had less margin during a string of overcast days. Wind over *thirty mile*, especially but not only in winter, could really do a number on her. I tended to get tense with demanding guests or with the noise and unpredictability of young children whom we received the first half decade. Each of us found that the long day of provisioning on the mainland, especially when begun or ended with an anxious crossing, followed by preparing dinner for guests, could really have us exhausted by 10:00 PM.

It is interesting to speculate as to the broader contextual causes of psychological depletion. First, much would depend on who the guests were at a given time: certainly not all were created equal in that regard! A guest might be demanding, dismissively ignorant of village culture, very full of himself/herself, or simply sour that he or she had been sentenced by the companion to this end of the Earth. We quickly learned that recipients of gift certificates were often less enthusiastic about their visits than were the donors.

As indicated, Sharryl and I assumed an unwritten contract with our guests that entitled them to our respect, courtesy, consideration, and when needed, tolerance. But dutiful courtesy is almost always more exhausting than the kind that flows, and I would sometimes feel myself drifting toward not wanting to see another human being for a very long time. On such days, I would not likely be crooning Barbra Streisand's *People*.

Guests Who Became Our Friends

Guests who returned repeatedly and became our friends, in several cases dear friends, raised interesting issues. These good folks, while offering both friendship and sizable checks, the latter because they often came in fours or sixes for multiple nights, and multiple years, often related to us *a la* family in a way that crossed time, space, and familiarity boundaries important to our sanity. The fact that Sharryl and I often encouraged and enjoyed this altered ambience was no insurance that we would not end up being depleted by it.

Furthermore, unless such a party had bought the entire house, which some would, there would be first-time guests present as well, to whom we would relate differently. Some such visits of guest-friends were simultaneously very enjoyable and very exhausting for us. There probably is no resolution available to this quandary: friendship and love at whatever level always entail risk, loss of control, and, sooner or later, pain. We were, more often than not, grateful that we had the problem.

Depleted by Dynamics Outside the Inn

Occasionally, everything in the Inn was affected by something transpiring outside it. For example, our fifth season and the first part of the sixth were dominated by the U.S. Army Corps of Engineers' building of a new bulkhead, two thousand feet of barrier against drowning and erosion on the shores of Tylerton Island that face north, west (us), and south. This was a development of sheer grace, given the village's minuscule population and paucity of electoral votes!

Anyway, for a fifteen-month period, heavy tracked machinery went back and forth just outside our screened porch, reaching crescendos when meals were served with the pile driver near. That their machinery never took out our trellis on the lane seems, well, impossible. During precipitation, the lane past the Inn simply disappeared, with passage nigh impossible. That chapter's dust remnants in the crevasses of the Inn would be years in the extricating. During this period, Sharryl and I toyed with refunding deposits and closing the Inn for an interval, but in part because of the astonishing gameness of guests, we never did.

Once in a while, nearly everything possible went wrong at the macro level. October 25, 2005 remains in our memories as one of these "layered-crises" days. This was the fifth day that the village's waste treatment plant was down, the sanitation engineer having dictating that only "urgent" commode use was allowed. (This came but two months after a fortnight during which the village's water system incrementally died, with guests being issued plastic buckets with which to draw water from the "overboard" beyond the bulkhead for those same commodes.) That October 25 was also the confluence of the remnants of Hurricane Wilma and a nor'easter, resulting in tides reaching the cap of the bulkhead, putting nearly the entire village underwater. The innkeepers joined guests walking the bulkhead cap, a heavy plank but a foot wide, to the Market. A consequence of the storm's high winds was cancellation of the ferry's second run with two guests, dislodged by noon arrivees but unable to de-isle so as to make their San Francisco flight, needing to be billeted in the village. Oh, and the innkeepers were having a spirited marital snit. October 25 was, well, both memorable and forgettable.

At other times, we became snagged in interpersonal conflict among villagers, affecting our availability to guests. Contacts with villagers at the dock, in the Market or post office, or in the lanes would generally pump us up, and the town would always provide that fascinating tableau to which the vast majority of our guests were drawn. But occasionally, discord in the village managed to suck the energy out of the two of us, leaving us little margin.

And sometimes, of course, Sharryl and I simply had less to give guests for reasons having nothing to do with either guests or villagers. A difficult telephone conversation the previous evening with a family member, a dark dream during the night, the no-show of a guest with whom one of us had been too generous with the cancellation policy, or tension between the two of us—any of these, or a score of others, might leave me with less to bring to the guests in the Inn. And I, more prone to oscillating moods than Sharryl, might range from euphoria to misanthropy, at least interiorly, within a fairly short time. Since guests, and Sharryl, were constants in my life, I might play off on either one moods and dispositions having origins unrelated to them.

My Depletion Symptoms Set to Music

Over time, I began to note symptoms within myself of psychological depletion. My role as innkeeper, at least during the high season, was a highly verbal one, and that is where the fatigue might show up. I, a lifer regarding talking for a living, would have a kind of out-of-body experience in which I seemed to be listening to my own tapes, only from a distance. Occasionally one of the oft-asked questions would trigger switches to several tapes, which then became snarled, with the most bizarre combinations of words resulting. It was both relieving and disconcerting when no one seemed to notice the combinations of words probably unprecedented in the history of the cosmos. This experience was an indisputable evidence that beast fatigue was licking his chops in the corner of my psyche.

Or fatigue might find expression in whining. During perhaps season number four I would occasionally frighten Sharryl by emoting out loud in our quarters at the end of the day: "I'm exhausted and it's only June!" or, "I just don't enjoy this anymore." Or, "why can't we have an ordinary B&B where people just crash to sleep or whatever, and then are elsewhere the rest of the time?"

During my thirties, I became aware of a propensity within myself toward depression, making me vigilant regarding this danger throughout my subsequent life. Earlier I had often responded to darker moods by moving out among people. But that strategy required some tweaking at the Inn. As the decade proceeded, I became increasingly aware that terms like "psychological depletion" or "social fatigue" were but penultimate explanations at best; almost always there was something more fundamental that had to do with my interior life nearer to or at the center. This, of course, made these symptoms no less serious.

Perhaps the most amusing index of psychological depletion involved, not inappropriately, music, often as I entered the kitchen during table detail. If I was weary yet reasonably jovial, I might be yodeling "git along, little dogies," the latter my term of endearment, a pet name, for guests. Farther down the slope, I might transfer from porch to kitchen, singing the words of Emma Lazarus' poem:

> Give me your tired [they come here tired!],
> your poor [middle income, actually],
> Your huddled masses yearning to breathe free,
> The wretched refuse of your teeming [western] shore.
> Send these, the homeless, tempest-tost [in Tangier
> Sound] to me. . . .

A few steps lower on the musical fatigue index might have one of us launching into Marty Haugen's *Gather Us In,* often sung in our parish, especially these lyrics: "Gather us in—the rich and the haughty, gather us in—the proud and the strong . . . ," only with more colorful words substituted. And yet deeper down the slope? Well, I might be going about with clenched jaw trying not to glimpse the Christ in anyone, and certainly *not* singing.

2006: The Ultima Season

And then there was our last season, without doubt our most stressful. Basking amid the bouquets of nearly a decade of kudos, we were unprepared for the minuscule trickle of potential buyers interested in purchasing the Inn, either as an ongoing business— our preference—or a second home. We learned that, while a fine dinner before the pastel palette of the western sky amid stimulating conversation and imported spirits might elicit from guests words like "idyllic," "paradisiacal," and "Shangri La," they would not necessarily climb over each other to make our wonderful life their own.

Nor could we have known in early 2006 what was beginning to happen in the housing market and the economy in general.

In retrospect, the number of potential buyers was further winnowed by both the ratio of income to workload, and the risks of owning real estate two feet above sea level just off hurricane alley. Midway through that final season, Sharryl and I conceded that we may well have created something which would not survive us, and we opened ourselves fully to the possibility of selling the Inn as a second home.

In the end, after escrow period as well as mortgage closing in which many things that *could* have gone wrong actually *did*, the property was purchased by two splendid people from Kremmling, Colorado (elevation: 3,681 times our own!). The Inn of Silent Music lives on.

Now, into our retired lives, Sharryl and I occasionally muse about why our final season became so difficult. There were many factors: the 2006 real estate market was sagging and going to flat; I struggled with chronic health issues that intermittently had Sharryl operating the Inn alone; only in retrospect could it be known that the ominous 2006 hurricane predictions would not be realized, even though Ernesto gave us a big scare the last weekend we were open; and unlike previous seasons, we were now already looking ahead, thus finding it a bit more difficult to be fully present.

With all the uncertainty, it was difficult to know how, and how many times, to say goodbye to the dear people of Tylerton. All of this made us more vulnerable in the face of the wall-to-wall uncertainty that comes with the territory of any real estate/business sale. While I was disappointed that we had not handled the entire transition better, running the gauntlet of that final year did generate a greater clarity—a confirmation—that we were exhausted, and that a "ten," in addition to perfection, was *enough*!

C. A Bizarre Susceptibility: The "Isle Virus"

Among the many strange and exotic maladies afflicting folks in these parts, whether waterfolk or *fúrr-ners*, is the Isle Virus. I have never known it to be authenticated by a pathologist, but I know its most vulnerable victims to be tidewater types, particularly islanders with anatomical girth greater than the elevation. Rumor has it that the symptoms of the Isle Virus have been linked with those of locoism among the bovine on the western plains.

It's a Dirt Thing!

Anyway, the virus has a long incubation period, during which the victim is infused with a sense of well-being, occasionally euphoria, with even levitation occasionally reported. However, after perhaps several years, the symptoms of a second stage begin to appear: presumption of the isle as coterminous with reality; viewing the struggle against tide, that ubiquitous wolf at the door, as the moral equivalent of the war against terrorism; having nightmares populating one's bed with crustaceans; flirting with offering sacrifices to the savage deity Wind; etc. But there is one common strand in these virus cases: dirt. A visceral craving, an existential hunger for . . . dirt. Whereas on the mainland thoughts of the tender of heart in April turn to sentiments of love and fecundity, on Tylerton they turned to thoughts of . . . dirt. Elevation-enhancing dirt.

Sharryl may have already displayed symptoms of the Isle Virus shortly after our purchase of the property. August of 1997 was her first birthday in residence, and I should have been alerted when she asked that I give her, for her birthday, her heart's fondest desire: forty bags of dirt. In helping me unload the delivery from the ferry to my handcart, Capt'n Larry delivered a memorable monologue on the incomprehensibility of my judgment, after which he wagered as to the chances that he would soon give his wife Marge such a gift. Sharryl appeared to exhibit both surprise and pleasure when I presented my earthy offering.

Our celebration that August gave rise to an ongoing conversation about perhaps throwing a party in this otherwise dry paradise, a B.Y.O.B. affair where the terminal "B" would be understood as a bag of dirt. Needless to say, we would have had to invite mainland guests; inviting locals would only have served to rearrange the elevation-challenged terrain of Tylerton. I remember a tranquil winter evening, Sharryl and I each reading in the kitchen in our well-worn wicker chairs, when, exploding out of a P. D. James mystery, she exclaimed, "LeRoy, *LeRoy*, we live in a *fen!*" I'm sure it was the Virus! By the way, I never heard her call anyone in Tylerton a "dirt bag," at least not derogatorily.

Coveting Ma Margaret's Dirt

And then there was the passing of Ma Margaret Marshall, one of my dear friends. Sometimes I would bike over, bringing my guitar, and sing for her. More often, I or we would be received in her kitchen, former schoolhouse on (disappeared) Shanks Island just below the state line, where we would ply her with questions about the past. She was one piece of work: a splendid memory, great stories, but a refusal to drift across the line into gossip. One of the few people I have known who would look you in the eye and say, "I love you." Often. That, in the end, is irrefutable evidence of a good life.

In our seventh season Ma Margaret, in her ninety-third, went to the One. After grandson Capt'n Larry, himself already a grandfather—there were five generations for several years!—brought her back from the Crisfield mortuary on the ferry's stern, there was a joyful funeral service. Ma Margaret's daughter Mina had invited me to bring a brief tribute to her which I shared together with those of various others, after which she was committed to the ground—was it "dirt to dirt," or do I just remember it that way?—just outside the window by the choir loft.

Two days later—two days!—Sharryl and I were riding past Ma Margaret's grave, the pile of earth to the side still festooned with the remnants of innumerable bouquets celebrating her life. "What do you think," Sharryl began, her voice slipping into that more sensual range signing persuasion, "Might we try to get that dirt?" I responded with expansive indignation: "Sharryl, not only is this rank covetousness; it is also irreverence! Why, the body hasn't even had time to cool yet!"

Sharryl was not dissuaded, and would lobby me intermittently over our remaining seasons, surprising me that she did not try once more as we walked to the dock for the very last time. Thus, whenever we opted for Bugeye as we rode our bikes to church, I'd try to speed up as we passed the dirt. But on one occasion, I just lost it: "Just look at what's happening to us, Sharryl! The two of us are going crazy!" It was the Isle Virus, sometimes simply called Marsh Madness. Highly transmissible and potentially fatal, this terraphilic compulsion. I knew I would never again hear the words "from dirt to dirt" intoned on Tylerton without wondering if Sharryl and I, and our marriage, would survive its contagion.

The Gift of a Triaging Memory

To conclude on the matter of depletion, whether physical, psychological/emotional, or viral: the memory, it may be argued, is not an equal opportunity employer. Even though I worked intermittently across the decade with one form of depletion or another, to one extent or another, with the exception of the final season, I have had to dig hard to ferret out the more stressful particulars for this section.

What rather has risen to the surface, and remained there at a level disproportionate to the actual experience, has been the good, the beautiful, the nourishing, with a little of both the idiosyncratic and the scarcely believable, plus but a sliver of the disgusting thrown in. I do not fully understand that selection process, but I am not about to look this gift horse too hard in the mouth. I am grateful for my selective, my prophylactic, memory: it has been my friend seemingly looking out for my well-being, and I am counting on it from here on in.

20. Care at the Boundaries: Professional Competence

A discussion of the care of the hospitalier in the face of various stresses and pathogens begins here with the repository of wisdom that the guild of innkeeping has accumulated over the centuries. This is basic, common-sense counsel of the sort available to all in the trade. It is the level of self-care that might occasionally make it onto the agenda of the annual guild conference. I explore here four expressions of the profession's wisdom toward the end of sustaining the innkeeper—Private Space, Private Time, Reducing the Workload, and Having a Life.

A. Private Space

Sharryl and I had learned during our seven years at Davis House in Washington that boundaries between space private and common were absolutely essential to our survival and wholeness, even though the two of us sometimes disagreed about where those boundaries should be. These learnings were reinforced by research we did in the B&B literature during our Inn renovation. We were convinced that, with minor pre-opening floor plan modifications, and development of personal quarters on the third floor not long thereafter, the important common space/private space issues could be managed on the Crick property.

Showdown at the Parlor/Kitchen Interface

Two months after we opened, however, I made a unilateral decision to purchase French doors that I installed between the living room or parlor (common space) and the kitchen (generally private). Sharryl neither supported nor objected. So much for our hope that guests would respond to our metaphorical shocker fence, including a discrete "private" sign, particularly during the press of dinner preparation!

One draw on guests was the fact that the kitchen was site for the single-line telephone service into the Inn. (It would be two years before I installed our third-floor phone.) We asked guests to use the phone only in urgent situations, a policy that occasioned some tension with them as well as between the innkeepers. The growing proliferation of cell phones across our decade actually waxed rather than waned this issue: many could get nary a signal in our "end of the Earth" except, possibly, at the utility pole in front of the Market. However, the heightened expectation generated by cell phones would be redirected at the innkeepers. Our efforts in both advertising and conversations with guests to spin "remote unreachability" as romantic ambience were roundly lauded in the abstract but repeatedly disregarded in the concrete.

Less than six months after I installed the French doors, I was fully engaged in the third-floor project. In retrospect, it is difficult to exaggerate the importance of completing the latter for the well-being of the hospitaliers. Although passage from the kitchen, our principal work area, to our third-floor quarters had us moving through the living room and the central staircase, both common areas, once we reached the third floor stairway we were largely isolated from guests. Only after the third floor became our personal quarters and business center during our third season were we able to focus attention on the next front: setting aside private *time* on an intentional basis.

"I'm Outta Here!"

The issues of space seemed pivotal in the saga of a couple we came to know during our renovation who owned a lovely B&B in Crisfield. Having put four years into a meticulous restoration of a grand Victorian with seven bedroom/bath options, they appeared to be majestically steaming along at the top of their game. They were in all respects a class act, and we learned much from them, both before and after they closed.

In the course of a lovely morning as their day-guests just prior to our own opening, we learned that, after but four seasons of receiving guests, they would soon be closing. As the two of them walked and talked us through every cranny of their mint-condition operation, I tried to understand why these two charming, sharp, and seemingly healthy hospitaliers were calling it quits sooner than anyone expected, themselves included. Indeed, I found their ratio of years of renovation (four) to inn-keeping (four) unnerving.

As the morning wore on, I began to notice things. First, the two had no staff, most unusual in an inn the size of theirs. The woman, who prepared all the rooms (he the bathrooms), was a perfectionist, probably dispositionally unable to delegate. Second, the physical separation between private and common space appeared diaphanous, and it was apparent that their own private quarters, like ours the first season, had been nomadic. Third, their shared generosity and, especially in her case, gregariousness, suggested that they would go far out of their way to please guests, including spending much time with them. Fourth, and relatedly, they alluded to numerous guests becoming their personal friends, a claim we found most credible.

At the end of the morning, I found myself less surprised that after four years they had found themselves exhausted. I wondered whether they had not gotten swallowed up in the rush of having all of these fascinating guests, some of them long since their friends, and then actually getting paid for their own rich social life!

Upon returning home, Sharryl and I discussed the implications for ourselves of what we had learned. Later, during one of this couple's several visits as guests at our Inn—always with friends whom they had come to know in theirs—yet more clarification emerged. The woman's comment on our porch one evening said it all: "One morning, I looked at all of those people in my kitchen, and I said, 'I'm outta here!'" Neither Sharryl's mother nor mine raised dumb children, and the lesson our friends embodied—an extraordinarily important one, in retrospect—was not lost on us.

The space issue, of course, assumes a different configuration in every inn, and there was only so much tweaking we could do with the hand we had acquired. In a relatively small building like our own, with single staircase, not all problems of separation and floor plan can be solved. For example, we never were able to devise an access to our washer/dryer/utility room under the stairs without going through the Sassafras Hammock guest room and bath. Many an incorrigibly curious guest finally *had* to ask us where in the world it was. Like life in general, a decade in an inn is lived forwards, not backwards, so we had to address private space concerns within the confines of the hand we had been dealt.

The Race Is Less to the Swift than the Paced

But the setting off of innkeepers' quarters where we were not casually accessible to guests was *nonnegotiable*. Some innkeepers get greedy in their choice between another revenue-producing room and a better solution to privacy needs. The wrong decision here is one for which we pay dearly! Sharryl and I were fortunate that, when converting one guest room at the decade midpoint into an additional bathroom (thus being able to offer a private bath with each of our three rooms) plus gaining some storage space, we were nearly able to recoup our previous income. The crucial value here, as in nearly everything else in our trade, is sustainability: the race is a marathon, not a sprint; it is less to the swift than the paced.

A concluding comment regarding the word "space." In the discussion of "construct" in chapter 8, space was understood as the raw material which, engaged by the visitor's imagination within the context of existing cultural memory/narrative, can be transformed into "place." I use the term "private space" here solely in that raw material sense. The issue here is that a space/time-tethered occupation like innkeeping requires breathing space, time-out space, simple extent in three dimensions, room to roam, where demand and obligation are largely checked at the door. Not the perfect space, not qualitative space, not *the* space, just some extension shielded from the tether of duty, functionally speaking an isle St. Kitts, at least virtually. Of course, such private space can become a place—witness our third-floor balcony—but that is the issue of chapter 8, not this one. Space, as in "private space," has in fact a single criterion: it must offer the possibility of disengagement. It is space cleared out and dedicated to un-use.

B. Private Time

My days at the Inn of Silent Music always began at 6:00 AM when I would set out stout coffee and tea options on the porch for guests. The workday generally ended shortly before 10:00 PM when the kitchen had been cleaned following dinner, the table set for breakfast, and the flags brought in. (We had seasonal banners flying from the four Victorian porch posts, a large Maryland state flag from the balcony above.) It was self-evident from the outset that we needed to block out and protect significant time away from Inn responsibilities during that sixteen-hour interval, and the third-floor renovation made it possible for us to actualize that commitment. Although we often would retreat to the third floor together, it was almost always with the understanding that one or the other of us had the phone and the infrequent knock at the third-floor door, thus completely freeing the other.

Sharryl often began her downtime around 2:30 PM, after returning from the social whirl of the Tylerton post office and the stop at a crab shanty and/or the Drum Point Market. She would often read fiction, an activity both restful and powerful in transporting her to an alternative reality. Or, phoneless, she would work with her beautiful flowers, an activity which might have her just outside a porch full of guests, and yet far, far away in one of the chief joys of her life.

If I did not board my skiff during my downtime, I might journal, read, or do non-innkeeping work at the computer, including this manuscript, at least on the shoulders of the season. Even when events swallowed up our personal time on a given day, as when guests both arrived and/or departed on each of the two ferry runs, it was restorative to know that our downtime would be there again the next day.

The Wedding of Freedom and Form

A huge lever in protecting some private time at the Inn was the relatively predictable pattern of daily events. The ferry arrived from Crisfield around 1:15 PM and again at 5:45 PM. Except for the few guests (under 5 percent) who arrived on their own craft, and a few more I had to pick up in North End with my skiff, having arrived there from the Bay's western shore, arrivees would appear only at those two times. Sharryl and I smiled about how few walk-ins we had.

Although the phone was almost always a tether for one or the other of us, we could plan blocks of time between the end of the breakfast cleanup (c. 10:30 AM) and the beginning of dinner preparation (c. 4:15 PM). And, unlike Davis House, where we periodically had 3:00 AM arrivals via Dulles on red-eyes from places like New Delhi, here we were able to sleep all night.

The issues raised by time were not unlike those about space: structure could become an ally, and the instructuring of each of these dimensions liberating. Gestalt, rather than the enemy of freedom, could become its necessary collaborator, its sidekick.

But opportunity is not yet fulfillment, nor do private space and/or time necessarily run to respite. The possibility always existed that I could emerge from three hours on the third floor, having never left either the time or space of the Inn. Thus I sometimes selected particularly absorbing downtime activities—music, fiction, and spirituality come to mind—precisely lest, whether via intention or carelessness, I end up with a sixteen-hour Inn day. The availability of *external* time and space needed to be complemented with an *internal* separation as well. The urgency of being fully present in the downtime now—not in this morning's past or tonight's future—is central here. Innkeeping has been a good tutorial for this value.

Issue: Using Guests to Meet Personal Needs

In retrospect, I suspect that I spent slightly less time with guests, outside of meals, with each passing season. Awareness of self-depletion was part of this trajectory, and reduction of the *gung ho* coefficient closely bundled to it. There were times when my desire to continue enjoying most of our guests most of the time had me monitoring how much I was with them—I did it less, perhaps to do it better, and longer. While I would sometimes go to the porch because I was somewhat down and drawn to an interesting person out there, I was wary of crossing into common space for reasons of my own needs. A visa for such crossings was not part of our implicit contract. Periodically, I would grow weary of both guests' questions and my own stories, and then shy away from settings where these tended to surface.

In a manner closely analogous to space, the principal glory of private time for me was its disengagement, its exemption, however brief, from the relentless tide that was the life of the Inn.

C. Innkeeping Smarter: The Decade's Chronicle

During our second off-season (1998–1999), numerous major projects yet before us, Sharryl and I initiated an informal annual review of the season completed. Following this came the tweaking of our operation for the season ahead in the interest of greater efficiency, wholeness, and sanity. Our occupancy had doubled that second season, and would nearly do so again the third, and we began to have more fiscal room for playing with pace in the interest of sustainability.

Early Tweakings

That third season (1999), the Inn was open but ten months, as we were finding our stride not only regarding family obligations but also the need for greater self-care, including retreats, recreational travel, and periodic removal from Smith Island entirely. The length of our Inn season would stabilize at seven-and-a-half months (April through mid-November) for our last three seasons. This incremental movement toward a shorter season had multiple parents: our desire to be with family more; our need of a respite from Tylerton's tether; the volatility of the Bay's winter weather (including the possibility of being sequestered here by wind or ice and/or reduced ferry schedule); and the moral aspects of inducing the public onto the Sound between Thanksgiving and the Vernal Equinox.

We also made decisions that reduced our work per guest. In our fourth season (2000), we began requiring a two-night minimum stay on all holiday weekends, a decision we extended to all weekends in 2001. This change, in addition to reducing room preparation on Saturdays (when I was with my Carmelite fraternity in Salisbury a day each month), also protected desirable two-night openings for those desiring the full weekend.

The Issue of Young Children

As we neared the midpoint of the decade, we began to accept children only age twelve and above. Part of this decision was driven by the modest size of the Inn. Babies crying at night and children running up and down the stairs could often be heard in adjacent spaces. The importance of this issue grew as our clientele increasingly was constituted of urban professionals working too hard and badly in need of rest, persons explicitly drawn by the words "silent" in our name, "remote" in our brochure.

Earlier, we had accepted families of two adults and two children in our Black Walnut Point room, meaning our common spaces were even more strained. And there was also the safety issue. Early on, I had watched in mute horror from the porch as a hyperactive two-year-old motored to the end of the dock before the father, preoccupied in the lane, raced out to scoop him up just in time. I never forgot that experience.

But there was another issue in the policy change regarding children, and it was my own. I found the tempo and noise level generated by children to be stressful. I had long known myself to be less a child person than an adult one, and the first years at the Inn confirmed that. Sharryl, an early childhood education professional, would sometimes smile at me noting that I had obviously never been a kindergarten teacher in that I had difficulty multitasking. My greater stress level at hosting children at the

Inn than adults was another indication of this. I discovered that my management of stress as an innkeeper was largely calibrated for adults.

As the seasons passed and we became more experienced, confident, and unflappable, I could handle almost whatever came down the pike with adults. It wasn't easy for me to admit that children upset this calibration, this during the very period when I was becoming a grandfather for the second time. But that is what happened. Sharryl supported this policy change, despite the fact that the issue was not ours so much as mine.

Decisions in the Race's Second Half

Over Christmas in the off-season following our fifth year (2001), the midpoint of our decade, we enjoyed a three-week pilgrimage to Italy—Siena and Assisi. We returned having made two more change decisions.

First, we converted our fourth, smallest, and least-rented room to a bathroom so that we could offer three rooms, each now with private bath. During our first half decade, we had had beds for a maximum of nine guests, a number too large for the common areas such as the living room and porch. The crowded conditions became more pressing on the two shoulders of the season, when weather drove the serving of both breakfast and dinner into the kitchen. The fact that most of our guests were in the building much of their visit had also brought pressure on our common areas.

Second, in the spring of our sixth season (2002), we hired a local woman to help with room preparation for two hours three mornings a week, a change that benefited Sharryl in particular. The person we hired, Joan Corbin, in addition to repeatedly providing perspective on Tylerton for guests and innkeepers alike, helped to embody the vocation understanding of hospitality.

The famous eight-layer Smith Island cake is a treat we wanted to serve as often as every second dinner. To further reduce our labor, in the 2003 season, our seventh, we began to purchase these cakes from women of Tylerton. This decision, which reduced the baking Sharryl had been doing, would also enhance drama on the porch as the cake would routinely be delivered via golf cart by its baker shortly before the meal was served. Also that year, Sharryl became *persona non grata* in the kitchen before 8:15 AM on penalty of being de-isled.

Our eighth season (2004) found us tweaking our operation in yet more ways. First, in the interests of protecting Sunday as a day of at least some rest and increasing the chances of morning worship with Tylertonians, we stopped receiving one-night reservations for Sunday night. Second, both my work station at the end of our dock and I retired from filleting rockfish for the dinner table after a seven-year career, in favor of near-octogenarian Waverly Evans, a decision which left me with more relief than guilt. And third, while continuing to meet all arriving guests at the ferry with the luggage cart, my previous practice of escorting all of them back as well when they left became optional.

We approached our final season confident—the winter had generated our highest off-season reservation total ever—with full intentions of enjoying the last dance. We were, fortunately, shielded from knowledge of how difficult that last one would be.

The Issue of In-Season Respite

A comment about two self-care options for brief rest amid the season: closing the Inn or hiring staff allowing us to absent ourselves. On various occasions during the second half of our decade, Sharryl and I, for reasons of respite, would simply block out the last day within an approaching month or two-week period not yet reserved. But interestingly, this proved unsatisfactory as a policy, this for several reasons.

First, a single day away from guests, necessarily including preparation for the next arrivees, resulted more in income loss than either rest or disengagement. And we generally judged the blocking out of two contiguous days during high season to be financially unwise. Second, whenever we blocked out a day, a four-day reservation request for two across that block was liable to appear, and we, always after consultation, would generally accept it. This decision was made for reasons other than greed; having to supplement Inn income from other sources to make a living did make us cautious about losing multiday reservations.

A second possibility—hiring someone to cover while we removed ourselves— was also financially problematic. The one occasion when we did this across a four-day Labor Day weekend for an out-of-state family wedding required the entire income generated for staff remuneration. In addition, we were not sure that the arrangement had been fair to either staff or the guests.

In retrospect, the trajectory of these sundry tweakings appears to have offset the two interrelated curves of our aging and subsiding adrenaline. Having broken out of the blocks in 1997 in a sprint, we had, in the interest of survival, learned much about pacing and cadence in the second and third quarters. I have little doubt that this incremental recalibration across the decade was what gave us just enough fumes in the tank to absorb the unforeseen demands of the final season. In a profession where more than a few crash and burn, I think that Sharryl and I, all things considered from a safe perch beyond the finish line, just managed to pluck victory from the jaws of defeat.

D. Having a Life

Perhaps more important to the wholeness of the innkeeper than either space or time issues, or even rendering the operation more efficient, was having a rich and satisfying life *apart* from the job. Such a personal and interpersonal life provides a pole that—in oscillation with work, whether across an off-season or in an August moment—offers nurturing distance and diversion, allowing the innkeeper to return refreshed after an interval. It is in the interest of my well-being *as an innkeeper*—to say nothing of my roles as spouse, father, grandfather, person of faith, neighbor, friend, and citizen— that my profession *not* be the Earth and sky. Stated otherwise, it is paradoxically in the interest of my survival as both innkeeper and person that I not strive to succeed in the business *at any cost*.

This appeal for balance, realism, and humility rooted in self-knowledge should be part of the boilerplate wisdom of the professional hospitality guild, not viewed as esoterica or prerogative of the spiritually elite. Unfortunately, because it shows up only indirectly on the bottom line—and show up it does!—work/life balance gets inadequate attention in the hospitality fraternities, and then too often halfheartedly. Here again, the surrendering of issues with profound ethical and spiritual dimensions to the vagaries of the marketplace reflects a grossly inadequate understanding of the meaning of being human. For direction and support regarding such matters, innkeepers need to look without the guild, or more likely within themselves.

It is my conviction that while this "Having a Life" theme flows back and forth across the profession/vocation interface, it is rooted primarily in the latter. That it is neglected in the professional guild means that Sharryl and I here were largely on our own. In some aspects of self-care, she and I worked collaboratively; in other respects, each soloed. For all of these reasons, I address the theme of the nurturing of this hospitalier primarily in terms of vocation. In fact, an alternative title for the remaining chapters of Part V might be "Having an Actual Life."

21. Care at the Center: Vocational/Spiritual Wholeness

Self-care, even for anchorites and other recluses, has social components. And it is in one's sociocultural existence that the fruits of self-care are chiefly evidenced. In few settings is this more self-evident than with innkeepers. Thus, some might have addressed self-care by emphasizing personal support provided the innkeeper by players in that social context—for example, the co-innkeeper/spouse, family members and friends, the host community, the episodic interaction with guests both new and not so new, one's faith community. That I write chapters 21 through 27 with a focus on one's own care of self is to presuppose rather than to disregard this rich list of caregivers without. Pervasive in this entire book is a sense of indebtedness to each collective support named.

A. The Self Is Where the Buck Stops

And yet, self-care at the center is a profoundly personal matter, linked with self-knowledge, the identification and excision of false satisfactions and attachments, the urgency of intentionality and commitment, and the astonishing inimitableness that is each person. The person's journey to the center and one's DNA or fingerprints share a uniqueness that is both scary and the object of wonder. Thus, the "stranger at the gate" in Part V is the one within, the one too awaiting attentiveness, valuing, compassion, and yes, hospitality. This one also can drift into disillusionment and despair, having found no room in the inn of his own life. This one's preciousness is neither less nor more than that of any stranger encountered without, but the circle of responsibility and agency here is much smaller. Careless failure to pursue self-care with intentionality is probably as high among innkeepers as in the general population.

In the scheme of things, each of us is primarily responsible for the wholeness of our self, and this requires proactive, not merely reactive, efforts. Just as basic as the truth that we do not make ourselves whole is that we are nevertheless the moral agents primarily responsible for allowing, or not allowing, this gift to be given us. Assuming the vast webbed interconnectedness, the profound and nonnegotiable *betweenness* of human life, each of us nevertheless is a place of aloneness, a place where one *solus* is agent, chooser, will-er. Taking Jesus' words about the Great Commandment (Lk 10:25–28) as our guide, our reason to be is neither reducible to, nor possible without, loving care of the self.

It is difficult to conceive of wholeness, whether for the innkeeper or anyone else, where some intentionality is not given to this lonely task in which central responsibility cannot be shifted to another. In the remaining six chapters of Part V I discuss as many areas of vocational self-care, quite aware that the onus is on myself as agent: self-care is a buck that cannot be passed.

Finally, by way of introduction, care of the self at the center should never be merely subsumed under a heading such as "Ten Ways to Outfox Burnout" or "Depletion Self-Inoculation for Dummies." Utility is surely but a tertiary reason for addressing a matter that gets at our basic understandings of what it means to be human.

At the same time, the spiritual life—whether its definitive metaphor be journey to the center, ascent of the mountain, or preparation for the dark night—does not occur in a vacuum. The practical matter of personal survival *is* also an argument for self-care. In a word: the rigors of innkeeping have heightened for me the practical urgency of this interior journey, even while other reasons for it remain dominant.

B. An Overview of This Hospitalier's Self-Care

The following chapters address six ways in which the nurturing of this hospitalier has taken place:

Chapter 22: Nurture Via Care of the Body
Chapter 23: Nurture Via Nature's Beauty
Chapter 24: Nurture Via (Audible) Classical Music
Chapter 25: Nurture Via Tylerton's "Class Meeting"
Chapter 26: Nurture Via Spiritual Disciplines
Chapter 27: Nurture Via the Monastery of Aging

22. Nurture Via Care of the Body

The care of the body, as we often belatedly discover, involves a whole lot more than we expected. For those of the Christian tradition, with its anchor in Bethlehem and Incarnation, the sacred preciousness of the corporeal is nonnegotiable. The belief that in the enfleshment of the One a splendor has been laid bare in all nature and physicality—from the galaxies to the subatomic quarks and everything in between, including human beings—has profound implications for the care of the human body, and of course the entire natural environment.

When St. Paul refers to the human body as the "temple" of the One's Spirit (1 Cor 6:19), he is merely pushing out one of the innumerable sides of the meaning of divine visitation in Bethlehem in the Christian faith tradition. A disembodied spirituality, whether now or in the Greater Life, is foreign to the Christian faith. Bethlehem has rendered embodiment nonnegotiable. Rather than merely *having* bodies—to say nothing of the notions of either briefly *borrowing* bodies, or devoting our lives to *escaping* their confinement—biblical faith teaches that we are as much inspirited bodies as we are embodied spirits. In Bethlehem, the One has self-bound to the creation, including its materiality; for Christians, this embrace is understood as irrevocable. Mortal life is too short a time to sound the depths of what all this means, including the significance of our own embodiment.

A. Physical Exercise

Sharryl and I had used the 1995–1997 Inn renovation period to put in place several exercise decisions germane to care of the body. Although in the relatively prosperous 1990s many Tylertonians had ascended to golf carts, we chose not to join this further reduction of opportunity for exercise. We also chose not to partake in the lamentable invasion of dilapidated undersized pickup trucks in the second half of our decade. While respecting the need of a graying population to move beyond the bicycles and walking of an earlier time, we were recurringly uneasy at how the use of powered vehicles further reduced the already cramped exercise options presented by the size of Tylerton Island.

During the 2003 off-season, Sharryl and I began a pattern of vigorous walking with weights to a video, four half hours a week. Although this began with a group of village women on the second floor of the firehouse, the onset of the crabbing season in May left the two of us to exercise alone. We then transferred to the church basement, which was cooler in the summer. We maintained this pattern year-round until health issues tripped me up, well into our final season.

Our decision not to purchase a golf cart also meant that I transported all of the decade's garbage and other refuse to the collection cage at the back harbor a quarter mile away via bicycle, handcart in tow. Throughout the decade, my responsibilities included escorting guests from the ferry to the Inn—frequently four round-trips daily, until the eighth season—and I enjoyed it. Generally attired in my uniform of shorts, tank-top, and sandals, I found the sun, wind, and exercise to be a pleasant part of a typical day. Beyond that, I thrived on the pedestrian life and its bantering in the lanes and on the dock.

B. Diet

Food was another issue where Sharryl and I sought to distance ourselves from some village patterns. Eating is a really big deal in Tylerton, whether at the groaning tables in the church basement and fire hall or in private homes. In fact, I have mused about whether the strong abstinence position on alcohol has not resulted in a compensatory orality, consisting of smokin' (males), eatin', and yarnin', in the latter two cases savorily.

On one occasion, when Sharryl returned from Ladies Aid, I inquired as to the fare. "The main dish was cut-up chicken with a block of butter, a cup of sour cream, a can of cream of chicken soup, and a package of Stove Top stuffing, this served with mashed potatoes and mashed sweet potatoes, together with a seven-layer salad with a cup of mayonnaise." And dessert? "Several kinds of cheesecake." The fact that pervasive obesity in the village is taking a terrible toll in numerous joint replacements, with nearly half the permanent residents diabetic, is not unrelated to the dietary, or exercise, patterns.

Unfortunately, I brought to the Inn project dietary patterns less robust than those for exercise. I found it difficult being around meal preparation, service, and cleanup twice a day, and struggled with my weight intermittently during the decade as I had throughout much of my adult life. Although I always prepared the oatmeal breakfast for the two of us, Sharryl did the preponderance of the cooking, and she cooked most healthily, shielding me somewhat from myself. I would concede that the bricks which I here hurl at some of the self-evidently poor dietary patterns in Tylerton are delivered via the arm of one who lives in a well-windowed house.

C. The Alcohol Issue

During virtually all of our decade, a glass of wine and a "happy [half] hour" were shoehorned in somewhere in the late afternoon. It was time that Sharryl and I had together in the kitchen, the French doors closed, before the dinner push began. However, near the end of our seventh season I stopped using alcohol, first for personal and then medical reasons, both of which could be subsumed under self-care.

While Sharryl, never intemperate, would continue the pattern, I had become less sure what was controlling what, and mounted the wagon as a kind of penance. I suspect that isolated islanders everywhere are vulnerable to alcohol abuse—Smith's non-church population would serve to support that hypothesis, an abuse with which I also had flirted. The decision to reverse my lifelong dispositional preference for *via media* over total avoidance turned out in this case to be enormously freeing. My change did mean, however, that Sharryl and I needed to be more intentional about our daily shared hiatus in time.

Incidentally, anti-alcoholic zealotry, particularly the kind present in the Tylerton congregation, was not the spur of my personal decision. Across the decade, I had observed the way in which spirits would often catalyze interaction both before and during dinner, how the initiative of offering to share a packed-in bottle of wine could transform the social dynamics at a table. I did not find it necessary to proselytize others to my lately found abstinent wisdom.

At the same time, I was gaining the impression that our guests did not represent a true cross-section of either the American population or the spectrum of its alcohol use/abuse. When we opened, I would not have expected that across the decade I would be able to count on the fingers of but *one hand* the episodes when alcohol abuse had become problematic among guests at the inn.

23. Nurture Via Nature's Beauty

Sharryl and my initial forays into Smith Island's nature during our pre-purchase honeymoon, much of it via canoe, were generated by both great curiosity regarding a topography simply off the scale of our previous experience and a tendency to lock on to its haunting siren of serenity. Our August of 1994, not yet encumbered with the decision of the following month, had a carefree and lilting character about it. We would sometimes take a picnic and canoe into the salt marsh, tying up wherever impulse dictated, or just drift with King Tide in a gut, crick, channel, or canal totally removed from any evidence of civilization. It was a most intoxicating experience for us urbanites, and the way it made us feel about ourselves, each other, and just being alive would not be insignificant in the life-changing decision bearing down on us at the end of that month.

A. OK, So Her Beauty *Did* Seduce Me!

In my introduction to Part III, on "place" as metaphor, I sought to contrast Richard Nelson's emphasis in his *The Island Within* on the import of loving deeply *a* place, *whatever* place, *any* place, with my own experience of being quite improbably seduced by the inimitable—albeit severe, understated, and vertically challenged—qualities of this one *particular* place, Tylerton.

Now, having mused further about what has spiritually nourished me across the decade, that contrast appears less sharp. Granted, the lady's beauty is unconventional, judged by the values of the culture's runways and silver screens; hers is the sort that required time to grow on me. And even then, rather than *Vogue* beauty, she is the sort for whom one needs to acquire a taste. Yet she, the isle, is beautiful. Admittedly there was in the affair some *eros*: love not indifferent to the attractiveness of the other.

Is there not something about the beautiful way everything is—the entire cosmos, from the Initial Ignition through all of its subsequent unfoldings—that lures us to respond with love and not merely knowledge? Isn't this love at least partly *eros*, a response to beauty which engages the heart and body at least as much as the mind? Isn't this the case especially if one has domiciled for a time with the possibility that the entire cosmic saga is one grand love story, from the Original Overture to the writing of this sentence, and beyond?

Is there not a distant analogue between how we know the One only as the fruit of having responded in kind, however brokenly, to that One's Love, and the view that one can only know a place by loving it? And is not *eros*, that response to the beauty in the other, operative in both cases? Yes, I was musing about parallels between my experiencing of a place and my experiencing the One, and the way in which both beauty and love seemed to be a part of each experience.

While I thought I had loved other places before, it had usually been their historical/cultural ethos that had enamored me, and then but for a season. While historical culture was also part of the Tylerton package, I discovered that culture to be amazingly attuned to, and an actual part of, the natural place. No mere peg on which to hang historical events, did not the Tylerton I came to love turn out to be some green and vital crystal whose haunting silent siren was seducing me to look down into her? And did she not thus become for me a stumbled-upon peephole offering glimpses into the kaleidoscopic mystery, the Mystery, of all that is?

As first love is prone to do, I sought to read and hear everything I could find about her, Tylerton and her environs. I became interested in her flora and her fauna, her geological and estuarial history, her vulnerabilities and catastrophes, her strengths and triumphs. And as with all love, first or ripe, I wanted to be with her. To use the words of *The Song of Songs*, "While I was asleep, my heart was awake" (Sg 5:2). As early as when Sharryl and I were moving into the purchase process in late 1994, it was all beginning to feel like an *affaire de coeur*.

B. My Fifteen-Horse Magic Carpet

Late in the summer of our opening season, just before my amphibious descent into darkness beneath the house, I purchased a used sixteen-foot skiff and fifteen-horsepower Yamaha outboard motor from a North End waterman whose sixteen-year-old had graduated to more powerful and less boring things. It proved to be a magical carpet!

Rendezvous on Swan Island

That first autumn, when our guests were only intermittent, Sharryl and I would occasionally clear a late afternoon, board the skiff, and take a picnic, including a discrete bottle of wine, to a sandy beach on the Bayside's Swan Island above North End. There, gazing west toward Maryland's Point Lookout to the right, Virginia's Smith Point upland to the left, we'd watch the sun easing down into the Potomac between them, perhaps the silhouette of an oceanic tanker floating above the horizon against a variegated sky.

It wasn't hard for us to feel the explorer's tug and, for an infatuated moment, swear off landlubbing forever. There was something about the Bay's beauty, Swan my perch, that made me simply feel wonderful. All my reading and research, the years of winter evenings in the Drum Point Market with the men, flow into that feeling. But centrally, it comes down to what the five gates of my sensorium let in, and then activate beyond themselves. I would sometimes pinch myself or weep for joy out there on the isle, whether Swan, Tylerton, or whatever. No, I had not loved a place so before, not like this.

Huck Finn on the Mississippi

After some scary misadventures in which, failing to read the tide and almost catapulting myself into the marsh by running hard aground, I became marginally proficient at knowing how much draft I had in various passages in the tidal cycle. Smith Island today being a lace-work of erosion-cut pieces sometimes only inches above sea level, the possibilities for exploring in a given moment are endless. Thirty minutes later, the tide rising or falling, a whole different set of possibilities presents itself. I enjoyed calling to Sharryl as I bolted for the dock to exploit a fifteen-minute hiatus, "I'm off to the Commonwealth!"—the Virginia state line cuts through the southern part of Smith, less than a mile to the south.

Part of the rush of being on the water was the complete disconnect from utility: doing something and, especially, being some*place*, for the sheer joy of it all! I would sometimes think of myself as an overly ripe Huck Finn a-boomin' down the Mississippi on the raft, Big Jim at my side. When our grandson Jacob came on his annual week-long visit from Atlanta, he was Huck, I Big Jim. Or we would do our own take on "Captain and Commander": he, the captain, in his best ten-year-old bellow, would let go with "Hard to port!" or "Bring me *abouuuuut!*" while I, dutiful helmsman, would comply with "Ay, ay, sir!" A magic carpet that skiff was for the two of us!

But the real kicker, the *ultima,* was that I could head out on an impulse, on an absolute whim. Traveling to Salisbury from the Inn might take in excess of two full hours, on three kinds of conveyance, preceded by two days of planning and list-making. But if I could shoehorn a few minutes open before setting tables on the porch I could be gone, cutting through the late afternoon slants of sunlight, heading for Fishin' Crick or Peach Orchard Point, Amen Corner or Merlin Gut, before I had time to know better. And the only critters out there were my delightfully non-human kin!

The sun, wind, and splashing water working my body; the profusion of birds wheeling above and around; the near total absence of any vestige human; the tiller comfortable in my hand while negotiating the cross-seas coming in from West Africa; and the road ahead created *ex nihilo,* wherever in the next moment I choose it to be: I may never have, nor ever again know, freedom so nakedly, so sensually, so purely, so joyfully! Ah, at least momentary deliverance from the memorized life!

I kept the skiff in unsheltered moorage in front of the Inn, where it could safely swing from the bow in winds up to fifty mile from a freestanding pile I had driven for that purpose. The craft would have been safer in the protected back harbor a quarter mile away, where I had kept it before the bulkhead was completed, but junkets from back there were both less frequent and impulsive. You see, while one cannot schedule the spontaneous or serendipitous (to say nothing of the numinous), one can nevertheless prepare the way for it. One can create the conditions under which it is more likely to spark into being. And, yes! Living on the Crick had that preparation written all over it!

Voyage into the Sun

I remember a late Sunday afternoon in mid-November early in the new century, the long season having ended with the 3:30 PM ferry departure but an hour or so before. I was on the front porch celebrating with a Friday newspaper a guest had left for me, intermittently glancing up to track Sol's descent through complex levels of clouds out over the Potomac. Suddenly our star broke clear into the remaining narrow gap over Hog Neck. The perfectly still water between the horizon and me exploded into fiery and burnished brass. And my entire being cried "yes!"

In minutes I was speeding through the now rapidly cooling damp air, aiming the skiff's proud prow directly into that line of fire igniting the water all the way to the suspended globe of fire which energizes our life at the speed of light, and in the process coming close to hitting the land mass opposite! Only after the inferno behind every last window in Tylerton's houses behind me was extinguished as Sol's last sliver surrendered to the Potomac, did I return to the porch, my dated paper, and now compounded contentment. The thrill would not soon subside as I reveled in the fact that, living in this place, I had both the agency and the opportunity to do that, and on an impulse!

C. Sharryl and Her Floral Companions

I learned in myriad ways that beauty is its own nourishment, healing, and empowerment. For Sharryl, that was no less so than with me, only her particulars, in addition to the interior design of the Inn and presentation of food, tended to center in flora she sought to shield from the ravages of depraved salinity and pestilential wind. The machinations of that debauched duo drove her to tactics previously unknown: I once found her trying to restore our wetlands to its status as "lawn" with our Shop-Vac! And yet, it was that very wet and wild desert, or the pots and half-barrels of dirt raised above it, which she caused to bloom, and very little of it seemed to feel like work to her. Sharryl's flowers' canticle of praise consisted simply of being what they were created to be.

I think it not exaggeration to say that Sharryl might not have reached ten without her floral support group. And while my worthy opponent King Tide might have a surprise for me around the next bend of Indian Crick or Sheep Pen Gut in our ongoing three-dimensional chess game, Sharryl's blooms extended only consideration to her. And after dealing with guests, tide, wind, and me all day, Sharryl was profoundly grateful for that prelapsarian harmony.

D. "The dearest freshness deep down things"

But while this accolade to beauty requires nothing more, more there is. As the cycle of our decade rotated, I became more and more aware of the translucency of what I continued to find so beautiful. The economy and elegance of the great egret feeding just beyond the bulkhead at low tide; the consternation *in perpetua* of the kingfisher up on the utility wire; the magic of a night ferry trip from North End during Advent with Tylerton, decked out in thousands of lights for Christmas like some regal lady, softly stepping out of the fog for her curtsy; the young waterman in the deep rose-hued dusk of a Saturday night passing before the Inn to the soft throbbing of the engine, his lady joy on the engine housing at his side; going to sleep on a foggy windless November night to the melancholic contrabassoon sonata of the leviathans' foghorns in the Susquehanna channel six miles away: any of these experiences, or a thousand others, has brought tears to the eye, ache to the heart, joy and gratitude to the spirit.

In a world often driving people to hand-wringing over why so many things go wrong, a practice from which I am not exempt, it has been a spiritual rush a thousand times over to have occasional experiences in which *everything* is pristine, harmonic, and luminous of the One, at least momentarily, at least for that "one brief shining moment." The hardest week is awarded a kind of lilting perspective with the Saturday night suspicion that one did a heck of a lot of marveling during that seven. One person's beauty is not necessarily that of another, but what is nonnegotiable is the urgency of allowing oneself to be seized by that which is her beauty and to be drawn by it where "lives the dearest freshness deep down things," in the words of poet Gerard Manley Hopkins.

It is probably only human to desire to seize and prolong indefinitely such moments of indescribable joy, especially when they provide inkling of much more than what the senses capture. Peter the disciple speaks for me when, amid the ecstasy of the transfiguration of the Christ, flanked by heroes Moses and Elijah, he blurts out that he will forthwith build domiciles for each of the three (Mt 17:1–13). I understand how he wanted to render permanent what in this life is always ephemeral, for I too have often wanted to bronze the rainbow or bottle a moment of indescribable synchronicity. It is a temptation not entirely unlike that of idolatry: rendering one's fealty via that which one can clutch, control, *possess*.

But so much beauty, particularly in the case of music, is held in but a moment, for it is *event*, a gift that can only be extended in time in the ache of memory, the gratitude of heart. Like Moses' insistence to the ancient Israelites that they gather manna *each day,* rather than hoard it across time (Ex 16), on the Crick I came to see more clearly that sufficient to the day is the beauty thereof. The suspicion that I was becoming increasingly receptive to, and more moved by, beauty's fleeting episodes as they unfolded around me, was itself repeatedly a source of both hope and joy.

E. Shiva Attired in Beauty

But sometimes, nurture via nature's beauty can become quite complicated. Witness Gustavus Adolphus, a feline whom familiarity trimmed first to Gustav and then, a tip of the hat to T. S. Eliot and Andrew Lloyd Webber, simply Gus (although never "Aspara*gus*"). I had given him to my ethnically Swedish bride for her birthday the year of our nuptials. Before we adopted him at Davis House, Gus had survived an adolescence and early adulthood on the streets of Washington, D.C., and with time, I concluded that he viewed my unconditional love ethic with a sneer.

Anyway, he was large, orange-blond, and might himself have passed for Nordic or Scandinavian. Indisputably, he was a creature of surpassing beauty, and well he knew it. After we moved to the Crick, where he was a kept cat, not fraternizing with the local riffraff, I lovingly built various passages for him so that he could have his way about the Inn, as well as unnerve guests by passing mysteriously through walls. There is no doubt in my mind that a properly reared pet—a hearth- or lap-cat in this case, or the beautiful black lab of our successors—could bring pleasure and ambience to guests in the Inn. And the challenges of allergies among guests were probably not insurmountable. There at the bottom of the stairs each morning, Gus would be waiting for me, ever inscrutably sphinx-like, as I descended to feed him and make coffee for guests, in that order.

Yes, I would have hung in there with Gus, I with my unconditional love ethic, had he not lacerated our stuffed chairs, sometimes after first carefully securing my full attention. Nor was he above drawing blood when intervention ensued. Finally, Gus was who he was, a street cat, an incorrigible who carried. Alas, while a Nordic god without, indisputably of the unblessed within; on the exterior immaculately groomed, the interior of the unwashed; malevolence dressed to the nines, he did not reform. Nor did I, I suppose, in that by his later years, thinking of Shiva the Destroyer when I saw him and musing about his marauding genes, I was alternately euphoric and perplexed that the One had unfolded such a mixed piece of work. By the time the end came, I knew him for what he was: a rapacious Viking cat!

Yes, Gus did constitute for me a kind of faith crisis padding in on cat's paws. In mid-decade, he mercifully went the way of all flesh—no, it was natural causes, the fruit, no doubt, of his earlier self-absorbed and debauched life. I turned the other cheek by agreeing to dig his burial chamber under our patio's statue of St. Francis, one who would also have been in over his head with Gus. Over his enshrouded remains Sharryl read from Judith Viorst's *The Tenth Good Thing about Barney*. Other words, appropriate, some even true, were solemnly intoned before the two of us left the back patio and returned to our guests.

Anyway, the marriage was providentially spared, and keeping the Inn clean of cat hair became a long-term possibility. Since I live with the hope that the scale of the One's salvation is cosmic, is it not possible that a macro healing of what the novelist Walker Percy called the "human predicament" ("original sin," in churchese) could also include the likes of a feline who had lived his entire life crossing wits with those same humans? Even though an *Imago Dei* he surely *warn't*?

But sometimes in recent years, perhaps a frigid winter evening, when we are reading in our wicker chairs in the closed-off kitchen, Mozart piping at my side, I think I see him out of the corner of my eye. He is sitting there on the chair's arm, as oft he would, looking me full in the face, and surely behind those great yellow eyes, conniving yet new calamities . . . drat it, I miss him! I miss the handsome son-of-a-bitch, rapacious Viking or no! I miss the not inconsiderable joy he brought to my life, and all—O, how I hate this to concede!—by simply being the critter the One unfolded him to be! I mean, what's the big deal about another six hundred bucks for a new sofa? If Anne Morrow Lindbergh was right when she wrote that "it is only framed in space that beauty blooms," then Gus by his very being generated such an ambulating space, one implying an invitation: "Here, experience *this*!"

I conclude this chapter on nurture via nature's beauty by quoting Wendell Berry's "The Peace of Wild Things." Few writers have a feel for the spiritually nurturing powers of nature as does he. For a time the following graced the hall bulletin board of the Inn:

> *When despair for the world grows in me / and I wake in the night at the least sound / in fear of what my life and my children's live may be, / I go and lie down where the wood drake / rests in his beauty on the water, and the great heron feeds. / I come into the peace of wild things / who do not tax their lives with forethought / of grief. I come into the presence of still water. / And I feel above me the day-blind stars / waiting with their light. For a time / I rest in the grace of the world, and am free.*

24. Nurture Via (Audible) Classical Music

During our Tylerton decade, "music," beginning with our establishment's handle, served as the metaphor of choice. That choice extends through this work as well, my earlier olfactory foray notwithstanding. And implicit in this metaphor is the auditory as the sense gate of choice, in contrast, for example, to the visual employed in much literature, mystical and otherwise.

The harmonic of nature's vast orchestra, the very atmosphere this book breathes, is but the most obvious example here of the metaphorical centrality of "music." There are innumerable others:

- the cadence of the haunting calls of tundra swans, seemingly arriving from another galaxy;
- the *adagio* of an August afternoon, humid, hot, and *slick cam*, and I humming "Summertime" from George Gershwin's *Porgy and Bess*;
- the fierce opera of storm replete with cymbals, all manner of stage effects, a raft of notes well above the diva's register, a downright scary plotline, a climactic cacophony;
- the bassoon of the waterman's workboat engine as he slowly churns right to left in front of the Inn in the predawn darkness;
- the first notes of the improvisation, *jammin'*, by a half dozen guests randomly tossed together in close quarters for a weekend;
- the occasional near-perfect silence, like the lauded composition of John Cage (1912-92) entitled *4'33"*: silent music for piano in three movements, stuck on "repeat."

A. Loving Music Before Loving Its Meaning

But the Inn of Silent Music was also the arena for much non-metaphorical, *auditory* music. As with Dostoyevsky's distinction massaged throughout this book, between that experienced via the sensorium (the thing) and that in its depth to which it is translucent (its meaning), I must, and most assuredly do in this case, love the thing itself. Although the rich metaphorical depth of music pervades this work, there was first, and abidingly, the simply love of the thing in and of itself. And love the thing I do, music both classical and auditory, and with passion. What would the cosmos, the miracle of music silenced, be like? I recall the saline sting in my core as Sharryl, re-entering the Inn after having engaged four day-trippers in the lane, three of them deaf, mused pensively, "I suppose for them the music is *always* silent . . ."

My Own Musical Fantasy

By September in life's arc, one has earned the right to move beyond trendy eclecticism and the homogenization of all things, and embrace publicly and shamelessly that which one has truly come to love. I love classical music that way, notwithstanding the extent to which it has been disproportionately male, white, programmed, and elitist (aesthetic, social, or economical, occasionally to the point of snootiness). In the august kingdom of the arts, where there is no king, I consider this music to be queen, some of her offerings the greatest art ever crafted. Indeed, I rank music near the very summit of humankind's expressions of aspiration beyond ourselves.

And to erase any remaining uncertainty as to my bias, my ultimate fantasy would be to conduct before a large and full house—Washington, D.C.'s National Cathedral, perhaps—a work of opera, but one spilling over into a bevy of adjacent genres including *liturgy*. It would be my musical composition, set to a libretto from the Apocalypse (from chapters 4, 5, 19–22), and including the following: a massive orchestra at the crossing in concert with the cathedral organ; a chorus of a thousand (*a la* Mahler's Symphony No. 8) ensconced in the arms and balconies of the transept; a children's choral ensemble filling the choir back into the apse; multiple levels of cantilevered sets rotating out above the chancel; phalanxes of dancers moving up the nave and aisles; more brass in the three balconies; incense ascending into the dimness; and, joining the baritone and the contralto before the screen, a tenor simply divine as the Lamb who is the Lamp (Apoc 21:23). Possible title: "*Agnus Dei*: A Resplendency" (Heb 1:3). Paul Manz's Advent anthem, "E'en So, Lord Jesus, Quickly Come," hints of the text, spirit and beauty, but not scale or magnitude, of my fantasy.

I could imagine no greater expression of natural human powers exercising co-creatorship: participating in the prerogatives of the Creator. While my experience of both the audible and metaphorical power of music is not limited to the classical genre (as will become more apparent in Part VI), this is for me music's center of gravity, and unless otherwise qualified, determines how I use the term "music" here.

The Rest of the Music Repertoire

As a child, my mother having earlier introduced me simultaneously to her milk and gospel songs, I would wonder about music not yet written because its composers had died prematurely, songs nevertheless, of course, known to the One. Only the particulars changed during first the popular music of my pubescence, and then the belated discovery of classical music in my midthirties.

What did the ripe works of Mozart (1756–91), Schubert (1797–1828), or Mendelssohn (1809–1847) sound like? Or Symphony no. 16, whether Beethoven (1770–1827), Bruckner (1824–96), Mahler, or Shostakovich? It was almost as if the musical pieces were eternally preexistent, outside of time, stored in some Platonic celestial repository with some of them getting stolen now and then, Promethius-style, and, like fire, stingily shared with us mortals. Perhaps music was simply too precious, too much ethereal visitor from another less foibled and more sunnied realm, to be subject to the coarse vagaries of contingency and mortality.

Yet for example, while Mozart died long before he could pilfer his full allocation, nothing is ultimately lost! No, it is all *still there*, piping and bowing and sounding in the mind and heart of the Maestro! And among the tertiary gifts of the Greater Life would be the prospect of hearing for the first time all of that gorgeous, *not-yet-stolen* music!

As I look back on this curious pattern, I detect a proleptic hint of the role music would occupy throughout my later life. The theologian Karl Barth (1886–1968) mused that, when relaxing together with family, the One listens to Mozart. I would trump that: the *ripe* Mozart the One listens to, awash with joy before this lush and confirming fruit of the risky option toward freedom for the cosmos.

B. Music in the Inn

It is clear that this music factor was involved in our very decision to craft and open an Inn. The surviving list of pros and cons we began to assemble in the days following our tour of the Morgan house in late August of 1994 had in the plus column the strong NPR station in Salisbury, Maryland (WSCL), which features classical music. We had been impressed with the efforts at Salisbury University to establish the station in 1987 for what would always be a limited listenership.

Music in Tylerton's History

That station was critical, because we knew from the outset that living on the island would largely preclude attending live concerts. Frequenting the Kennedy Center's cheap seats was over. It was also self-evident that, with the exception of a North End waterman who was an opera aficionado, Smith Islanders' tastes for music were different from our own. In Tylerton, as in the Mennonite Brethren congregation of my youth, most music is gospel songs imported from another era. That music was, nevertheless, very important to the islanders was always symbolized for me by the durable "The Lord is my strength and my song" (Ps 118:14) bumper sticker through-out the decade on the golf cart of Fred Marshall, himself the steward of a beautiful tenor voice.

According to Adam Wallace, the revival movement led by Joshua Thomas in the early nineteenth century in time expressed itself in the burning of fiddles and the "sweet strains of their catgut," the forbidding of "levity and frolicking," and the silencing of the culture's own musical tradition before 1807. It was only in the first decade of the twentieth century that a musical instrument, a pedal organ in the Union church in The Pines, appeared. I lamented the indigenous music outside the church that was lost with the burning of the fiddles. And my vote for the Inn project would have been more ambivalent had WSCL-FM in Salisbury, and its signal across the Sound, not existed.

Throughout our decade, I would play recorded classical music during dinner preparation and dining, whether in the kitchen on the shoulders of the season, or on the porch before the setting sun during high season. I might put on Schubert's string quartets, flute music with James Galway, concerti of Joaquín Rodrigo (1901–99), or perhaps Yo-Yo Ma on cello playing Johann Sebastian Bach (1685–1750). I prudently kept my distance from music choral, atonal, or overtly religious; requiems, operas, Gregorian chant, oratorios, and serial music never made the cut.

Occasional Discordant Notes

I would sometimes play a piece because I hoped it would be appreciated by a par-ticular guest, a gesture on occasion warmly received. But there were other nights, such as the one when I sought to honor a young Russian couple with a dinner tribute to their country's inimitable musical tradition by playing a selection of well-known works of Tchaikovsky (1840–1893), Rachmaninoff (1873–1943), and Prokofiev (1891–1953)—only to learn after the meal that the two had heard nothing they rec-ognized. On occasion, I would have qualms about whether I was descending into either proselytizing or highbrow Muzak, but gamely I forged on.

There was, unfortunately, a casualty for Sharryl in this mingling of music with meal. For reasons beyond me, she would forever identify *Minuet* by Boccherini (1743–1805) with hearts of romaine salad with lemon, olive oil, and freshly grated parmesan; Mendelssohn's *Italian Symphony* with rockfish with tarragon and fennel; *Nocturne for Strings* by Borodin (1833–1887) with chocolate mousse tart with fresh raspberries. On more than one occasion, during off-season motoring, the beginning of one of these pieces on the radio, or any one of various others, would cause her either to salivate, or, more likely, become mildly indisposed. Precious Pavlovian moments in the truck, these.

C. Music in the Perch

But it was primarily in our third-floor quarters that audible music catered sustenance and joy, either at day's end when dinner was over and we were alone, or during one of our infrequent open days. Although I wanted to hear the audible sort more often than did Sharryl, there were many times when what we listened to was all the richer because we did so together.

Room Preparation to Puccini

I remember a glorious April morning when Sharryl related to me how an NPR segment that morning on the cherry blossoms in Washington had concluded with the aria "Si, Mi Chiamano Mimi" from *La Bohème* by Giacomo Puccini (1858–1924). I turned our recording way up on the third floor, programming "repeat," opened the doors, and we prepared the rooms and bathrooms on the second floor with every corner filled with the glory of Mimi's "love, of Spring, of dreams and visions and the things that have poetic names."

And then in our final off-season, a time when manuscript rewrites dominated my days, Sharryl and I subscribed to Netflix for evenings at the cinema. Half of our orders were for music: opera, concerts, and musical theater. These we would hear and see, wedged into our third-floor gable—even popcorn!—before our computer screen. And there, ambience provided by the wind buffeting and flexing the building, we seethed at the malevolent Scarpia in Puccini's *Tosca*, exulted in the triumph of *amore* or whatever in *Carmen* by Georges Bizet (1838–1875), and wept in the face of either Rodolfo's loss in the finale of *La Bohème* or Calaf's aria "Nessen Dorma" in *Turendot*, also by Puccini. "Nessen Dorma" ("No One Sleeps"), inexplicably our aria of choice, would seem an odd favorite in an establishment specializing in sleeping, but that it was. Part of my interest in opera, particularly a work like *Parsifal* by Richard Wagner (1813–1883), grows out of the way in which the union of time-bound music with space-bound visual, plastic, and dramatic arts—dance pirouetting betwixt—can beget progeny which I experience as seemingly boundless.

Music: Beauty Tethered in Time

Finally, however, audible classical music was *my* music, and I relished it in my solitude. I listened to it whenever I could, monitored music developments in the *New York Times* and via Amazon.com. I always looked forward to a longer ride in the truck when I traveled, because I could listen to an entire work straight through on what was our best sound system. I rarely allowed a growing personal collection of recordings to pull me too far from our rich FM station, a tutorial broadening and deepening my experience. Like travel, good music has the power to transport, to take one to distant places, whether exotic and lush or dark and disturbing, without leaving one's confines. Uncannily suited it is as travel agent for one tethered to a journey in place.

But music, like the other arts, is also tethered, confined within finitude, limitedness, of which space and time are but the two most obvious expressions. If the visual and plastic arts are tethered in space, music is sequestered in time. Like the glimpse of a bald eagle just before it alights in its nest on Sassafras Hammock, the rainbow in the fleeting equipoise of light and droplets, or the mysterious green flash at sunset (which successfully eluded me), music is all about moments. True, its composition, like prose and poetry, involves writing, but its performance is happening, event, rather than object possessed. And if music is akin to rainbows, it is not the sort I can bronze.

Music is the exotic fruit of that sequesterment in time; within that narrow cell it blooms riotously. Indeed, music is the transformation of that tetheredness, that confinement, that bondage, into rhapsody. The gestalt within which music's freedom pipes is time. There is a dark irony in the *Quartet for the End of Time* by Olivier Messiaen (1908–1992), composed and premiered in a Nazi prison camp on a theme from the Apocalypse ("time shall no longer be" [Apoc 10:6]), for it could only be performed prior to the end of time. Music, at least the sort familiar to us, outside of time is an oxymoron.

What has all this to do with the notion that music is in some special way spiritually evocative and nurturing? Why include classical music under "Vocational Wholeness" rather than clumped with surfing for sports scores or reading Michael Connelly mysteries under a catchall "relaxation" heading in the "Professional Competence" section? Indeed, what is the very meaning of the words "music can be spiritually evocative"? I am not confident that I can adequately respond to these questions, for my challenge is to make the case for a profoundly trans-verbal phenomenon with mere words. However, my toolbox here contains but words, so here goes.

D. Spiritually Nurturing Music: *Via Negativa*

I begin to address this question of the meaning of "spiritually nurturing music" in the easier way, the *via negativa*: eliminating three possible responses, all of which are finally unsatisfactory.

A Triad of Nonstarters

First, to restate a prior point: music as metaphor of that beyond itself is *not* a Trojan horse designed to showcase "religious" or "sacred" music, whether composed for the church in genres such as oratorio, musical settings of the Ordinary of the Mass, or choral settings of holy text. I make this point despite the fact that much of my favorite music can be so categorized.

Second, my argument is *not* a side window through which I hope to sneak a notion of *performer*—I am less clear regarding *composers*—of a certain moral or spiritual ilk. Good music requires good musicians, not necessarily good persons—even though I suppose I would prefer all musicians in my Camelot, like all non-musicians, to be morally good and spiritually sensitive persons. But generating spiritually nurturing music goes far beyond merely getting good persons together.

And third, my citing music as "spiritually nurturing" is *not* the proclamation of some new musical messiah, one whose works encompass the totality of reality including the Reigning in full flower.

Mahler as Musical Messiah?

On the heels of that denial, I nevertheless acknowledge the efforts of one like Gustav Mahler. Words attributed to him regarding his Third Symphony might well represent a summation of his life's output: "Imagine a work so large that it mirrors the entire world. One is only an instrument the universe plays upon!" For me, Mahler's symphonies stand alone, possibly joined only by those of Shostakovich, in being both Promethean constructs erected on the scale of nothing less than the cosmos itself, and stunning, indeed, *bleeding*, efforts to sound the depths of the tragedy of the human situation in the modern era.

Allow me to elaborate on this third nonstarter. After a passionate fling with Mahler's music in my midforties, I mounted the wagon: what with the hangovers, I could no longer afford to drink him straight. His sonar canvasses reflected the fierce integrity with which he looked into the bleak face of early modernity, and sometimes what I heard bore me down. Alas, his integrity was not enough.

However, during our decade on the Crick, I began listening to Mahler again, but now only sipping. Now he seemed to be piping the existential questions to which the Lover, pointed to by the Bethlehemite and John of the Cross alike, was the answer. While I was now aware that Mahler's music would not, *could not,* bring me home, listening to it midrace in the 1980s had helped me discover that I was of a homing sort, and that I wanted, above all else, to move in that direction.

I live with the hope that, in the Greater Life, the music of Gustav Mahler, perhaps more stranger at the gate than musical messiah in his abbreviated life, will yet be completed. Until then, Karl Barth's celebration of Mozart notwithstanding, I have yet to identify *the* musical messiah.

E. Spiritually Nurturing Music: *Via Positiva*

Having cited three understandings of the phrase "music as spiritually nurturing" that finally are *not* adequate, allow me to take a modest step in the *via positiva* direction. Music is a language—but, given its vocabulary in the piping, a quite different language, particularly for those of us who fill much of our lives with words and ideas.

Music can include words and ideas also, of course. *The Dream of Gerontius* by Edward Elgar (1857–1934), for example, is the setting to music of the words of a poem by John Henry Newman (1801–1890); the work as a whole represents a distinct point of view regarding the themes of life, death, and the Greater Life. Furthermore, a treatise could be written on both the acoustical physics of the vibrating sound waves set in motion by the performance of this piece and the physiological process whereby these waves become sound in the ear and are actually heard. In fact, the structure or vehicle of music, on surface examination, may be accounted for *solely* in terms of mathematics and physics, reason and science!

Yet I am always amazed at how little the knowledge of such matters has in common with actually experiencing the piece performed, how the music itself seems to billow into flowered fields under, above, and beyond any of this data or analysis. The reading, piping, bowing, and singing of music entail the majority of the sensorium, but this is but the vestibule.

More than the Physics of Its Vehicle

What music really is involves something almost miraculous that is slipping around under the mathematics and physics on the surface. Music is qualitatively and immeasurably more than the sum of these parts—it is a miracle, in which less is actually more. It is almost as if music were a sacrament, like bread or wine or water, an outward sign (albeit received by the *auditory* portal) via which is transfused a mysterious power, one for which the vehicle's data cannot account. (Note that the Latin *sacramentum* is a translation of the Greek *mysterion*.)

Music points toward and opens the way to the spiritually evocative in part because it constantly reminds us of the narrowness of the portals through which we more ordinarily receive from outside ourselves. Music stretches those portals, it forces them to open more widely, and for those recognizing only what can be experienced via the sensorium and the intellect, it can iconoclastically shatter those portals.

What does the logical positivist, one restricting the meaningfulness of statements to what can pass through the sensorium portal, do with the majestic organ music of Charles-Marie Widor (1844–1937)? What does the devotee of scientism, one restricting reality to that which can be verified via the scientific method, do with the aching beauty of Richard Wagner's *Siegfried Idyll*? Are these pieces mere physical sound? Noise? Are they not "miracle," at least in the sense of being outside the grids insisted upon by such hearers?

Music as Window into Life's Open-Endedness

And this is the point: music is a constant reminder that reality is immeasurably more rich and encompassing than what our thoughts, words, and systems can demarcate. Music, like the sudden chanting of a Sanskrit poem amid cocktail party banter, is ever reminder that our sensorial dialect is not the only language, that our common tools do not gain us access into all the corners of what *is,* and that there is more, more, *always* more.

In short, for those giving it careful attention, music is self-transcending; it hints of dimensions infrequently visited, faculties not commonly exercised, places not otherwise known to be. This does not yet bring us all the way home to spiritual evocativeness, but it does break open encapsulated universes, relaxes retentively dogmatic certitudes, and allows the plot to thicken.

F. Music as Beautiful, Truthful, and Good

Beauty

Sometimes I image music's self-transcending *modus operandi* in terms of the solar flares of our local star. Music's most obvious flare, one receivable without filter, is beauty—exquisite, sometimes palpable, often bearing but never requiring meaning beyond itself—and for some, hinting of Beauty itself. Sometimes that beauty finds expression in sheer playful delight, like a child in toyland, as in some of Mozart. A very different expression of beauty would the setting of the medieval text *Magnum Mysterium* by Morten Lauridsen (b. 1943); the piece's hushed expectancy is intersected by the gorgeous dissonance on the first syllable of the word "Virgo," signing in that threshold the very realignment of the cosmos. What am I to make of the sort of cosmos that includes the beauty I can gaze at on the Hubble website, in the beloved's eyes, in the bird feeder just outside the window, or Alice Walker's fresh peaches?

To make a metaphor of Jessica Powers' earlier line (188), is it not in the favor of *something* that the uni-verse is strewn with gaily plumed singing "birds," among other beauties, in whatever direction we turn, with whatever sense we use? And that we humans have the capacity to receive, respond to, and celebrate beauty, whether in procreation, relationships in general, liturgy, or string quartets? And that it can bring such amazing joy to our spirits as humans? Beauty is the bougainvillea that snags the eye; the major seventh chord, the ear; the bouillabaisse, first the olfaction and then palate; the beloved's body, the hand.

But beyond its own splendor, beauty, aura'd in wonder, bears and bares a question among religious and areligious alike: *what all else is there?* And it elicits, sometimes *demands*, response: first, amazement; later—often—gratitude, and beyond. For this entire sequence, I found the Crick to be a candy store, with music ever piping at my elbow: in some seasons I lived a-marveling nearly each day, and while often three steps forward, two back, I did become more grateful. And for the person increasingly frequenting gratitude, all manner, *all manner,* of things become possible.

I suppose I respect music subsequent to the Romantic period more than I exult in it. I salute the impulse for exploration, and the new giving rise to the early twentieth-century lurch away from the tonal, harmonic, and rhythm givens largely presupposed since the Renaissance. And it is self-evident that amid those very seismic shifts away from classical forms, impressionistic musical works true to the darkness, contradictions, and horror that lace the modern period were created. This is music which the Romantic period, the century between the middle Beethoven and Mahler's death in 1911, neither did nor could have delivered.

Yet, I unabashedly cast my personal lot with the beauty of previous music—the Romantic period—experiencing it more with my heart than my head. In this regard I resonate with the words, "Above all do not analyze my music—love it!" attributed to Francis Poulenc (1899–1963), which sound more like the century in which he was born than in which he lived. And part of my affection for Mahler grows out of the way he approached, indeed *teetered* above, that very crevasse that would succeed him, yet never quite losing himself in it.

There is little music in the Romantic period that I do not appreciate, to say nothing of love. And I marvel at the extraordinary density of quality music surging throughout that century. How did that come to be? And how is it that so much of it, whether in the church (a small minority) or concert/opera hall (the vast majority), is able to elicit from me emotions and hungers which seem distantly akin to those drawn more immediately by the One in prayer? Might at least some of this music be a kind of tutorial in transcendence, a preparer of the way for the life of faith? How could one listening to the Requiem of Gabriel Fauré (1845–1924), whether musician or physicist or metaphysician, conclude that this was merely music deemed beautiful by those socially conditioned to think that way?

I remind myself that all great music was once "new." That of the Romantic century was no less so than any preceding: it was avant-garde, indeed radical in its time, drawing listeners where they had never been before. Perhaps because I view both the fact of, and the rich possibilities in, tonality as clues that the light will prevail over the darkness—and/or perhaps because I am not particularly coura-geous—I find the freedom *within* the confines of tonality to be sufficiently heady. Music whose primary characterization is that it is "pretty" is little more than deco-ration: "elitist Muzak." On the other hand, music that makes no meaningful claim to beauty may indeed still be good, even music both great and true, but I will often pass on it. If I have hereby confessed a greater allegiance to beauty than to truth, at least regarding music, so be it.

I have been fortunate that in the aftermath of my stumbling upon classical music in the midseventies, there has been a resurgence of new works more strongly influ-enced by the forms and values of the earlier periods, chief of these being beauty.

Truth

A second solar flare of music, less obvious and often needful of interpreters, involves the matter of truth: a relationship of integrity with what is. Again, for some, mu-sic generating this flare includes moral truth as well; for others it perhaps points in the direction of Truth itself. As hinted above, the music of Mahler, particularly as it plumbs human angst in the frightening transition to modernity, or that of Shostak-ovich, a triumph of the human spirit in the catastrophic confluence of totalitarianism and war, is truthful music.

This "conformity to reality" is not, of course, a photocopy, a replica of what is, but rather a recapitulation involving perception and reinterpretation, a creative and interactive construct emerging out of a profound grappling with the context in which the artist lives. A live performance of a symphony by either Mahler or Shostakovich has thus always left me disconcerted, even shaken, yet with the consolation that in a world of spin and sham there is at least one artist who really *got it*. It may well be that the public's penchant for "pretty" music has consigned to the dustbin some of the modern period's most truthful music, which in its atonality and dissonance was hold-ing up a mirror, an inconvenient truth, to our age.

Truthful as well is the music, a telling portion of it sacred, that has flowered among composers in Eastern Europe in the aftermath of the Soviet hegemony. Ex-amples include the works of Poland's Henryk Górecki (b. 1933), Estonia's Arvo Pärt (b. 1935), and Finland's Einojuhani Rautavaara (b. 1928). This music, much of it mini-malist and stark, simple and ethereal, and some of it nothing less than gorgeous, testi-fies to the tenacity of faith and has been no small inspiration to me.

The truthfulness of these composers' music, crafted by persons who personally experienced probably the seismic ideological shift of our time, is a confirmation of the Evangelist's words that "The Light shines in the darkness, and the darkness did not extinguish it" (Jn 1:5). I was incredulous when, during an evening in our last season on the Crick, I discovered first one couple and then another, strangers to the first, who loved the music of Pärt. Indeed, one of these individuals conducted Pärt's choral works from time to time!

Good

Finally, music flares of what is good, of musicological excellence, but farther—much farther—as well. It flares of the sheer goodness of the uni-verse, perhaps in the direction of a realm of moral goodness, for some even the Good itself. Rather than color within the lines, music is ever-flaring, self-transcending, yearning, leaning out of what is, toward what could be and actually *is,* opening new transverse portals through the walls of our compartmentalized cosmologies, ever activating unexercised parts of ourselves and our powers.

Music: opening, beckoning, sometimes luring, always preparing for that beyond our solipsistic cells and systems. In this sense, music can be tutorial, antechamber, to all that is the astonishing depth of life, whether human love, human freedom, human dreaming, or beyond. Engaging less the head than the heart, much less thought and understanding than desire and love, arguably the most Dionysian of the arts—music, particularly for me from the Romantic period, predisposes toward all that is analogously engaged and apprehended. Sometimes the hearing of music simply bleeds into prayer, and I neither know, nor care, in which I am.

It is my judgment that the chief human faculty engaged in relation to the One is desire: we hunger, we thirst, we long, for we are no less creatures of *eros* in our relationship with the One than in sexual love. Music, particularly from the Romantic period, does not find the faculty of desire to be a strange land: that province is its home.

And then, infrequently—and perhaps for some, never, at least knowingly—Beauty, Truth, Good, and so much more align, albeit momentarily, in the listener's experience of a segment of music. And then, in the words of the Jessica Powers, "all to splendor run" (123). That splendor is what the mystics have called the beatific vision; Belden Lane the "snow leopard." Music in this fleeting moment is nothing less than sacramental: audible sacrament, exuding the numinous, nudging the hearer toward awareness of the presence of the One.

G. Music as Tutorial in Transcendence

I do not believe in the One solely because music eventually emerged from what began as primordial plasma 13.7 billion years ago. But had it been all I encountered,

I suspect I would have given it a very long listen. And I still do. For me, music has been nothing less than an escort, varyingly beautiful, truthful, and good, into more self-transcending living.

The Joining of Text and Score

The powers of score and text reciprocally enhance when their matchmaker is truly an artist. It is not coincidence that the joining of music with texts of adoration of the One goes back at least as far as the liturgical settings in ancient Israel, giving rise to the Psalter. Nor that new settings of these same texts were chanted from near the beginning of the Christian tradition, especially by monastics.

The first of two examples of such score/text matchmaking, both involving Georg Friedrich Handel (1685–1759) and arguably "made in heaven," involves the words of exilic Isaiah: "and all flesh shall see it [the glory of YHWH] together" (Is 40:5). For me this text has become, in addition to an unabashed petition for universality, a fierce prayer of hope, a tenacious act of will in rejection of both cursing and succumbing to the encroaching darkness. But, tell me: what are the chances of this text, buried in the lengthy work of an ancient Hebrew prophet, becoming *my* prayer apart from its inclusion in the musical cadences of Martin Luther King, Jr.'s "I have a Dream" speech in 1963, to say nothing of its decisive musical setting *The Messiah* by Handel more than two centuries earlier?

A second example is from a scene at the end of the film of Dinesen's *Babette's Feast* in which the pious elder, long since bereft of words in the face of the gift this French woman had given him and his co-sectarians, steps out into the night, gazes into the sky, and cries out "Hallelujah!" Could anyone doubt the role of music in enhancing that particular cry of the human heart?

The point here is certainly *not* that musical settings need sacred texts to be spiritually evocative, but rather that music and text, artfully paired, can and sometimes do take on a level of power neither could generate alone. I remember how moved I was the first time I participated in an Easter Vigil where the Mass, most memorably the *Exsultet*, was sung by the priest, and sung *beautifully*!

While refusing to equate spiritually evocative music with the religious or sacred, I have long suspected that the greatest challenges to and accomplishments of music have been in compositions overtly piping of and toward the One. As a person who across decades, whether in the classroom or closet, has repeatedly knocked head and heart with the limits of language in reference to the One, I strongly believe that sensitively composed music, when wedded to texts precious yet inaccessible to many, can gain them a fresh and wider hearing.

I, for one, had my first vital experience with texts such as that of the five-fold Ordinary of the Mass, the Requiem, the *Stabat Mater*, the *Benedictus* and *Magnificat*, and the *Magnum Mysterium*, via musical settings. Thus, works as varied as Tchaikovsky's and Rachmaninoff's choral settings of the *Liturgy of St. John Chrysostom*, Bruckner's *Te Deum*, the *Mass in G Major* and *The Dialogues of the Carmelites* by Francis Poulenc, the Requiem of Fauré as well as of Duruflé (1902–1986) (both of which I have been able to sing as a choral member), all seemingly more at home in the cathedral than the concert hall, are among my traveling companions for the duration. This clutch of co-journeyers is no mere theoretical list on my part: coming to love this musical corpus was part of my discernment to enter the Catholic Church.

Music: A Gift Drawing Us Beyond Ourselves

My musical interests are not in all respects harmonious or consistent, but then, such is not the final criterion as one moves into the precincts of mystery. It has been suggested, for example, that the severe musical minimalism of the sort composed by Estonia's Arvo Pärt is akin to contemplation understood as prayer, less and less dependent upon words and images, a gravitation toward the apophatic or *via negativa* in prayer, the prayer of silence. The fact that I love the music of both Pärt's sparse and ethereal *Litany* and Mahler's over-the-top Symphony No. 8 reflects both my apophatic and kataphatic sides, respectively. Neither, nor both together, is adequate in piping of the One, whether in closet, cathedral, or cosmos.

The hymn "O for a Thousand Tongues" by the Methodist Charles Wesley (1707–1788), perhaps exuding both exasperation and ecstasy, needs to be kept near at hand. I know that I tend to be deeply affected subjectively by the overall ambience of a work while being insufficiently trained to appreciate much of the more objective musicological theory. A conductor friend of mine opined, almost enviously, that I seemed to know classical music just well enough to love its forest, but not so well so as to focus on and get lost in its trees (as does he, I inferred, on occasion).

Dorothy Day, inspiration in my own journey toward the Catholic faith, quoted Dostoevsky's "The world will be saved by beauty" frequently enough to make it partially her own. Music's "beauty," that which pleases and ignites joy, can draw us beyond our minimalist selves, in which we are tempted to cower. It can repeatedly awaken us to the fearful splendor with which we, and our home cosmos, have been crafted (Ps 139:14). In the Christian tradition, Beauty, together with Truth and the Good, has been one of the names for the One. Whether encountered in a heavy yet gentle snowfall on the marsh, the trusting smile of a child, or the "Pia Jesu" from the Requiem by Andrew Lloyd Webber (b. 1948) sung by Sarah Brightman (b. 1960), expressions of beauty are, I believe, part of the One's healing and re-creation—indeed, *salvation*—of the cosmos.

The haunting theme of *apokatástasis* ("restoration"), found here and there in the Christian tradition, raises prayers to the One that the entirety of the cosmos ultimately be drawn into the loving embrace. My own prayers identify me as part of this strand, except that I am more inclined to see the cosmos as having been for 13.7 billion years, and in this moment continuing to be, drawn by the One from out of our future rather than "re-stored" to an Edenic past. But it is surely for that healing, that comprehensiveness, that haste—how long?—that I pray. As well as pipe and sing.

Music When "Time Shall No Longer Be"

Finally, I know now that I want music to be among my companions as I travel the autumn of my life and then move into the winter that is the eternal spring, the theme briefly raised in chapter 27. I pray that waning powers will not soon rob me of my auditory faculty, that I will be allowed, in the paradigmatically receptive mode that is listening, to continue so to celebrate creation, human co-creatorship, and Creator until my time is ripe and full. But if that gate be closed, may the gift of memory of the silent music be sufficient for me to marvel and be grateful still.

On the basis of what I have received through music in my life, I have this inkling regarding its place in the Greater Life. Not surprisingly, that hunch is beset by paradox: music, a dance in and with time itself, in the Greater Life when, in the words of the Apocalypse, "time shall no longer be" (Apoc 10:6). Might indeed the references to a "new song" in that same book (Apoc 5:9, 14:3), following on numerous such references in the Hebrew Bible (Ps 33:3, 96:1. 144:9; Is 42:10), be music no longer sequestered in time? And what might such music be? What might such music be!

25. Nurture Via Tylerton's "Class Meeting"

My previous references to the Methodist "class meeting" were as a garden of rich and revelatory stories, most notably that of Dwight Marshall and the fish hawk. This gathering is nothing if not narrative, but it is more, much more. The class meeting is the first of three modules at the Tylerton Union United Methodist Church on a Sunday morning. Lay-led, informal, occasionally attended by fewer than ten of the faithful, visibly gray, inimitably Tylertoniana, the class meeting is arguably the oldest vital artifact of Wesleyan revivalism dating back to the autumn of 1808, and before that to Methodist founder, John Wesley (1703–1791) himself. Methodist class meetings thus significantly predate, for example, the Camp Meeting that has met annually in North End since 1887.

I include the class meeting in my nurture as an innkeeper because—well, this artifact of the distant past *lives!* The meeting did not fit the Inn schedule—it convened but fifteen minutes after guests sat down for breakfast at 9:00 AM, so I was often absent or tardy early on. Nevertheless, participating in it gradually became part of my week on the Crick.

A. What is a "Class Meeting"?

Just what is a class meeting? It is about neither educational nor social class. The answer I offered to guests at the Inn was this: it is an opportunity for all persons present, including guests and/or visitors from Smith's diaspora, to say something about their previous week in the light of their faith in God. Adam Wallace's phrase for it, "experience meeting," is helpful. The result is a tossed salad, wildly different each week, of sorrows and joys, tears and laughter, platitudes and serendipity, repetitions of last week's words as well as stories still singing well into the next week, all served with the balsamic vinaigrette which is Tylerton.

Not unlike my own life, sometimes class meeting was scintillating, sometimes simply bristling with eccentricities, and sometimes flat big-time, but most often it was a bit of all the above and more. While each person present is expected to contribute, and might be explicitly so invited if holding back, there is respect for silence if the previous week had been unspeakable or nondescript. My attendance began more as curious and distant observer; it ended with this innkeeper being increasingly nourished in my spirit. That the meeting became the clearest window into Tylerton's soul embraces both.

B. What Took Off as Curiosity . . .

My initial attendance, weekends during our 1995–1997 building renovation, piqued my interest despite the fact that I thought I had long since filled my life quota for "testimony meetings." However, this one, a short-cut way of catching up on village developments during the previous week, was a fascinating sociological window into village workings. Although but a small portion of the village participated, they did so in a way unlike that encountered in the Market or the crab-picking house. Here the tone was straight and serious, rather than the widespread bantering. Words here conveyed vulnerability rather than serving as buffer. And although several women were very active, the class meeting—more than any other Tylerton collective except the Market's liars' bench—was primarily male, both in composition and leadership.

From my very first Sunday on the Crick I was enamored by the class meeting's format. After being opened by a member of the rotating lay team (to which I, in time, was invited), the meeting was declared open. As the first person rose to speak in her pew (*always* Miss Evelyn!), the convener moved to a position directly before her, listening intently. When she had concluded her words, the two would exchange a blessing, accompanied by at least a handshake, after which most other persons present would rise, approach her, and exchange the same. The phrase of blessing, whether "bless you," "pray for me," or "I love you," was always tactile, whether handshake, hug, occasionally kiss. Then a second person would rise, triggering a repetition of the sequence.

During my first such meeting, I reverentially calculated that, with a dozen persons present and all participating (a few tended to remain in their seats), there would be 144 exchanged blessings—surely a critical mass of benediction! The class meeting's physicality was one of my early indicators that this conservative community did indeed have its rituals of intimacy. I found the *content* of some attendees predictable, with others the *format*. An example of content was the waterman, who seldom found the United Methodist vessel sufficient for his Pentecostal zeal. (He would exercise his mainland option mid-decade, leaving the meeting both more peaceful and less interesting.) An example of format predictability was the person who could deliver a nonlinear stream-of-consciousness blizzard worthy of none less than James Joyce. Sharryl did not attend the meeting; thus, I would often report to her over Sunday dinner as she would to me after women's events.

C. . . . Landed as Engaged Participation

What first hooked me into taking the class meeting more seriously involved its theological dynamics. While Calvinist codewords might be heard here or there, the collective body language at class meetings clearly was, as is Methodism in general,

Arminian. That is, rather than the playing out of predestination, the Christian life is a struggle toward sanctity; human freedom is very real; grace can be and often is resisted; and the hazard of backsliding is ever the wolf at the door. While the village clearly was not above responding to deviant behavior by holding grudges *a la* the Hatfields and McCoys, the mood of the class meeting seemed to presuppose a common flawedness—indeed, needfulness, brokenness—such as is implicit in the hymn "There's a Wideness in God's Mercy." Grace, mercy, forgiveness, second chances: these were not strangers here. Granted, attendance being viewed as a sign of spiritual vigilance, the faithful did not always resist the temptation to judge those who were elsewhere Sunday morning.

My appreciation for the class meeting also grew as I began to see it as an opportunity to share of myself and my faith with my new neighbors. In our life together with Tylertonians, Sharryl and I were hardly ever asked questions about who we were, what positions or values we stood for, or what our life experiences had been—and then only by one or two persons, and primarily during the second half of the decade. I confess that several years were required for me to come to peace with the realization that the *content* of the interface between our lives and theirs would be overwhelmingly defined by them and their world, rather than via some reciprocity.

But in the class meeting I could volunteer to my neighbors what it was that mattered most to me. And there I spoke of my family including son Chad living in a group home in Indiana, encounters with guests, my repugnance for war, the generosity of a villager which had illumined my week, my struggle with the darkness, and the uneven terrain of my life of faith. In all of this I usually felt that I was among the like-minded and like-hearted.

D. An Arena of Accountability

But do the above qualify the class meeting as a source of nurture for this hospitalier? Was more going on within me than the satisfying of my sociological curiosity, pegging the group theologically, and stumbling upon a format for self-disclosure? Yes, there was more, particularly in our last several years there.

I gradually became convinced of the integrity of a vast part of what happened in the class meeting. Whether it was failure being courageously addressed ("I know God has forgiven me, all of you have forgiven me, but I can't seem to forgive myself"); breakthroughs tearfully bared; grinding loss grieved and lamented; profound concern aired for family members not of the faith; aridity acknowledged; or an impromptu prayer clustered over one member, with the music of tactile intercession in (about) twelve parts: it was repeatedly real, fresh, unscripted, and *without pretense*. I intermittently found the configuration of my own life confronted, challenged, chastened, and occasionally wood-shedded by another's shared word that was true to a lived life. My discipline of offering these who had vulnerably opened themselves to me, to the One, will continue after our departure. At no other place did I, as a Roman Catholic, feel as close to these progeny of Wesley as in class meeting.

In short, the class meeting gradually became for me an arena of accountability. Most of the participants evidenced a commitment to live their lives more transparently before the One and the One's people. While the class meeting was not for me equivalent to the sacrament of reconciliation (confession), to which I did not have frequent access, it did surely overlap, and face in the same direction: living honestly and accountably. By the last several seasons it had become for me a kind of check-in time for which I would prepare during an *examen* in my silence earlier Sunday morning. The meeting would also prove to be a setting in which I could offer an incremental farewell across the months before we finally de-isled.

I did occasionally succumb to the temptation to use the hour to enlighten my siblings in Christ—perhaps exemplified by my explosive condemnation of the Bush administration the Sunday after Hurricane Katrina struck—but I usually sought to join the other members in speaking honestly, gratefully, and humbly.

It is only in retrospect that I realize that most Tylertonians named in this book were in that small class meeting group. I also see more clearly now that I will miss the accountability, forthrightness, and closeness of the class meeting more than I do the Sunday morning or evening services, perhaps even more than the off-season Bible teaching opportunities I was generously given. I expect that on most Sunday mornings after I reside in Indiana, a part of me will still be with them in the class meeting.

And finally, in *An Island Out of Time,* Tom Horton quotes his first wife Cheri. Having completed their two years on Tylerton and being back on the main, they had just departed a Washington, D.C. party when she mused to Tom: "Compared to the islanders, they all seemed dead from the neck down." Cheri died in her late forties, just weeks before we opened the Inn, so I must wait to meet her. But it was her vibrant Catholic faith, known well to the islanders, that left doors ajar all over the place among them, doors through which Sharryl and I would repeatedly pass throughout our decade. Her quote has been for me a shorthand for an aspect of the genius of Tylerton, one which I quoted back to them (with Tom in attendance) at our own farewell. That her words apply not only to the annual watermen's banquet skits, the banter of the liars' bench in the market, and the scarcely believable things that can transpire in the picking house, but also in the class meeting is evidence of a consistency which is one of the highest compliments I can give to Tylertonians.

26. Nurture Via Spiritual Disciplines

I am the product of a rural Mennonite religious ethos that was very "low church" liturgically, and yet relatively regimented regarding ethics and lifestyle. I packed this not unusual confluence of fluidity and form into the life of faith in my early adulthood, albeit with different content, this being the 1960s: an aversion for what I called "wooden formalism" or "theological clichés." Even then, however, I was beginning a decades-long eyeing—seemingly from the safety of distance—of monasticism in the Roman Catholic Church, a paragon of structure and discipline.

With the decades-long experience of becoming more aware of the scale and depth of the human predicament, throughout the planet and within myself, generally in that order, I found myself nudged during the backstretch years toward the non-negotiability of structure as a complement to the freedom I experienced my life to be.

It is Sharryl to whom I am indebted regarding a deeper understanding of the gift of freedom within form and gestalt, whether in corporate worship or marriage, an innkeeper's sanity or personal prayer. A very weighty decision following our marriage, jointly entering the Roman Catholic Church, had already seen this freedom/form issue receiving considerable attention. Thus, one of the underlying strands running throughout this section on spiritual disciplines involves the relationship between freedom and form and the way in which each both requires and can enhance the other.

During our Tylerton decade this creative tension found expression for me in numerous settings including the following four: my membership in the Discalced Carmelite Order as a secular, construction of the Oratory on the Inn's third floor (a prayer gestalt in space), building the Green House in the pines behind the Inn, and our annual silent monastic retreat. I present each of these below.

A. Membership in the Discalced Carmelite Order as a Secular

A first spiritual discipline nourishing me during the decade on Tyler's Crick was my identity as a secular in the Roman Catholic religious order called the Discalced Carmelites (OCDS for the Latin *Ordo Carmelitarum Discalceatorum Seculorum*).

Seculars, in earlier times called "third order" or "tertiaries," and tracing their origins to St. Francis of Assisi, are laypersons (also a few diocesan priests) who nevertheless discern within themselves a vocation of prayer in the tradition of one of the historical religious orders. The Discalced ("barefoot") Carmelite Order (OCD) is a sixteenth-century reform. Initiated by Teresa of Jesus in collaboration with John of the Cross of the Carmelites of the Ancient Observance (OCarm), it goes back to the geography in the late twelfth century near what is now the Israeli city of Haifa.

"For the Rest of My Life"

I began exploring this reformed order, the Discalced, in the St. Joseph Community in Washington, D.C., in 1993, making temporary profession as a secular three years later and taking the name "LeRoy of the Wine of God."

Upon moving to Tylerton in 1997, my Carmelite "formation," a journey encompassing both heart and head, in that order, continued within the OCDS Community of Mary convening in Salisbury. In part because our innkeeping precluded weekend Mass attendance at St. Francis de Sales, our Salisbury parish, except during the Inn's off-season, this Carmelite community of a dozen became increasingly important in my faith experience during that decade. It provided a powerful spiritual resource for deepening my innkeeping vocation as well as my experience of both the natural environment and culture of Tylerton. At the conclusion of our third season on Tylerton, I concluded the five-year beginning of my Carmelite journey making the permanent promise, which includes these words:

> I, LeRoy Friesen, inspired by the Holy Spirit, in response to God's call, sincerely promise . . . to tend to evangelical perfection in the spirit of the evangelical counsels of chastity, poverty, obedience, and of the Beatitudes . . . for the rest of my life.

My formal obligations as a Carmelite secular included daily prayer (including both the Divine Office/Prayer of the Hours and silent contemplation), an annual retreat, and participation in a monthly Saturday with other members of the Community of Mary. These monthly days together began with parish Mass followed by both silent and then verbal prayer. The day always included two formation classes generally centered in the texts of Sts. Teresa or John as well as scripture, the sharing of concerns, and the concluding praying of Vespers. The ferry schedule just barely allowed me to meet this Carmelite commitment; the winter passages provided more than enough prayer practicums.

I Want YOU!

But for me, far more central than these formal obligations is the cry from the heart of the Discalced Carmelite order and its members: "I want You!" Not this or that, not sense-candy nor intellect-toys, not method or discipline, precept or dogma, not even primarily consolation or peace, joy or satisfaction, heaven or beatitude. *Nada, nada, nada*, intones John of the Cross: nothing, nothing, nothing. Nothing but *You*, O Lover, YOU! I am a Carmelite because of the correspondence between that simple focus, arguably shaped by St. John of the Cross more than anyone else, and that issuing from the very center of my own being. My cry, long misunderstood, only belatedly named and subsequently owned, and the one reverberating through the centuries of Carmel, are one and the same. That correspondence is conclusive: I'm home.

It is both an audacious and frightening matter, this cry, one which thumps palpably in my thorax every time I offer it, even while I write, but one for which the stalking Hound of Heaven had been grooming me for a lifetime. And it is a human's last and farthest cry. There is no "after" or "beyond" here, for this cry, and its being heard in faith, is itself home. It is the destination rather than merely the road, the end leading nowhere (else).

Because this cry is oblivious to the boundaries of the land of words or images, silence as a life's receptive stance is prominent in this tradition. Carmel became my hut, its prayer rug my place within the wide embrace of the vast and variegated Roman Catholic communion. Carmel's numerous saints became my mothers and fathers, its simple cry belatedly recognized to have been my own since forever. If the query, "What's it all about?" in the 1966 movie *Alfie* was *the* question, then the "You" in Carmel's "I want You!" was *the* answer.

B. The Oratory on the Inn's Third Floor

A second spiritual discipline on the Crick involved space and, derivatively, time. Back on August 21, 1994, when Sharryl and I had walked through the Morgan building that would become the Inn, I pointedly asked to see the attic, the space I would subsequently renovate into our personal quarters during our second year. But as much as for potential living quarters, I was looking that morning for a corner of space that might serve as a place reserved for silence, solitude, and the life of the spirit.

A Prayer Gestalt in Space

Sharryl and I had only recently shared a lovely evening at table in Bethesda just outside Washington, D.C., with a group of friends, including Tilden Edwards, a founder of the Shalem Institute, an organization in greater Washington committed to resourcing the life of prayer. In the course of the meal, Edwards, who had recently moved into a new house, suddenly had my full attention when he mentioned in passing that he had protected a corner under the eaves on the top floor to be dedicated to prayer. Now in the Morgan's foul-smelling attic, a sow's ear *sans* windows, ceiling, or floor, I was reconnoitering.

Completed as part of the third-floor renovation, what I chose to call the "Oratory" (*ora,* Latin for "prayer") would become an important part of the self-care of these innkeepers. It was ten feet square, but rendered even more intimate by the angle of the roof on both left and right *a la* a cathedral. To the rear was a large window with a stunning view to the south, all the way to Tangier Island, seven miles away. Flanking the rear window on the one side I would hang a painting of St. John of the Cross, and on the other, an abstract piece I had done twenty-five years before on the text "For YHWH your God is a consuming fire" (Dt 4:24). On the floor was an Egyptian rug, its motif the forest of minarets that is Cairo. And at the front of the space, hanging over a large banner in the color of the liturgical season, was an image of the *Risen* Christ, one signing for all times and spaces the expansive embrace which is the cosmic triumph of the One's inimitable *modus operandi* of the cross.

A Jesuit Blesses Our Secret Oratory

Father Larry Madden, SJ, previously our pastor at Holy Trinity Parish in Georgetown, visited the Inn when the Oratory was nearly complete in 1999. He celebrated the first Mass in the space, and then led us in a special rite of blessing. Since 1991, I had each morning prayed the Divine Office, the Psalter-based prayer offered throughout the worldwide Roman Catholic Church and beyond, and that activity now had a spatial home, a gestalt first in space and then time. Aside from being grandson Jacob's bedroom when he visited, an exception proving the rule, the Oratory was solely for prayer and dialogue about the life of faith. It was a dedicated space.

Although I found Sharryl to be ambivalent initially about the Oratory, musing not unreasonably that space in the sailboat-like confines of our personal quarters might have been put to better use, she joined me in the Oratory at the beginning of 2001 in the morning Office. This practice would thus become one of the points at which our respective self-care efforts were firmly intertwined. It was with this discipline that we began each new day as innkeepers our last six seasons.

The Role into Which the Oratory Grew

Following the setting out of coffee and tea for visitors, I had most of an hour in the Oratory, the first half alone in the silence, the second with Sharryl and the Office, before we attacked breakfast and the day. Her joining me immeasurably strengthened and rendered more concrete what transpired in that space and time. Several years later, we would also incorporate the lectionary readings of the day into the Office, insofar as attendance at Mass where these are read was limited by our work and location. A small, inconspicuous sign on our downstairs bulletin board invited interested guests to join us in this discipline. Their visits, while not frequent, were often both moving and memorable.

There are seasons in the life of prayer when the spirit soars and there is little need for external reinforcement, when adoration is the song and we want nothing as much as simply to *sing it*. But there are other seasons, more numerous for most, when we need all of the support we can get, when the unintelligible groans deep within us require the efforts of the One's own Spirit (Rom 8:26) so as to be given wings. For the myriad situations between these two poles, the bulk of us benefit from channels, gestalts, and patterns: disciplines. For me, this particular time (sixty minutes) in that particular space (ten feet square) became scaffolding in support of commitments I had and would continue to make to the One and to my dear ones. And to myself, the wagerer that this One above all others was both my Lover and Destiny.

In addition to the cadence of discipline, the Oratory was also the space to which I could repair when the chaos crowded me in, when Sharryl and I were making more dissonance than music together, when the One who is Night seemed only to compound my more ordinary darkness, when desperation was metallic in the mouth and palpable in the gut. The shelter in the storm is the One: "It is to have a place to hide / when all is hurricane outside," Jessica Powers pipes (92). The Oratory, a dedicated space, has been reminder that it is so, *everywhere*.

Interestingly, an oratory or chapel in one's private home is not historically unprecedented in the state of Maryland, that colony of the thirteen whose origins were most Roman Catholic. In 1688, the "Glorious Revolution" took place in England, in which William of Orange and his wife Mary seized the throne and permanently reestablished Anglicanism as the faith of the realm. Within a year, repercussions in the colony resulted in the fall of the proprietary government of Lord Baltimore at the hands of Puritan rebels.

During the following period of nearly a century, ending only after the Revolutionary War, the public practice of the Christian faith in the Roman Catholic form was illegal in Maryland, the Act of Toleration promulgated with such promise in 1649 null and void. Roman Catholic landowners in Maryland, including the Eastern Shore, built secret or discrete chapels inside their houses where Mass could be celebrated by itinerant and incognito priests, often Jesuits. Sharryl and I have visited such a house outside Cordova, near Easton. I would occasionally smile about our recapitulation of a hidden Catholic worship space in the house, especially one also surrounded by low-church Protestants on low-elevation land, aided and abetted by a *Jesuit*!

C. The Green House Behind the Inn

A third element of spiritual discipline, like the Oratory, involved an enclosed space that then sheltered time, only in this case primarily for use by guests. I was brainstorming and sketching for this structure as soon as the third-floor project was completed in late 1999. In the spring of 2001, I both exchanged e-mails about the project with an interested guest, Fred Schroyer, and received a splendid article on my obscure interest from a friend, Bill Hocking. In a sense, all of this represented but a continuation of the pre-opening discernment that Sharryl and I had carried out as to the niche that the Inn would occupy, and in particular the extent to which spirituality impulses could find room there, however low in profile.

A Place More Remote Than the Inn

In the end, I decided to build a structure elevated six feet above the ground, measuring eight feet square in the interior, and located where the loblolly pines and cedars interfaced with the *Phragmites australis* about a hundred feet behind the Inn. The structure's legs were sixteen-foot 4 x 6s embedded in three feet of concrete in the ground. Having windows, some salvaged from village retrofittings, on all four sides and covered with a shed roof, the structure faced east-southeast with a view of Glennan Marsh, Tylerton's Back Cove, Tyler's Creek, and the open Tangier Sound, respectively. The principal view was thus in the one direction where Tylerton is not shielded by landmasses from the seas of the open Bay, precisely the corridor through which Dame Isabel passed at dusk on September 18, 2003.

A stairway along one side provided access to the building, which included a fifty square foot raised deck and a yet-higher "Crow's Nest"—it was the decade of the perch—for an elevated view. The vista from the "nest" was awesome at dawn, and perhaps even better just before sunset when the marsh version of "alpenglow" generated colors for which I never did have adequate words. The interior was furnished with two comfortable chairs, a prayer kneeler, a hinged writing table on one side, a small stocked bookcase, a rug, a pillow, and a small representation of St. Francis' cross of San Damiano.

Borrowing from the rich labyrinth tradition, I cut a serpentine path through the *Phragmites,* which in some places were ten feet high. Enriching the metaphorical power of the journey, this path was rarely entirely free of poison ivy (*Toxicodendron radicans*) in the late summer, and for reasons of low elevation and the water absorbency of the vegetative detritus, was often impassable after heavy rains without boots. My mind would remain inside the metaphor as I regularly did battle with the *Phragmites* so as to keep the path open. In retrospect, a machete from the outset would have been prudent. Being in Tylerton, the Green House was, of course, suitably difficult to get to from here.

Although I had hoped there would be guests who would want to use this enclosure for prayer, the earlier commitment of Sharryl and myself to target the mainstream B&B market held firm. While earlier name candidates included the "Hermitage," the "Poustinia" (Russian for "desert of the soul," popularized by Catherine de Hueck Doherty [1896–1985]), or simply the "Desert," I ended up opting for a name describing appearance rather than recommended function. Having painted it a dark cedar green, I dubbed it simply the "Green House," and sought to offer its multiple possibilities to guests.

To our web listing we added the following in 2001: "For those finding both Tylerton and the Inn too cosmopolitan, we have created an elevated structure called the 'Green House.' . . . It is suitable for reading, bird watching, meditation, or simple solitude. Available without charge to interested guests, it can be reserved for half days."

The Manifold Use of the Green House

Many guests reported using the Green House for silence and prayer. Some reserved the space when they made their reservations and came prepared for a personal retreat. An incomplete list of reported usages included yoga on the deck in the early morning; bird watching among the trees, which hosted numerous songbirds; writing projects; naps; much reading; and conversation. A stay by Philadelphians Mary Agnes and Thomas Parker Williams in 2004 gave rise to his "Island," a suite of three impressionistic musical compositions, one of them based on the songs of birds recorded on the Green House deck, and including brush and ink drawings. Tom's CD pipes at my elbow as I write.

We know of at least one engagement that took place in the Green House, this following the reading of Gerard Manley Hopkins' "Pied Beauty" ("Glory be to God for dappled things . . ."). The fact that I would ask other guests to honor the party having reserved the place for the half day, hoping thereby to reduce interruptions, is part of the reason I do not know much about what transpired back there. Although I was making a day retreat in the Green House the morning of September 11, 2001, the project having been completed just weeks before, it was overwhelmingly used by guests rather than the innkeepers.

So How Did the Green House Nurture Me?

Why discussion of the Green House, a facility built primarily for guests, in a chapter devoted to the innkeepers' self-care? Were not the "strangers at the gate" in this case without (guests), rather than within (innkeepers)? I did weigh including the Green

House in Part IV. Yet, although offering the enclosure to guests was clearly an expression of hospitality, equally important to me was the self-nurturing benefit of dreaming it up, constructing it, and then, across six seasons, interacting with guests who had used it.

Although I had experienced some of this in the building of the Oratory, I came to see the planning and construction of the Green House as analogous to writing an icon (one *prays*, not paints, it), or a medieval cathedral (its design and construction are its first two prayers). The journey—dreaming, constructing, and interacting with guests—turned out to be the principal prayer, not the destination, for me in this case. The crafting of an enclosed space for the purpose of prayer (among other things) was itself a prayer.

Granted, awareness of the project's benefit to my own wholeness came to me largely in retrospect. Although I labored on the Green House with unusual self-engagement and joy under adverse conditions (poison oak, difficult access, tension with Inn responsibilities, villager incomprehension, rough off-season weather), it has only been with the writing of this chapter that the music of that endeavor has reached the threshold of words. In short, the Green House project gave me the opportunity to push out the walls of our vocation here on the Crick, to engage guests on aspects of the hospitality enterprise for which I had the most passion, and that made the entire endeavor sing! The guests' use of the Green House gave me more occasions to interact with them at levels that left me both nurtured and refreshed. Whatever their accumulative benefit from the enclosure, my own via them was greater. Seldom was my sustenance via our guests as apparent as here.

And now, near the end of the decade, I wonder whether this paradigm, serving the stranger within via the ones without, is not applicable to virtually all aspects of innkeeping, all aspects of life. Of course, that did not in fact always happen, or even usually. I completed many tasks and responsibilities as innkeeper with minimal awareness of personal benefit, apart from a sense that I had either done my duty or, short of that, had somehow managed not to lay waste the situation. Being able to accept the latter kinds of outcome, however, would become easier as I sensed that from time to time I would, inadvertently, receive far more than I had given.

A "Dog House" for Exiled Spouses?

Finally, on a lighter note, crafting the Green House, a structure of enigmatic utility, generated perplexity among Tylertonians. During construction, they would pass by in their golf carts, monitoring developments, furtively eyeing the structure from the lane. Watermen viewing it from the water might inquire about it in the store that night. Capt'n Larry, seldom at a loss for an angle, was most curious, finally conclud-ing that the structure was a "dog house," a shelter for exiled spouses. On one occasion, I jocularly offered to make for him, in the interests of his comfort, an open-ended reservation for that use of the building. He would never act upon my generous offer.

Ironically, although several village women admitted to sneaking a visit during one of our off-season junkets, I know of no male visitor to the Green House until our very last week, when nearly a score of them showed up in response to my appeal. Alas, a required survey confirmed that I had encroached four feet into our neighbor's land when I enthusiastically built the structure. We sawed the legs off at ground level, re-braced them, and used posts and pipes as rollers to move the building fifteen feet. The entire experience, while socially memorable, was humbling for both the Green House and its architect. The men? They were unusually kind: nary a smartass remark.

D. Our Annual Silent Monastic Retreat

Following our first two off-seasons, both dominated by the third-floor project, Shar-ryl and I began what would become an improbable and serendipitous annual fixture: a week of silent retreat in a monastery. Our first such venture was in January 2000 at Mepkin Abbey, a community near Moncks Corner on the Cooper River north of Charleston, South Carolina. We would return there during three subsequent off-seasons. In between, we arranged similar stays at Holy Spirit Abbey outside Conyers, Georgia (2001) and St. Benedict's Monastery near Snowmass, Colorado (2003). During the 2002 off-season, we made a Christmas pilgrimage to Siena, Assisi, and Cortona in Italy, taking our accommodations in convents; we did the same during two weeks in Avila and Segovia, Spain, in June 2005.

Why Silent Trappists After Silent Music?

While I had been slipping off to monasteries since 1968, they constituted a new frontier for Sharryl. But a number of factors converged, both for her and us together. First, one of our explicit needs upon completion of a season was liturgical immer-sion. While one can no more hoard the Eucharist than could the ancient Hebrews manna in the desert, or disciple Peter transfigured moments, fast can surely fuel the yearning for feast.

All the monastic houses we visited in this country were of the Order of Cistercians of the Strict Observance (popularly known as Trappists), tracing their origins to a twelfth-century renewal movement within the Benedictine family. They followed the ancient pat-tern of the Divine Office (Prayers of the Hours) seven times daily, beginning with Vigils around 3:30 AM, in addition to daily Mass. This strength of the entire Benedictine tradition regarding corporate prayer and liturgy was certainly a factor in our choice.

A second draw involved Thomas Merton. Even though our visit to his community, Gethsemani Abbey in Kentucky, motherhouse of both Mepkin and Holy Spirit abbeys, was only a day-trip, I have little doubt but that his impact on the two of us, both before and after we became Roman Catholics, was a factor.

I interject that my status as a Discalced Carmelite secular precluded my consideration of that option for our off-season retreats together. Sharryl was already moving far into new territory with the whole monastery thing, and the Trappists would, at least in some sense, be neutral turf for the two of us. Co-ownership, Sharryl's enthusiasm being no less than my own, made it work.

A third factor that drew Sharryl and me to the Trappists was silence. The name of our operation notwithstanding, innkeeping involves an enormous amount of talking, particularly in my case, with the major interpretive component. By the end of the season, we were always weary of words—our own, each other's, and everyone else's. The Trappist patterns of minimal speaking throughout much of the day, including meals, in addition to supporting our individual retreat plans, were a wonderful change after the season's mounds of verbiage. By November of the season, the two innkeepers at the garrulous Inn of Silent Music were nothing less than crying out for some silence! The rhythm, the cadence, of the Divine Office, immersed in a sea of near silence, was what each of us hungered for.

Being Alone Together

Finally, Sharryl and I found that our monastic weeks met our needs because, in each case, we were able to arrange separate although adjacent accommodations. The monastery week, usually scheduled shortly after the end of our season, was thus a *personal* time alone, yet with companion near. The reader will recall that Sharryl and I had originally stumbled upon innkeeping in part because we desired to work together. From a perch seventeen years later, it can be said that this desire had been, in a word, *sated*!

At the monastery, we would begin daily by rejoining each other and planning the day as we walked the half mile in the starry, starry night to morning prayer. We would then spend the day apart, rendezvousing periodically yet silently in choir or refectory. It was a restorative rhythm, a fresh and satisfying way for the two of us to be together. Only as we drove away from the monastery at the end of the week might we turn on NPR or look for a newspaper, to discover what had happened to the One's cosmos during our week in the garden. An exception would be major concerns that surfaced amid prayers in choir, this being how we learned of the catastrophic tsunami in Asia on December 26, 2004.

27. Nurture Via the Monastery of Aging

Life, not unlike space or chronological time, is in some respects a Rorschach test: what we experience it to be is significantly shaped by what we bring to it, whether assumptions, traits of character, patterns of behavior, or faith. Life's meaning is not manifest, not self-evident: it will not, *cannot*, communicate an intrinsic meaning to us, in and of itself. This is not only to say that life's meaning is a mystery. It is more than that: the experience of life apart from transcendence has no intrinsic meaning.

Meaning, too, is always a construct. Thus, the way we live life says at least as much about what we are given, and have thus brought to it, as what life is, in and of itself. I understand all three of the Abrahamic faith traditions to be in agreement that the meaning of life is profoundly affected by that brought to it, values not in all respects self-evident in it. In short, each of the three confesses the One to have self-disclosed, albeit via very different means.

A. Menu Options for Life's Summit

Life's meaning as construct is nowhere as obviously the case as with the issues brought to life by aging.

Physical / Athletic / Sexual as Peak

If the meaning of an unfolding life centers in our physical attractiveness, athletic prowess, and/or sexual desirability, for example, then it is self-evident that we humans peak curiously early, spending our remaining decades declining until we are in decrepitude. Unlike Cana (Jn 2:1–11), the best wine here is served very early in the party. In a society of tennis players and gymnasts who might retire in their late teens, models in their twenties, and team athletes in their thirties, the notion that "the best" is both early and ephemeral is in the very air we breathe.

It is thus not surprising that advertising, at least before the baby boomers' purchasing power bellied up to the bar, was dominated by the huckstering of images of youth: a range of cosmetic, apparel, and lifestyle goods and services fixated on the contrived prolongation of the early peak. The fortunate few cash in before the peak subsides, and are then said to live the good life for the duration—which is descent.

Prestige / Power / Profit as Peak

A second model would link such meaning as there is to either intellectual vigor or professional accomplishment and its rewards. Peaking, in this case, generally takes place in the middle of the life span with the financial and power rewards garnered, again allowing one to prolong the good life in the decline to follow. With either model, life post-peak consists for the duration of managing the portfolio of previous peaks, the major variable being that some have more resources with longer shelf life than others to buffer their pain.

Of these two models—the quests for perpetual youth and financial/material security—we received in the Inn far less of the first than the second, with the latter group bringing the perfect depletion/affluence ratios to provide the innkeepers with an income. As an innkeeper, I tried never to forget that Sharryl and I were living comfortably because such a large bulge in our census came from persons to some extent in this second category.

All of the Above

For the sleek, gifted, tenacious, and/or lucky, these two models get bundled together sequentially in what then becomes the *credo* for the super American dream. These double winners are forced by the calendar to move from the first into the second step, even while grasping for elements of the first as long as remains credible, and briefly beyond.

It is not my objective here to disparage entirely these two paradigms, for each of our own developmental trajectories takes us through these countries. The problems have to do with both arrested development and the weighting of one or both of the models as embodying the decisive meaning of life. In the case of either peak, life's later years can be "golden" only in the vicarious sense of feeding parasitically off the goodies of yore.

I have been, and remain, profoundly shaped by this American two-step. Although I came out of a Mennonite culture with a distinct countercultural stance (although with its share of blind spots regarding application and practice), I have yet bought into, and continue to be tempted by, the two models cited above. The fact that I have a section on "aging as nurturer" should in no way be understood as putting me outside the siren's sway of these models in our culture.

B. A Case of Premature Mortality

At the same time, something happened to me and to my extended family that, in retrospect, thrust before me end-of-life issues long before I would likely have given them attention. At age thirty-seven, roughly three decades ago, I was diagnosed with cardiomyopathy. In contrast to my father's sudden death at age fifty-three due to a coronary blockage, I had a congenital and developmentally emerging condition. I would learn much later that this was passed to me via my mother.

A younger brother would subsequently also be diagnosed with the same condition, and would succumb to sudden death at age forty-four. Both of that brother's sons and one of my own would later be diagnosed with the same. Three of us have undergone defibrillator implants. In contrast, my remaining brother's miraculous return from a near-death experience at age fifty-one in our fourth season was rooted in a diagnosis similar to what had taken our father thirty years before.

In retrospect, existential awareness of my mortality, experienced earlier than most, was a heavy load to carry, one that affected various subsequent life choices—some positively, some otherwise. I believe that awareness also contributed to placing in question the cultural paradigms shaping my life. The fact that I am writing this section on aspects of aging, and doing so in my sixty-seventh year, is something that for nearly three decades I had viewed as virtually impossible. In short, my health situation both rendered improbable that I would reach anecdotage, and brought urgency to its issues much sooner than I might otherwise have done. I believe that my response, later more than sooner, to what I learned in April of 1978 has contributed to what I now write.

C. A Biblical Image for Aging

Back in the 1980s, a colleague at the Associated Mennonite Biblical Seminary, Harry Martens, a man of extraordinary wit and the *joie de vivre*, was diagnosed with Alzheimer's. Since he was still able to be on campus from time to time, I invited him to visit a Peace Colloquium I convened, and he was able to come. Assisted by his caretaker spouse, he spoke movingly about an active person like himself confronting divestiture, detachment, the surrendering of control. It was a precious hour for all of us.

Later, I read to Harry the words the Fourth Gospel has Jesus speaking to Peter: "Truly, truly, I say to you, when you were younger, you used to gird yourself and walk wherever you wished; but when you grow old, you will stretch out your hands and someone else will gird you, and bring you where you do not wish to go" (Jn 21:18). A committed peacemaker throughout his globetrotting life, Harry was most concerned lest he descend into violent behavior as his condition deteriorated.

Although the principal interpretation of this passage has been as a prefiguring of the incarceration and martyrdom of Peter, Jesus can also be understood as spinning out an image of relinquishment applicable to each of us as we grow older. The diminishing of our powers of self-care, mobility, and freedom in general is a given. Spared the sudden death that has plagued my family, I and/or

Sharryl can expect at some point to be dressed and transported by others, per-haps against our wills.

D. The Case for an Alternative Summit

Dr. Jane Marie Thibault, a clinical gerontologist and student of the spiritual journey, in her book *A Deepening Love Affair*, refers to aging as life's "natural monastery." In a manner not unlike that of the person entering the novitiate, aging is a time of incre-mentally relinquishing control over the spheres of one's former powers, whether physical, sexual, intellectual, social, or psychological/emotional. This surrender re-quires no less courage at sixty-seven than at seventeen: "Getting old is not for sissies" was the way friends Jean and Jim Matlack put it as her mother was nearing her jour-ney's end well into her tenth decade.

Thibault raises the question whether the frightening aging process can be trans-formed into ally in moving us toward centering in the One in whom alone rests our security, destiny, and peace. Playing with Thibault's image triggered a raft of fruitful questions within me:

- Can the waning, and even loss, of powers actually be requisitioned toward the goal of honing a heightened thirst for and awareness of the One?
- Can we, at the very centers of our beings, allow the fearsome face of the final turn to nudge us toward the words of the prayer in Matthew 6:10 that the Christ taught all his followers—"Thy will be done"*(fiat voluntas tua* in Jerome's *Vulgate*)?
- Can faith utilize fading capacities both to channel our prioritizing and infuse us with hope that this detachment is, rather than decline, anticipatory lean-ing into the wonder that is to come?
- Can one in the season of divestiture, the concluding movement, the finale of which is death, believe fiercely that, because of the One, "the best is *ever* yet to come" in a way which is the antithesis of sentimentality and self-delusion?
- Can not the viewing of aging as an unyielding and yet supportive novice master, one strangely suited to ready us for the transition to come, allow us to join in the singing of the "Canticle of the Sun" with St. Francis of Assisi: "Praised be my Lord for our sister, the death of the body"?

Do not confuse the preceding with the notion that the One *causes* the decline of powers ending in death toward some greater good. The record of the One as source of life rather than death, wholeness rather than disintegration, requires no defense.

Rather, I believe that in all things *of whatever mysterious causation,* the One is working for the well-being of those thirsting for the One (Rom 8:28). Stated otherwise, in a paraphrase of Joseph's words in Genesis 50:20: although it was intended for evil, by Joseph's brothers in this case, the One used it for good to bring about the desired result.

Encapsulated in those two texts, Romans and Genesis, is the towering truth that the *modus operandi* of the One, paradigmatically glimpsed in the cross and resurrection of the Christ, is the transformation of tragedy, loss, and *death of whatever causation.* Christ transforms these into the splendor that, in the words of the Apostle Paul, neither eye nor ear—indeed, not even human imagination—has ever entertained (1 Cor 2:9).

During my decade in Tylerton, the marsh, sea, and host village culture conspired to form me in the journey, in the need to slough off, and to become more single-hearted, more honed for the final lap. But I also found myself receiving teaching from the aging of my own body, mind, and spirit. I was not nearly always receptive to this demanding tutor, but by now, I knew that from my reception of the medical news back in 1978, and before, that the One has been tenaciously doing the good work.

Granted, the very notion of becoming receptive to compulsory deprivation, and viewing it as needed honing for life's paradoxical peak yet ahead, constitute a complete inversion of our culture's pervasive paradigms. But it is to this inverted cosmology, this upside-down kingdom, that all faith in the One points. Part of my intense joy about the entire Tylerton experience is rooted in the way in which this paradox became clearer to me there.

As I conclude this section on the nurture of this hospitalier out of the resources of vocation, I cite the words attributed to Pierre Teilhard de Chardin, SJ, theologian and cosmologist: "Joy is the most infallible sign of the presence of God." Not mere happiness, nor about this or that, but the response of my entire being to all that is, and to the One whose joy birthed, unfolded, and will consummate that cosmos. I may be sized up as a pessimist, and that I am—regarding, for example, aspects of the unsustainable house of cards that is the present American way of life. But there is a far larger picture, one embracing the entire cosmos, both including and transcending what my sensorium and intellect can engage, and I am both fiercely hopeful and quietly joyful about *that!*

The vocational nurturing discussed in the chapters above, resourced via care of the body, the beauty of nature, the miracle and splendor of music, habituated patterns of celebration and adoration, and the chiseling and honing of the years, cohere in joy in the face of the stunning notion that I am a participant in the sure-to-emerge New Heaven and New Earth, which is even now coming to be. All of this is central to the sustaining of this hospitalier on the journey.

PART VI
THE COSMIC DANCE AS ARENA
FOR ADORATION

". . . as it was in the beginning, is now, and will be forever. Amen."

As a boy, he loved the daytime sky. He might pass part of a summer afternoon lying in the grassy pasture out beyond the vegetable garden and apple orchard, looking up into that sky with its multivalent cloud shapes drifting into and out of his imagination's enhancement. And at dusk, after the chores, those same clouds could become the canvas on which glorious colors appeared in the west and northwest through the grove of willows. It was from these colors that he first learned that delight and pain, his responses to beauty, travel in tandem.

However, apart from an occasional glimpse of the aurora borealis to the north of his family's Minnesota farm, the night sky was another matter. In his earliest memories, especially on cloudless nights, that sky was cold, empty, *inhospitable*. Well before adolescence and the confusing ache of first love, the sight of clouds racing before the moon on a frosty and windswept autumn night would nudge him toward melancholia.

But it was out beyond Earth's satellite, beyond the solar system in the Milky Way galaxy, that he encountered a heartless frigidity that would have him casting his eyes down rather than up. Thus when in his twenties he first read Albert Camus' *The Stranger*, especially the protagonist's experience in the night sky of "the benign indifference of the universe," he was in familiar territory. Although as a boy he did not yet know the word "contingency," the night sky did elicit from him feelings of *angst*—a word commonly heard in his parents' melding of English with the *Plattdeutsch* of their Friesland origins—as well as questions like, what would it be like *not* to have been?

Dis-ease with the night sky might have been finessed, at least negotiated, had the dreams not commenced, perhaps at age seven or eight, well before *Sputnik* caused everyone to look up. The setting was unvarying: a point somewhere in galactic space where he was rendered immobile by perfectly balanced forces of gravity. There was neither up nor down, north or south, day or night, in this emptiness. But it was on the peg of *time* even more than space that terror chiefly hung: it was always, and ever, too late. The nightmare began and ended the same: he was irrevocably tethered to this point in space with time having already run out.

Newly acquired in school, the image of the mathematical symbol of infinity (∞), large, metallic, and *literal*, began appearing regularly in his nightmares. Whether applied to space or time, personalized or in the abstract, this symbol was terrifying, the notion of undelimitedness in the strange world of dreams concussing. A child, he could not deal with that represented by the symbol ∞, and he felt too overmatched to seek help. Other symbols encountered in his dreams—such as a spurred boot and silverware, both also literal, metallic, and gigantic—served, unlike the sign ∞, more as props than players in the drama.

His most tender memories of his father would be of being held in the darkness, gently coaxed back to earth after his horrific space odyssey. Surely the family's periodic subjection to hellfire and brimstone sermons contributed significantly to his nightmares, but long after he had become a man he would puzzle over the way in which a bizarre scenario regarding both time and space had been his common morning detritus, the residue after nocturnal flames had blasted the beaker of his being. He became acquainted with terror decades before the word became a trump card in political discourse.

Later, in his pre-pubescence, he and a favorite cousin would hole up from time to time on winter Sunday afternoons in either of their upstairs bedrooms. The activity was the boys' serialized space voyage that they yarned out like a brace of dueling banjos. He would take the craft through zillions of light years of space out to the edge of the universe, after which his cousin would seize the baton and spin the next leg through a billion-mile wall of titanium or perhaps quartz. Back would come the baton in this competitive antiphony: Don Quixote and Sancho Panza in turn sallying forth to tilt with an infinite forest of cosmic windmills.

To this arduous voyage the two Argonauts would repeatedly return on the day of rest. On one occasion, they brought the ship to the yet farther edge of the universe, this time being blocked by a great cosmic throne consisting of . . . *shit*, one of them blurted out. Both navigators were taken aback: the darker side of tilting with the seeming infinity of the universe had surely won that hand.

A poem he would write in his midforties suggested that what he brought to the space of the night sky continued to make it a disconcerting place:

> how old was i when first beyond
> galactic stunning ice

i touched as though an open nerve
the question that is i?

Then already in the July of his years, he continued to experience the character of the night sky as residing in its coldness and emptiness; it remained a place of loss. The eyes of his body, mind, and, especially, spirit remained largely averted.

In retrospect, my use of the grammatical third person in the above narrative of the terrified dreamer evidences the discontinuity I feel between the two chapters of my life regarding the night sky. Whether reading now the words about the night sky by either the boy or the middle-aged man, I still experience both to be persons I chronicle more than am.

28. Prayer in an Exploding Cosmology

A. Nudges to Look Up in a Vertically Challenged Land

Parts II and III of this work are punctuated with references to Tylerton as vertically challenged. Indeed, on one occasion I did a far reach for thunderheads to generate some verticality, on another the depths of the Sound's Puppy Hole as inversion of the same. This vertically challenged line, tongue partially in cheek, was intended as neither ridicule nor chauvinism, but rather compliment, term of endearment: must be quite a place if but *two* dimensions will suffice! Besides, if the economic and minimalist qualities of the apophatic vision pertain—that less can often be more, that what really matters may be better hinted at by the stark than the superlative—then introducing a spiritually evocative place as having but length and breadth might be just about right.

Although generally aware upon moving to Tylerton that there had been astonishing developments in the vertical disciplines of astronomy and astrophysics since the summer of 1962 when I had shifted from scientific to theological studies, other priorities had kept me from serious reading in either the former or the hinterland betwixt.

So how was it that I moved beyond decades of dis-ease with the night sky and began, on the Crick, *to look up*? How was it that the vertical's ship finally came in, and in such a vertically challenged place, one in which verticality was seemingly only virtual? In retrospect, it appears this shift involved a village of mothers, five of whom I cite here.

The Contagion of Attentiveness

I began to look up precisely because I had been learning to look down, and with greater care. The marsh made me do it! More of the Isle Virus, more getting high on marsh gas! I am speaking here of how the islescape, approached with growing curiosity and respect, seized me by the scruff of the neck: "Hey! Pay attention!"

A blizzard of bio-factors was weighing more heavily upon me as the decade turned.

- I was living, unprecedentedly, in daily contact, cheek-to-jowl, with my living fellow fauna.
- I was observing, and pondering, their frenzied oscillation between copulating

and procreating, the process whereby they were passing perhaps slightly enhanced genes to progeny.

- I now had daily experiences of the "food chain" as a sphere of violence, suffering, and death; the survival of the fittest, a drama red of both tooth and claw.

- Fossil sites, such as the Calvert Cliffs opposite Dorchester County, were reminding me of the past existence of massive numbers of fellow species having long since become extinct in this bloody fray.

- The emergence of increasingly powerful astronomical instruments, complementing major strides in molecular biology and archaeology, was allowing me to look back into time, thus shedding light on both the context and antecedents of critters' ubiquitous struggle to live. Indeed, I repeatedly found myself awed, humbled, and *respectful* of the fauna's ferocious will to live, both as organisms and species.

- And I was for the first time morally restless regarding my own prime predator perch atop the bio-pyramid, my meeting of needs and wants at the expense of fellow fauna whose distant relative status was taking on existential weightiness.

Moving to the Crick taught me that I had not previously cultivated skills of careful observation of the natural world, whether flora or fauna, animate or inanimate. In this regard Tylerton was a candy store: every square meter was a bio-habitat; the seasons were bountifully varied; *every* Sound crossing was a faunal tutorial if I cared; and nightly professorial briefings on the critters took place in the Market's seminar. The place was incredibly *fecund*!

My point is that I found the experience of becoming a more careful and attentive observer of flora and fauna near at hand to be *contagious*. Living on the land/sea membrane, it was only a matter of time before attentiveness regarding the isle and its environs served to thrust my eyes upward, toward and beyond the earth/sky frontier as well. Indeed, after decades of being largely ignored, that thrust would assume a major role in the dilating of both my person and my faith.

But, while becoming a more careful horizontal observer has me profoundly indebted to the watermen, many of whom paid for their attentiveness on the breast of the bright sea with glaucoma and/or cataracts, they as a group were not among my mentors as to what I was seeing *up there*. The fact that I found only one or two particularly interested in the night sky may reflect either that culture's penchant for practicality, or intimidation in the face of what all that verticality might have to teach us.

Falling into Tylerton's Night Sky

A second nudge to look up was, of course, Tylerton's night sky itself, the space above the place, that space that was now *also* becoming a place! Our decade mid-Bay, largely removed from urban pollutants including light, afforded me in multiples my own thousand and one nights, nights crystal-clear, gorgeous, and so deep that I would grasp the perch railing lest I fall in. And whether my vantage point was the balcony, the Oratory window, the dock, the decks off either kitchen or Green House, or that sweet spot beyond the right field foul line of the softball field where the faint Crisfield skyline nine miles away was the only artificial light, the night sky simply commandeered my attention. More often than not, that sky was clear, unoccluded, unsullied, and stunning!

I recall rising in the pre-dawn darkness on March 23, 1997, to watch from one of Black Walnut Point's windows the splendor of the Hale-Bopp comet. Late the following evening, leaving the isle the last time before moving to Tylerton, Sharryl and I pulled off Route 50 between Cambridge and Easton to gaze wordlessly into that phenomenon yet again. Being so close to sea level, not unlike the Sinai whose night sky had wowed me back in 1974, Tylerton could not match the reduced atmosphere and pristine clarity of the Trappist monastery site in Snowmass, Colorado, at an elevation of more than eight thousand feet where Sharryl and I spent a week in early 2003. Nor was the Inn's starry, starry night book-ended by wolves singing first vespers and then lauds as they had there. Nevertheless, our isle's night sky warranted no apologies.

The second half of our decade saw a growing trickle of information becoming available about the Chesapeake Bay Impact Crater formed thirty-five million years ago just a couple dozen miles south of Tylerton. That event, and its aftermath, began to constitute a tether for me between the two dimensional bayscape I had come to love, and forces far beyond our planet, indeed, our solar system. I would ponder the irony of this link: on a slip of isle marooned within an estuary almost certainly nudged toward being by a celestial visitor, I had begun to cultivate a relationship with the outer reaches of the uni-verse from which that gate-crasher had come, sensing in so doing that I was completing the circle. After all, an island, a speck of shoal in this case, surrounded by a vast emptiness interrupted by the lights of a ship or two, is not the least promising setting in which to ponder a night sky having similar characteristics but with exponentially greater scale. Thus before turning in, I would often slip out onto my perch to check the lights . . . both kinds.

What I was discovering was that the night sky, like all other places, whether Jerusalem or Tylerton, was a construct, one melding a certain cosmological givenness with a pre-text that I was bringing to it. But rather than static, my pre-text now was shifting. The childhood construct had been one of emptiness, loss, and terror. Now, more than fifty-five years later, the experience was bending toward wonder, awe, and, in time, adoration. Thus Part VI of this work has been both occasioned and shaped by transition from night sky as nightmare to glimpse into the dream of the One, by the journey from Milky Way as precinct of fear to that of prayer shawl.

Guests on the Science / Faith Nexus

A third nudge to look up more came from particular persons. Two of these had been Washington, D.C. friends first, guests subsequently. Bill Hocking, Goddard engineer from the dawn of the space race and my sponsor on entering the Roman Catholic Church, had me looking up for reasons of his trade, tales, and temperament. Another, Jean Matlack, by vocation a spiritual pilgrim, drew me into the writings of cosmologist Brian Swimme. While I would not find all of Swimme's correlations of the Roman Catholic faith with science helpful, I received much from him. He helped me to move toward both a more holistic understanding of the cosmos (hence my borrowing of his hyphenated word "uni-verse") and a deeper appreciation of its preciousness in my biblical / theological tradition. My response to Swimme's work included both reflecting upon and praying more intentionally about my *place* in that whole.

From time to time, whether triggered by the rising of the inflated peach moon in the east, the brilliant lantern of Venus hanging amid the dusk's charcoal wash in the west, or the milky river cleaving the dome above, the languid conversation following dinner would adjourn to lane or dock. On one such occasion a guest, armed with stronger binoculars than those of the house, invited me to view for the first time Jupiter surrounded by his four most visible wards. After I had purchased my own Oberwerk 20x80 binoculars with tripod, I would often revisit that sight. A guest couple—both ophthalmologists, not surprisingly—generously donated a new telescope to the inn which I immediately began to turn on the ascending moon from the Oratory window.

Our guests included numerous scientists, some from agencies such as National Oceanic & Atmospheric Administration (NOAA), others defense contractors, yet others from science faculties of major universities. Several would email me from time to time about aspects of our overlapping astronomy interests. While I was circumspect about initiating shoptalk with guests, scientists' animated interest in Tylerton's environmental challenges repeatedly ignited fruitful exchanges. A weekend with an evangelical astrophysicist out of Cal Berkeley, who talked about cosmogenesis/faith issues, was inspiring.

Also germane to my interest was intermittent NPR coverage and commentary regarding the National Genome Project, completed in 2003 under the leadership of Dr. Francis S. Collins, also an evangelical. On the other hand, a younger physicist guest lamented how some of the guild's graying members, "especially if they have a Nobel under their belts!" would wander off to dally in the "why question." He seemed embarrassed by such geriatric proclivities.

Yet, more than with the reductionism of "ideological scientism" or "materialism," I had long been impatient with the advocates of creationism including Intelligent Design, its latest proxy. Religion unhooked from mystery tends to wield the hammers of literalism and dogma upon poetry, myth, and metaphor, with the result being the savaging of sacred texts filled with awe and wonder. Creationists' stonewalling and tortured manipulations of scientific data has long struck me as tragically unnecessary, as ideological self-indulgence in a world filled with very real needs, as a transparent prizing of certitude over faith. My suspicion—that I would not find kindred spirits for my emerging enthusiasm for the night sky amid creationists in Tylerton's sanctuary or store—was also confirmed.

Finally, a "might-have-been" addendum: in the mid-1980s I had served as handler for Dominican Fr. Matthew Fox during a series of lectures he gave at the Mennonite seminary where I was teaching. This had allowed me quality time with him, including discussion of his recently published and widely celebrated *Original Blessing*, a work explicating creation spirituality, a subject not unrelated to the journey being sketched out here in Part VI. However, the two of us were moving in different directions: my inclinations were seemingly more Incarnation-centered than his; he would leave the Roman Catholic Church about the time that I entered it; and what might have been a major influence on my journey was, for reasons including timing, not to be.

Personal Study and Reflection

These experiences with the biosphere, the night sky, and scientist guests gradually propelled me into books and websites wrestling with the spirituality implications of discoveries in the fields of astronomy and cosmogenesis, a fourth nudge toward looking up. From Brian Swimme's 1995 audio tapes entitled *Canticle to the Cosmos*, lent to me by Jean Matlack, I moved on to his *The Hidden Heart of the Cosmos: Humanity and the New Story* (1999) and then the work he co-authored with Thomas Berry: *The Universe Story* (1992). Berry's *The Dream of the Earth* (1988) and *The Great Work: Our Way Into the Future* (1999) followed.

My interest in the implications of cosmogenesis for a Christian anthropology got me into the writings of Georgetown University's John Haught, particularly his *God After Darwin: a Theology of Evolution* (2000). The reciprocal enrichment of science and faith in the vision of Harvard astronomer Owen Gingerich's *God's Universe* (2006) increased my courage, as did *Making the Shift: Seeing Faith Through a New Lens* by Elaine M. Prevallet SL. Across our last five years guests had been introducing me to Jared Diamond's books, each fleshing out in broad, and occasionally simplistic, strokes an aspect of a developmental understanding of all of life: *The Third Chimpanzee* (1992); *Guns, Germs, and Steel* (1997); and *Collapse* (2005).

I came to understand cosmology as a guiding gestalt, a collective construct, a crafted "multi-struct" for thinking about *everything*, whether inanimate matter/energy or denizens of the biosphere including ourselves. The Ptolemaic multi-struct holding sway in medieval Christendom had been geocentric: Earth, and humankind, were central to the movements of the heavenly bodies and, presumably, the interests of the heavenly One. It was a comforting, reassuring cosmology for pedestaled humankind, one also conveniently in harmony with a literal reading of Genesis.

My exploration of the disturbing of that Ptolemaic construct was triggered by Gingerich's *The Book Nobody Read: Chasing the Revolutions of Nicolaus Copernicus* (2004) as well as Dava Sobel's *Galileo's Daughter: A Historical Memoir of Science, Faith, and Love* (2002). The subjects of these two works, Copernicus (1473–1543) and Galileo (1564–1642), began the torturous supplanting of a geocentric gestalt with a helio-centric one that relegated both Earth and humankind to a less obvious centrality even while arguably implying a far greater grandeur on the part of the One. The passion with which that reconfiguration was both espoused and opposed, and the duration of resistance to it—Galileo, convicted of heresy in 1632, was only formally acquitted by Pope John Paul II 360 years later!—did not suggest that issues cosmological were passé. Incidentally, I was delighted to discover that John of the Cross, in his culminat-ing Living Flame of Love (1586), implied support for heliocentrism, this perhaps the result of his 1564–68 study at the University of Salamanca with its astronomy chair.

What sixteenth–century Christendom faced in the challenge of Copernicus and Galileo and what we people of faith face today are not entirely dissimilar. In my life-time the heliocentric configuration, still clutching the earlier anthropocentricity, has become the obsolete construct, having been inundated by a deluge of discoveries in the disciplines of astronomy and astrophysics as well as molecular and evolutionary biology. Even more unsettling for many has been the emergence of virtually irrefut-able evidence that all that is in the cosmos, including our human sort, has evolved from earlier forms, and that *process* is everywhere operative. It is ironic that while the emerging cosmology is received by many persons of faith as showcasing the Creator's grandeur vastly beyond that of the two previous models, many others remain uneasy regarding the relationship of either ourselves or the One with such a construct. Nor does the fact that the new cosmology, a work in progress, must remain open to repeated tweaking into the future lower the anxiety level.

Mid–decade I also came upon the text of Pope John Paul II's 1996 address to the Pontifical Academy of Sciences entitled "Truth Cannot Contradict Truth." Here he elaborated upon the Church's openness to viewing human development within the "physical continuity" of both cosmic and biological evolution as supported by scientific inquiry, *provided* there is acknowledgment of a mysterious "ontological leap" in the human spiritual distinctive, one which cannot be fully accounted for by scientific inquiry. John Paul II wrote that this human discontinuity, including "the experience of metaphysical knowledge, of self–awareness and self–reflection, of moral conscience, freedom, or again of aesthetic and religious experience," looks to philosophy and, especially, theology for its ultimate meaning. For me his address, one implying the importance of the theme of freedom in all aspects of the unfolding of both the cosmos and humankind, represented a broadening of Vatican II's groundbreaking "Declaration on Religious Freedom" in late 1965. Living amid Tylerton's biosphere and under its night sky, I joyfully embraced the Holy Father's words as confirming a place where I could, and do, stand.

It was only gradually that I glimpsed more clearly the scale of reconfiguration called for at the interface of my faith and a developmental understanding of the cosmos. I can best provide glimpses into that process by remaining in the interrogative of my journaling at the time. If the horizon of my vision is merely my self, nation, species, or planet, awareness of the larger cosmos might seem largely irrelevant; but what if all such parameters are removed? Does an expanded cosmology merely mean that my faith has gained a more spacious venue within which to arrange its same beliefs, or is there something far more seismic going on at the spirituality/cosmology interface? How is the living out of my faith altered by knowledge that my very capacity to do so is fruit of an unfolding and recycling of elements now approximately 13.7 billion years old, and counting?

What difference does it make if the locus of the tabernacling of the One is expanded from Bethlehem to the cosmos at large? While all places may well be alike insofar as they are constructs—spaces engaged by us humans, whether that space be island or stable—what happens when the space engaged is a massive, elegant, unfolding cosmos and the human engagement a peculiar sort called prayer, raised from a point embedded within that space itself? Must not such prayer to the One be profoundly affected by my relationships with, and obligations to, the star–stuff elements, the local energy–nurturing star, and our inimitably calibrated planet, the host of antecedent organisms from all of which/whom the framer of this question has sprung? Yet if so, what does prayer seek in such a uni–verse where all, including the pray–er herself, is fruit of eons of fine–tuning? Such questions were often in both my thoughts and prayers during the second half of our decade.

But particularly urgent for me was the issue of how the One of the biblical narrative is understood to be actively present in a cosmos, the unfolding of which science is learning more about every day. How this question is handled hinges largely on whether one equates the taking seriously of scripture with literal interpretation only. Such an equation, not unlike the Church's sixteenth–century position, makes it difficult for religion and science to engage in dialogue toward the goal of greater understanding. It was my emerging conviction that in contrast to being merely tacked onto a traditional belief system, the new cosmology required a re–formulation of the worldviews in terms of which we have understood the faith. The new cosmology did not merely provide a more capacious stage for the drama: it was as much part of the drama as were we humans.

The Role of the Cosmos in the Biblical Story

The compounding of growing observation skills; the haunting mystery beckoning above; the stimulation of guests, study, and reflection: all these served to "re–mind" me that the defining narrative of my life, the biblical one, was not disinterested in the natural world, whether planetary or cosmic, and the human relationship with it. Not only did scripture, explicated and interpreted in an unfolding tradition, declare the One to be Creator of all that is, but this One's abiding interest in and engagement with the creation was a foundational assumption of biblical faith. Scripture, bundled with the tradition of its interpretation, thus constituted a fifth, and not insignificant, nudge toward looking up.

I was particularly drawn to sacred writ regarding the *scale* of the redemptive initiative at the center of the biblical story. What was I to make of accounts of the One's postdiluvian covenant with Noah and "every living creature that is with you, for all successive generations" (Gn 9:8–17) or the Mosaic legislation regarding the Sabbath Year and the Year of Jubilee (Lv 25), both expressive of divine interest in the creation far beyond the merely human? Or Hosea's prophesied covenant, characterized by complete safety and the abolition of war, with living creatures right down to the critters creeping on the ground *included as covenantal partners* (Hos 2:18–20)?

Was there a Freudian slip in my repeated temptation to substitute "species" for "nations" when the Office included Psalm 147:20: "He has not dealt thus with other nations; he has not taught them his decrees"? Did we humans have a vocation to convey to the other creatures, indeed, the entire cosmos, their inclusion in the One's favor, this analogous to that of the Hebrews to be a "light to the nations"? Was not the psalmist implying such inclusiveness when he wrote, "Let *everything that has breath* praise You" (fr Ps 150:6)?

And was not the Apostle Paul alluding to such expansiveness when he wrote that the whole creation groans in anxious anticipation of its participation in "the freedom of the glory of the children of God" (Rom 8:18–25)? Is it not a *cosmic* vision of healing underlying his Ephesians reference to the "consolidating of all things [*ta pánta*] in the Christ, things in the heavens or things on the earth" (Eph 1:10), or that in Colossians: "For it was the Father's pleasure to reconcile all things [*ta pánta*] to Himself . . . things on earth or things in heaven" (Col 1:19–20)? (In the latter's context [verses 15–20], equivalents of "all things" [*ta pánta*] occur seven times!) And is it not the *télos,* the goal, of this consolidating and reconciling "that God may be all in all" (1 Cor 15:28)?

And do not both 2 Peter (3:13) and the Apocalypse (21:1) echo the "on earth as it is in heaven" linkage in the "Our Father" prayer (Mt 6:9–13; Lu 11:2–4) in speaking explicitly of "a new heaven and a new earth"? Indeed, is not the "new Jerusalem," the Apocalypse's sociopolitical image of life shared with the One beyond time, described as both "coming down out of heaven" and the One's permanent domicile among humans, the fruition of that One's declaration, "Behold, I am making all things new" (Apoc 21:1–5)?

Although some of the heresies with which the Christian church struggled during its early centuries were Gnostic—that is, denigrating the natural or physical in favor of the spiritual—did not the Christian movement emerge from those conflicts retaining much of the Hebrew Bible's robust embrace of physicality reflecting the divine interest in the larger creation? Finally, was not this biblical tradition of the creating and engaging One foundational in shaping the vision of one such as Dante Alighieri (1265–1321) when, Ptolemaic though he was, he concluded his *Comedy* with reference to "the Love that moves the Sun and the other stars"?

Carl Sagan answered his own famous question, "Who speaks for Earth?" by rightly pointing to ourselves: humans. But for us of biblical faith, must not the answer be enlarged? For is not the One issuing the seven-fold imprimatur of "good" in Genesis, the One wooing the cosmos toward wholeness, the One "tabernacling" amid it both in the Christ (Jn 1:14) and permanently beyond time (Apoc 21:3), one and the same, the uni—verse's chief advocate and defender in solidarity with whom we human are invited to stand?

B. Growing Edges at the Spirituality/Cosmology Interface

In the spring of 2001 the evangelist in Tylerton's annual revival meetings was Rev. Jim Riley, pastor of one of Crisfield's numerous Methodist congregations. Although ambivalent about such meetings and attending but infrequently, I had enjoyed him as a guest at the Inn, and I decided to chance it.

Amid his sermon Pastor Jim recounted a past experience: how he, amid forty thousand persons in a religious gathering in an Atlanta stadium, had yet again prayed for liberation from self-absorption in his life of prayer. Suddenly, he continued, he had heard himself addressed, and with the boyhood nickname long since shed: "Binky, I want you to sing me your song; I want you to climb up into my lap and sing me your song." Hesitating, albeit briefly, Pastor Jim had stood and begun to sing, learning only later that many people around him had joined in his song.

From a deep place within myself I felt a soft "yes" rising as I heard this story, and it rises within me still as I write this several years later. Most obviously, I resonate with the musical imagery, with the invitation extended to me to respond antiphonally to the One's silent music infusing all that is. Relatedly, I celebrate both the freedom, the agency, implicitly ceded me as to whether I participate in the Song, and the prizing of something unique which I *alone* can generate. Although we Roman Catholics intone the *Kyrie* together, sing the *Gloria* together, recite the *Credo* together, speak the words "Lord, I am not worthy to receive You" together, I compose and sing my inimitable song to the Maestro *all by myself!* And finally, I warm to the way both invitation and response in Pastor Jim's story emerge from within the confines of a loving embrace.

Part VI of this book is, among other things, an expression of my desire to sing my own song to the Embracing One, and to do so in a manner also *less self—absorbed, less minuscule of heart and mind.* The night sky, the now increasingly vast yet friendly skies, helped me to do that. Rather than linear and orderly, the growth at the spirituality/cosmology interface, initially below the horizon of my consciousness and intentionality, brings to mind the image of snowflakes: each unique and yet all of a kind, mysteriously appearing almost simultaneously at a time meteorologically ripe.

What follows is an overview of four such points where my song discovered its voice, progressing from what might be the least to the most weighty. What the four issues have in common is that each was the fruit of both prayer and reflection, each was but a point on a journey, and each was a different glimpse of the Mystery toward which cosmology no less than spirituality is both pointing and moving.

Perspective and Dilation

First, cosmology became increasingly relevant to prayer, the singing of my song to the Embracer, because of the matter of perspective. In chapter 10 I alluded to the usefulness of the microcosmic perch of living on an island with a population of but fifty-eight. The second part of the "think globally, act locally" slogan is seemingly more manageable at that scale even as the isle's environs provide metaphors for a larger vision.

The night sky greatly expands that dynamic. Whether as antidote to *hubris*, provincialism, anthropocentrism, or religion *sans* mystery, I found that positioning myself in the village, and then in turn the Island, Bay basin, planet Earth, Milky Way, Local Group of galaxies, and uni-verse both humbled and inspired me. The gerbil runs of my routines, trivialities, and preoccupations got put into perspective when I pondered, for example, the magnitude and distance of Sagittarius' trove in the lower southern sky.

In chapter 19 I jocularly designated the insular dangers of island life with the term "Isle Fever." "Think islely and act islely" might then be the slogan for a collective solipsism and self-absorption, for life turned in on itself. All of us are susceptible to the temptation to draw in our horizons to the shores of our respective islands, of projecting the smallness of our minds, spirits, and hearts onto the face of the cosmos. In contrast, as with both music and human love, the night sky dilates, stretches, and prepares us for what is greater rather than lesser about ourselves. Its awesome grandeur nurtures both our capacity and our hunger for transcendence. Indeed, the night sky was becoming for me tutorial for the One. I was learning *existentially* that I would be a creature of smaller spirit without its recurring hush.

But beyond the argument that the night sky expands the human spirit is the question whether I as a person of faith have the courage to allow that faith and the new cosmology freely to have at each other. I find the query of the psalmist to be helpful: "What is a human being that You should take thought of her, a mortal that You care for her?" (fr Ps 8:4). For many of my siblings in the faith, a developmental understanding of human origins and the implications of cosmogenesis for our understanding of how the One is active in the world are both so frightening that the psalmist's question is answered in the static categories of a cosmology having *twice* been rendered obsolete.

For others confessing the One as self-disclosing in the two books—that of religion and that of science, each having its own methodologies, jurisdictions, and questions—the present period is arguably the most exciting ever. I see the first group as requiring greater certitude and the second as open to a more central role for mystery. In the second half of our decade on the Crick, I identified with this second group with growing intentionality: the expansion of the sounding box of the silent music to the space and time of the cosmos as we are coming to know it cannot but enhance the stature of the Maestro!

Lectio Divina and the Text of the Cosmos

A second interface between spirituality and an emerging cosmology involved for me the traditional Benedictine method of *lectio divina* ("divine reading"). This ancient practice of praying the scriptures might be summarized as reading (*lectio*), reflecting (*meditatio*), responding (*oratio*), and resting (*contemplatio*). The summit of prayer so practiced—prepared for by engagement of the eye and other senses (*lectio*), the reflective and meditative capabilities of the intellect (*meditatio*), and both the capacity and freedom for response from the reader's center or heart (*oratio*)—is a state of intimate rest in the One who is, finally, beyond words, thoughts, or images (*contemplatio*). This goal of *lectio divina* is realized by allowing the reading of words on pages in the text to be transformed into a reciprocal and loving conversation between author and reader.

As one believing the two books—scripture/tradition and nature—to share the same author, I found myself drawn into *lectio divina* beneath the night sky. Here encounter with nature, as in reading its companion volume, requires attentive observation (*lectio*). Although enriched by the use of a bevy of excellent instruments as well as the photographic trove offered by the web in particular, the unmediated experience of the naked eye beneath the night sky cannot be supplanted. Yet observation needs to be enriched by research, reflection, and integration (*meditatio*) in what is arguably the most rapidly advancing period in the history of astronomy and cosmology. *Lectio* should not be deprived of this *meditatio* lest the reader be marooned, either in terror in the face of immensity as was I as a child, or in a cul-de-sac of mere astonishment as millions are in this privileged era when access to deep space is but a click away.

But *lectio divina* beneath the night sky beckons yet further, soliciting response (*oratio*) on the part of the reader from her very center. And as with scripture/tradition, it is not only response to the "text," not merely to this or that, but to the One out of whose loving embrace that night sky has come to be. This step in my case unfolded gradually and inadvertently, but in time would break forth out of the first two steps. Finally, there is rest in the Source (*contemplatio*), a teasing increment of satisfaction, one neither guaranteed nor of duration, often beyond both thoughts and images, where all is decisively well and the appetite is whetted.

Indeed, I found it just as possible to "pray the cosmos" as the scriptures. The two books, having the same author, cannot contradict each other; scientific inquiry and faith, each properly exercised, the jurisdictions and methodologies of each both differentiated and honored, have nothing to fear in each other. In contrast to the argument from design of either deist or creationist, in which the intellect extrapolates from pattern to patterner, *lectio divina* beneath the night sky is the heart incrementally wooed by the One in the direction of relationship, adoration, and union.

The Night Sky as Apophatic Desert

A third interface of prayer and the new cosmology returns to the distinction between language *kataphatic* (with images) and *apophatic* (without). Instructive here is Psalm 19:1 which, thanks to Franz Joseph Haydn (1732–1809), is for me always *heard* thus: "The heavens are telling the glory of God, the wonder of his work displays the firmament." This is an uncomplicated kataphatic statement: the night sky showcases both the artisanship and grandeur of the One. This is in principle not unlike my childhood experience, only then my senses assessed the night sky as seemingly infinite, cold, and indifferent, words which bludgeoned me in their literalness. And to the extent to which that night sky was image for the One, that One was then boundless, cold, and indifferent, essentially a deist god, or worse.

I am reasonably sure that I would never have gotten past that take on the night sky had I not received help from another quarter. The Apostle Paul seems to concur when he cannot move beyond "eternal power and divine nature" in summarizing what of the One gentiles are accountable for knowing *from nature* (Rom 1:20). For me evidence of the infinitude, power, and artisanship of the One just wouldn't cut it, for these provided no hint of the One's disposition toward me. In retrospect, my childhood nightmares were a prolonged series of exposés of just how discomforting immensity was to me, how little ∞ satisfied this hungering heart.

However, having been seized in the backstretch by the unequivocal disposition of the One toward me disclosed via the Bethlehem project, I had been able, rounding the far turn, to return to the night sky. The kataphatic majesty and stunning handiwork were still there—neither the compelling nor repelling would ever be entirely removed—but now mine was primarily an apophatic "reading" of that sky, one dilated to the boundlessness of Divine Love.

Regarding that which matters most, the apophatic is *never* content with the surface, the literal, but *always* seeks to peer down into the Mystery deep down into and beyond all that is: the One. Indeed, the apophatic was transforming for me the cold, void, and indifference of the night sky, as it earlier had the sea, into *desert*, the arena stripped of similitude and analogy, and increasingly denuded of all else but the self and the One with whom I have to do. Among the images in the Carmelite tradition for that One encountered in this desert is the Furnace of Love: implicit in John of the Cross, explicit in Thérèse of Lisieux OCD (1873–1897).

A strange thing began to unfold in my prayer life beneath this stark celestial desert: I began to hear myself addressing the One with improbable names, including some laced with irony or paradox: Mystery, Abyss, Thicket, Desert, Torrent, Furnace, Night, Lover. But especially *Fire*. Each name was a different surface on the multivalent crystal, each a reminder that neither one nor all *together* could name the Whirlwind ensconced beyond all names. And the more I donned the Milky Way as my prayer shawl, allowing its silent music to draw me down into, through, and beyond itself, the more frequently prayer became, rather than the striving across a lifetime, something *being done within me* rather than merely *done by me*. It was wonderful when for the first time I cried uncontrollably—another kind of weeping now—under Tylerton's night sky!

To repeat, my experience had seemingly been *the reverse* of the extrapolation from clock to intelligent clockmaker often associated with the book *Natural Theology* published in 1802 by Anglican divine William Paley (1743–1805). No, the sequence along which I was being drawn was from Lover to beloved cosmos.

Freedom and the Cosmic Dance

But the growth issue at the frontier between a spirituality tethered to scripture / tradition and modern cosmology receiving the most attention from me was the intriguing role in each of some expression of "freedom."

Although the terminology differs widely—from the capability of moral agency, volition, or deliberative choice with humans, to randomness, contingency, probability, and chaos theory's exploration of the inherent lack of predictability with inanimate objects or systems—I experienced neither jurisdiction as scripted or mechanistically pre-determined. There seemed rather to be an openness to varied possibilities in human beings which is not entirely unlike that of the cosmos itself.

Freedom, of course, is not a new issue: both religion and science had each long addressed it within their respective jurisdictions. What became important for me for the first time on the Crick was the crucial role of freedom when the two jurisdictions, spirituality and the emerging cosmology, were allowed to inform each other. What is the role of freedom in each of the two processes that I attribute to the One: the Christ event and cosmogenesis?

Freedom in the Christ Event—Looking first at the one born in Bethlehem, a motif rising out of scripture and orchestrated in the Roman Catholic tradition, the

311

theme of freedom is present everywhere. From the divine side, we believe that the One freely chose to bring into being that which was not, to give that creation being outside the One's self (contra pantheism), and to allow it a measure of independence to be itself rather than function as mere machine.

Furthermore, we believe that the One freely chose in Jesus the Christ to "tabernacle" among (Jn 1:14), establish solidarity with, humans in particular, the cosmos in general. But on the human side, the role of freedom in this event is no less prominent: first, paradigmatically and astonishingly, in Mary. Not only the angel Gabriel, but all humanity and the entire cosmos—indeed, none less than the One—awaited her response (Lk 1:38) in the Annunciation. The One, it seems, extends and then honors freedom.

But this is but the beginning of the freedom strand in the tale. Implicit in the birth, ministry, teachings, associations, and solidarity with humankind even to the death on the part of Jesus, was his freedom to set aside, abdicate, divest of presumed prerogatives. Even the cross itself appears to be subject to his agency. From Bethlehem to Golgotha there was in him a consistent pattern of *relinquishment* in which less somehow became more, and in which what was presumed to be weakness became expressive of divine power. This is kingship, to say nothing of "deityship," on a road less traveled!

The Apostle Paul speaks of this characteristic of the Christ as his "pouring himself out" (Phil 2:7), as, while having been rich, becoming poor, this for the sake of us humans (2 Cor 8:9). The carol "Hark! The Herald Angels Sing" alludes to this theme with the phrase "Mild he lays his glory by." Perhaps the most poignant expression of this relinquishment are words attributed to the Christ on the cross, words taken from the Psalms (22:1): "My God! My God! Why have You abandoned me?" (Mk 15:34; Mt 27:46). The challenge confronting first-century Jews is not unlike that facing us: the "pouring out," the relinquishing, profile of the Christ, *sans* omnipotence and companions, cuts across nearly all existing models of messiahship, to say nothing of deityship.

But there is even more at stake in this messianic opting for relinquishment, much more than merely the shape of the messianic kingdom Jesus proclaimed and inaugurated. The Christian scriptures claim that the relinquishing, self-out-pouring profile of the Christ is no less than that of the One, both Creator and Consummator of the cosmos. In the Fourth Gospel the Christ responds to Philip: "The one having seen me has seen the Father" (Jn 14:9). The Apostle Paul in his letter to the church at Colossae (Col 1:15) represents the Christ as "the icon of the invisible God," a theme he repeats in his second letter to the church in Corinth (2 Cor 4:4). In the introduction to the

Epistle to the Hebrews (Heb 1:3) the Christ is referred to as "being . . . the express image of the essence of God."

The message is both simple and momentous in its implications: what we see in the Christ is what we get in the One! The relinquishment style, the pouring out of himself on the part of the Christ, is indicative of the character of the One. Thus on Dark Friday *the One* relinquished; more specifically, *the One* suffered, *the One* was crucified, *the One* died.

The cumulative effect of the previous sentence triggers the question I consider to be the definitive shibboleth of our religion-lacerated time: is the principal *modus operandi* of the One that of relinquishment and self-giving Love rather than power, immensity, and sovereignty? Is not the very content of the divine power supplied by this relinquishment? Needless to say, the implications of this relinquishing understanding of the One, whether for "just preemptive war" or how I respond to my neighbor, are both vast and theologically incendiary. But our interest here is to push out neglected aspects of freedom present in the One's solidarity initiative.

The freedom and willingness of the One to relinquish, even to the death, is the precondition in the Christian faith creating major space for *human* freedom. Implicit in the One's freedom to relinquish is mine as *imago*-bearer to do the same, or its opposite. The One of the self-outpouring is not a deterministic deity, one by whom my assigned responses are locked up in some predestinated vault. What is implicit in the Christ's appeal to me to pattern my life after the Relinquishing One—namely, freedom on my part so to choose—is matched by my own experience as having received that freedom.

In the words of T. E. Lawrence in *The Seven Pillars of Wisdom*, "nothing is written" irrevocably in stone; my choices, whether large or small, are real, frighteningly real, rather than merely apparent. Human freedom is not a farce. The call to accountability and responsibility presupposes freedom as does the warning of judgment. In short, the Christ is the One's loving embrace of the human family, but in a way which honors our freedom. On the Crick I was increasingly praying to the One whose *defining* characteristic, rather than infinitude or omni-something, was that of Lover who was both Torrent and relinquishing respecter of my freedom.

But why this foray into the subject of freedom? Is it mere tangent? What is at stake here? While the psalmist infers splendor, artisanship, and righteousness from the night sky (Ps 19:1), and the Apostle Paul is left with but the One's attributes, power, and divine nature that can be derived from creation (Rom 1:20), neither claims that the One's Love is also so deduced. That was exactly my own experiential conclusion across the first half of my life.

Rather, that disclosure of the disposition of the One *toward me*, one of Love, while not restricted to, has been centered in the Christ. Relinquishment, divestiture, and abdication are words for the other side of Love, that which the One not merely does but *is* (1 Jn 4:16). The Christian scriptures, showing their Hebrew origins, particularly that of the late prophets, speak of this divine Love (*agape*) as motivated primarily by neither the object's attractiveness (*eros*) nor the desire for companionship (*philia*), but by who the One is, the One whose principal name in the Hebrew Bible, YHWH, is translated as "I AM WHO AM." In contrast to all human loves, this Love has no "reasons": it flows out of who "I AM WHO AM" is.

In the subsequent Christian tradition, this *agape* (the Latin *caritas* in the West), is showcased for me most clearly and powerfully among two millennia of mystics for whom the One is frequently both Torrent and Fire, Tracker and Lover. Above my desk, midway between the inn's perch and Oratory, is a small sign: "It's a love story, stupid!"

During my decade on the Crick it became increasingly apparent that this Love embodied in the Christ, absent freedom on the part of respondents, was an oxymoron. Consistent with the range of our human loves which serve as prep tutorials, the Love of the One presupposed the prerogative of freedom. Whether in the One's relationship with ancient Israel and Judah, the Christ's conversation with the Samaritan woman at the well (Jn 4), or my own experience as trekker, the One respects human freedom in a way much better hinted at by words like Lover, Wooer, Inviter, and Beckoner than Coercer or Determiner or Infinitude. Indeed, we might say that the One is no more able to spin out Love without freedom than square triangles. *Coerced love, Love, or love, is not*! In this matter the Lover is pro-choice! No exceptions!

This nonnegotiability of freedom implicit in the divine Love has not, of course, been inconsequential. It has seemingly provided opening for the murky mystery of evil, tragedy, suffering, and destruction that the cosmos has absorbed. At several points in my earlier life the issues of theodicy—the attempt to justify belief in the loving One in the face of evil—had ensnared me. But now on the Crick I was pressed by hard counter-questions: Was it not suspect to wring my hands over the massive costs of human freedom even while, in so doing, exercising that very freedom which had rendered that cost possible? Was it not cheeky for me, the clay, to bemoan the disfigurement of the pot when from the outset I had been granted freedom, in effect a co-potter's apprenticeship role?

And although in a younger season I had once flirted with praying in desperation, "O Infinite One, make me automatically holy!" did I really want to go *there*? Did I really want to pay *that* cost and become a secure and innocent *pawn*? Or was my tripping over that freedom's cost hint of just how niggardly was my surrender to the One's whole initiative, from the Flaring Forth of Fire to the "new heavens and new earth"? And so on the Crick I would, sometimes in a single day, even nearly adjacent moments, both exult in the One's shimmering gift of freedom so as to be swept into adoration, and find my spirit concussed that the One would embrace this absolutely terrifying *risk*. But what would low-risk love, to say nothing of the no-risk variety, look like? A square circle?

Somewhere in that decade the image of dance began to grow on me. I had packed it into Tylerton back in 1997, but its use was restricted to the *personal* spiritual journey. I had known that that to which the One who is Love invites us is not a relationship predetermined or mechanistic, but rather one in which each party exercises freedom. The relationship is like a dance, one between two agents, two choosers, two co-creators. Granted there is asymmetry, in that the two dancers share but distant similitude, are decidedly unequal, and one of them leads with the other invited to sing her song. Yet their shared Love is nevertheless rendered concrete in the space of their overlapping freedoms.

Was not the most neglected image of the divine/human relationship, not Judge and violator, nor Redeemer and redeemed, even Parent and child, but collaborators, dancers who together shape what will be? As a dancer I freely bring what no other party, including my partner, could bring: namely, my freely chosen response, my very own song. I even thought in 1997 that the dance image had possibilities for the relationship of the whole human family with the One. However, the enlarging of that image to include *the entire cosmos* would not blossom within me until my spirit had ripened for some time beneath Tylerton's night sky.

Freedom in Cosmogenesis—As my person grew beneath that night sky, I was giving more attention to three interrelated developments across the previous quarter century: an unprecedented expansion of knowledge of the cosmos due, in part, to availability of new technology; an emerging loose consensus that there were strands of directionality in the unfolding of the uni-verse; and, improbably, what many from both religion and science deemed a more promising setting for interactions between their two perspectives.

I realized that the terrain surrounding questions of origin, both cosmic and human, had shifted since I had last been preoccupied with them in seminary nearly forty years earlier. Hypotheses positing both complete randomness and infinite time had been chilled by converging data from various sources suggesting a cosmos age of about 13.7 billion years, a most finite number.

Answers to my earlier uneasiness about other hypotheses had not emerged in the interim. Pantheism positing the cosmos as self-directing, having a homing instinct and an intrinsically purposive grain, remained unpromising for me as a Christian because of how it confused the One and the One's handiwork. Creationism remained unacceptable because it bludgeoned one book while straitjacketing the other in literalism. And deism, while acknowledging the divine regarding cosmic origins, had remained mute regarding the divine's disposition toward or present engagement with this cosmos.

The sole possibility which remained alive for me was one which could grow out of serious interaction between the perspectives of religion and science. An approach to origins positing the cosmos as the fruit of two collaborating subjects, the One and the One's work, each bringing to the adventure both freedom of some sort and receptivity, neither exercising determinative power nor mere passivity, became increasingly attractive. Significantly, such a model did not appear dissimilar to that which I had encountered in the Christ in whom the One, particularly in the cross, had relinquished a measure of control out of respect for human freedom and reciprocity.

Many of my subsequent thoughts remained interrogative, as they do in what follows. Most foundationally, had not the cosmos, birthed in the Flaring Forth of Fire, been given being as that outside the One's self? Had it not subsequently, in effect, been extended the opportunity to take the bit and run with it, be a partner at some level in the shaping of a life of its own, be itself, *become* itself? Did not such an invitation imply something analogous to human agency or freedom, in each particular—whether quark, galaxy, invertebrate, or chimpanzee—proportionate to its capabilities, to the extent of the potentiality of its unfolding? Was there not a variety of categories—contingency, probability, randomness, and unpredictability, for example—each of which sought to address some aspect of this cosmic openness to the unfolding? Indeed, was there not in the cosmos' part of the dance arguably more flex than determinism, probabilism than certitude, option than prescription, contingency than necessity, yet never the total absence of either form or freedom? Had there not been in the unfolding of the cosmos a wide spectrum of expressions rather than one tightly confined, evidences of the cosmos' own participation in its unfolding rather than a role passive or inert?

Furthermore, I found that the cosmos in its unfolding seemed to exercise a capability for problem solving. I noted several examples, from the dearth of heavier elements in the first generation of stars to emergence of *Homo sapiens*, where repeated cul-de-sacs and dead-ends were finally surmounted by some improbable breakthrough. In the case of our planet, sometimes the deck was seemingly rearranged enough by climate shifts or bolide impacts or continental drift or genetic mutation for the breakthrough to ride those coat tails to an improved hand. The cosmos *itself* appeared to exercise qualities of suppleness, subtlety, opportunism, almost plucki-ness. One of my images is of an uneven plowed field being slowly yet steadily flooded from one side, the water, thwarted here, turned to the side and back there, continu-ing to be energized by the momentum of the whole, ever probing, pressing, and re-directing in search of advantageous channels until it has traversed the entire plane.

Tylerton was ever supplying examples of this flex in our corner of the cosmos. From our first visits I was learning about ruthless aspects of the unfolding among my fellow fauna: a random event like a hurricane could severely impact the season's entire crab population; a species' constant adaptation, whether vis-à-vis predators, disease, salinity, or weather, could propel it into either more favorable survival odds or a crisis cul-de-sac for thousands of individual critters or even the species; the zoosphere's state as a whole was in constant flux, its delicately balanced equipoise nudged by far more species and variables than I could know. And as my interests grew I learned that antecedent flora and fauna species now extinct in the continental basin which would become the Bay vastly outnumbered those still resident there, with the counter ticking.

I also learned that some advocates of the unfolding, not unlike creationists, tended to overlook its ragged and chaotic dynamics, inferring directionality only from a perch high above and far away from the particulars. In reality, I experienced the details of the unfolding to be extraordinarily *messy*, whether the indescribable violence of the first generation of stars; the rough sex of later intergalactic rela-tions; the multiple periodic extinctions of significant percentages of our planet's species (including dinosaurs); the actual playing out of that to which euphemistic terms like "food chain" refer; increasing pollution since the onset of the Industrial Revolution, the full impacts of which we are now still only discovering; and violent human deaths at the hands of other humans, in the twentieth century alone, accord-ing to various studies, approaching two hundred million.

While what skewered my attention about the violence of the uni-verse's first ten billion years was its unimaginable scale, that beginning with our planet's Precam-brian time came closer to home because it involved life, critters preying on critters. Archaeology's fossil trail, its incomplete record now being increasingly enriched, or corrected, by disciplines as diverse as genome analysis, paleolinguistics, and pale-oneurology, undercuts any notion of linear and clean progression, whether regarding humans or anything else. Survival of the fittest may appear sublime to some, but only from a great distance, a luxury Tylerton denied me. I found the struggle for survival of millions of critters in a fructive and thus crowded bio-habitat to be a glimpse into a disturbing aspect of the cosmos actively participating in its own becoming.

Add to this the seeming wastefulness of the notion of the emergence of a cosmos, perhaps as much as fifty billion light years in diameter, in service to a goal of a relationship between the Lover and a reciprocating population successfully unfolded in perhaps but one tiny corner of that uni-verse. Yes, the freedom which comes with the territory of being in the dance can be terribly untidy, indeed, costly, even while retaining an element of playfulness in its "Let's toss for snake eyes yet again!" predilection.

In all of this there is present something akin to choice. Not conscious choice or deliberation, but response at some level to forks in the road, a penchant for exploration and experimentation. Given the frequency of cul-de-sacs in the fossil record, the time necessary for even the most modestly advantageous mutation to unfold, it must be concluded that many—or overwhelmingly *most*—of those adaptations have had ill consequences, with the result often being organism or species extinction. To a degree not unlike with humans, the exercising of analogues to freedom in the cosmos at large comes with a high and disturbing price.

Such perplexing aspects of the unfolding notwithstanding, the One's relationship with all of creation was beginning to enter my awareness in terms of the image of dance. After all, what could be a more appropriate image for first the One's unfolding of a gorgeously physical uni-verse, and then the One's embedding in that very physicality in Bethlehem, than physical dance?

I also found this metaphor to be very promising for the joining of the purposive and the spontaneous. Dance is a hybrid, a two-part invention, an example of creativity wedded to order, freedom to gestalt. On the one hand, it embodies playfulness, improvisation, exploration, experimentation, spirit, and zest, and the way in which it is not the dance apart from the free exercise of creativity on the part of each partner. On the other hand, dance is also form, gestalt, configuration, and parameter within which freedom can strut its finery. That form would include the music, either relatively fixed or less so as with improvisation. And while in this case the form is strong insofar as the other dancer is leading, such an asymmetry is not incompatible with the experiencing of freedom within it. Gestalt stripped of all creativity, and freedom bereft of form, are the co-finalists for the Worst of Show award. Commonly perceived as opposites, form and freedom are actually improbable collaborators, sidekicks, traveling in tandem. The two in their mysterious equipoise can be elegant, explorative, and just plain *gorgeous*.

But what of the cosmos' dance partner with whom this creativity wed to gestalt is spun out? How do I even think about this One who has invited the cosmos to bring both its gifts and its freedom to the ball? The image "Lord of the Dance" seemed a safe direction; ballet's culture, less so. I went with the latter.

But rather than explosive and riveting, a Rudolf Nureyev (1938–1993) bursting on the stage, I knew from the Christ that this lead dancer, *Le Premier Danseur*, brings strength to lift and carry, as well as nurturing for the ballerina in apprenticeship known to fall in midpirouette. Rather than flamboyant and dominating, this lead melds patience and support with invitation to excellence in drawing the emerging partner into ever greater stature in the art. Indeed, might not the signature verb of this lead be "to draw," as in the Christ's words that none comes to him except the One "draws him" (Jn 6:44)—only now that action is broadened to embrace the very cosmos itself? In contrast to its bogus use, is not the true meaning of the slogan "Be all that you can be!" *Le Premier Danseur's* invitation to join all parts of the beloved cosmos in moving into the full flower of their potentiality? As with my sort as disclosed in the Christ event, has not the Relinquishing One who is Love ceded the cosmos ample space in which to sing its own song and share in the choreography of the dance? Counter to all precedent, expectation, or reason, could *Le Premier Danseur* actually be a loving, and enabling, servant?

While I believe there is a *Premier Danseur*, one supremely (albeit not solely) represented in the Christ, and that whether to make this confession is my free choice to make, there are numerous scientific findings which for me *tend* to align in parallel with that belief. Already cited is the argument that 13.7 billion years is rather short a time for the random generation of amino acids, much less human beings of the likes of Dante Alighieri, Teresa de Jesús, Vincent Van Gogh (1853–1890), or Dag Hammarskjöld (1905–1961).

Additional examples of *directionality*, understood here as evidences of the response of aspects of the cosmos to the Lover's drawing from out of its future, can only be sampled here:

- the equipoise immediately after Initial Ignition between the speed of subatomic plasma and the emergence of increasing gravity as tiny irregularities in that expanding flow became clumps and then, finally, the first generation of stars.
- the manner in which heavier elements, particularly the carbon and oxygen necessary for life, were generated and then deposited back in the public domain only via the density-induced nuclear fusion in the first generation of stars.

- the smaller size and slower burning rates of subsequent generations of stars serving to delay the possibility of life about ten billion years until a suitable and stable environment such as Earth had unfolded.

- the temperature of Earth's bio-habitat, totally dependent on radiation from its local star, which any variation in the planet's size, rotation, angle of tilt, orbit, distance from that body, absorbency, or atmosphere (as with greenhouse gasses), would raise or lower, thus jeopardizing flora and fauna alike.

- the mutation of very early forms of life on our planet's surface allowing them to gain the capacity to trap sunlight and become photosynthetic, apart from which the possibility of nearly all subsequent life, possibly excepting chemosynthetic life on the seafloor, would almost certainly have been aborted.

- the complementary roles of photosynthesis (flora) and respiration (fauna) in maintaining the necessary levels of oxygen and carbon dioxide, respectively, in the finely calibrated cocktail which is Earth's atmosphere.

The list of examples of such balance or equipoise could be supplemented by another of several dozen so-called Fundamental Physical Constants, each of which if minutely tweaked could jeopardize or extinguish life on Earth. Each of these calibrations are knife-edge traits walking a fine-tuned wire between tandem catastrophes. Each appears from the 13.7-billion-year milestone to have been necessary to provide the prerequisite stability/form as well as openness/freedom for the cosmos to have been drawn into its own future and destiny by *La Premier Danseur*.

C. Prayers Elicited by the Silent Music

Several comments are in order about the prayers making up the last three chapters of this book. First, forms of both themes and texts initially surfaced in my spirituality journaling on the Crick, whether in the Oratory, the perch, or computer station betwixt. The prayers are all in the first grammatical person addressing the second, reflecting the incremental shift which took place in that journaling across 2002 and 2003. This change was crucial in my ongoing struggle to allow prayer to become more listening and responding to the One than something *about which* I thought, studied, or talked. That the prayers retained their vehicle of *words* hints at either the incompleteness of my shift or the inflexibility of this medium, or both.

Second, the prayers following are almost entirely in the interrogative mode. Both inspiration and model here is Karl Rahner's atypically slim *Encounters with Silence*, a book of prayers largely in this interrogative mode, as well as the first grammatical person addressing the second. On the one hand, this mode seems appropriate to me given both the One to whom they are addressed and my novice status regarding matters at the spirituality/cosmology interface. The choice of the interrogative, whether query or rhetorical, signs my awareness that I, in addition to being *apprentice* dancer, am also clay rather than the potter (Jer 18).

At the same time, I acknowledge that I hope the interrogative provides a bit of margin, cover, license even, in exercising the participatory mandate given to the entire cosmos, myself included. After all, I am invited to be a free and not merely compliant dancer, one moving to music which I have been invited to help compose and choreograph. Thus I have wanted my prayers to embody honestly, in both form and content, the song of this particular piper with whom the Lover desires to be in relation. If my prayer on occasion is cheeky, betraying excessive *chutzpah*, I remind the reader that establishing the rules of participation in the dance is not my area. If there be either applause or boos for such, I defer to the One. Jessica Powers, in her "The Second Giving" (133), bares the audacity of this part of the human birthright:

> God seeks a heart with bold and boundless hungers
> that sees itself and earth as paltry stuff;
> God loves a soul that casts down all He gave it
> and stands and cries that it was not enough.

Third, a comment regarding how I, as comfortable as I purport to be with what science teaches about cosmogenesis, can practice prayer—confession, thanksgiving, adoration, but particularly *petition*—to the One. Does the One I address as Thicket, among other handles, actually grant petitions in the uni-verse illuminated by the cosmology I describe as "exploding" in the last several decades?

Above other reasons, I pray because I am invited to do so by the Christ, most directly in the "Our Father" texts (Mt 6:9–13; Lk 11:2–4). Although in his first language, Aramaic, Jesus would have addressed the One as "*Abba,*" an intimate word best translated as "Daddy," that word is found only once in the Gospels' Greek text (Mk 14:36, Gethsemane), and but twice elsewhere in the newer Testament (Rom 8:15, Gal 4:6). It is highly probable that the frequent appearance of *patér* in the Gospels' Greek text, and thus the more distant "Father" in most English translations, carried the much more familiar and relational nuance of *Abba* in the initial oral form. Thus Jesus invites us to pray within a safe and trusting relationship not unlike that a small child would have with a loving parent.

In addition to being invited, I pray because throughout my life I have been part of a community, and story, that testify to the good life as lived vis-à-vis the One who so invites me. I know of no competing case for the good life meriting serious attention.

Being a Carmelite has helped me to pray more because of who *Abba* is, whether Source, Lover, or Destiny, than because of questions answered, petitions granted, or goodies delivered. John of the Cross in particular is teaching me to give myself to the One of consolations more than the consolations of the One. That my cosmology, lacking a *deus ex machina* pulling the strings behind the scenes to secure such goodies, may not in all respects fit neatly with my belief in and practice of petitionary prayer does not unduly concern me. With us finites relating to the Mystery, there will always be loose ends; their absence might well be more troubling than their presence. When in doubt amid such loose ends, I pray, and leave the messiness for others to sort out. Prayer is thus something I do because I have long since freely chosen to do so. In my flawed and foibled way, I have sought to follow the Christ in this regard, setting "my face like flint" (Is 50:7).

Aware that no one else could have written the prayers which follow, I view them as part of my acceptance of the invitation to come to the dance, to sing my own song to *Abba*. In these prayers, that song may be lament, venting, exasperation, gratitude, or, occasionally, simple adoration characterized more by desire and silence than words or images. That my body's matter and energy were probably present in the Flaring Forth 13.7 billion years ago, and wondrously mediated to me via countless recyclings so as to be nurtured into receptivity to spirit, only enhances my desire to respond to the One's invitation to offer my song, and myself, *precisely as I am.*

And fourth, the prayers that follow are not organized chronologically according to how they initially surfaced in my journaling. Rather, the sequence flows from my confession that origins in the primeval past and destiny in the mysterious future, for both myself and the cosmos, are decisively illuminated by the Christ in the "center," the core, *kairos* (ripe time) rather than *chronos* (measured time), of the tale. It is via this itinerant minstrel, whom I generally dub below as the "Troubadour," that I decisively heard the silent music, the *chanson d'amour,* of the One.

It is thus at this center, in regard to both *kairos* time and meaning, that the following prayers begin. Only subsequently do I move first to prayers having to do with what precedes (cosmogenesis), and then to those regarding continuation into what is yet to be (cosmic culmination), each viewed through the lens of that same center. I understand this sequence, from the Troubadour who poured himself out to the Creator inviting the creation to join in shaping its own unfolding, and only *then* to the glorious destiny of the Lover/beloved relationship, as separating me from both deist and designist.

29. Prayers Offered Out of the Center: The Troubadour

A. O Lover!

O Source of all that is, were You not in my earliest hearing of biblical stories as a child, above all else, immense? And as I grew into adolescence and beyond, was not that ongoing biblical formation corroborated by my own experience, namely that Your splendor and artisanship could be inferred from the night sky; Your invisible attributes, eternal power, and divine nature deciphered from nature?

Of course, there were also other divine characteristics attributed to You, like mercy, forgiveness, and compassion, but were not they, perhaps via some trinitarian gymnastics, somehow attributed to Jesus of Nazareth, with You remaining distant, pallid, and immutably immense? So that any loving kindness having to do with You was experienced more as something I qualified for by meeting the conditions than was inundated by? So that Your mercy was unnecessarily dispensed when I was performing well and self-contained rather than when I was in free-fall and desperate? You were merciful, but in a qualified sort of way—surely an oxymoron, mercy that I repeatedly experienced as measured, measily, and, yes, damning? Did I not understood You to be Love (1 Jn 4:16), yes, but always with an asterisk?

Pray tell me, do You know what it is like for a mere child, or a mere man—one finite, foibled, and flawed, one small in every respect—to be confronted with Your enormity, Your boundlessness, this on a scale dwarfing the sea, the night sky, the cosmos itself, or anything I could imagine? Do You know how ill-prepared we mortals are when encountering primarily Your omni-whatever? And when, decades beyond my childhood, I read in Deuteronomy 18:15-20 how the Hebrews at Sinai had petitioned You to supplant Your thunderous voice, Your great fire, with a spokesman of their own sort, *lest they die*, did I not know that I had company? Does not immensity, naked, faceless, and unmitigated, simply elicit fear? Does not the memory of that visceral terror of childhood remain even as I write this?

How could any of my vessels contain You, O Ocean? Could it be otherwise but that You, Deluge, would not only fill and overflow them, but buffet them, dislodge them, threaten to sweep them all away? And are not those vessels, my faculties, who I am, my self, and did not Your immensity jeopardize that self? Was I not already as a child mysteriously intuiting that I was simply not equipped to countenance Your exhaustlessness, overmatched, simply out of my depth? Was not that immensity, eclipsing face, heart, and disposition, in and of *itself* ominous and dread-full and thus, seemingly, malevolent? And my endangered self all I had, I not having been crafted with back-up?

Did I not discover only much later, O Immensity, that throughout my life, I had had but a single question to address to you: what, *really*, was Your disposition toward me? More specifically, *did You love me*? Did You, Immensity, ∞, unconditionally *love* me?

OK, perhaps a second also: how could, or why would, You love me? Your Troubadour offered promise, what with his valuing and embracing of all manner of marginated, insignificant, and fractured of my ilk. But this too could get very dicey: how helpful was he, part of a trefoil of uncertain cohesion, whose disposition told me little about Yours? He, proclaimed by some as the "compassionate face of God," merely begging the question who was *really* behind the mask? He, propitiating Your wrath or acceding to Your demands or otherwise shielding me from Your disapproval, leaving me back on square one? He, pertaining to personal and interpersonal jurisdictions, or vowed religious life, or some other spiritual lacunae, leaving to illimitable You the immense task of running of the cosmos? He, distracting or diverting me from You even while ostensibly disclosing You, he tortured to death while You silently, immutably, and immensely, looked on? Or, *a la* Hagar (Gn 21:16), away?

No! Was it not You with whom I had to do? *You*? But was who I encountered in Your Troubadour really You? Was what I received in his song, what I got in You? Rather than solving my conundrum, did not he merely shift the question to his relation with You, to the matter of the integrity of his iconic depiction of You? Years later did I not recall hearing the words of Johann Kepler (1571–1630) to the effect that he viewed his astronomy as thinking Your thoughts after You? But Your thoughts, were they not, like everything else about You, immense, cold, and *sans* comfort? Did not I, without actually being aware of it back there, really want to be "desiring Your desires after You," "loving Your love after You," if these You actually possessed?

Enter Your saints, Your holy fools, many of them Saints. While some, whether in their writings or in others' accounts, were addressing the Troubadour, others the Holy Mother or even their own selves, were not they thereby really addressing You? Was it not You they were either thirsting after or inebriated with, You with whom they were having this love affair or desiring to do so? Did not Jessica Powers in her "But Not With Wine" (17) write that if she got too looped with the choice vintage of Your goodness, we could all blame You for the open tap? Was not Catherine of Siena, a scarcely believable piece of Your finery, also into her cups, repeatedly addressing You with the likes of "O Loving Madman"? John of the Cross, by all measures neither a Casanova nor Don Juan: did he not in *The Living Flame of Love* play the beloved, begging You to quit fooling around and *consummate*? And did not some of these saints, a fair portion of them celibate religious, interestingly appropriate from the Song of Songs in invoking imagery of the *boudoir* to depict Your passion for us? For me? Immense, perhaps that too, but were You not above all else to these saints the passionate Lover?

So then, why did You do Bethlehem? So that my sins would get died for? To satisfy demands, whether Your own or another's ransom scheme? To defeat evil and death in some cosmic "High Noon" scenario? Most, and yet none, of these, not primarily, I suspect. Rather, did You not do Bethlehem to disclose Your disposition toward my sort? Was not the tabernacling (Jn 1:14) Your hug, both of me and the cosmos? *Abba*, did I not want—no, *need*—to know whether You loved me? And did not the one whom we confess to be the Troubadour in his very being answer that question? And did not who he is in relation to You, repeatedly confirmed by Your fools, clinch the matter for this trekker?

Did this disclosure appear to me full-grown beside a first-century road outside Damascus or in a garden in late fourth century Milano? Or did You, O Hound of Heaven, need to pursue me across the decades, down the arches of the years, finally and inexorably running me to ground, I Your fearful prey finding myself, counterintuitively, within Your embrace?

But is it not the case that Your communication, Your disclosure, finally "took," and I, overwhelmed, exhausted, and in regard to Your mercy, in way over my head, surrendered? And am I not persuaded today, at least as fully as I am persuaded that I exist, that You Love me, that I am among Your favored? And were You not aware from the Flaring Forth of the Fire of Love that I would *have* to know that, that I simply would not be dissuaded? May I personalize René Descartes' *Cogito ergo sum* thus: *Amatus sum ergo sum:* "Having been loved, I am"?

O, Lover!

B. O I AM WHO AM!

Knowing well both my sort and me, are You not also familiar with our propensity to contextualize? You know, the myriad factors surrounding anything only in terms of which it can be properly understood? Like the way I crafted the context for Tylerton in Part II? Is it not appropriate to do this, given the fact that nothing can fully self-account, nothing in this webbed-connectedness called a cosmos You have spun out, known in isolation from all else? Indeed, was it not part of my academic formation to position everything, whether idea, object, text, phenomenon, or person, inside a larger whole within which it could better be known for what it was?

Now then, have You not always been a problem to me in this regard? Already as a wee child I was wondering, "Who made God?" (In my evangelical origins, I didn't even have access to the *Mater Dei* non-solution!) In time the question evolved in form and complexity: did You have a genealogy, a metaphorical navel, a résumé, perhaps a precipitating antecedent event, a formative experience, a *raison d'etre*, a paper trail? *Any kind* of trail? Perhaps a defining principle You adhere to, or an external perch or perspective from which You could be accurately sized up?

Then in my early theological studies, did not Paul Tillich via Robert Scharlemann teach me that You simply could not be so objectified, could not be placed within the "subject/object structure," as I might a butterfly pinned to a board or a chemical sample in a beaker? And had not *all* of my questions to date presupposed that You could be so held for examination, if only I could find the right method? But if You had no context, if everything proposed as such was derivative of Your Flaring Forth, were You not then simply unanalyzable and therefore unaccountable? And, back then, wasn't all of this simply maddening?

But did not accounting for You remain a persistent issue, particularly as Your profile, whether via study of the texts of ancient Israel, the Gospels, or the traditions of the churches, became increasingly apparent? For example, when the Hebrew people, having just been delivered from the Philistines, demanded a king "like all the nations" (1 Sm 8:5), when they already had one, You, why did You give them what they wanted, despite the fact that it was both insult to You and self-destructive to them? Or amid the seemingly interminable oscillation between idolatrous faithlessness and judgment following Solomon's death and the division of the kingdom, why did You tirelessly continue to woo this most ambivalent people to Your self? Why this tenacity, this dogged determination, regarding the covenant with Your chosen people in the Hebrew Bible?

Or if he called Your Word was indeed "the radiance of Your glory and the exact representation of Your nature" (fr Heb 1:3) and thus displaying Your heart to us, why would You have a special compassion for the broken, marginalized, and those sinners in some public sense which he embodied? And what are we to make of Your longsuffering and patient wooing of the Christian churches, we sword-bearers in the name of the nonviolent Troubadour, we of the grounding of all manner of discrimination in religious values, we of the preferential option for the respectable like ourselves? Why are You so . . . inimitably, so cantankerously, You?

Why are You this suitor seeking, hat in hand, to persuade us of Your love? Why are You not appropriately judgmental and punitive, like we would be and are with each other, particularly in the face of how we have squandered Your gifts of life and freedom? How did You become this way, so unyieldingly, so incorrigibly this way? Don't You ever give up and back off? Are You helpless to alter Your *modus operandi*? You, source of all that is, might You, like all of us You joined, have come to be different than You are? What kind of deity are You *anyway*? And what is this thing about You and relationships? Sometimes my frustration gets too much and I just scream out within myself: Why are You the way you are? WHY ARE YOU THE WAY YOU ARE?! And do I get any satisfaction except the reminder that Your handle is YHWH, meaning, "I AM WHO AM" (Ex 3:14)?

If indeed in Bethlehem You have joined me in the finitude of my humanness, do You know what it is like to be invited to reconfigure my life around One who is entirely self-sustained, self-contained, self-contextualized, self-accounting, self-explained, and self-disclosed, One who cannot be assessed in terms of *anything*? You who are who You are simply because You are, self-contained like some infinite set of matryoshka dolls? You, the Word *sans* foreword, the text lacking context, the inside unaccompanied by an outside? And who You are is least inadequately communicated by our most transmogrified word of all: "love"?

O I AM WHO AM!

C. O Real Presence!

In Advent, that magical time of light amid the encircling darkness, do we not repeatedly speak of Your *coming* in the Troubadour, both the first time and the last? Are not both Paul's use of the Aramaic *maranatha*, "come Lord Jesus" (1 Cor 16:22), and its Greek translation concluding the penultimate verse of the newer Testament (Apoc 22:20), evidence of the earliest faithful's longing for You? Have not Your people ever since employed forms of that word used by lovers throughout the ages—"come," "coming"—because we weary of our darkness and isolation, because we long for You, our Lover, to disappear the separation and be fully with us?

But had You ever really left, or been away, as the plea "come!" implies? How could the Flaring Forth of Your Love have transpired, the emergence of something out of nothing, had You not been fully "here" the moment time began? How could the cosmos, Your love-child astonishingly kissed into being—my image: Gustav Klimt's "The Kiss"—have taken place, have remained in being, have unfolded, had You not been and remained fully present? Or Your Spirit's "brooding over the face of the waters" (Gn 1:2), that, for me, sensuous image of the unfolding, had You somehow withheld Your self? How could the uni-verse have been nurtured from subatomic particles to the glory of Anton Bruckner's music, or the miracle of human love, without You having been fully present to it at every turn of the journey? How could You have brought into being and then ever-wooed Your beloved creation, the only such love affair we know anything about, without being fully engaged? Yet does not our observance of Advent presuppose an absence, almost a deist interval, for which Bethlehem is the penultimate satisfaction, the Reigning in full bloom the *ultima*?

O, the experience of separation from You is very real for us, we, in the words of the Easter Vigil's *Exsultet*, of the "happy fault," but might that be more the fruit of our fearfulness than of the delayed arrival of the heaving ocean of Your Love? Who actually needs to arrive, You or we? Is not Advent an opportunity for us to meld disciplined preparation with greater receptivity to You who have never not been *brooding* over the face of Your beloved, never not been *Immanuel*, You-with-us? Is it not more a matter of our coming to see what is—within, without, enveloping—than of Your needing *to come*? Have You not been here from the foundations of the cosmos, from the Flaring Forth of the Fire of Your Love, not so much for reasons of damage control in the face of our rendering grotesque of the freedom central to Your Love Project, but as the culminating expression of Your 13.7-billion-year effort to draw this cosmos into a more intimate relationship with Your self? So this Advent season I ask: who needs to come to whom? Who is already here? And who isn't?

But wait, do we not already have a feast, and a season, which focus on Your proclamation, Your rolling out, Your showcasing, Your laying bare, Your *advertising* Your eternal presence with us? Is not that the meaning of the Feast of the Epiphany, literally "manifestation," show-time, arguably the very summit of the Christmas season? Do not the texts associated with that feast, whether the visit of the Magi or baptism of Your Troubadour, to say nothing of Your table, in different ways trumpet to us of the stopped ears that You are fully, astonishingly, *really* present? Rather than more waiting for that which is not yet, O Ocean of Fire within which I swim, would You dilate my heart so that I can more fully receive You, You who have never not been here?

O Real Presence!

D. O Sacred Heart!

Am I not the prophet Isaiah, bowed before You high and lifted up, Your splendrous wake enveloping the temple, crying out, "Woe is me" (Is 6:1–7)? Or the psalmist, "What are we cosmics that You give us a thought, offspring of mortals that You make contact with us" (fr Ps 8:4)? Or Simon Peter, upon initially encountering the power of Your Word, fearfully blurting out, "Get away from me, Lord, for I am a wretched man" (Lk 5:8)? As Your Troubadour guides me via his teachings, life-style, death-style, and resurrection-style deeper into the abyss of Your Love, the questions of these on whose shoulders I stand become my own: why do You bother with my sort? Why do You bother with me? Why all of *You* . . . for this? Was not some form of this question present in either my consciousness or regions just below many days here on the Crick?

But is not this also a rhetorical question, one exploding out of me in the face of Your splendor, one demanding more to be aired than answered? And isn't it similar to my other questions in that it seeks to identify an explanation, a motivation, a rational for Your lavish Love, in this case perhaps lodged in some attractive quality of myself or my sort? In other words, what is so precious about us so as to cause You to proceed in the first place, and then continue to extend Your self in Your Love toward us? What is so intrinsically, so innately, prized about us so as to account for Your extravagance?

Ah, but am I not here again trying to identify a good in terms of which I could then account for You? And do I not again receive no help from You, none aside from the "I AM WHO AM" handle? Your heart's burning fire, O Hound of Heaven, driving You "down the nights / and down the days," driving You "down the arches of the / years," driving You "down the labyrinthine / ways / of my own mind," to quote Francis Thompson's *The Hound of Heaven*, was it not eternally laid in You rather than in my worth? And despite the preciousness of my sort, despite our beauty, our being in Your image, our election as consciousness and voice of the entire stupendous unfolding, do You not at the end of the day love us sight unseen, as if You had conducted no appraisal?

I, for whom the purist human love, whether received or extended, has always been touched by the gray grit of the shadow, how do I come to rest in a Love which is unwavering, unqualified, unqualified *for*, un-*anything*, nothing but the contents of Your heart? Do You understand why this is so difficult for me? I have neither parables nor parallels, examples nor experiences, analogues nor . . . *Nothing*! Only that Your heart is the way Your heart is. Is that what "Sacred Heart" *really* means?

O Sacred Heart!

E. O Solidarity Initiator!

Although You have invited me above all else to love You (Lk 10:27) rather than merely think about You, may I nonetheless exercise here my intellect as well as my heart and will? Have I not, for more than four decades, loved to *think* about the Incarnation?! The sheer luminous beauty of the *notion* of the "enfleshment" of Your self-disclosing Love, of Your "tabernacling," pitching tent, amid the human community and expansive cosmos (Jn 1:14)?! Is not the Incarnation a stunning master stroke, a dazzling *tour de force*, an exquisite beauty to the intellect as well as the heart? More than yet another piece of legislation, codicil, apparition, prophet, surrogate, or proxy in Your long saga of wooing us of the happy fault, what could be more tactically dazzling, brilliant in communication, and momentous in scale, than Your embedding Your self in and among us, *and for the duration*? Talk about a strategy: Wow!

O Lover, is not the message of John's prologue (Jn 1:1–18) about deep core union on Your part with us humans, to say nothing of the entire creation? So that any notion of Your Troubadour merely "appearing" to be human (the heresy of Docetism), only "slumming it" with us for an interval, is rejected? And though the etymological meaning of words like "Incarnation" and "enfleshment" leaves them vulnerable to mis-interpretation—as an exterior appareling only, as an actor donning a costume—has not the central meaning of Your Bethlehem initiative remained that of identification and solidarity *at the core* with our sort and the larger creation, a kind of embedding for aye?

And is not the very center of Your Solidarity Project the matter of the communi-cation of Your message, Your Word (*logos,* Jn 1:1, 14)? Was not my needfulness to know Your disposition toward me, to know whether You loved me, broadly representative among my sort? But vastly more than wanting merely to fulfill an obligation to issue such a communiqué, were You not fiercely committed above all else that upon arrival it "take," that we recipients would have a decent chance to "get it"? That the *infiniti* message would be delivered in such a manner as to offer us of the fragile *finitum* an actual opportunity to receive it, and You?

Did not we of my sort discover the vehicle, the medium, of that communication to be ourselves, Your Word articulated in our vernacular, in the humanese tongue? So then, did You not in effect cause the medium to become the message, the vehicle and its freight one and the same? And was not all of this terribly important to me, O Lover, I who across much of my life have found the full *humanity* of Your Living Bread to be the more difficult half to swallow?

But wait, am I here again making complicated something above all else extraor-dinarily simple? Is it not the character of all true love, whether Yours of the relentless Torrent or our own distant and shadowy derivatives, to seek intimate and binding union? Always? Indeed, is there not in the coupling of all fauna reproducing sexu-ally a dim harbinger of the uniting which is love, a union which can bear the fruit of abundant life? And thus have not we vulnerable to the shadow nevertheless contained within ourselves this marker of Your passionate and tenacious drive toward union, intimacy, and covenantal commitment? Were there not within our own loves—and *not* excepting the shabby ones!—distant hints of Your resolve to bind Your self to us forever? Were not we prepared by our human loves to be able to identify Your Bethle-hem mission as transparently, indeed, *blatantly*, amorous? And if we didn't, shouldn't we have noticed that our own couplings were both analogous to Yours and examples of the mechanism whereby You were patiently drawing all life toward what shall one day be?

O Wonder of Wonders! In words shaped by those of Elizabeth, kin of Your Min-strel, how has it happened to us of my sort, that You would come *to us* (fr Lk 1:43)?

O, can ever again despair be seen to triumph, can ever again the darkness be thought to have extinguished the light, when *THIS* has happened?

O Solidarity Initiator!

F. O Sign of Contradiction!

Are there not, O Lover, *two* scandals in Your entering into solidarity with us in Your Troubadour, each of them boggling to mind and heart alike: *that* You identified with us, and *how* You did so? But can it not be argued that we of the happy fault have choked even more on the bone of the second than the first?

Did not the disclosing of Your Solidarity Initiative toward us via Your Troubadour take place amid intense and varied expectation? And although this expectation might have aided both the preparation for and identification of its fulfillment, did not much of it in fact obstruct rather than facilitate? After all, do not we humans, O Sovereign of the Galaxies, have some definite ideas as to what You deities are like, how You are to conduct your work of ruling the cosmos? And are not many of those ideas just plain wrong? Indeed, has it not been quipped that ever since You created in Your image, we have been creating You in ours? Are not humans, we Abrahamics *not* excepted, incorrigibly certain that we know how You are to behave?

Thus, is it not the second scandal of Your Solidarity Initiative that You operated almost entirely *outside* what we understood Your character to be? How? May I count the ways? Born in a cave, Your Anointed, to an unmarried and illiterate girl who failed the "just say no" test? His arrival announced first to socially-challenged herdsmen, and serenaded by mid-level mammalian hosts? Hounded out of the country by a real king, did not the family-to-be make a night flight to Egypt—of all places!—ultimately landing in the village of Nazareth in Galilee, unmentioned in the Hebrew Bible and, arguably, the armpit of the ancient world? Are these not auspicious beginnings for this one dubbed by some nocturnal foreigners as "King of the Jews" (Mt 2:2), later to be touted as inaugurator of Your Reigning?

And did not things only get worse in the Troubadour's adult and public life? Was he not chronically more comfortable with bottom-feeders than our finest? Indeed, apart from religious bureaucrats, was he not remarkably understanding and empathetic of the foibles of my sort? And what was all this about loving the enemy, turning the other cheek, and forgiving as a lifestyle? Indeed, did not the Reigning he came inaugurating just about *invert* all of our values, embodying our own politic, only *stood up on its head*?

And then, did he not have the vinegar to tell us that his teachings, manner, and vision were what the Reigning really looked like, because You, YOU! were that way?

You, Sovereign of all that is, generally addressed by him as mere "*Abba*"? Indeed, is it any wonder that ancient Simeon, holding Your infant songster at his temple presentation, predicted that he would be a "sign of contradiction," a sure bringer of sorrow to his mother (Lk 2:34–35)?

But was it not the meaning attributed to Your Troubadour's execution as a blasphemous felon, and the Resurrection as Your imprimatur on that very meaning, which represented the apex of Your departure from our expectation? Would not our finest have done it *opposite* in nearly every respect? And yet for those giving themselves to Your Way, was not the entire story, from Bethlehem through Golgotha to the empty tomb, received as Your showcasing for all time how much You loved us of the fault? And that Your love was stronger than evil and the darkness, stronger than death itself?

Is it any surprise then that the Apostle Paul, for whom the Troubadour was none less than the *eikon* of You (2 Cor 4:4; Col 1:15), would describe his song as offensive to Jewish thinking, incomprehensible to its Gentile counterpart (1 Cor 1:23)? He who "poured himself out" (*kenosis,* Phil 2:7) rather than saving himself via divine prerogatives? "Poured self out" kingship? "I lay down my life" (Jn 10:15–18) deityship? What kind of almightiness is this *anyway*? Is Your heart, above everything on the omnia list, the "pouring out" heart? And all to communicate a quality and scale of Love as never before laid bare, a Love nothing less than to the death? Is this not simply off the scale of more with less? Why don't You just bludgeon us into accepting Your largess the way we, whether individuals or nations, do? Why do You have to be so *other*? If a Fire of Love, then are You not most certainly a *dark* Fire, One most opaque to my understanding?

So what, O Lover, did You "pour out" of Your self in Your Troubadour? What Olympian powers did You, "Greater than the roar of mighty waters, more glorious than the surgings of the sea . . ." (Ps 93:4), lay aside? What Herculean prerogatives did You abdicate? What the content of Your divestiture?

On the one hand, may we not infer from the Gospel narratives that in submitting Your self to the vagaries of human freedom, to the delimitations of life in space and time, You *freely* sluffed off aspects of both your power and freedom? Indeed, was not the die already cast in Bethlehem? If this Solidarity Initiative was to have any integrity, was it not only a matter of time before the death card would show up from the deck?

Or, on the other hand, did You set aside nothing, having been since forever the Lover bent on wooing and persuading rather than the brandishing the mace of infinitude and coercive power? Had You always stooped, indeed *bowed*, upon entering our humble gestalt, our finitude box, although until the Passion Week rarely actually credited as doing so? In which case, would not the "sluffing off" be our own, it apply-ing to expectations previously, and erroneously, projected on You? Was Your self-out-pouring the constant, the few of us finally beginning to *get it* the new development on Easter morning?

Either way, O Lover, have You not forever changed my understanding of both power and love, Your Love, and given to me a center, an *axis mundi*, which holds, one around which You are reconfiguring my life? And now do I not know that it is precisely Your abdication, Your self-out-pouring, which is Your grandeur, Your reliquishment "the effulgence of Your splendour" (fr Heb 1:3)?

O Sign of Contradiction!

G. O Relinquisher!

Were there questions about You which occupied me more during my ten on the Crick than those involving "freedom"? Like, how is it that You freely chose to submit Your self to *both* our finite enclosure *and* our fearful freedom's fruit, this all the way to the cross, to the slow death? Given the biblical narrative and subsequent Christian tradi-tion, must we not but conclude that Your Love intrinsically presupposed freedom, both for You, the Addresser, and for the cosmos and its residents, the addressees? That in the face of Your amorous overtures, we humans always had agency, choice, freedom, whether or not to respond, and how? That with You, freedom was a *nonnego-tiable* component of Love? Coerced or determined love, Love, Your Love, was *not*?

As the *scale* of this freedom slowly penetrated me, did I not have several reac-tions? Astonishment in the face of Your profound respect for our agency, You who could just as well have crafted us to be automatically *whatever*, although not, appar-ently, "automatically loving"? My, couldn't You have put on grand gigs, You and Your polished marionettes, performances flawless and unmessy, involving neither risk nor cost, insurance nor Plan B, cramped space / time nor the torturous cross?

Instead, what? You wanted, more than another perfect performance, to dance with us, it seems? With us of the fault You wanted a partner more than perfection, to dance rather than dominate? Granted one dancer leads, *Le Premier Danseur,* one Lord of the dance, if You please, but *two* moral agents, *two* freedoms, *two* dancers, *co*-choreographers in the one dance? You, Flinger of Galaxies as so many Frisbees, submitting Your self to our finite freedom? Relinquishing, pouring out, surrendering to that freedom, not only on the cruciform, but in every nook and cranny of the dance?

Including Your table as well? As I make my way toward Your Troubadour's body and blood, am I not sometimes nearly immobilized before the prospect that You should imminently submit Your self into my hands, I of the species that uses and abuses all that we touch? That not unlike the original Apostles, I am allowed "to handle him with my hands" (1 Jn 1:1), hands, not unlike lips and heart, unclean?

Astonishment repeatedly, yes, but did I not also have a darker reaction to Your radical gift of freedom, one laced with fear? For did not this gift mean that I could simply refuse to dance with You, just walk away? Select as my new partners from the appetites, objects, ideologies, persons, ideas or obsessions, rent a set of glad rags, and dance the night away? Or perhaps just clone myself and have the most charming partner of all? Yes, has not my darkest fear in this regard been that I now know myself to have both the capacity and freedom to gather my entire being into one great "Fuck You!" to You, the only lover I've always wanted since forever?

O Torrent, having been patiently nurtured across 13.7 billion years of recycling by You, the Dark Abyss of Love, having received a personal invitation to be a participant in the dance into a future which simply defies description or imagination, have I not also been enabled by You to decide rather to peak out as a portfolio peruser, an aging sexual athlete, or a sheikh of shopping? Did You lovingly unfold, nurture, and draw us across the long arc of Your 13.7-billion-year Love Project so that we could emerge as resplendent . . . consumers? Could there be anything more supremely tragic? And dreadful?

Does not my freedom thus sometimes frighten the hell out of me, press me against dread, in the face of the gravity of choices which Your relinquishment has placed in my stewardship? That, having encountered You, the indefatigable Lover of the long journey, having encountered You who are the answer to the question, "What's it all about, Alfie?" I should rather fritter away my being with this or that creation of You? Or me?! Did I not get the impression from Teresa de Jesús that while frightened by neither You nor death, she had a healthy angst about herself, of her capacity to choose away from You? Is it not so with me as well? And do I not sometimes, upon hearing the piece *In Truitina* ("In the Balance") from the slightly wicked *Carmina Burana* by Karl Orff (1895–1982), about the delicious yet precarious, indeed, humongous, stakes of freedom, find myself awash in both the lighter and darker precincts of wonder *at how You have set it all up?*

O Relinquisher!

H. O Contingent One!

O Silent One, while during the first half of my life I found my principal hope in the divinity of Your Troubadour, in the more recent half has it not been in his humanity, specifically in Your solidarity in him with the entirety of the cosmos, including my sort? Is not all my hope grounded in that identification, not merely a thirty-three-year hiatus, but extending from the inception of time to and beyond when it shall be no more? Is not this identification—*Ave verum corpus*—the substratum of my faith?

I am not speaking here of a solidarity in regard to the *tenebrae*, the corruption, the surd: I accept that in the Triune Mystery it was You who were "tempted in all things as are we, yet without the shadow" (fr Heb 4:15). No, I am referring to the state of being creature, finite, mortal, being in and of space and time. Do You know what it is both to be told, as I will be this Ash Wednesday, "Remember, man, you are dust and to dust you will return" (fr Gn 3:19), and to live each day at some level exploring what that means? May I hope that the psalmist's words that "You Your self know our frame; You are mindful that we are but dust" (fr Ps 103:14), mean that You actually know my experience of mortality *from the inside*? Is it part of the meaning of Bethlehem that You, Unfolder of nebulae, cosmic dust clouds measured in light years, are Your self also, in some sense, *dust*?

Even more to the point of my struggle, do You know what it is like to *be*, even while never having *needed* to be? To be, philosophically speaking, "unnecessary"? Having once not been, to face the prospect of again no longer being? And to live each day with the weight of the *knowledge of this*? You, whose *raison d'etre* resides fully within Your self, You who are "necessary," You for whom every "why?" question ends up with us reciting again Your Hebrew Tetragrammaton, can You know what it is like to have been flung into being *sans* consultation? What it is like to be incidental to extraneous forces, those both known and unknown?

Could it be that You share with my fraternal fauna the *absence* of the burden of that question, one with which my human sort alone, *alone,* is saddled? Are you more like the other critters *in that respect* than like us? And am I to believe that we of the *Imago* are better outfitted to be in relation with You because we, perhaps we alone, have that burden? Might You pardon my citing words Teresa de Jesús is alleged to have said: "If this is the way you treat your friends, it's no wonder you have so few"?

Or am I underestimating yet again Your Bethlehem stratagem, Your proclivity for the road less traveled? Am I failing to open myself to Your *modus operandi*, one never previously encountered among the spectrum of deities before whom cultures, ancient or modern, collectively bow? Did You not in Your relinquishment forever enter our neighborhood, our time and space delimitations and all of the other facets of our finitude, subjecting Your self to its laws and anxieties, its loneliness and fears and, yes, its death? Among whom of the other deities, whether on Mount Olympus or Wall Street, has anything of this sort happened? Indeed, how can this be?

May I find solace in Your Troubadour's cry from the cross "My God, my God, why have You abandoned me?" (Mt 27:46) May I presume that just as *You* died that slow death, just as *You* bore the dead weight of the surd on the cross, so also did *You* agonize with contingency, especially in Gethsemane and then on Golgotha? If we, the flung-into-being sort, find ourselves having been bound to You, by You, and this for the duration, as C. S. Lewis put it, as over against a mere thirty-three-year aberration, might that mean that there is no cranny of my finitude, *not even contingency itself*, which You, *You!* do not know *experientially?* CAN I BANK ON THIS?

Although, to the best of my knowledge, I am not playing games here, must I not know that it is so with You as well, that the Incarnation was not a farce, that the solidarity of Bethlehem was, is, and ever shall remain, *total and irrevocable?* Is this, Your self-binding to us of the contingency, what Dante sought to put to words as the human likeness integrated into the very image of who he glimpsed You to be in the culminating canto of his *Paradiso?*

Do You understand that it is precisely because I know that there is only the surd outside Your embrace, that there is such urgency for me in pressing You with these questions? Have I read Your identification aright? As one himself only too susceptible to exaggeration, is it the word of grace this day that overstating the extent of Your solidarity with the creation *is simply impossible?* Have You identified with me in *all* that I am, so that I might address You, also, as O Mortal One?

Or has this urgency regarding Your companionship in my finitude, my contingency, my mortality, been but the underside of Your gift to me of my desire, my hunger, my thirst . . . for You? In the words of Francis Thompson, having been brought to ground by You, O Hound, "Is my gloom, after all, / Shade of [Your] hand, outstretched / caressingly?" Could it be that my very greatest precariousness, my contingency, is marker of my destiny not merely *with*, but in, *in!* You?

O Contingent One!

I. O Sacramentalizer!

Did I not come to Tylerton, this shrinking shoal surely no stranger to relinquishment, a believer in Your Troubadour? That You had in him showcased unprecedentedly Your Real Presence, both "the radiance of Your glory and the exact representation of Your nature" (fr Heb 1:3)? That via him You were, for the duration, my Source, Guide, Model, Reconciliation, Peace, and Destiny? That in Your Solidarity Initiative via him there was *an implicit yet resounding compliment* extended to all, whether the physical, psychological, intellectual, spiritual, relational, or communitarian, contributing to what is human? That in You via him, in ways and degrees far beyond my words, images or understandings, was the healing of the human, the cosmic, predicament?

O Honorer, may I work the phrase "implicit yet resounding compliment," this acknowledgement of my sort as provider of suitable material for both Your Hut (the Holy Mother) and the Troubadour himself who is Immanuel, You-with-us? Am I even capable of overstating the honor dealt to our species, to our physicality, to our sexuality both procreative and covenantal, by Your pitching tent among us? How could You have possibly hoisted Your fists to the sky and thundered "Yes!" to our humanity any more clearly and powerfully than You did in Bethlehem? Or, given this book's title, done so with "a tiny, whispering voice" (*a la* 1 Kgs 19:12)?

Tell me, how could the dignity, integrity, rights, and preciousness of each of my sort have been any more passionately declared and anchored than in the stunning news first announced to herders of sheep? And how could the case for war, its reduction of human beings to "collateral damage," have been any more forcefully condemned than by Your binding of Your self to us, we of the damage, for the duration? May I not use terms like "rendered sacred," "ennobled," "honored" for the entirety of humankind swept up in the self-disclosing Love of Your solidarity's embrace? And although in much of the literature of Christian mysticism, John of the Cross included, individuals in their entirety are often referred to as "souls," should not we, out of respect for Your ennobling of our physicality as well in Bethlehem, restrict that word "soul" to its more precise usages?

Thus far, it seems, I had come by 1997 in opening myself to implications of Your Love Project; thus far I had allowed You to begin dilating the reluctant and retentive aperture of my heart. For did I not know, given the collective images in the Christian scriptures, whether the Reigning (Kingdom) , body of Christ, *koinonia* (community), *ekklesia* (assembly), or the New Jerusalem, that if we of my sort were to be saved, we would be saved *together*, as aggregate, as collective? Did I not step off the *Capt'n Jason II* with this *credo*?

But was not what remained, and remains still although now less so, the significance of Your Troubadour, Your Solidarity Project, *for the cosmos at large*? Indeed, was it not this aspect of Your inverted Reigning—may I use the term "Unkingdom"?—announced and inaugurated by him, which expanded within me across that decade? Will I soon forget that spring dawn when, upon entering the perch, all before, around, and within me seemingly perfect as the Flaring Forth on the first day, I suddenly, arms flung into the air, bellowed out, "All this, *all this!* You have embraced in Bethlehem!" only to sink tearfully into my chair, oblivious to anyone walking the lane below?

As in many other instances, did not the richness of life on the Crick remind me of neglected themes in my definitive narrative, scripture, hinting at the implications of Your Love Project for *EVERYTHING*? Are not our Hebraic roots forceful in acknowledging Your concern for the physical and not merely the spiritual, whether in Your imprimatur, seven-fold and comprehensive, of "good" regarding the cosmos (Gn 1), the five-fold inclusion of every kind of living creature for all generations in the covenant with Noah (Gn 9:8–17), or Mosaic legislation regarding the Sabbath Year and the Year of Jubilee (Lv 25)? Are not these but the most obvious examples in the Hebrew text of Your inclusion in Your Love Project of far more than merely the human? So that when Mark the evangelist draws together the words of Your Troubadour before he is taken from the disciples, they include these: "Go into all the world (*kosmos*) and preach the Good News *to the entire creation*"(Mk 16:15, EA)?

And was not the vision of Paul, reared and formed amid that very Hebrew text similarly cosmic in scale, whether his repeated references to "all things" [*ta pánta*] in heaven and on earth, the anticipatory groaning for its redemption on the part of the cosmos (Rom 8:18–30), or his discussion of Your Troubadour's stripping of the "principalities and powers," Paul's language for disordered structures and systems, of their evil potency, especially in his letters to the Ephesians and Colossians? Were not both the individual human heart and sphere of religiosity venues far too small to contain the scale of Your Love Project? Given the life-long duration of my own struggle to open myself to this Your scale, should I not have gained some understanding of the churches, including my own, all of which have struggled to embrace the full magnitude of Your redemption, You who are the infinite, oceanic Fire of Love?

The implications of Bethlehem for understanding the cosmos: are they not virtually endless? How is the Bay, still appearing as pristine pearl from where I write, to be cared for if we give ourselves to Your preferential option for the cosmos? How do we atone for ravaging our resident fellow fauna with whom we share common forebears? How need I change my relationship with my distant critter cousins once I have begun to view them as, like myself, partners with You, O Cutter of Covenants? Can I be seized by awareness of the participation of my own matter/ energy in this 13.7-billion-year recycling saga, and then live as if I emerged in June of 1940 *creatio ex nihilo*? How do I view the myriad of secular/sacred demarcations in a cosmos in which Your Solidarity Initiative renders *all* things holy, *all* as potential material for sacrament, *all* as lavishly blessed and destined to participate in the splendor yet to come?

And, to allude to the words of Your Troubadour (Lk 16:13), how is it that we surrounding the Bay who bear Your name continue to serve both You and the mammon of planet-lacerating consumerism? How, O Tabernacler, are we to find our way back, we who, having befouled our nest, the inimitable and irreplaceable planetary palace You have unfolded for us, are now doing more of the same beyond that earthly neighborhood? How can we continue to speak with such earnest familiarity about Your "salvation" while actively opposing it, and You, on so many fronts?

O You who are loving and merciful above all else, accept my repeated prayer of this decade, that the *totality*, *ta pánta*, of Your cosmos, not only we bearers of Your image, but all of the other fauna, all citizens in Your astonishing league of life, all of the nebulae and galaxies, all of the minerals and compounds, elements and subatomic particles, even the surd and its henchmen, be wooed and swept up into Your healing and saving embrace? O Lover, may it be? Is it too late? May it yet be?

But is there not even more? O You, both Source and Embedder, are not all of Your traffickings, those of which we have knowledge, with us creatures who both have and *are* materiality? And do we not acknowledge You as Agent of this feature of our Unfolding? Did not You cause our materiality to be so? Does not the résumé of our race contain the Hut of God item? Although You may well have other stories—how could it surprise me if You did!—is not materiality intrinsic to us of the *Imago Dei* rather than that from which we require rescue or graduation? Is it not the case that there is *nothing* involving Your fraternizing with us humans, we of the "predicament," that does not include our physicality? Indeed, may it indeed be that present at the Initial Ignition was that matter / energy quantum from which all subsequent unfolding and recycling proceeded, and that this includes not only Your Hut, the *Mater Dei*, but Your Troubadour, birthed, tempted, tortured, executed, and glorified, like ourselves partially derived from the plasma of the first subatomic particles? O Lover, You who have so honored the galaxies and the nebulae, why is it that we have made this issue so difficult? Why, when You have lovingly unfolded all that is, tabernacled amid it, and, in the words of the Apocalypse, declared your intention to make Your permanent abode here with us when time is no more (Apoc 21:3)?

Now does not the Roman Catholic Church, together with its more liturgical siblings of both the East and the West, have a practice, a dogma, a vehicle, a materiality, via which You come to us of the fault, predicament, and loneliness, something called the *sacraments*? And somehow, in a manner permanently ensconced in mystery for me, has not that materiality been graced with the capacity to convey to us *You,* whether in font, at table, beneath oil, or in marriage bed? Yet, while "seven" signs completeness, perhaps perfection, are not the seven but the beginning? Does not all that You have unfolded possess the potential of sacrament, a potential activated by Your gift of faith to us? In short, is not the cosmos itself, both in its components and in the whole, sacrament via which You expand Your hut among us, deepen Your solidarity with us, envelop us in Your Real Presence, and prepare us for our destiny within Your Community of Love?

Finally, O Suitor of the Cosmos, may I confess a slip of self-doubt? Have I overdrawn here the scale of the concentric reverberations of Your Bethlehem Initiative?

Does scripture indeed support what I have sketched out here? Does the unfolding Christian tradition? Is not my response to these last two questions in the affirmative, although the evidence be more implicit in both cases than explicit?

But is there not a third question needful of airing: is it even *possible* for one of my sort to overstate the scale of the triumph of Your Love Project? O Mad Lover, as Your Catherine endearingly addressed You, is not the burden of proof on those *delimiting* the reach of that Love which You embodied to the Cross and beyond? When it comes to You of the self-divesting Love, must we not, when in doubt, *always* seek to err towards big, always wagering on the side which transcends both eye and ear, indeed which points toward precincts not so much as approached by human imagination (1 Cor 2:9)? May I simply rest my prayer here, having asked forgiveness in advance if my attempt to open myself more in that direction has, in reality, been *hubris*?

O Sacramentalizer!

J. O Translator!

O *Abba*, may I describe a dilemma I have regarding You, one having two distinct horns? On the one hand, do I not, as J. B. Phillips argued in *Your God Is Too Small*, hold You in my finite heart and head in ways chronically undersized and inadequate, repeatedly lapsing toward creating You in my own paltry image? And here on Tylerton have not first the sea, and then the night sky, teased both my head and heart out beyond the patterned ruts of my little world, the laziness of my false contentments, the urgent gerbil runs of my passions, and my miniaturizations of You, in the direction of grandeur awash in awe? And in the process, have not these two tutorials in transcendence been transformed, the sea on occasion into a libation to You ushering me into adoration, our galaxy's river of light across the night sky a prayer shawl preparing me for the same? And has not some of that stretching been painful and, on occasion, frightening even as I thank You for it with all that I am?

On the other hand, have not both Your grandeur and otherness been far too much for me to receive, I being creature, You Creator? Am I not mere earthen vessel with modest orifice, You Torrent? I reed basket, You Ocean of Fire? Does not the book of Exodus have You saying to Moses, "You cannot see My face, for no one can see Me and live!" (Ex 33:20)? How could I have exercised my *capax Dei* agency, my having been equipped to be able to receive You, had You remained ensconced in boundlessness? How was I able to begin to climb up into Your lap, *Abba*, and sing You this my own song, had You remained shrouded in immensity and infinitude? Oh, is it not my prayer these decades that the destiny not only of myself, but of all of your handiwork, be to wander for the duration within the rarified air of Your boundlessness? But could I have ever offered You my first trembling and fearful "yes" in that stratosphere?

And so, would not I, my entire sort, have remained precisely there, impaled for the duration on both horns of this dilemma, seemingly condemned either to miniaturize You or concede to futility, or both, *impossibly matched* with the One with whom we, yet, *had* to do? Damned if we did, damned if we didn't, as were perhaps some of the Hebrew prophets or the psalmist on occasion?

And into this gulf, this cosmic conundrum, did You not step with Your Solidarity Initiative, Your Love Project? And whatever else the Embedding meant, was it not a diminution, a calibrating down of the scale of the presentation of Your boundlessness in the direction of ourselves, so that I could activate that first tentative "yes" to You, itself Your gift? Diminution of boundlessness: like Fire in a reed basket, it's an oxymoron! Not to worry, but isn't that precisely the point? Is not Your Troubadour the very center as well as foundation of belief that *finitum capax infiniti*, that the finite has the capacity to receive the infinite? That Your boundless Word could be incarnated in my sort, oxymoron or no, is that not the central Mystery of our faith? All so that we of the modest orifice, the reed basket, the earthen vessel, could somehow receive You, Mother, Suitor, and Hospitalier to all that is and ever shall be?

Is not all of my sort's unbelievable unfolding from subatomic plasma and starstuff via aquatic critters and all manner of other illustrious ancestors to our present status as human "persons," preparatory to being encountered by You, O Lover?

Is not cosmogenesis, among many other things, Your incremental provision of womb, nursery, playpen, and kindergarten toward the end of patiently equipping us with the consciousness, agency, and voice to fashion a first halting "yes" to You? And when the mismatch was still too vast, did You not relinquish and surrender Your self to self-diminution? I know well that you are not "person" as am I—there is no accounting for You that way *either*—but have You not in Your Troubadour *come to me* as "person"? And is it not that coming which both prepared and emboldened me to respond, to address You as Father, even to climb up, *Abba*?

Thus, do we not encounter You vis-à-vis ("face-to-face") in Your Troubadour, in him translated into our language, "humanese"? Do we not encounter in him Your preferential option for the poor, this in a form which our ears can hear, our eyes see, our hands handle (1 Jn 1:1)? In the proclamation of the Gospels do we not hear, in quadraphonic sound, the graphic, indeed, torturous description, rife with relinquishment, of You, Lover, scaled-back so that we could both encounter and respond to You?

Is it not irony of ironies: that my sort, since forever plagued by the propensity to miniaturize or reconfigure You, this for reasons of both our finitude and the malignant surd, should encounter You in the Troubadour, *shalom* walking, You scaled-down to, translated into . . . *ourselves*?

O Translator!

30. Prayers Offered Out of the Beginning: Cosmogenesis

A. O High Roller!

Although in Your Troubadour You accomplished an exquisite equipoise for the ages between creation and Creator, is it not the case that this symmetry does not yet extend to the cosmos itself? Are not we of the *finitum* contained by walls, one of which is time, another its double-cousin space, which, among other things, determine our box? Indeed, are not we *intrinsically* of the finite box: of material/energy, locked into contingency, philosophically unnecessary, our agency uninvolved in our having come to be? And is not each of us fruit of about 13.7 billion years of ever-recycling formation, with how much yet to come?

But You, on the other hand, while uncircumscribable, boxless, and *sans* beginning, did You not freely choose to love our box into being, draw it through its development, tabernacle within its tiny stage to showcase Your Love, nurse it toward greater wholeness, and declare it to have a heart-boggling destiny? And even more improbably, did You not embrace, surrender to, and voluntarily make the box Your own? And why does this matter? Well, as starters, do we know *anything* about You other than that which has issued from the Flaring Forth of the Furnace of the Fire of Love, a.k.a. the birth and the unfolding of the box?

Yet, O Fire, do I not remain curious about "before," an odd word, there having been no time "then," pre-box? Does not even musing about that require that I do so "outside" the box, where, however, we mortals cannot go except, perhaps, via imagination? Speaking of which, did not You, more than "accounters," for example, spin out poets, musicians, artists, dreamers, who could, in the words of poet John Frederick Nims, employ metaphor "which can suggest much by stating nothing," in part because You knew we would want to try to get "out" and "back" there? Poetry, like music, having some mysterious links with the timeless celestial repositories? Does not Your Troubadour, in the Fourth Gospel's "high priestly prayer," say to You that "You loved me *before* the foundation of the cosmos" (Jn 17:24, EA)?

Does not John of the Cross, in his poem, "Romances," roll back the tape of Your traffickings with us box-ers to the beginning, and then "farther," so as to sketch with broad strokes the relationship between You as Lover and Your Word as beloved, the Love between being Your Spirit? And does not Jessica Powers, in her "For a Lover of Nature" (165), play with "earth's sad inexperience and youth"—earth being a relative newcomer on the block—compared with Love which has no beginning? O Dark

Ocean of Fire, are there not present in these poets' words inklings of a thrice-hallowed community of intimate and overflowing Love "before"? A community nevertheless a unity, for, in the words of the Spaniard, "the more love is one / the more it is love"?

But "did" You not in pre-time proceed "out" of Your self? "Did" You not "move" from that which had never not been to that which, while about to be spoken into being, "was" not yet?! Raised to You from inside the box, the question is this: why is there something rather than nothing? Or in the words of physicist Stephen Hawking: "Why does the universe go to all the bother of existing?" Clothed in the idiom of poetry, You, the Triune Community of Love, an unending melding of initiative and response, differentiation and union, reciprocity and rest: why . . . why "did" You proceed forth so as to prepare the stage for the beginning?

Pardón, but may I, neither poet nor artful, speak brashly in matters of which I know little? Given what all has transpired in the wake of Your proceeding, what all would flow through the opening fashioned by Your insistence that Love among Your creatures, like that around the celestial table, be free rather than mechanized, *why did You proceed*? Surely the compromising of Your dream for the cosmos by my sort, compounded by the poisoning of all else as well, did not catch You by surprise, did it? But then, You *knew* what would transpire?

What "was" . . what *is* that dream in You, O Sacred Heart, that would warrant this titanic risk? Yes, O Ocean of Fire, is not *that* the question I have wanted my entire life to bring to words and then raise to You: WHAT DREAM, WHAT GOOD ENVISIONED IN YOUR HEART, WOULD WARRANT THIS STUPENDOUS RISK WHICH HAS EXACTED SUCH AN OBSCENE PRICE?

O Lover, You, *ar-Rahman* (the Merciful), *ar-Raheen* (the Compassionate), You who know all hearts, do You not know that I have no interest in the insolent queries of theodicy? Have I indeed a lofty perch from which to summon You to account?! Are You not my judge rather than vice versa?

Yet, *yet*, am I not a dancer, O Fire, am I not a dancer? And You made me to be a dancer? As part of Your dream for the cosmos, the dream out of which *everything* proceeded and hangs, did You not make me a dancer? I, sitting back there against the wall, had I not always presumed that it was a performance gig and that You were doing the honors? Was I not reasonably content with that arrangement, since that was the way it had been, was, and ever would be?

But, did You not then, via Your Troubadour, invite me, all of us, to step out onto the floor and dance? Preferring just to listen, did I not require coaxing? But did I not, admittedly gradually, step out there, and now I am learning to dance? I, prize exhibit *uno numero* of the predicament, one totally dependent upon Your mercy, yes, but the fact that I am a dancer, did that not come on Your watch? Is it not on Your plate? Am I not one of Your fiercely free co-creators who longs for nothing more than the music of Your Fire? Is not this entire chapter expressive of my dance? So, once more *that* question, the one You don't have to answer, *but I do have to ask*: what "was," what *is* that dream in Your heart which would warrant the risk inherent in the cosmos project? You, I AM WHO AM: what kind of High Roller are You?

But, O Dark Fire of Love, is not submissive silence only my last resort? Do I not know You, not because I sleuthed You out but because You, O Stalker, O Tracker, self-disclosed to me and the entire cosmos, most decisively via Your Troubadour, *and invited me to step out and dance?* So I and my sort are entirely dependent upon You, right?

Yes, but are not You also dependent on us of the box, although in a most different way? If my sort, and others You may have unfolded, had not come to be, either because you chose not to proceed from Your Love Circle or decided midcourse to bail out and not draw us to present capacities, how would You have been known beyond the Circle? Does there not need to be someone around capable of encountering and coming to know You? If we of the *Imago Dei* have the potential to bring You satisfaction, O Lover, would this not have been diminished had Your unfolding crested with mere centipedes, sans *Imago*?

You know, the tree falling in the forest making no sound unless there is someone nearby with an active auditory faculty? Well, is not the tree falling in the forest *You*—who You are and what You do? And we the witnesses to what we have heard and seen? Pray tell, where would Your Procession Project be without us, if there had been no creatures here with the capability of whispering *"Abba,"* let alone just "hearing"? If my hunch is right, that what You are always up to is trying to give Your self away, then has not *everything* been about Your nurturing into being agents with whom You could do this, those to whom You could give Your self? In short, is not your self-disclosing Love, like all our derivitives worth the trouble, also a *construct*?

What if You, O Torrent of Love, threw a love banquet lasting seven Earth-days, replete with all that You are, but there were none unfolded beyond paramecia to fill the guest list? Or might You then have unfolded some entirely different creatures, perhaps extra-solar types, with capabilities far superior to ours, and thus not be dependent on us so as to be known? But then might You not have faced all of these questions in relation to *them*? *Ergo*: as in any dance, don't *each* of the two partners, admittedly in very different ways, need each other? And if You need us in that way, must it not be because you unfolded us so?

But I return to my central question, stated as only I, a common box-er, can state it: what warranted Your proceeding from the Circle in the first place when well You knew that the role of freedom in Your sort of Love meant a relinquishing of tight control over all aspects of the project, and thus opened a humongous Pandora's box?

Might not the beginning of an answer lie in the direction of You wanting to have more recipients upon whom to unleash the relentlessness of Your Sea, the naked splendor of Your Night Sky, that is, Your Love? O I AM WHO AM, do You not want us so as simply to be more expansively and expressively *You*? Yes, what does a merciful, long-suffering, patient, forgiving, just, and loving *Abba* do if there are no existent daughters or sons to climb into Your lap and begin to receive the One You want to give away? Did You not proceed, venture forth into what had not been, so as better to be You? So that You could initiate a journey to bring the entire cosmos to Your celestial/terrestrial table? Did You not take on this entire incredible risk simply because of who You are, a passionate, risk-taking Lover, one seemingly not free to be otherwise? Am I on to something here?

O High Roller!

B. O Flaring Forth Fire of Love!

O Source of all that is, with Edwin Hubble's findings in the late 1920s suggesting that the galaxies were moving farther and farther apart, was not the "Big Bang" theory, together with its rival static models, in the air during my collegiate pre-med studies (1958–62)? Having said that, is it not also the case that the curiosity-challenged state of my faith at that stage resulted in little interaction with such a hypothesis?

Against that background, do I not recall that day on the Crick forty years later, when, while reading about the "Flaring Forth" in Thomas Berry and Brian Swimme's *The Universe Story*, I suddenly stopped and blurted out aloud, "*Hey*, I know You! I recognize You! I'm *LOVED* by You? Isn't the whole blooming thing Your Love story?" Oh, I had *thought* something like this before, but never before been *seized* and *moved* by it! And, O Torrent, did I not then recall Thomas Merton writing that with You the *lingua franca* is Love rather than the workings of either sensorium or intellect? Is it so that Your heart is unknowable, and You refuse to be known, *except* via this one language, You for whom communication has always been such a big deal? Are You, O Relinquisher, indeed monolingual, only that language being Love rather than, as my Teutonic forebears opined, *Deutsch*?

And was not that day on the Crick one when my capacity for Love was invited to step forward, a Rubicon I never would, nor could, uncross? Generally familiar with the differences between the jurisdictions of physics and metaphysics, science and faith, was I not aware that day, that, unlike both deists and designists' penchant for proof, I had not made a scientific so much as a faith statement? Was not the only trace of shadow that day my wondering why it had taken so long for this awareness to *seize* me? Why my slowness when I had already come to know You as, of all things, *Fire*? At my center I was filled with awe: was not this a step toward *rapprochement* between science and faith, the very different and tragically estranged sibling offspring of a single Mother, You?

Had not Fr. Ronald Rolheiser, OMI used the image of each of us humans having been kissed into being by You? And as we grow from infancy into childhood, do we not retain a dark subconscious memory, an aura, of that first kiss, of having, in the words of Rolheiser, "been caressed by hands far gentler than our own"? And as adolescents and then adults, does not each of us have a "first love" which really isn't, as we look everywhere, mostly in the wrong places, for that *first* first love which is somehow coterminous with being alive? Each of us Your love-child, is not the wholeness of our lives dependent on whether and to what extent we experience a *re*-union with You, the Parent, the fruit of whose lovemaking we are?

But is not this kissed-into-being quality of each of us individuals applicable as well to the entire human family, indeed, the entire cosmos? Might this primordial "memory" in the very matter/energy of galaxies and nebulae, the cells of flora and fauna, be the seeming homing device being massaged by Your Love from out of their, our, future? How could one, having encountered at the center Your Troubadour, he of the self-relinquishment as index of Your Love, come to any conclusion but that all that is, from the Initial Ignition through the innumerable paths, cul-de-sacs, and burgeoning meadows of the unfolding, is love-child of Your passion? After all, are You not the One joyfully Flaring *Forth*? And are not the chorus of kudos in our time accompanying breakthroughs in the disciplines of astronomy, astrophysics, cosmology, and molecular biology reverberations of that first event to which Job's question referred: "Who laid earth's cornerstone, When the morning stars sang together, And all the children of God shouted for joy" (Jb 38:6,7)?

O Ocean of Love, to paraphrase the psalmist, how can I possibly absorb, how can I find words to express my gratitude for what You have done (Ps 116:12)? That You proceeded forth *at all*? That there is something rather than nothing? That rather than remaining ensconced in the splendor and safety of the Triune Community, You ventured into that which, not having been, was ignited into being, including matter, energy, time, and space? That You determined to enlarge the pool of recipients of Your lavish Love, the invitees to the dance, the guest list for the celestial/terrestrial table, so as to be more expressively, more expansively, more lavishly, I AM WHO AM?

That You embarked on what, in some of my darker moments, looks like a cosmic crap shoot, so that Your Beauty, Goodness, and Truth could be laid bare, and received?

And *appropriated*? O You of many Names, vastly more magnificent than any and all, how do I thank You for having proceeded so that this elegant and beautiful cosmos could be, so that a hospitable planetary palace for such a fevered vitality as is life could unfold in our solar neighborhood? How is it that I, once terrorized by nightmare forays into the night sky, can now experience its canopy as oratory for adoration?

Was not part of what You were nurturing within me on the Crick an awareness that I could not fully inhabit this cosmos, make it my "place" in terms of construct, if I failed to acknowledge and respond to the way in which it had been loved by another before me? And in a way distantly analogous to the love of this place by centuries of waterfolk, and millennia of Amerindians before them, had You not loved it, loved it into being, leaving Your tell-tale hum as witness into my own time? How could I have my little thing with the cosmos without acknowledging, and responding to, its own memory of that first kiss?

How is it that I, a common and contingent box-er, could be inundated by awareness that I am Your love-child, that I could both hear and be part of the reverberating "Yes!" which, analogous to the Cosmic Microwave Background Radiation—ubiquitous hum of Your song, lingering scent of Your love-making—*is* the silent music? That I, awash in adoration, "lost in wonder, love and praise," in the words of the hymn of my origins, am myself reduced, however briefly, to silence?

O Flaring Forth Fire of Love!

C. O Journey Spinner!

O Lover, as I was beginning mid-decade to look up, whether into Tylerton's night sky or the Hubble photographs on the web, did not my most fascinating, and urgent, questions have to do with the *significance* of what I was seeing? What, *really* now, was I witnessing? Was I viewing cosmic context bracketing *the* focal piece of furniture in a salon, the sets and curtains framing a theater stage? Was the night sky mere aesthetic decoration serving up beauty to us terrestrials, hormonal enhancement for us mammalia at rutting time? Perhaps the nocturnal dome was a *tabula rasa* mysteriously supplied to mortals so we could project upon it, zodiac style, our understandings of ourselves, our planetary digs, and our transcendent itches? Or was the tapestry of the night sky merely the random, inadvertently beautiful, flotsam of earlier stages of a journey which had culminated in, *Voilà!* ourselves? I ruminated over such hypotheses regarding the night sky: why did all of them seem to supply Alfie's question, "What's it all about?" with the same answer: *ourselves*, human beings? Did the entire cosmos, *a la* much of American culture, exist for humans, *numero uno* in particular?

But what if the cosmos, both that known and that yet to be known, were more player in the drama than mere accoutrement, more part of the cast than merely the set? What if the cosmos were less a bucket of pieces than an "it": not a "he" or "she," but an "it"? And, furthermore, what if the cosmos, the whole enchilada, were doing something *as a whole*, a unity, whether that be expanding, entropically cooling, seemingly aiming itself, or somehow responding to that without, or ahead? Was not this deeper unity of the collective cosmos something Swimme had been nudging me toward? Might the Apostle Paul have been hinting at some such unity with his *four* references to "the creation" in Romans 8:19-22, possibly also the writers of exilic Isaiah (65:17), 2 Peter (3:13), and the Apocalypse (21:1) regarding "new heavens and earth"?

But if the cosmos were an "it," a unity, an aggregate, what might "it" be doing? Given that to look "out" (space) is also to look "back" (time), was not the most self-evident answer be that the cosmos is on a journey, nearly all elapsed stages of which we are now able, *literally*, to see? And because of technology developments, did we not possess gorgeous photographs from all stages of that journey save the very first billion years, with reason to hope that that period too will continue to shrink?

For those of us believing in You, could there ever be a more graphic display of Your *modus operandi*, your penchant for process and flow, than cosmogenesis: the unfolding of the cosmos, a journey with an aura vastly more of spirited and suspenseful adventure than paint-by-number lockstep? But then, as I study Your schooling of ancient Israel or Your Troubadour's formation of the twelve or his parable about You as Loving Father (Lk 15:11–32) or the mysterious role of Your Spirit in the shaping of the tradition of Your Church or Your patient stalking of me, whether before or after bringing me to ground: what's novel about You and adventurous *process*?

While You are the Unbounded, attributable to none but who You are, is not *process* Your mode of choice, at least in the uni-verse project? Is it thus surprising that the cosmos should be found to be on a journey? Would it not have been much more out of character had You crafted it as we know it by fiat rather than across 13.7 billion years, You for whom time does not pass as it does for us? And yet, O Unfolder, You on whom time has no claim, did You not nevertheless surrender Your self to it, indeed, self-ligating to huge blocks of it, so as to enter, and then settle into, our finite box?

And, of course, does not "journey" embody the additional benefit of laying down rich strata of Your mode's markings—partly decipherable via astrophysics, archaeology, paleolinguistics, and genetics, to begin a list—allowing us better to learn about the journey, indeed, the many journeys? That of the nascent cosmos in its first moments; of the initial generation of stars; of the formation of our galaxy and, later, the solar system; of the greening life with its surging differentiation and proliferation; of our emerging awareness as humans, first of ourselves and each other, and later, of You; awareness of our intertwined mortality and destiny? Are they not journeys, all? In terms of the titular imagery of Part VI, was not the entire cosmos, *in some sense,* itself an entity which You, *Le Premier Danseur,* invited to dance? And did not that entity, that aggregate, possess in its contingency and box-ness, *in some sense,* the capacity to respond to the massaging and drawing power of Your Love brought to bear upon it from out of its future?

Although the primary thrust of Your Troubadour's parable of You as Loving Father (Lk 15:11–32) engages us as individuals and the secondary as humanity at large, might there not be a tertiary application as well: the cosmos itself? Is not the freedom intrinsic to Your Love also operative at this macro level? Are there not everywhere in the cosmos evidences which point away from the mechanistic and predetermined model Paley's watch implies? Can we not pile up words and phrases—like "flux," "change," "contingency," "subtleness," "suppleness," "forks in the road"—all hinting of the limited yet real capacity of the uni-verse to contribute to its own becoming?

And is there not in Your love-child energy/matter an astonishing emergent potentiality ever thrusting new and fructive combinations into the arena? Who could have anticipated that the combining of two gasses, hydrogen and oxygen, could have resulted in a hydro-environment out of which the first single-celled organisms, distantly sharing with You what we call life, would emerge? Might we not infer that you withhold determinism from Your beloved cosmos not unlike how You did with the crucifiers of Your Troubadour, or ourselves, Your headstrong sons and daughters in far countries? All this because of Your respect for what all of us of the love-child creation could bring to the dance? Has not the unfolding of cosmos and life alike had an aura of adventure, exploration, and *Eureka!* about it with You refusing to dotingly bail it out as a more controlled model would have required?

Yet, despite the occurrence of the unspeakable, whether at Chicxulub in the Yucatán (sixty-five million years ago), Jerusalem (587 B.C.E.), Krakatau (1883), Auschwitz (1942–45) or Hiroshima (1945), do I not fiercely believe that the cosmos has had a dancing partner on its long journey, One drawing it toward its fully flowered future, One passionately amorous rather than deistically distant? Are not You, who honor Your own gracing of the cosmos with the potentiality ever more to become itself, ever drawing it home, to Your self? And do You not remain as passionate about that process as about its destination?

O Journey Spinner!

D. O Jammer!

May I make a confession? Did I not across much of my early life tend to image You as conducting a grand symphony employing instruments from all ranks of the unfolding, each of us musicians bowing, piping, drumming, or singing, however well, the score before us? As Herr Maestro, were not both the interpretive conducting and orchestration Yours as well, to say nothing of us instruments and voices, the box-like hall itself, and the very possibility of music?

And had You not also previously composed the score, our role being that of faithfully playing the music placed before us? Of course, we being creatures of free agency, wasn't there occasional opportunity, above and beyond the interpretive always present in the playing, for one of our virtuosi to spin out a cadenza, a brief, bracketed improvisation, mysteriously also part of your score? In short, was not my model of You the maestro/symphonic one?

While across the years this model had sometimes left me restless—was it not more tidy than warranted by either Scripture or experience?—was not its music, after all, varied, spirited, expressive, and beautiful?

And had not John of the Cross' explication of the principal image of this book, "silent music," *thrice* employed the term "symphony"? Ignoring until much later the question what the word "symphony" even meant to a contemplative Castilian friar in 1584 (!), one who might well have had both Jewish and Moorish ancestors and thus been a *converso* squared, one who nearly starved to death as a child, was not my orchestral model reinforced by both my personal musical preferences and its secure and clear-cut roles for both myself and You, Herr Maestro?

After all, had I been one of the disciples after the Resurrection, would not I too have opted for awed *spectator* of the Troubadour who stayed on and on rather than faith-exercising *participant* after he left? Although our sort had been invited to contribute creatively to the dance with You, was not the music itself of Your inspiration, score, interpretation, and conducting? Wasn't it reassuring that You were in charge of the music, Herr Maestro?

But on the Crick, the whirling dance going on all around, above, beneath, and within, the haunting hum of Orff's *In Truitina* ("In the Balance") picked up in marsh and gut, in the night sky and both guests and villagers, was not my restlessness about this imagery on the wax? Was I not becoming increasingly suspicious that Your unfolding was not only preparing us to join the dance, but the composing of its music as well?

But if so, would that not mean that rather than the score being checked out of some past "classical" repository, the music to which You were inviting us to dance was a collaborative effort in the present, in the succession of "nows," in box-time? And that *both* You—chief composer, *Le Premier Danseur*, Unfolder of the Gig—and we—co-composers, co-choreographers, co-dancers, apprentices all—were eager to see how it was turning out? And was not the central issue here, again, the freedom, the open-endedness, which Love of Your sort required? And might not my need to grope toward a far more open model be both sign of the integrity of Your Project Solidarity and hint of the *télos* of Your dream? Indeed, was not the collaboration between You and ourselves, whether my sort or the cosmos at large, at least as much like a combo doing improvisation as a maestro conducting an orchestra from a fixed score? Pray tell, O Lover, was I on to something here?

What is "improvised" music anyway? I asked myself. Is it crafted entirely in the present? Do terms like "random," "tossed-off," off-the-cuff," "slapped together," "impromptu," "extemporaneous," or "ad hockism" do it justice? In the form/freedom tension, is improvisation solely freedom, creation *ex nihilo*, formless, having no memory, and solely in the now?

Or, is improvisation rather built on the *interplay* between form and freedom, in this case both *within* each of the dancers/musicians and also *between* them? Cannot improvisation be lustily free and yet centering in tonality, for example, thus tapping into a lengthy historical consensus, at least among those beholden to Europe's musical legacy at least through the Romantic era, around which notes, intervals, and chords are built, outside of which all is mere noise and cacophony? Might we think of the Fire of Your Love functioning as such a tonal center, a tonal key, in the music of the cosmic dance?

Furthermore, might not the genius of improvisation include freewheeling yet recurring musical themes, *leitmotifs a la* Wagner, repeatedly re-presented and reworked in the rolling event called the present, motifs like covenant, promise-keeping, fidelity, *kenosis*, and, yes, volition? Indeed, were not tonality and motif each possible expressions of form within the space of which freedom could spin its magic, gestalts both offering venue and lending shape to the frolic of the muse? Freedom and creativity thus being channeled and shaped, not dictated? Does not this image have promise in pointing toward how things are between us, cosmic apprentices, and You, the Lead? Does not improvisation, O Lover, so understood, get at Your thing about freedom being nonnegotiable in Love *in any context*? And does it not also mean that You value freedom so much that You have left the final result this wide open?

And so, O Fire, was it not suddenly holy ground that sunny off-season morning mid-decade when, in the Atlanta home of my daughter, Tiffany, and her husband, I chanced upon their CD of John Coltrane's *A Love Supreme,* and in one setting knocked back the entire piece for the first three times in my life? Did I not intuit immediately that *this*, my snootiness about classical music notwithstanding, might be my least inadequate image of the music to which You had long since invited me to dance? That You had not merely invited me to dance with You, but also to give myself to jammin' with You? That You and we cosmics were making music together, and that both of us were finding out how it was turning out, even as it was turning out? That the entire sweep of cosmogenesis was a collaborative adventure, an exploration in harmony, a conspiracy to go to ever more wonderful and relational musical places, a thing delectably, deliciously, *joint*? That You of the Fire and we, cosmics of the combustible, were making music together *a la* lovemaking? Yes, although Your cosmogenesis surely included sight-reading Tchaikovsky under Slatkin's baton in the Kennedy, was it not *also* jammin' with the Trane in some more dim and ambienced venue, the music being born *now,* harbinger of splendor to come?

After all, wasn't Your invitation aimed straight at my agency: an invite not merely to concur, ascent, obey, or even imitate, but *dance*, this freely and inimitably, to embrace and appropriate my own co-creatorship birthright? Not as an equal, of course, You having gotten the combo together and being its lead dreamer and soliloquist and all, but rather, perhaps, as an enrollee in Your in-service class for aspiring dancers and jammers? Yes, and recognizing that Yours were the underlying motifs of both our age and the ages (Love, also known as Beauty, Coherence, Truth, etc.), Your M.O. one of *improvisation*, of jammin' toward the end of discovering what the music's glory was yet to be? And not only I, not only my sort, not only the faunasphere, not only the planet or our galaxy, but the entire cosmos? And was it not slowly dawning on me that there would be no music but that which all of us, You and we cosmics, would compose together, and it would not be heard except at its premieres, a wondrous series of nows?

How often, O Jammer, having initiated my day by stepping into the perch, running my eyes here and there before the host of bio-kin, minerals, and elements which had come to the dance, Your dance and our dance, did I resoundingly proclaim yet again Your seven-fold "good!" of Genesis 1?

Yet, O Wild One, must I not confess that jammin' with You has sometimes been unsettling for me? You see, haven't we cosmics since forever spoken of "Your music" as if You knew the composition cold, we not, and we needed to get it down the way You had it down? And yet, have I not been learning on the Crick that I can *never* make music with You when checking my agency at the door? Do You understand that Your decision to grace us with this measure of freedom is not only a soaring honor, but sometimes a frightening burden?

Is it not better to have a preexistent score, even *sans* advanced access to it, better that at least *You* have such a score, than that we craft as we go? Haven't we of my sort always *loved* a solid and sure thing, like simply repeating the tunes and lyrics of yore? Do You know that sometimes Your being so *pro*-choice is a load for us? Don't I have days when I wish You'd just hand me the score and make me bow it right on my instrument, *automatically* right? Or to use, and possibly abuse, Augustine's image: make me chaste, *automatically* chaste?

Is not my other misgiving about jammin' with You that the musicianship on the side of my sort, to state it in Tylertonese, *really ain't much*: so much cacophony, so much *noise*, whether within or between? Are there not days when the shadow's toll on both us cosmic dancers and the dance in general leaves me concussed? When, despite it having been embraced and absorbed by You in Your Troubadour (2 Cor 5:21), the impact of the *tenebrae* on what my sort brings to the gig seems hopeless?

And isn't that impact, more often than not, rooted in our choice of jammin' partners? We being inclined to drift off promiscuously, whether into some masturbatory rendezvous with a clone of ourselves, an attached other, some prized notion of You, or some vacuous tryst with freedom herself? Sometimes knowing what we do, often not, to the point of continuing to address our partner *du jour* as You? Doesn't it sound stupid, You having crafted the very possibility of collaborative music as well as being the combo's Lead, that the shit You have to put up with has *me* feeling sorry for *You*?

Has not my gravitating toward a more improvisational model, the unfolding cosmos as a collaboratively crafted construct, for understanding the music-making between us, deposited me on a road which sometimes feels like a high wire? On the one hand, don't we cosmics need to keep in mind that we are in the combo because of Your invite rather than our virtuosity? It's a grace gig, right? On the other, does not the very content of that invitation, that we freely show up as musicians, dancers, choreographers, orchestraters, *however apprenticed*, require that we assertively claim, *and assert*, that astonishing role? The gig's rules are Yours, right? While there is no question but that the show is Yours, have You not invited us into its very core as fellow jammers? There it is again, strains of *In Truitina*, in the balance, but then is not that precisely as You crafted us to be?

So given my fears, what would I do without Your Troubadour, the one forever designated by J. S. Bach (1685–1750) as "joy of [*our*] desiring," the one who, in addition to embodying Your Love as well as living (and dying) out the depth of Your identification with us, freely poured himself out for the music, for the dance, *and for the dancers*? So in Your Troubadour's song, have not we apprenticed cosmics had opportunity to hear strains of our own future, that toward which Your Love is drawing the entire unfolding dance?

In a great improvisational piece, isn't there often that event, that moment of magic, perhaps occurring but once, when it all really comes together? With the Coltrane foursome, did not that take place in Englewood Cliffs, New Jersey the night of December 9, 1964, and a master tape, subsequently lost and then, much later, found, *got it*? Well, is it not my confession of faith that Your Troubadour began singing his *chanson d'amour*, also known by some as *A Love Supreme*, on a starry, starry night around the dawn of the first century in Palestine, and that a quadraphonic take, repeatedly almost lost, *got it*?

Despite my fears, I acknowledge that there are other times, mostly days or just minutes, when I'm following Your lead, and we're making music together: whirling, flying, me high off the ground and thinking I can see forever, and absolutely lost in the music both Yours and ours, momentarily just lost *in You*? And with the psalmist, am I not singing out with my baritone, "I will make music to You as long as I live" (fr Ps 146:2)? And in those brief fragments of time, don't I know as totally as I know *anything* that there's something wonderful afoot, something which both You since forever and I, but of late, treasure?

O Heaving Ocean of Dark Fire, could You not have crafted an infinitude of wonderful things to emerge *automatically*, with predictable and methodical, costless and painless, regularity: galaxies genuflecting at every singing of the *Gloria*; scholae of nebulae chanting the *Magnificat* antiphonally across the chancel of light years; planet Earth's nations conducting ourselves like so many denizens of Edward Hicks' Peaceable Kingdom; innkeepers effortlessly garnishing the apple strudel dessert with renditions of Mozart's *Exsultate Jubilate*; I, this writer, loving You, my neighbor, and myself with all that I am all of the time with no exceptions? Could there be anything more wonderful, more glorious?

Yes, actually, and is not that precisely the point? How could I ever thank You for Your gift to us, one both terrible and sublime, of freedom?

O Jammer!

E. O Beauty Herself!

Have not many references to beauty in this memoir emerged directly out of Your unfolding with minimal evidence of human collaboration? A pastel sunset over Rhodes Point at one solstice, the variegated lanterns of Orion at the other, the pale purple flower of the salt marsh aster at the autumnal equinox, the return from South America of the osprey but days before the vernal equilibrium? Is not exilic Isaiah emphatic that "Look for me in an empty waste" (Is 45:19) are words You *never* spoke? And then is there not a second category of beauty, whether Sharryl's flowers, a community's character, the disposition of a guest, or a captain's generosity, where the collaborative nature of the dance, the co-choreography, is writ large?

But then, is there not yet a third category where we of my sort emulate You in a more nearly pure creatorship, where both the journey and destination of the crafting of beauty are its own, sometimes *only*, reward? Whether Sharryl's hand-stitching of a quilt each of our last two off-seasons or Maurice Ravel's *Le Tombeau de Couperin,* the artistry of the yarnin' in the Market or the simplicity of a Zhang Yimou flick, my satisfaction over a porch table well set or Claude Monet's paintings of his Giverny gardens? (Indeed, is there in the entire world a more powerful image of the delicious dialogue between freedom and form in the dance than an impressionist painting?!)

What does our passion to create and/or enjoy what is beautiful show us about ourselves? Could it be that part of what being in Your image (Gn 1:26,27) means is that we have an itch for image-making ourselves, for interpretively re-presenting that interior to ourselves in terms accessible to the exterior senses, and thus sharing it? Does not our likeness to You, O Connoisseur of Beauty, include our hunger for co-creatorship, itself an expression of our playfulness, our freedom, our delight in flaring forth, *too*? How is it that You have unfolded us so as to have this fascinating and delight-ful capacity to create, O Fire, yet one never devoid of struggle and pain in the bringing to birth of the new? Are we like You in *that* respect as well? Living several years as I have in this book project amid the cosmic unfolding, need I have even asked?

What are we to make of the fact, O Aficionado of Beauty, that earliest evidences of artistic activity—whether drawing materials at the Nauwalabila site in the Aborigi-nal Homeland of Australia's Northern Territory dated to more than forty thousand years ago or the stunning paintings of herds of mammals in the Chauvet Cave in southern France dating as early as thirty-five thousand years ago, for example—show up just a few millennia after what many paleoanthropologists view as the onset of a flurry of development of the anatomically modern human, the Cro-Magnon, in tools, language, and a zest for innovation, each with a growing aesthetic flair?

And how could anyone familiar with Your penchant for covenants, communica-tion, and relationships in both testaments of scripture not take note of the emergence of the art of language among my sort during that same general period? Is it not this astonishing *Homo sapien* emergence, a *kairos* mysterious and glorious, that John Paul II described as an "ontological leap" above the "material continuity" of evolution?

O Source, is a part of what the Genesis 2 account images as You breathing into what You formed from the dust "the breath of life" (Gn 2:7), our love for beauty, beauty in and of itself? Is not this capacity, largely unlike that of the other fauna in-cluding our nearer kin the Neanderthal, a marker of the expansiveness of Your gift of playfulness, creativity, and freedom? Is it such a reach to ponder the possibility that in this mysterious threshold our Cro-Magnon forebears were evidencing the *Imago Dei*, a distant similitude to Your own explosion in self-expression in hue, timbre, scent, taste, and texture through all stages of the unfolding? Yes, is not Your own free and playful delight in color, form, harmony, and crescendo in the sphere of matter/energy distantly mirrored in our own? And does not our primary lapse, perhaps our only, then consist of absolutizing what we have crafted, whether object, self-image, relationship, idea, or spiritual value, rather than giving ourselves wholly to You and Your way less traveled? In matters of art and beauty, is not our flaw immediately adjacent to our splendor? Has not image-making occasioned both our glory and our surdish idolatry?

And, O Beauty Most Ancient and Most New, to cite the African Augustine, when I am in a space dedicated to the adoration of You, whether closet, cathedral, or cosmos, am I not repeatedly moved to tears at the way in which the free and creative resources of all of the five sensorial ports are marshaled in the raising to You of my *Hallelujah*? Am I not taken aback by our propensity—indeed, our urgent *need*—to generate beauty in whatever ways available? Whether in movement, gesture, speech, food or space presentation, visual representation, or, especially, music, does not the human being frequently seek to fill her pocket garden of the cosmos with what is a delight to the senses, the intellect, and/or the heart? Is not this capacity, but especially the eagerness, the playfulness, the profusion, the hunger, to generate, an expression of our co-creatorship with You? And do You not delight in this, our delight?

Living amid the evidences of our co-creation here on the Crick, has not part of my *Adoramus Te!* been in recognition that, rather than having been crafted to do this by fiat, formed so as to do no other, You have given us the capacity *freely to choose* to do this?

O Beauty Herself!

F. O Love that Moves the Sun and Other Stars!

O Source, do I not see everywhere in the cosmos, micro to macro, process, flux, contingency, change, probability, unpredictability? Have You not freed the cosmos to be itself rather than march in some lockstep cadence? Is not some analogue to human freedom evident in the pattern of the primordial subatomic material in the aftermath of the Flaring Forth, as if the cosmos itself were endowed with some participatory capability in choosing what it would become? Is not the cosmos' sharing in the dance glimpsed in the formation and life-spans of the first generation of stars? In galaxies such as our own coming to be from the enriched elemental mix disgorged from the nuclear furnaces of those first stars? In the emergence of our solar system with its central nuclear heating? In the improbable appearance of this mystery called life? In the mutation/adaptation dynamic ever pressed forward by critters' will to copulate, propagate, and survive? And in the arc among some higher primates toward ever more ingenious tools so as to remain engaged in the fray?

Can we indeed look at the Bay's food chain or star nurseries in distant nebulae or Your "star . . . come forth from Jacob" (Nm 24:17), Your Troubadour's humming of You, and conclude that all that is, is as You alone "designed" it, the cosmos itself reduced to the concretizing of a static blueprint? Can we bearers of Your image live the experience of life without suspicion that the galaxies, like ourselves, can and do contribute to shaping the dance? Could we honestly argue that You, the Loving Father in Your Troubadour's story (Lk 15:11 ff), "designed" the younger's experience in the far country, causing it to unfold according to "Your plan," when in reality what You did was financially *enable* that headstrong youth to use and abuse both You and *his own* agency, refusing to intervene even when he was starving to death? Is not "design" far too *tight,* too *static,* a word for Your M.O. with us and the rest of the cosmos? How can we speak of either a designed or predetermined cosmos, or life, when You have invited us freely to make music and dance with You?

Yet is not the other extreme—that this glistening, elegant uni-verse came to be solely via the random encounters of subatomic particles, celestial bodies, galaxy groups, and, later, rutting critters—equally bleak? Does not the statistical improbability of life emerging by mere randomness within the relatively short period of 13.7 billion years cause some to conclude that the cosmos was somehow "aiming" at a possibility such as Mozart's *Ave verum corpus?* What are the chances of the human genome, including the sequences of its more than three billion chemical base pairs, coming to be by sheer random chance?

Can one, after studying the development of the first generation of stars from pre-atomic plasma, the emergence of a planetary environment called Earth suitable for life, or the unfolding of self-conscious creatures possessing both the capability and the need to press this question, conclude that there is a void of directionality in the uni-verse? Or, in the language of the Troubadour's tale about You, Loving Father, is it plausible to argue that having respected Your child's decision to go into the far country, You subsequently had no further relationship with her? And that she remained unaffected by the subconscious memory of that Love which kissed her into being, or a conscious recall of nurture and affection received in Your house, or the burning Ocean of Hope in Your heart that she would yet *choose* to come home?

But if words like "design," "plan," or "engineer" throttle Your love-child's freedom threatening to reduce the dance to mere parody, indeed, farce, and if the deity's distantness and indifference renders deism dead on arrival, how then are we to understand the nature of Your role in the cosmos? Are we abandoned to the hopelessness of this chance/necessity dichotomy, this dice/design dead-end? *Le Premier Danseur,* You dance both with us aware of the fault, and with the rest of the cosmos, but, pray tell, how is it that You *lead?* Yes, O Lord of the Dance, how is it that You both *lead* in the dance and yet respect the freedom with which You Your self have crowned us?

Or has the answer to that question been in front of us all of the time? Does the content of Your self-disclosure through the life, word, death, and resurrection of Your Troubadour—that You in Your Love draw us, invite us, court us, lure us, to Your self—apply to the entire cosmos as well? While I believe that You so "lead" my sort via Your Love, is it so as well for chimpanzees? Amphibians? Paramecia? A copse of hackberry trees? A ridge of rock on a star's planet in a yet-undetected galactic group? Might the unfolding subatomic plasma of the Initial Ignition have begun to evidence lack of homogeneity, which then developed into concentrations of gasses and, later, the first stars, because of the lure, the tenacious draw, of Your Love? Do You call a stone to Your self and, freely, *in some sense*, it possesses a shadowy capacity to respond? Cannot "the Love that moves the Sun and the other stars," as Dante concluded his *Commedia*, act upon a cay? An ecosystem? A *cosmos*?

Do You not, *Abba*, indeed stand in our future, *a la* the Father in Your Troubadour's canticle (Lk 15:20), squinting back to us in time across the unfolding yet to be, arms and heart aching, mysteriously wooing us to come to our only home, beckoning us and our befouled cosmic palace to Your self? Do You not indeed run back against the flow of the dusty road of cosmogenesis toward Your wounded and violated cosmic love-child, longing to draw it, us, to Your breast? O Lover, You who rejoice in us as a bridegroom in his bride (Is 62:5), do You not lean amorously into our freedom, yet never violating it? And is not the fruit of that Love the directionality, the *grain*, apparent in all that is and a support to my dark hope in You, both for myself and for this ravaged speck of cosmic garden?

Is it not amazing, O Fire, how today confessors and non-confessors of You alike are grappling with the way in which each of several dozen fundamental constants of physics is seemingly calibrated to the equipoise necessary for the sustaining of our biosphere? Is not human life, including the possibilities of the beautiful, the fascinating, the mysterious, and the *reality of love, freely and consciously extended*, indebted to this grand staircase of symmetries, this cascade of so-called coincidences? That were but one of these constants to have been minutely higher or lower, I might not have been so as to form this question? Is it at all surprising, given the paucity of hope in pure randomness, that the power of Your Love, brought to bear on the cosmos and wooing it into possibilities unaccountable via science, would be mistaken for an intrinsic homing device whereby the uni-verse aims itself?

Yet, if Your love could and indeed is seducing me with joy, drawing me toward Your self even as You fortify my freedom allowing me to enlarge my "yes," could You not have affected the early stages of cosmogenesis so that, the lean elemental cocktail of the first billion years notwithstanding, carbon-based life could in time emerge? Ah, is it not more difficult today not to confess You than to do so? Or need I be cautious here lest I forget that I am persuaded—help my *unpersuadedness* (fr Mk 9:24)—only through the lens of Your Troubadour, that matter/energy possesses no *intrinsic* meaning? Was not my experience a common one: failing to infer Your disposition of Love from the cosmos, I was nevertheless later able to recognize it there, having in the interim been bear-hugged by You via Your Minstrel?

But, some might counter, is the image of the loving Father in his parable as one who merely persuades, draws, passionately yearns for the love-child to come home, a sufficiently adequate one for Your role in the cosmos *in general*? Is loving persuasion, O You, the Alpha and Omega, the One from whom I come and to whom I go, Your primary, perchance Your *only* mode?

Or do word combinations like "merely persuades," like "merely love," betray how my sort sees Your heart through the pale lenses of our own paltry and pathetic loves, when in reality a metaphor like Fiery Ocean of Love only *begins* to inch in the direction of a less inadequate representation? Do I really think it is possible, let alone conceivable, to overstate the power of Your Love, O Relinquisher, Self-Emptying One? What are the chances that Catherine of Siena or John of the Cross would ever have mused about the power of Your "mere love"? O Torrent, Ocean, Night Sky of Love, would You "dilate my heart" (Ps 119:32) lest my measly diminution of Your Love cause me to doubt what you have prepared for Your cosmic garden home?

But so what, O Lover? So what if faith in Your Troubadour's singing of You serves both to underscore and personalize evidences of Your wooing of the cosmos ever since the Flaring Forth, accounting for what is in a way which science cannot match? Might this mean that I yet again must allow to be stripped from me notions of separation from Your gorgeous creation, theologies of finding salvation *from* it, You *beyond* it?

Might it mean that I am invited finally to accept fully my materiality and my implicit kinship with the entirety of that cosmos, especially given it as the arena of Your Bethlehem trafficking, the locale of Your ultimate and final residency (Apoc 21:3)? And might it also mean that, *once and for all*, I can acknowledge that the only "spirituality" relevant to us of the fault is that in the arena of matter/energy, this not so much because of who we are as because of who *You* of the proceeding forth, the settling in, and the permanent residency, are?

O Love that Moves the Stars!

G. O Cornucopia of Green!

O Torrent, my question to You this dawn, while not original, is urgent: why are there so many things? Has not the bio-rich Crick itself pressed this query, this despite both its restricting salinity and shallow depth? Even more, was it not pressed by looking up on a moonless night into the edge of the river of light which is our galaxy, estimated to contain hundreds of billions of stars, one of an even greater number of galaxies in the uni-verse?

Even when restricting ourselves both to our own planet and to entities bearing the mysterious gift we call "life," are not the numbers staggering? While perhaps 1.8 million flora and fauna species have been scientifically named and classified, do not estimates of the species presently existing range wildly from perhaps twice that num-ber as high as one hundred million? And do not the named/classified species inhabit-ing the Bay at least part of the year, including the many I encountered daily during my decade, number more than 3,600, and counting? Furthermore, has not analysis of Earth's fossil record suggested that presently existing species number perhaps in the high single-digit percentages of those ever having been on the planet? Is it not thus plausible that across just the most recent third of the unfolding, Your drawing Love has nurtured into being on this planetary speck the larger part of a *billion* species, to say nothing of the number of individual organisms? Where might the numbers go as we learn more from both the fossil records and extra-solar planet possibilities, past or present, to say nothing about counting the inanimate?

Hence my query, now downsized: why are there so many *living* things? Why did You not invite forth but one specimen of one "kind" (to use the more inclusive term of Genesis 1 rather than the scientific term "species") to showcase Your glory? A splendid critter, beautiful, regal, and singular, and also a paradigmatic botanical specimen with commensurate charms? Or, if that were not enough, numerous individuals belonging to each of these two kinds? Would that not have resulted in more with less, part of Your *modus operandi* in other respects? Why was even this seemingly not sufficient, O Artesia? And would not that same question need to be raised in reference to any other bio-scenario I might imagine?

So what is this wild profusion in our planetary place, this lavish and extravagant flourish of plentitude, this dazzling proliferation of life? Are not the skies, the seas, the streams, the mountains, the deserts, the very dust of which we box-ers are crafted *teeming* with life, a vast horn of plentitude and diversification arcing toward complex-ity? Is not the entire planetary garden a can of worms, a kudzu-like frenzy of life, ever moving, ingesting, excreting, coupling, procreating, seeking to pass its perhaps slightly enhanced genes on to the future, as if each sort were sweating beneath the hot breath upon its neck of wolf extinction? Why this kingdom of vitality, the half of the photosynthetic alchemy nursing at the tits of parents planet and star, the other, directly or indirectly, nourished by the bodies of the alchemists themselves? O You, ensconced in Mystery, to my faculties both impenetrable Darkness and Thicket, to use two of John of the Cross' terms for You, whence this plethora of life, this cornucopia of green?

Is not the entire garden Earth *green,* a cacophony of green run amuck? Is it not *rigged,* indeed *hard-wired,* for a million shades of green? Are not the skies and forests, mountains and fields, even the rivers and seas, a seamless carpet of *Spartina* green? As if You were one Jackson Pollock at work on a cosmic canvas with a palette of an infinite variety of *verde,* whether flora or fauna? O Tree from whom we spring, what is Your thing about *green?* And given Your propensities to proliferate life on our planet, what fool would wager against You having done so elsewhere as well? Pray tell, why do You find green *so* very interesting? Are You not the God of the Green? Were you possessing of "pigment," would it not most likely be that represented by Hildegard of Bingen's word: *viriditas?* Does not all of this verdancy tempt me to trot out Catherine of Siena's "madness" term yet again?

Again my question, O Cornucopia: why? While no single thing can mirror Your presence, cannot Your vast and varied multiplicity of them, Your orgy of differentiation throughout the cosmos but especially here, do so slightly less inadequately than could but one thing? Is there not in the plethora of Your profusion, the torrent of Your bounty, hint of Your lavish generosity, Your astonishing fecundity and creativity, Your sheer delight in variety and inimitableness, Your childlike exuberance and playfulness? Indeed, does not the night sky remind some of us far more of a child at play than an engineer methodically rendering concrete a blueprint?

But is there not more here than Your desire to give of Your self to yet more things, a criterion the cosmos at the nine-billion-year mark might arguably have satisfied? Did You not want, beyond that, for at least part of the cosmos to flower, indeed, bloom, toward the end of making the journey increasingly its very own? Beyond the less obviously active and receptive materials, did You not desire flora and fauna exercising their respective measures of choice, freedom, and agency? Creatures having the capacity to respond more expansively to Your invitation to become co-creators? Yes, You could have created ever-more beautiful mountains or plains or rock formations, but was it not *life* which You brought forth, life with a larger, potentially *much larger,* capacity for the exercising of freedom and co-creativity, companionship and intimacy? O, You loved Your creature siblings all, but was not *life* Your Rachel, Your favored (Gn 29)? Was there not from the very Flaring Forth this qualitative bio-vector, earlier dormant yet preparational, later manifest, in retrospect relentless, amid the quantitative profusion?

And beyond my piling up adjectives for You like "fertile," "fecund," and "fructive," did You not draw some bearers of the miracle of life toward even higher levels? Do not

Your self-disclosure to, relationship with, and love for my sort, three values permeating all You do, each presuppose in us centeredness and separation, individuation and differentiation, qualities You were nurturing across the epochs? Given our inference that Your proceeding grew out of Your longing to give Your self away more freely and widely, is not this plentitude, especially of life, some measure of both the urgency and scale of this Your passion? Have not our enormous numbers as creatures offered more opportunity for the Torrent of Your Love to affect, cause to blossom, *and be reciprocated?*

Have I ever before really thought how different life would be, how altered would be our ways of conceiving of *You,* were there but seven celestial bodies, six elements in the periodic table, five varieties of flora, four musical tones, three species of birds, two seasons, and but one hermaphroditic human gender? Can we not glimpse within ourselves a remote shadow of Your unabashed joy in a creation of Yours *turned loose to take on a life of its own,* and in so doing possessing the capacity to choose to offer You praise and reciprocate Your love in innumerable ways?

But has there not been a major issue awaiting me amid Your orgy of green? Have I not been repeatedly pressed by the comment of many of Tylerton's watermen, harvesters of the sea, on one or the other side of the church door: "They were put here for us to take"? While living on the Crick, did not my heart awake to the possibility that all of these citizens of the biosphere, the fauna, were my kin, that we all had common ancestors? That we were all together *respondents* to the magnet-like draw of Your relentless Love, all of us united in having been embraced by at least one of Your covenants? Is not a sense of our webbed interconnectedness with these kin why Chief Seattle said, "If the beasts were gone, man would die from a great loneliness of spirit"? Is not what we hold in common, life, the basis for all of us to cry out both *"Abba!"* and *"Magnificat!"* (Lk 1:46–55) *on behalf of* all that is?

O Fructive Womb of us all, what are my obligations to these whom I now know share with my sort in being blades rising in Your greening of the planet? Must I not extend to these my siblings rights or considerations due them? Do I by my lifestyle continue to be complicit in extinction from the planet at rates which may be approaching fifty thousand species annually, not dissimilar to rates resulting in the extinction of dinosaurs sixty-five million years ago? Do I not find myself humming the words of Jimmy Webb's 1968 song *MacArthur Park* whenever I think of extinction:

> *I don't think that I can take it*
> *'Cause it took so long to bake it*
> *And I'll never have that recipe again.*
> *Oh, no!?*

Do I slay and eat my brothers and sisters, these to whom I have learned this decade you have also bound Your self? Or do I become a vegetarian, not for reasons of mere somatic health, ideology, or idiosyncrasy, but because I am learning how better to love my kin? How do I allow You to "dilate my heart" (Ps 119:32) sufficiently so I can embrace fully the meaning of Your unfolding of life for my relationship, my shared greenness, with these others? How do I share life with them cognizant of our relatedness, both derivationally and covenantally?

O Cornucopia of Green!

H. O Lord of the Green!

O Vivifier, may I, again, offer confession to You? It has to do with how I have responded to this question: toward what is the dance to the silent music, our *shared* silent music, the dance including Your entire green garden, the cosmos, moving?

Was not my initial response to that question here on the Crick focused on the image of "crest": the arc, the trajectory of the surge, was toward the unfolding of a creature who, mounting the last green mountain, would be able to cry, *"Abba!"*? Was that not my "crest stage," the idea being that we of the *Imago Dei* were the culmination of this journey because we were unfolded to an extent allowing us to receive, be conscious of, and reciprocate Your Love?

After all, was not such a "crest" notion faithful to both the Genesis account and John Paul II's insistence that the embracing of "physical continuity" include allowance for an "ontological difference," an "ontological leap"? Was there not an implicit "crest" as well in the so-called Anthropic Principle with its focus on the numerous fine-tuned variables requisite to the possibility of life, particularly *human* life, as we know it?

But later in the decade, did I not come to find this crest hypothesis suspiciously self-congratulatory, too triumphalist, too anthropocentric, too *species-ist*, too *us*? Had it not been my sort's self-understanding as so privileged and special which had gotten us into the terrible crisis we find ourselves today, most obviously in relation to the ecosphere? Was it not arrogance on my part to presume that the fact that we humans exist is equivalent to our being the *télos* (goal) of the entire unfolding? Was it not increasingly uncomfortable for me to think of us humans, crying out *Voilà!* upon mounting the summit of this 13.7-billion-year journey, including the perhaps four billion years of greening, when, among many other things, that journey has entailed violence, suffering, waste, and death at simply unimaginable levels? How can the reader avoid suspecting that in this my "crest stage," cosmogenesis was still all about *us,* about *my sort*? And should I not have learned a thousand times, a million times over, that nothing, *nothing!* is only about us or me?

Furthermore, did not my crest mentality serve to reinforce the human separation from the rest of the green garden, to say nothing of the inanimate cosmos, an alienation for which the Crick was the beginning of Your healing of me?

And perhaps most importantly, did not my "crest stage" conveniently ignore what is not yet, what Your unbaring of Your Love is yet to bring about, that which we humans have not so much as imagined (1 Cor 2:9)? Rather, ought not we as *Homo sapiens* see ourselves as singers of a traveling song, road music, raised to You *en route*, at a point somewhere between the Ignition and the Consummation along the cosmic journey? Stated otherwise, is it not *sacrilege* to designate our own sort, hands bloody from the wars of the last one hundred years, as the goal of the unfolding? Is not the crest hypothesis yet more *hubris*, even when trotted out in hair shirt? And does it not slide too easily into the claim that I, or my sort, rather than You, is the Lord of the green?

And this is the hinge on which so much in our world hangs: do we of my sort understand the gifts uniquely given us as distancing us from, and ceding us dominion over, the verdant tangle from which we have sprung, in effect self-congratulatorily enthroning ourselves as lord of the green in the process? Or, do those same gifts serve both to bind us to our journey's companions, and to exercise a deputyship, a stewardship, on their behalf, in our shared accountability to You, the Lord of the Green? Who—we of my sort understood as crest, or You—is Lord of the Green? Which will we, self-designated *Homo sapiens* ("*humans of wisdom*") having now ascended to "modernity," choose?

O Lord of the Green!

I. O *Lumen* in *Tenebrae*!

May I make further confession of fault to You? Have not I, both clay and dancer, repeatedly across the first half of my adult life called to account You, the Potter, seeking juridically to depose You regarding how there could be such pervasive shadow (*tenebrae*) across the cosmos given who You are? Have I not—whether amid the two Middle East wars I experienced (1973 and 1975), the otherwise-abled state of my second son Chad, the horror I encountered in Guatemala in the summer of 1981, the human propensity for war throughout the twentieth and now new century, and the resistance I find to You within myself—sometimes succumbed to the temptation to subject *You* to accountability? And has not the question of You and the shadow—what theologians call *theodicy*—found me living more in my intellect than my heart, doing more theologizing than praying? Was not I sometimes doing this precisely while protesting that I was not? Would You accept my remorse, forgive me this bent, and strengthen me against the temptation to recidivism?

Yet, O Potter, is it not also the case that this is no ordinary clay You have unfolded? Indeed, is it not part of our human splendor that we well know ourselves to be capable of being aware that we bear both Your image and the fault, that we are creatures of agency having been equipped to reciprocate Your Love? If humility is to see ourselves as do You, should not the word "original" be used only in relation to the blessing of Your Flaring Forth, self-depreciation always viewed as the trashing of Your consummate artistry?

But since Your Troubadour invited us to become whole and complete as are You (Mt 5:48), how can we be other than torn by the blight of that nonsensical surd—existence as if You were not—which is the *tenebrae*, by the terrible dissonance, static, and sheer noise distorting the silent music? Thus have I not long since resolved that, even when helpless to change anything, I simply must know of the cost exacted by the shadow; I cannot fabricate a contentment built on ignorance of the fate of my siblings and our palace? O Father out on the road, the risk of temptation notwithstanding, must not I, invitee to Your dance, raise to You my questions regarding the *tenebrae*? O Love dancing between Father and Son, will You bring to words these my groanings (Rom 8:26)?

Have I not reason to wonder whether, born as I was as France was falling to Hitler in 1940, I have lived in the shadow's darkest time? Babbi Yar, Theresienstadt, Dresden, Hiroshima, My Lai, El Mozote, Rwanda, Srebrenica, 9/11, Darfur? Ah, but the cost, O You whom I name as Dark Fire, the cost . . . shall I lower my eyes, my mind, my memory of millions of bearers of Your image being submitted to, of all things, fire . . . often literal fires ignited by those of hatred? And am I not today a citizen of a nation, its hands covered with blood, indeed standing in the pooling blood crying up to You from the ground? Is not this my country, having both opened the thermonuclear Pandora's box and, alone, unleashed its demons, thereby jeopardizing the entire unfolding on Earth—is not my country now shamelessly lecturing emerging nations regarding the same? And am I not resident of a fair and bountiful planet crowned with human ingenuity and creativity, one more than sufficient to provide food and clothing, health care and opportunity for dignified life for all, yet one which has been hijacked by an economic system *sans* commitment to the common good?

But has not the *tenebrae*, the surd, whether enmity, violence, wastage, pain, or suffering, long preceded my sort, indeed, seemingly touching all which You have unfolded? What do I make of the span of thousands of generations of cutthroat mayhem and devouring in the survival of the fittest required for the emergence of but one modest step toward consciousness? How many bloodied fangs and claws across the billions of years preceding hominids were prequel to my sort becoming capable of crying out "*Abba*"?

O Father on the road, is not the unfolding, whether in cosmogenesis in general or zoology in particular, distressingly violent? And although I lack certitude whether the *tenebrae* extends to the moon or the planets of stars in other galactic clusters, do I not have my hunches? Do I not seek in vain for inklings of the lion and the lamb (Is 11:6-9) in the first billion years of our cosmos, a period of unimaginable violence? After all, is not creation *as such*, according to St. Paul, having been "subjected to futility," in "slavery to corruption," and groaning in expectation of its redemption (Rom 8)?

Did not my awareness of the scale of the *tenebrae* expand during my decade on the Crick? In the ulcerated flanks of rockfish? The ubiquitous and ceaseless violence of the food chain? The obscenity of Tylerton's "Refrigerator Gut," the appliance cemetery across the Crick in Hunter Gut, visible from the Inn's kitchen table when we opened in 1997? The tons of non-biodegradable refuse—the fruit of generations of both residents' and sporting visitors' abuse of the sacred waters as a flush—pushed into the upland by the highest tide of year or decade? The opposition to regulating runoff from both poultry slaughter and cattle operations in the watershed? The tightening noose of condo/pavement/bulkhead encirclement of the Bay?

Add to this the shadowy aspects of interpersonal behavior on the Crick, whether random domestic violence or the strutting of grudges or willful refusal to forgive? Presumptuous claims to know who are the righteous and who not? The elitism and pompousness of some urban guests? And did I not glimpse the *tenebrae* most frequently and persistently within my own heart, whether in my vices or alleged virtues, even in my own claim to You? And, with Brother Martin, I asked, as I ask, how long, *how long*?

So, while eschewing any calling of You to account, yet with neither father Job nor mother Mary (Lk 1:34) modeling query as incompatible with faith, I *must* ask: might there have been another way, one with less risk and cost? O, forgive my impertinence, but did not Your Troubadour, he fully of what I am, raise the same in Gethsemane? And You who know all hearts, do You not know that at the end of the day I too want to embrace his "Your will be done" (Lk 22:42)?

Might there have been another way, one which scaled back both Your self-relinquishment and thus our burden of freedom? One whereby Your loving desire to unfold a cosmic garden containing elements of freedom in every sector could have been achieved at lower price? You, *Lord* of the Green, could You not have fashioned a slightly safer project, one with the realization of Your dream *more nearly* insured and lacking the nightmare of our accumulative bastardization of freedom? Oh, and perhaps round triangles as well?

In view of how shabbily we of the *Imago Dei* have played out our roles in the dance, pray tell, has it been worth it to You, given emergence of the *tenebrae*? Is it worth it now? O forgive me, but given the account of You having been fed up with the whole project once before, shielding but Noah's family and seed representatives of each of my faunal family (Gn 6–9); and on another occasion being talked out of doing the same by Moshe (Ex 32:7–14): have You at some points considered starting over yet again, perhaps this time with less relinquishment and a shorter tether on us critters?

Perhaps when the mob screamed "Crucify! Crucify!" with the fate of Your Troubadour in the docket? Perhaps when both Crusaders and Muslims were zealously slaughtering each other in Your holy name? Perhaps when millions of Soviet citizens, including some of my distant Mennonite kin in the Ukraine, were disappearing into the maw of Stalin? Perhaps at the ovens at Treblinka? Were You tempted to despair of us? Tempted to throw a new pot, whether from scratch or from discarded and recyclable materials?

Or perhaps, rather than start over, might You just have quietly *intervened*, a lighter touch, playing a more modest relinquishment exemption card? Like when Your Troubadour cried out, "My God! My God! Why have You abandoned me?" (Mk 15:34) Or when, in his story, the son told You, in effect, to drop dead and subsidize his profligacy in the far country (Lk 15:11–24)? Or during the early twentieth-century Armenian Massacre by the Turks? Or when German bishops walked the road more traveled rather than speaking truth to Hitler's power? Or during the massacre of Palestinians at the Sabra and Shatila camps in Beirut in 1982?

Oh, I know that on occasion You perform mighty acts which we of the small picture call "miracles," but don't these only reinforce the general rule, in addition to pressing the question where Your angelic hosts were in all of the *other* final acts? While I remain cautiously open to miracles, are not You the Furnace of Love, whether or not? Must not I as one invited to the dance with You be clear-headed about the fact that, at least in the short run, Your gift of freedom generally comes bundled with us creatures reaping the consequences of our choices? Can we humans not freely choose the package to which we sacrifice our freedom? Do not the names to which You answer *exclude* "Bailsman" and "Mariano Rivera," relief pitcher *par excellence*?

Must I not acknowledge to You that the extent of Your honoring of human agency can reduce me to fear, trembling, and tears? Do not I live each day painfully *lacking* any guarantee that, were we collectively to bungle into thermonuclear self-immolation or otherwise commit ecocide, that You would magically rescue us from the consequences of our free choices? How can we, originals or graftees, say otherwise after Auschwitz?

Having unburdened myself regarding the *tenebrae*, may I acknowledge that the central question of theodicy, "Where were *You* when tragedy struck?" has long since ceased being my own? Does not my heart know, both from Your way with the ancient

Hebrews and, especially, with Your Troubadour on the cross, that You die a thousand, indeed, a zillion, deaths? If this prayer has me intermittently in tears, what does it do to You, You who, like Hagar in the wilderness (Gn 21:16), turned tearfully away at the sight of Your own son dying a slow death? Indeed, were not the heavens filled with Your tears even as Conor Clapton plummeted, something his bludgeoned father Eric's song proclaimed far more than he knew? Were not *Your* tears my only balm after the horror of Guatemala and my ensuing darkness in 1981? Was it not *Your* tears which settled forever my question whether You in Your immensity were merely toying with us? Are You not again on the cross for every child who starves, every woman raped, every prisoner tortured, every estuary polluted, every wetland paved, every bomb built, every untruth spun?

O Self-Relinquisher, are You not the Suffering One, the One whose crucifixion is reenacted on the altar of the cosmos again and again and again, Your executors ever new and ever the same? More than with any other question, is it not regarding the *tenebrae* that I myself am in the dark night, all scaffolding and reinforcement having been stripped away, *annihilated*, with just You and I, and You in perpetual agony . . .? And I in that night? While in the vision of the Apocalypse You will one day wipe away all tears (Apoc 7:17; 21:4), for now are not Your own all that I have? Are not Jessica Powers' words (21) my own: "here in the dark I clutch the garments of God"?

No, O Dark Fire, I no longer demand, "Where were *You?*" While I will need to wait for the Greater Life, or its portico, for most of my purification, have You not done *this one* here? Regarding the shadow, the malevolent and death-dealing surd, does not my heart know exactly where You are? Do I not know well what You are doing: being offered up again and again, on the cross, on the altar of the cosmos?

Did not Pope John Paul II, himself a Discalced Carmelite secular, suggest that in our time John of the Cross' image of the "dark night" also had a "collective character" encompassing the appalling range of war, suffering, emptiness, fragility, and Your apparent absence? Indeed, do I not occasionally hear the entire planet humming, "Sometimes I feel like a motherless child / A long way from home"?

But is not this dark night for You also the "night of faith" insofar as, in the words of John of the Cross, You know "how to draw good from evil so wisely and beautifully"? Does not the extinguishing of up to 70 percent of the planet's faunal species—most notably the dinosaurs sixty-five million years ago, attributed by some to the Chicxulub impact, leaving a fauna lacuna within which mammals in time would unfold and we ourselves emerge—cause me to ponder just how You are drawing? O Alchemist, in regard to the *tenebrae*, do You not write straight with crooked lines, employ that intended for evil to bring about good (Gn 50:20)?

Is it not You whose Troubadour we invoke as *Lumen Christi* while standing in the Easter Vigil darkness, You who bring forth the Resurrection's light out of the *tenebrae*? May I petition, O Fire, that one day the entirety of the cosmos be filled with the knowledge of Your splendor as the waters cover the sea (Hb 2:14)? That, as Julian of Norwich (ca 1342–ca 1420) wrote, "all shall be well, and all shall be well, and all manner of thing shall be well"? And that hell, that is, existence as if You were not, consequence of our abuse of Your crowning gift to us, be forever vast, infernal, torrid and, with no exceptions, . . . *empty*?

O Love Supreme, do I not, with Job (40:1–5; 42:1–6), concede that You have the infinitely larger picture than I within which even modernity's dark night, the season of darkest shadow, is being wooed toward healing and the realization of Your dream? Yes, but would You strip the scales from the eyes of my heart and show me that dream? O, forgive me, for is this not why Your prophets introduced us to the lion and the lamb (Is 11:6–9), why You did Bethlehem *at all*, embodying Your loving word in humanese all the way to Golgotha? I know that the mode to which You call us is faith rather than sight, and do I not believe? Only, will You help my unbelief (Mk 9:24), will You show me more of Your dream?

Do You not know via Your Troubadour how terribly dark and lonely faith can be, how much we need all the help we can get? So would You show me how the splendor of the new heaven and the new earth, You being First Permanent Resident (Apoc 21:1–3), brings hope even to the present cosmic dark night? Even more than that, would You show me the Fire in Your heart? Yes, would You show me the Dark Fire in Your heart, I who must acknowledge that only "late have I loved You . . ."?

And having already said far more than enough, do I not repair to the words of Job: "What can I reply to You? I lay my hand on my mouth" (Jb 40:4)?

O *Lumen* in *Tenebrae*!

J. O Rouser of Self and Voice!

O Weaver of Wonders, is not the story of the cosmos, from the Flaring Forth to the present, but *one* unfolding fabric, a cloth of continuity? Is not *everything* related to everything else, all the blessed progeny of the Engendering Event? And especially among our planet's fauna bearing the gift of this mystery called "life," do not all of us have common ancestry and thus kinship? Are not even the mutations, nudging species into previously nonexistent channels of possible adaptation to changing conditions, part of the texture of that fabric?

Indeed, is not the recent discovery that we humans and our nearest surviving relatives, the chimpanzees, each with in excess of three billion DNA base units in our respective genomes, have only about 1.2 percent of which are different, yet another reminder of that cosmic continuity among us lifers? Am I not filled with wonder before the elegance of Your proceeding, O Womb, the cohesion of Your artistry, the cadence and shimmering beauty of the silent music?

And yet, amid that flow of a fabric of continuity, has there not been a threshold of discontinuity involving, to our knowledge, only my sort? Do not perspectives as diverse as those of Pope John Paul II and evolutionary biologists Richard Dawkins and Jared Diamond acknowledge a major transition during the millennia beginning fifty to forty thousand years ago ushering in modern humans? What transpired at that time that would propel our human ancestors into far greater dissimilitude from our closest living primate relatives than a 1.2 percent DNA differential might suggest? Whether referred to in terms of the *Imago Dei* or the threshold of the self and consciousness or the simple emergence of modern humankind, did not *our sort*, in contrast to other hominids now extinct, seemingly assert ourselves there? And does not the second creation account in the Hebrew Bible, the one having You forming us humans from the dust, the image that of the potter working with pre-existing materials, and breathing into us Your breath of life (Gn 2:7,8), offer rich metaphorical language for this defining threshold?

And have I not witnessed with excitement during our decade the growing accumulation of evidence, from those confessing You and those not, regarding what Diamond calls "The Great Leap Forward," this from various diverse disciplines: art history, archaeology, molecular biology, geography, and anthropology, among others? Did not our ancestors, shown by the fossil record to have been anatomically modern for many scores of millennia, suddenly begin displaying unprecedented progress in tools, the constructing and organizing of living spaces, art on the walls of caves, primitive musical instruments, and *language*?

Indeed, do not many scientists hypothesize that the language breakthrough, perhaps triggered by genetic mutation in either laryngeal tract or functions of parts of the brain, was foundational to other changes? In any event, did not yet additional flowerings unfold among what are sometimes called the Cro-Magnon involving the capability of planning, refinement of innovation, crafting of objects of beauty, affinity for symbols, and the beginning of abstract thought including awareness of the self?

Might not the emergence in time of the awareness of the self as an individual having one's own being, behavior, and thoughts be arguably the greatest and most consequential change in the entire bio-journey? And against the backdrop of life having been unfolding for several billion years, did not these seismic shifts take place within but a few millennia, with the impact being so powerful and swift that the remaining other branch of proto-humans, the Neanderthals, was completely displaced less than thirty thousand years ago? Can we not suspect that even this transition to consciousness, perhaps *particularly this one*, was a dance to which my emerging sort was contributing with flowering powers and freedom toward what was to be?

While the metaphorical accounts in Genesis 1 and 2 focus on humankind's creation by and relationship with You rather than on modern scientific queries, do not these stories nevertheless cast light on the latter? For example, You who are there described as speaking the cosmos into being, You whose Word (*logos*, Jn 1:1) was embodied in Bethlehem, You with this passion for communication and self-disclosure: how can we even think about Your *affaire de coeur* with us cosmics apart from language?

You who would subsequently show us that we were crafted so as to be in reciprocally loving relationship with You, was not the prerequisite the unfolding within us of that capability, that thirst, indeed, that urgency? And in order to return Your love, to offer ourselves to You, was it not first necessary that we discover that we had/ were a self to give, that each of us was an individual having her own being, behavior, thoughts, feelings, *and the freedom to choose whether so to give ourselves*? Is not this emergence of the "self" in a humankind capable of communication and thus relationship, all this invited forth by none other than Your Love, a core component of our self-understanding as being in the *Imago Dei*, as being in some respects in distant similitude with You? Does not our capability to address You as "*Abba!*" include this wonderfully multifaceted mystery?

But pray tell, O Unfolder of Selves, how could a species with such centeredness, such equipping for intimacy for which there were but the most dim antecedents, fail to emerge amid a vast cascade of additional marvels? May I begin to count the ways? Are not sheer delight in beauty for its own sake, wonder before the most common aspects of life, desire to create in form or sound or other media, a longing to know and be known, curiosity about how we are able to be curious, the capability of receiving You (*capax Dei*): are not all these things among the eruption of surprises garnishing our journey into the *Imago Dei*?

And, perhaps most obviously, our sexuality? Is there not much more than mere hint of the *Imago Dei* in our human sexuality as witnessed to by the words of Genesis: "In Your image You created us, male and female You created us" (fr Gn 1:27)? Granted, are we not similar to the more recent portion of our fauna forbears in our coupling, the mechanism whereby life has been both sustained via procreation and drawn via natural selection? Yet, although we are ever tempted to revert to the mere glandular rutting of our precursors, is there not in our male/femaleness always the possibility of intimacy, tenderness, commitment, and face-to-face self-giving as well as both fruitfulness and the relational stability needed for the nurturing of new recipients of the gift of life?

Do we not in all of this mirror distantly Your way with us? Is it not interesting how this male-female relationship is a major metaphor for Your relationship with Your people, whether in the Hebrew Bible (Hosea, for example), in Christian scriptures like Ephesians (5:22–33), or two millennia of mystical literature (John of the Cross' *Canticle* and *Living Flame,* sermons on *The Song of Songs* by Bernard of Clairvaux [1090–1153], for example)? Can we with straight face argue sex to be more central to our *modus operandi* than to Yours, You who pulled off *the* covenantal couplings of the ages with first matter/energy coming into being in the Flaring, then with the Hebrew people at Sinai, and finally with the cosmos in general, humanity in particular, in Bethlehem? And do not many mystics, both across and beyond the Christian tradition, point to *union* with You as our destiny?

Have I not across much of my adult life been astonished at how important sex, both literal and metaphorical, is to *You,* marveled about the sort of deity You are to have dreamed and unfolded it in the first place? O Lover, are You not, *in some sense,* sexual as are we, only in Your case both of the two "genders" and yet neither, and the cosmos the beloved? Is not our own lovemaking dim inkling of *everything* You are about?

And is not our emergent ability to distinguish our selves from the rest of the cosmos a precondition for then serving not only as its custodian and steward, but also its vocal advocate? Have not we of the *Imago Dei* a deputyship, a pastoral vocation on behalf of what Saint Francis called "our mother the earth," and by implication the rest of the cosmos, whose matter is not bereft of spirit, whose liberation into a shared destiny with us is part of Your intention (Rom 8:21)? And is not our having been equipped with voice, with language, also a mandate to render audible the silent musical praise to You latent throughout the uni-verse?

Might not we of the fault be the larynx of Your love-child cosmos, O Flinger of Galaxies? Might the mandate for husbandry and stewardship You gave our ancestors (Gn 1:26; Ps 8:6–8) be understood to include our human capacity for voice? Not merely understood as "proxy" or "surrogate," but as the cosmos *itself* singing its own song to You via its own laryngeal instrument, its voice, we of my sort? We, who sing "O For a Thousand Tongues" by Charles Wesley (1707–1788) or, like St. Teresa in her *Life,* wish ourselves to be "all tongues" so as to laud You less inadequately, might we not do well to recognize that, to our knowledge, the cosmos has but one conscious laryngeal instrument, and it is we? As in the line "Give the winds a mighty voice!" in the hymn of my childhood? How can I lend voice to the prayer of the uni-verse?

And as I gradually give myself to becoming a sounding box for Your green garden at prayer, do I not muse about whether this role *too* is part of the creativity and freedom which we humans are invited to bring to our side of the dance, the dance You are carrying on with none less than the heavens and the earth? Does not the *scale* of adoration in my paraphrased psalm, "Let everything that is green praise You!" (fr Ps 150:6), point in this direction?

O Abyss of Love, may I offer two petitions to You? First, in the spirit of Francis of Assisi's *Canticle of the Sun*, may I be faithful in my deputyship, my voicing role, even now: on behalf of all sub-elemental fruit of the Flaring Forth: *Abba*; on behalf of that first generation of stars whose nuclear ovens thickened the plot: *Abba*; on behalf of our star, brother Sun, whose self-immolating warmth remains the very incubator of all known life: *Abba*; on behalf of sister moon who lifts our seas while keeping watch over our lovers: *Abba*; on behalf of all participants in the surge of life, both flora and fauna: *Abba*; and, finally, on behalf of all of my sort whose long journey into capacities to know and love You includes the gift of freedom which is both our glory and our tragedy: *Abba*? Would You accept these prayers of praise and doxology as offered by the cosmos itself, raised to You by one of Your *Imago* bearers, one of the sort called to be cantors of the cosmic congregation?

And may I offer a second petition to You who loved the world (*cosmos*, Jn 3:16) to and through the cross? You to whom I pray that at the end of the day Your word will not have returned to You empty (Is 55:11) in one single case? May I bring to You my hominid kin, whether ancestors on whose shoulders I stand or those with whom I share forebears, but all participants in a luminous yet harrowing journey across per-haps six million years preceding this prayer? All of them *anawim*, Hebrew for "little ones," literally, metaphorically, or both: were not they *too* subject to the draw of Your Love? Did not all of them, as do I, respond to You within the range of agency nurtured within them? And as the millions of years unscrolled, did they not with growing awareness and intentionality come to care, protect, nurture, desire, marvel, and, in time, *love*, in response to Your massaging Love? Yet, excepting the ancestors of my stalk, did not all, alas, both individuals and species, become extinct, shorthanded today as hominid dead-ends, cul-de-sacs?

And do I not lift up to You in particular my Neanderthal cousins, co-residents of southern Europe and southwest Asia with my sort for millennia before they too were no more? Have I not been skewered by learning that the sacred geography of Mount Carmel central to both the confrontation between You and the fertility deity Ba'al in-volving Elijah (1 Kgs 18), and the late-twelfth-century origins of my Carmelite order, also contains Neanderthal burial sites? *Abba*, are not these Your love-children *as well*? Did You not kiss them *also* into being? Are not their names *too* inscribed on the palms of Your hands (Is 49:16)? On this day, rain falling outside, may I claim all of them as my family, O You in whom, I believe, nothing is lost (Jn 6:39), and hold them up to You: *Requiem aeternam dona eis, Domine. Et lux perpetua luceat eis?*

But is not the emerging of consciousness, of the self as an individual being possessing extraordinary gifts including freedom, as much fruit of relationship with You as it is precondition? If, indeed, as Augustine writes, "You have made us for Your self, O Lord, and our hearts are restless until they find their rest in You," then does not the emergence of the self, the "true self" rather than its sundry counterfeits, take place vis-a-vis You? Does not our creatureliness, our finitude, come to fullest bloom in a relationship of reciprocal love with You? Do not the words of the saint of my birth day, Irenaeus of Lyons (c. 130—c. 200), to the effect, O Fire, that "[Your] glory is a human being fully alive," make the point precisely: that Your greatest delight lies in our blooming in every capability for which we were unfolded? That we, self and voice of Your cosmos, be all that we can be?

And yet, does not our being in Your image, including awareness of the *tenebrae* and of our mysterious complicity, both collectively and as individuals, in it, multiply the complexity in our lives as well? Is not part of our distinctiveness that we are capable of imagining, for example, Your having unfolded other beings, whether in this or other universes, both far superior to ourselves and stalked by no shadow? And are we not also aware that Your crowning gift to us, that of agency and freedom, has been extraordinarily abused and transmogrified to the extent to which believing in the ultimate triumph of Your self-relinquishing way must be built on naked hope rather than empirical or analytical knowledge?

Do not we of my sort sometimes wish we had less awareness of the shadow, both without and within? Are we not susceptible to the temptation to yearn wistfully for a paradisiacal state in our murky human gestation, when, if it ever did exist, would surely pale compared with the destiny toward which Your Love is drawing the cosmos? You, who know the full extent of the *tenebrae*, You who in Your Troubadour fully experienced mortality, will You hang in there with us? You who know, in the words of the psalmist, both that we are "fearfully and wonderfully made" (Ps 139:14) and "little less than gods" (Ps 8:5), on the one hand, and yet of the cosmic dust (Ps 103:14), on the other, will You stay in the dance with us? Will You in Your long-suffering continue to hold us, we of the vice ambivalence, wanting both to share in Your life and fashion deities in our own image?

O Rouser of Self and Voice!

31. Prayers Offered Out of the End: Consummation

A. O Hospitalier!

O You, beckoning from out of our future, when was it that the image of innkeeper, purveyor of hospitality to world- and life-weary travelers, *Hospitalier*, first rose for me above the plane of us mortals, and pointed also to You? Might the notion have been planted already our initial season by a guest's thank-you note quoting from C. S. Lewis' *The Problem of Pain*: "Our Father refreshes us on the journey with some pleasant inns, but will not encourage us to mistake them for home"? The idea that You were the Host(ess) whose welcoming embrace, accommodations, tablefare, and self-investiture signed not merely yet another roadhouse, but final arrival, rest, and *home?*

But did I not need the entire decade for the seedling of this image of You as the Hospitalier to settle into my consciousness? And did not that *settling in* correspond with Your unfolding of my own identity as a hospitalier from profession to vocation, from remunerable services rendered to Your calling to me? Did not I experience the image of You as the Hospitalier and my own innkeeper identity as a dialectic in which personal growth in either, whether knowledge of self or experience of You, opened up correlative implications regarding the other?

So what were some of the settings in which this hospitalier identity, both Yours and mine, got *entangled?* When daily I apprenticed with alchemist Sharryl who, starting with pisces or crustacea, Delmarva vegetables and fruits, extra virgin and her ranks of spice, transformed nondescript circular tables into white islets of nutrition, celebration, and beauty, both dionysian and sacred? When, speaking of which, it became apparent that not all furniture was created equal: that the *table*, locus of nourishment, sensual delight, inclusion, and intimacy *vis-à-vis*, face-to-face, was not the piece of choice in both the (post-Vatican II) Eucharist and Your consummational banquet—*O sacrum convivium!*—without good cause? When I realized that both our dining and worship would be profoundly different were our tables ring-shaped, all of us *inside* facing *out?*

When I made my peace with the fact that, whatever the innkeepers' advertisements and promotions, each guest had to exercise her agency and *choose* to come to our remote venue rather than far more convenient ones? When my musings about innkeeping and the Troubadour's parable of You (Lk 15:11–32) got into dialogue, with Your strong-willed daughters and sons making their way back from far countries to Your house which was, of course, *home?* When I began to make connections between the hospitable tables of my Palestinian Muslim hosts and Your Eucharist, and everything in between, including the meal to be served on the porch that night? When, finally, my allowing the stories of Your cosmosgenesis and Your Troubadour to interpret each other sent me scurrying to enlarge my images of the *scale* of Your commitment to welcome home the creation?

And did not the image of You as Hospitalier thrive, although only with time, in the face of the rank irony of how our reluctant acceptance of being a Bed & Breakfast & *Dinner*, the major crisis of our launching, had given rise to the flowering of the entire project with that very meal becoming its heart? Indeed, was there not something uncannily paradigmatic about how all of that had transpired? And perhaps a hint of the transformational *modus operandi* whereby You are bringing the dispersed and death-weighted cosmos into a harmonious whole in Your Troubadour so that You will be all in all (Eph 1:10; 1 Cor 15:20–28)?

O Hospitalier!

B. O Promise Keeper!

O, I AM WHO AM, You whom we worship as Source, Proceeder, Unfolder, Vivifier, *Abba*, and Home: is not Your dream for the cosmos, the mystery teasing me throughout Part VI of this work, strongly hinted at by the arc of its journey to date? And have not in my lifetime the fraternities of both faith and the sciences had opportunities, both astonishing and humbling, to become more familiar with the contours of that journey?

Is not that arc, from the Flaring Forth of the Fire of Your Love to the writing of this sentence, characterized by a mysterious directionality: from simplicity to complexity, homogeneity to differentiation, subatomic particles to the full periodic table, the inanimate to the animate? Further, is not that arc glimpsed in the movement from ability to respond to sensorial stimuli to the separating of the self able to reflect on both the uni-verse and itself, from life preoccupied with the quest for food and survival to one including the likes of Diego Velázquez (1599-1660), Shostakovich, and Dorothy Day, from the attributing of the numinous to objects to the adoring of You?

O Spinner of Journeys, may I profess this arc, this 13.7- billion-year adventure thus far, to be for me an implicit promise, *Your* promise? Not a promise I *inferred*, but one which I, an acknowledger of Your trafficking in the box, *recognized*? And rather than futile flirtation with the notion of "proof," whether deist or designist variety, is not my prayer this day the outgrowth of awe, seeking to read the signs of the times, and *trust*? Is not cosmogenesis to date Your implicit promise *to*, Your implicit covenant *with*, all that is?

Speaking of which, have I not been intrigued by how the Hebrew prophets could play hardball with You regarding Your promises? Does not the prophet Jeremiah, for example, *thrice* challenge You in one verse: "For the sake of Your reputation despise us not, do not allow Your glory to be discredited, remember Your eternal covenant with us and break it not" (fr Jer 14:21)? Rather than arguing either the people's innocence or Your undue severity, does he not repeatedly pit You against Your self, warning You to weigh carefully the downside of breaking Your word? Is not Jeremiah seeking to remind You what's at stake if You provide the nations with occasion to wag their tongues and taunt the Hebrews with the likes of "Just where is your god?"

Buoyed by such prophetic company, my tongue partially in cheek even while conceding some fear and trembling, may I do the same regarding the promise embedded within the unfolding? May I hold Your feet to the fire and "call" You on the promise which I recognize in Your cosmogenesis, lest there be cause for some of my sort to jeer You and Your dream for having faltered at the 13.7-billion-year pole?

Having so indulged myself, I AM WHO AM, may I begin to "call" You by confessing my belief that the arc of Your promise in the past, fragmentarily reconstructed via the sciences, interpreted via faith, shall surely be brought to completion in the future? Cannot we who bear Your Troubadour's name in the present, our faith grounded in the nurtured memory of what You have already done in the past, extrapolate from that promise regarding both the *direction* and the *surety* of its fulfillment in the future? Indeed, is it not precisely *from* our future that You have been inviting, drawing, luring all that is, including me, in an unfolding toward that which neither human eye nor ear, indeed, not even imagination, has ever entertained (1 Cor 2:9)?

Is not the Hebrew Bible strewn with examples of such forward "leaning" in hope: "Do not fixate on the former things, nor be preoccupied with matters of the past. Behold, I am doing something new! Now it springs forth; do you not perceive it" (Is 43:18,19); or, "For the vision still has its time, is pressing on to fulfillment, and will not disappoint; if it delays, wait, it will surely come, it will not be late" (Hb 2:3)? Is not the entire sweep of biblical faith and its subsequent tradition sodden with Your promise in tension with the mixture of hope for and realization of fulfillment?

Rather than a Pollyannaish, pie-in-the-sky escapism, do not we of the long, long journey live *leaning* into that future, fueled by the hope that what Your Love has drawn the cosmos through since the Initial Ignition is but the beginning of our glory which is, of course, Your own? You not sequestered by time, do You not nevertheless draw us to Your self within *our* time, from out of *our* future? Is not the primacy of Your Love encapsulated *in our* time by the second part of the Church's most frequently offered prayer, the *Doxologia Minor*: "as it was in the beginning, is now, and will be forever. Amen"?

But must not we, of both dust and dance, fault and fulgency, be repeatedly reminded that the full realization of Your dream, the consummation of "all things" [*ta pánta*] in the heavens and on the earth in the Troubadour (Eph 1:10), what Teilhard de Chardin calls the "Omega Point," will come about via the drawing of You who are Relinquisher? Have we not good basis to believe that it is by way of the *modus operandi* in Your Troubadour, one of self-binding in honor of human agency and co-creatorship as in the cross, that with all of us cosmics you will complete the arc and realize the goal for which You initially proceeded?

Thus is not that cross not only a measure of Your passion for the cosmos, O Lover, but also a window into *how* all of the dissonance and noise will finally be disappeared in the cosmos' no longer silent musical praise to You? Will You not continue to transform and thus remove the dissonance, via the counterintuitive way, that less traveled, of Your Troubadour on the cross, the Lamb with the marks of slaughter upon him (Apoc 5:6), so that, finally, You will be "all in all" (1 Cor 15:28)? Will not Your *télos* (end), O Crucified Fire, of the hammering of swords into plowshares and spears into pruning hooks, be accomplished via the *means* of the hammering of swords into plowshares and spears into pruning hooks? Is not the *destination* of never again training for war to be reached via the *journey* of never again training for war (Is 2:4; Mi 4:3)?

Rather than a bracketed three- or thirty-three-year aberration, is not Your self-pouring-out Troubadour "the exact representation of Your nature" (fr Heb 1:3), the humanese translation of who You were, are, and ever shall be, *and how You are ever at work in the cosmos*? Is this not why we bearers of the name of Your Troubadour confess that he both inaugurated and embodied Your Reigning, the full blossoming of which is not yet? Will not the way of self-relinquishment, self-outpouring (*kenosis*), and the cross finally prevail in the cosmos, not primarily because it is disarming or cunning or ultimately more effective, but because it has been shown in Your Troubadour to be *Your* song, *Your* way? Is there a more succinct encapsulation of the *definitiveness* of Your Troubadour's song than that of John of the Cross in his *Ascent*: "In giving us his Son, his only Word (for he possesses no other), he spoke everything to us at once in this sole Word—and he has no more to say"? Is not Your Troubadour's song our guide as to how this 13.7-billion-year-long promise shall finally be brought home to its fulfillment?

So even as I petition for the patience which is part of hope, do I not also pray daily, and with growing urgency, holding Your feet to the Fire of Your promises: that "Your Reigning come, Your will be done, on earth as it is in heaven" (Mt 6:10)? "That the earth be filled with the knowledge of Your glory, as the waters cover the sea" (fr Hb 2:14)?

O Promise Keeper!

C. O Beautiful Dreamer!

O Lover, when I query about Your dream for Your cosmos finally at rest, am I not drawn to a huge word scattered across the Hebrew Bible, *shalom*, which points the way? Does not this extraordinary word embrace a host of the alienations in the existence of us of the fault: between the human and the nonhuman fauna, the animate and inanimate, the material and the spiritual, differentiation and harmony, gentleness and strength, peace and righted relationships (justice), celebration of creation and attunement with You, that desired by humankind and that dreamed of by You? Qualitative prosperity beyond anything we can imagine? Indeed, did not Your Troubadour embody this Your dream of *shalom* in what he called Your Reigning, that revolutionary politic which he inaugurated, lived and died, one to which You gave Your resounding imprimatur in the Resurrection, ascension, and the unleashing of Your Love at Pentecost?

Furthermore, to begin with *via negativa*, does not the Apocalypse indicate that the full realization of Your dream will spell the *tenebrae*'s absolute *end*: of the sea, ancient image for chaos and peril (Apoc 21:1); of fearful night (Apoc 21:25, 22:5); and of tears, mourning, pain, and, finally, death (Apoc 20:14, 21:4)?

Beyond that, does not that same book lay open a *via positiva* with the piling up of image after image of the flowering of this Your dream when the *tenebrae* shall be no more: the wedding of "the new heaven and new earth" in the new Jerusalem coming down to a healed Earth (Apoc 21:1); the gathering of the kings of the earth bringing to You and the Lamb their respective glories (Apoc 21:24); along both sides of the river of life, flowing from You and Your Troubadour, the tree of life, perpetually fruitful, its leaves "for the healing of the nations" (Apoc 22:1,2; Ez 47:12); and all bathed in Your effulgence, O "Light of Light," in the words of the *Credo*, of which Your Troubadour is the lamp (Apoc 21:23, 22:5)? Is not the destiny of the entire cosmos to be in such unity and harmony, and at rest? Has not a lavish and expansive embodiment of *shalom* ever been Your dream for the cosmos, from the Flaring Forth Fire of Your Love, indeed, even "before"?

But are not even such glimpses of Your vision, O Dreamer, but secondary at best, only the derivative fruit of what the cosmos already is in Your heart? And what then is within Your heart? O myriad of glories, are You not both Source of our human capacity to desire, indeed, thirst after You with all of our being, having ignited our potentiality and then drawn our unfolding across the eons, and ardent Responder to the same when in our ripeness we blurt out *"Abba"*? Is not this entire dance step, in some sense present throughout the cosmos, generated within Your heart? So that we yearn for neither this nor that, whether terrestrial or celestial, but for You, You Yourself? Just *You*? With St. Paul and the mystic saints at my elbow, do I not cry out:

Abba, the entire cosmos thirsts for *You*? Have we any other home, any other resting place? Are not Your hands' unfoldings, from the sublime Andromeda galaxy to the feisty *Callinectes sapidus*, joining us of self and voice in singing with the spiritual, "goin' home to live with God"?

Do not we of the embodiment, love-children of Your amorous coupling with the cosmos of matter / energy, expectantly await Your words once heard by the ancient Hebrews: "You have seen for yourselves how I have . . . brought you here to Myself" (Ex 19:4)? Is not the silent music to which I awake on this slip of shoal called Tylerton the cosmos achingly humming for home, for You? Is not that cosmos, homesick, heard to be groaning, "Only You, Omega, are *enough*"? And is not part of the *raison d'etre* of this book my desire to supply voice to this, none other than the prayer of the cosmos to You, Hospitalier of all that is?

Thus, are not for me the inimitably hopeful words of all Scripture, those balm, comfort, and promise-fulfillment to all of us journey-weary cosmics, Your words in the penultimate chapter of the Apocalypse: "Behold, at last, My final tent-pitching is among humans in the cosmos; they and I will share life together; they shall be my people *and I Myself will live among them*" (fr Apoc 21:3)? "Heaven" being nothing more (or less) than where You are, O Lover, is there any better news than this, all separations having ended, You, Immanuel, the One characterized by Your being with us, residing forever on our cosmic block?

Is it not *that* which makes the "new heaven" and the "new earth," the banquet celestial and terrestrial, one and the same, Your extending of Your inclusive table taking place *here* in the love-child cosmos? Are not the words in the *Exsultet* of the Easter Vigil, "[Oh] night truly blessed when heaven is wedded to earth" anticipatory of our destiny, that of the entire cosmos, with You? Is not *this* the fulfillment of Your impossible dream? And am not I, once myself terrified dreamer, leaning into that dream whenever, in the Eucharistic Prayer of the Mass immediately before the Doxology, I hear the words, "Then, freed from every shadow of death, we shall take our place *in the new creation* and give You thanks through Christ, our risen Lord" (EA)?

O Beautiful Dreamer!

D. O Deifier!

But is there not yet more to Your dream for both us of the self and voice as well as the rest of the cosmos, much more? (And could it be otherwise when You are involved, which is always?) Is not the assumption pervading the Jewish and Christian traditions that to be in relation to You is to be on a transformative trajectory, in the words of the prayer book, "to love You is to be made holy"? And does not that "holiness" consist in becoming increasingly imbued with You? No—may I not lose courage now—increasingly, in some sense, *becoming* You?

In the Christian scriptures, for example, does not the Ephesians writer yearn for his readers to "attain to fullness of being, *the fullness of You Your self*" (fr Eph 3:19)? Does not Peter's second epistle wish for his readers that they become no less than "*partakers of Your divine nature . . .*" (fr 2 Pet 1:4)? And does not John's first epistle read, "We know that when what we shall be comes to light, *we shall be like You*, for we shall see You as You are" (fr 1 Jn 3:2)? Most astonishing, what are we to make of Your Troubadour's petition to You: "that they may all be one, *as You, Father, are in me and I in You*, that they also may be in us, . . . The glory which You have given me I have given to them, that they may be one, just as we are one" (Jn 17:21, EA)?

Are not such texts hinting of a human destiny of becoming like You, to be, at the end of the day, drawn into the very Triune Community of Your divine life? Indeed, not merely to become similar to You, but to participate in You *a la* Your Troubadour? *A la* Your Troubadour? And is not this portion of our transformation Your work rather than our own, our role becoming less and less active, more and more receptive to You whose names include *Torrent* for good reason?

Granted, have not Your churches in the West, whether past or present, often distanced themselves from an understanding of human destiny as *divination* or *deification*, this squeamishness not infrequently draped in the sackcloth of humility? Indeed, could we of the fault *ever* get over the supreme irony that You have prepared such a destiny for our sort whose principal shadow has always been to displace You with aspects of our own selves as the deity?!

But has not my thirst across the journey increasingly attuned my heart to hints and glimpses in the Roman Catholic tradition which name and worship You as "*Deifier*"? Is not Your Spirit who is Love unabashedly addressed as "*O Deifier*" by poet Jessica Powers in her "The Spirit's Name" (35), she who in her "The Song of Distance," written shortly before her death in 1988, penned "I am with God and toward my godhead tending" (84)? She, already looking over in 1984, groping for words for the encounter with You: "light that the soul assimilates until / not witness but participant it stands, / taking of Godhead its amazing fill" (87)? And am I not repeatedly ambushed at the portal of the Eucharistic Prayer at Your table by the priest's words, whether silent or audible, always audible for me: "By the mystery of this water and wine *may we come to share in the divinity of Christ*, who humbled himself to share in our humanity" (EA)?

Does not my saint, Irenaeus, make the same point: "our Lord Jesus Christ . . . became what we are, that he might bring us to be what he is himself"? Might not this deified destiny have been that of which Dante sought to hint in the final canto of his

Commedia after having detected the image of my sort painted into You whom he was fleetingly allowed to glimpse? And does not John of the Cross, in both his *Canticle* (39:3–6) and *Living Flame* (2:34–35) distinguish between "God by substance," You, O Fire, and "God by participation," our human destiny, the latter a state in which the human "is absorbed in the divine life"? Is not to be increasingly of You, to be increasingly . . . *You*? And is not this destiny in You, our freedom and agency ever more robust, because You have unfolded us as capable of hungering and thirsting for You? Are we not crafted with the capacity of being seduced, and have not You, O passionate Lover, seduced us?

But did not my Tylerton decade compel me to take the matter but one step farther, regarding the implications of this human destiny for beloved cousin cosmos? Are there not those at the interface of science and faith, mathematical physicist and Anglican theologian Rev. John Polkinghorne (b. 1930), for example, who believe that Your dream includes also the cosmos itself being ultimately drawn into Your divine community? Ever wary of pantheism's equating of creation and Creator, does not Polkinghorne nevertheless follow the Eastern churches in awaiting a totally sacramentalized cosmos, one completely infused by You, one thus truly pan*en*theistic? Here again, rather than mere context or stage set for Your mighty acts of Love, is not the cosmos—including St. Francis' sibings sun, moon, wind, water, fire, earth to begin the list—recipient, actor, and beloved, according to the *capax Dei* of each, its capacity to receive You?

Indeed, is not this pan-sacramentalizing already occasionally glimpsed, albeit but momentarily and fleetingly? Such as one night in the perch when I, gazing into the Andromeda galaxy with my Oberwerk binoculars, found myself tearfully singing the Eucharistic hymn, "I received the living God, and my heart is full of joy"? You who mysteriously and unrestrainedly embrace us in common bread and wine, do you not, and will You not increasingly, do so as well via the spinning wafer of that galaxy or the contents of the cup of salvation splashed from horizon to horizon across the moonless night sky, the edge that galaxy's twin, our own? When our guides in these matters, the saints, speak of Your infusion as Creator of an aspect of the creation, is not the delimiting factor always, and only, the vessel, its size and its degree of emptiness and receptivity? Is it not so with Your Immanuel dream, O Furnace of Love, that You desire to fill each part of the cosmos, each person or creature or thing, with Your Self up to our respective capacities to receive You? And beyond? Is not this part of the meaning of the last words of Georges Bernanos' dying country priest, "Grace is everywhere . . . "?

Finally, does not the leaning of our living into this future, into the dream of Your domiciling Your Self, Your *Shalom*, Your Grace, Your Love, all who You are, in and with all You have unfolded, necessarily deposit us in adoration and worship? And, as exemplified by the *Missa Solemnis*, is not one of our loftiest vehicles of praise, the voice of both our exaltation of and exultation before You, not unlike the primeval hum of the Cosmic Microwave Background Radiation, pervasively *musical*? And in our anticipatory leaning toward Your dream's realization, O Beauty, is not the entire cosmos, bowing and piping, singing and dancing, all parts in concert, each according to its respective capacity, raising a vast *Venite Adoremus*, "O Come, let us adore [You]"? And as each is being drawn into the flowering of the beauty of its being, its inimitability, its fruitfulness, is not the song of the whole becoming increasingly more than the sum of its parts?

Still both graced and saddled as I am with my mortal biases, is not the music I recognize first amid that swell in Your dream perhaps Handel's "Worthy Is the Lamb" (Apoc 5:12, 13), an anthem of flush adoration before the majesty of Your self-relinquishing *modus operandi* in Your Troubadour? Then maybe the hymn "What Wondrous Love Is This?" And Paul and Ruth Manz's Advent anthem, "E'en So, Lord Jesus, Quickly Come," followed, perhaps, by Mahler's cosmic Symphony No. 8 with its majestic *Gloria*? But simultaneously the Trane's *A Love Supreme* as well? And strains originating in each of the Abrahamics, and beyond?

And then billowing in from all directions, do I not hear the music of every tribe and nation, tongue and orientation, era and color, from every one of Tylerton's creatures that has breath, from the *anawim* everywhere? And everything from the marsh and thorofare of Tylerton's neighborhood to the rocks and minerals of distant galaxies granted its thousand tongues, its exuberant musical *Gloria!* to You, at last delivered from silence? And is not all of this music, from the first Hebrew singers of the psalms to the combo doing their improvisational thing, from folks of distant isles to those of major cities, harmonious in a strangely wonderful way that has the freedom and creativity of all waxing increasingly vital and strong?

Is not the writer of the Apocalypse already hearing the music of this consummational celebration: "And *every created thing* which is in heaven and on the earth and under the earth and on the sea, and all things in them, was heard to be singing, 'To You who sit on the throne, and to the Lamb, be blessing and honor and glory and dominion forever and ever.'" (fr Apoc 5:13, EA)?

Indeed, is not in Your dream the entire cosmos jammin' with You in joy and celebration before the enormity of Your heart and Your Love? And, if I may employ one of *our* words, Your courage, O Dark Fire of Love, Your courage, *Your courage!*? And will we not ever be making more and better music both to and with You, I AM WHO AM, even as we are being made increasingly to become part of Your communitarian life?

O Deifier!

RESOURCES

The following pages offer information that I hope will be useful to you.

The first is an essay on my sources and method, which may interest more serious readers and scholars.

The second is a general index.

And the third is a scripture index, from Genesis to Apocalypse.

Please feel free to contact me with any comments, questions, or suggestions. Thank you.

LeRoy Friesen

1985 Creekbank Lane

South Bend, IN 46635

silentmusicfriesen@comcast.net

AN ESSAY ON SOURCES AND METHOD

This essay has two objectives. The first is to acknowledge the principal sources making possible the writing of this book. The more obvious type of source is that of text, whether books, periodicals, or materials on websites. Rather than footnote such sources, I chose, for reasons of readability, to include appropriate documentation in this essay. Included here as well are a handful of germane works either not directly referred to in the text or coming to my attention only after the major writing was completed.

It was self-evident from the outset of my research that I was learning at least as much about my subject from conversations with guests, villagers, and my spouse, among many others, as I was from texts. Many of these oral sources, particularly Tylertonians, are named in the body of the book with only a few elaborated upon in this essay. While such oral sources illustrate both the laudable and less laudable qualities of humans, I generally include names only in the former category. In several cases involving the negative, or where for other reasons I wish to protect anonymity, I employ pseudonyms which are then in quotes with first usage. It would be impossible to exaggerate the link between a decade of conversations and this book project.

The second objective, perhaps of interest to the more serious reader, is to identify various methodological issues I encountered in the course of envisioning and then writing the work. Again in the interests of readability, I decided in many cases to defer until this essay overviews of my thought trails. It is thus my hope that this essay will enrich the body of the text by shedding light on questions such as the following: Why does scripture play a major role in the book, and how is it used? What is my case for the cohesion of the book, which may seem to contain several genres? Why does this work about a slip of shoal both begin and end with cosmology? And to paraphrase the African Tertullian (ca. 160–ca. 225), what indeed has geography to do with spirituality? (In his *Prescription Against Heretics* [7], Tertullian queried, "What indeed has Athens to do with Jerusalem?") I trust that addressing such questions here will offer more clarity to the reader as to how I envisioned the entire project.

This essay, in which I move freely between these two objectives, listing sources and illuminating method, is exhaustive regarding neither. Acknowledgement of the role of all contributing sources to this book would have required the handles of hundreds of books as well as guests, to say nothing of the names of most Tylertonians: all the living and many of those deceased! I have needed to be selective in my citations, and I apologize in advance to any who feel slighted by this necessary abridgment. This essay is organized around the same headings serving the six parts of the book. Generally sources are cited here under the heading where they are first appeared in the text, and in the sequence of appearance.

Epigraph

My treatment of Psalm 19:1–6 is both hint of "music" as one of the work's two central metaphors at the geography/spirituality interface (the other being "journey"), and initial example of the method I sometimes employ in the use of scripture. For more regarding the latter, see the first four paragraphs below under Part I.

Scholars disagree whether to translate the text of Psalm 19:3–4 as indicating that what the heavens are telling is audible or silent. The audible interpretation has been popularized by the lyrics of "The Heavens Are Telling" from the oratorio *The Creation* by Franz Joseph Haydn (1732–1809), especially in his repeated phrase, "Never unperceived, ever understood." The more paradoxical translation—that despite permeating all that is, the "music" (*New English Bible*) of the cosmos is inaudible, silent—is supported by both the *Revised Standard Version* (RSV) and *New American Standard Bible* (NASB). The handles of both the Inn and this book, to say nothing of my treatment of Psalms 19:3–4 in the front matter, presuppose this second view.

Part I. The Genesis of the Book

An issue requiring explanation involves the cited texts of scripture including both the Hebrew and Christian writings. There are numerous such references in this work, particularly in Parts III through VI. Most such passages originally surfaced amid prayer and/or journaling, and the actual wording entering this book was frequently that which first seized me in that context. While at times the wording employed was shaped by Hebrew word studies or my limited knowledge of *koine* (New Testament) Greek, and sometimes from an amalgam of several translations on my shelf, more often it reflects my attempt to replicate the form in which the text rose from the page to confront me.

All biblical texts are referenced within the body of the work with book abbreviations those in *The Chicago Manual of* Style (15th edition, Chicago: The University of Chicago Press, 2003, pp. 578–579). Although I decided only rarely to specify a translation or version used, the Roman Catholic prayer book and lectionary both use the *New American Bible*. In contrast, my basic desk text during the writing was the *New American Standard Bible*, viewed by many as the most literal translation of the Hebrew and Greek available, and I tested all alternative readings against it. But the starting point for scripture entering the text of this book was morning prayer, meditation, and/or contemplation more frequently than it was study; an important goal for me was to preserve the wording which either first or finally addressed me there. Although I am aware of the hazards of this method, I judge the risk necessary to conveying to the reader the *fresh power* that emerged from scripture during our isle decade, one that seized me, would not be denied, and thus became my own.

My decision to exercise a measure of freedom with the biblical text assumed one additional expression. Near the midpoint of our 1997-2006 decade, I became concerned about how much of my spiritual journaling was in the third person. Rather than speaking *to*, and, more importantly, being addressed *by*, my prayer often consisted of talking/writing *about* the One with whom I have to do. In my journaling I was theologizing more than praying. At the same time, I was ever encountering biblical passages, especially in the Psalter, which I desired to graft into my own prayer. But with the text often in a grammatical person other than the first, I would find myself wanting to shift into what could become, at least episodically, an antiphony between myself as listener and then pray-er (both in the first person), and the One as speaker via inspirited text and then addressee (both in the second person), respectively. My shorthand for this shift is that I was beginning to learn *to pray the scriptures*.

This book contains many such transpositions of scripture, particularly in Part VI. Preceding each such transposed text reference embedded in the body of the book is the symbol "fr" (from). Some text citations begun with "fr" also include inserted italics for emphasis, this without further explanation. On the other hand, when for purposes of emphasis I add italics to ordinary quotations, whether untransposed biblical or otherwise, I indicate this in the citation with the letters "EA" (emphasis added).

For my understanding of the nature of *memoir*—creative recollection, bringing to words *consciousness* even more than experience—I am indebted to Patricia Hampl's *Virgin Time: In Search of the Contemplative Life* (New York: Farrar Straus & Giroux, 1992), and her "Sacrament of Self: The Catholic Roots of Contemporary Memoir," the 2007 Christian Culture Lecture at St. Mary's College, Notre Dame, IN which I was able to hear. I also benefited from Judith Barrington's *Writing the Memoir: From Truth to Art* (Portland, OR: Eighth Mountain Press, 1997).

The notion of "Abrahamic faiths," including Judaism, Christianity, and Islam, is one introduced to me by Roy Kreider, Mennonite churchman working in Israel, during the years I lived in occupied Palestine (1971–76), and nurtured during more recent study of the *convivéncia* era in medieval Spain. This term surfaces again at the beginning of the Part IV discussion of the art of hospitality.

An exasperating deficiency in books about places is inadequate, or nonexistent, maps! Insofar as this work was written with maps in both hand and head, the reader would do well to do the same. Maps of the Lower Chesapeake Bay, Smith Island, and

Tylerton village/island, generated by Jody L. Brown, are found preceding Part II of the text. Unless otherwise indicated, Chesapeake basin distances from Tylerton are expressed in miles, and "as the osprey flies."

Principal inspiration regarding the spiritually rich meaning of "place" is shared by Kathleen Norris' *Dakota: A Spiritual Geography* (Boston: Houghton Mifflin, 1993), and Belden C. Lane's *Landscapes of the Sacred: Geography and Narrative in American Spirituality* (expanded edition, Baltimore: Johns Hopkins University Press, 2001), and, especially, *The Solace of Fierce Landscapes: Exploring Desert and Mountain Spirituality* (New York: Oxford University Press, 1998). The latter work, in addition to the source (p. viii) of Lane's quote in Part I, also aided me in understanding the objective/subjective construct, of which "memoir," "impressionism," and "cosmos," in addition to "place," became examples. Quite late in our decade I also discovered Philip Sheldrake's *Spaces for the Sacred: Place, Memory, and Identity* (Baltimore: Johns Hopkins University Press, 2001). A second tier of varied works exemplifying the draw of the numinous in different geographies would include the writings of Barry Lopez, Annie Dillard, and Tony Hillerman.

I am indebted to no other Smith Island waterman as much as Jennings Lee Evans, a resident of North End (Ewell), with whom I had a series of rich conversations across the decade. In addition, during much of that period the Smith Island (elementary) school in North End circulated intermittently a photocopied rag called the *Smith Island Times* (not to be confused with a New York paper) to which Jennings regularly contributed outstanding historical pieces growing out of his research. Unfortunately the *Times* was discontinued late in our decade, and I am not aware of a repository of past issues other than that held by Evans himself.

With the exception of "The Place of Waters," found in her *The House at Rest* (Pewaukee, WI: Carmelite Monastery, 1984), all cited poetry of Sr. Miriam of the Holy Spirit, OCD, is contained in her *The Selected Poetry of Jessica Powers* (Regina Siegfried & Robert Morneau, eds., Washington, DC: ICS Publications, 1999). Because of how frequently I cite her, I have always included page numbers of her poems, like biblical references, in the body of the text.

The phrase "one brief shining moment" is taken from "Camelot (Reprise)" in the musical play *Camelot* by Alan Jay Lerner (lyrics) and Frederick Loewe (music), which opened on Broadway in 1960.

Additional works cited in Part I: Dante Alighieri, *The Divine Comedy* (John Ciardi, tr., New York: New American Library, 2003); *The Confessions of St. Augustine* (Rex Warner, tr., New York: New American Library, 1963); Dag Hammarskjöld, *Markings* (Leif Sjöberg & W. H. Auden, trs., New York: Knopf, 1965); Homer, *The Odyssey*

(Walter Shewring, tr., New York: Oxford, 1998); *Poems and Prose of Gerard Manley Hopkins* (W. H. Gardner, ed., Middlesex, UK: Penguin, 1971); Tom Horton, *An Island Out of Time: A Memoir of Smith Island in the Chesapeake* (New York: Norton, 1996); Nikos Kazantzakis, *Report to Greco* (P. A. Bien, tr., New York: Bantam, 1971); Thomas Merton, *The Seven Storey Mountain* (New York: Harcourt & Brace, 1948); Robert M. Pirsig, *Zen and the Art of Motorcycle Maintenance: An Inquiry into Values* (New York: HarperCollins, 2006).

Part II. The Place

The quotation with which Part II begins, and that resurfaces in Part V, is taken from the following in Albert Camus' *Carnets 1942–51* (Philip Thody, tr., London: Hamish Hamilton, 1966, p. 142): "We must love life before loving the meaning of life, says Dostoievski. Yes, and when the love of life disappears no meaning can console us for its loss." I understand this to be Camus' summary of the exchange between Ivan and Alyosha in *The Brothers Karamazov* (Constance Garnett, tr., New York: The Modern Library, 1950 [II,V,III], p. 274). I thank my brother Berry for first bringing the quotation to my attention. The William Blake quotation in the same introduction is from his "Auguries of Innocence," *A Selection of Poems and Letters* (J. Bronowski, ed., New York: Penguin, 1977, p. 67).

In 2002 several readings of Timothy Ferris' *Seeing in the Dark* (New York: Simon & Schuster, 2002) led to my purchasing a small reference shelf including the *National Audubon Society Field Guide to the Night Sky* (New York: Knopf, 1991); *Norton's Star Atlas and Reference Handbook,* 20th ed. (Ian Ridpath, ed., New York: Pi Press, 2004); and *The Essential Dictionary of Science* (John O. E. Clark, ed., New York: Barnes & Noble, 2004). I also began to monitor several NASA astronomy websites including Hubble, Cassini-Huygens, and "Astronomy Picture of the Day" (http://antwrp.gsfc.nasa.gov/apod/). In correlation with what I myself was seeing from the perch, these photographic resources on the web were too good to be true!

Regarding the C.B.I.C., see C. Wylie Poag, *Chesapeake Invader: Discovering America's Giant Meteorite Crater* (Princeton, NJ: Princeton University Press, 1999), and *The Chesapeake Bay Crater: Geology and Geophysics of a late Eocene Submariner Impact Structure* (Poag, Christian Koeberl, and Wolf Uwe Reimold, Berlin: Springer-Verlag, 2004). Carl Sagan's quote that we humans are "star stuff pondering the stars" is from his *Cosmos* (New York: Random House, 1980); his question, "Who speaks for earth?" is from the thirteenth and final episode of the PBS television series "Cosmos: A Personal Voyage," which first aired in 1980.

Part of my knowledge of the biosphere in which Tylerton is suspended was dependent on books shelved in the living room of the Inn where guests could access them as well. These included Christopher P. White, *Chesapeake Bay: Nature of the Estuary: a Field Guide* (Centreville, MD: Tidewater, 1989); John Page Williams, Jr., *Chesapeake Almanac: Following the Bay Through the Seasons* (Centreville, MD: Tidewater, 1993); Tom Horton, *Bay Country* (Baltimore: Johns Hopkins University Press, 1994); Tom Horton (text) and David Harp (photography) in association with the Chesapeake Bay Foundation, *Water's Way: Life Along the Chesapeake* (Washington, DC: Elliott & Clark Publishing, 1992); and Alice Jane and Robert L. Lippson, *Life in the Chesapeake Bay*, 2nd ed. (Baltimore: Johns Hopkins University Press, 1997). We relied on David Allen Sibley, *The Sibley Guide to Birds* (New York: Knopf) after its publication in 2000. The definitive work on the *Callinectes sapidus* remains William W. Warner's Pulitzer-winning *Beautiful Swimmers: Watermen, Crabs, and the Chesapeake Bay*. (New York: Penguin, 1984). Besides books, periodicals, and websites, my biospheric education came at the feet of Tylerton's watermen. Particularly during the off-season I would frequent the Market in the evening both to listen and ply them with questions. I have warm memories of those scores of hours.

My early interest in the Amerindians of the Chesapeake basin was snagged by Stephen G. Hyslop's major article "Life in America 400 Years Ago: When Algonquian Culture Ruled Our Region," *The Washington Post*, June 14, 1995, pp. H1-5. Charles C. Mann's *1491: New Revelations of the Americas Before Columbus* (New York: Knopf, 2005), provided me with a hemispheric perspective on pre-Columbian cultures. Most of my research regarding the history of human residency in the Bay basin was on the internet, with an important source being Robert S. Grumet, Lloyd N. Chapman, and Robert D. Campbell, *Bay, Plain, and Piedmont: A Landscape History of the Chesapeake Heartland from 1.3 Billion Years Ago to 2000*, available at http://www.chesapeakebay.net/pubs/gateways/plainandpiedmont/index.htm (accessed January 27, 2005). A yet narrower focus on Delmarva was provided by Helen C. Rountree (with Thomas E. Davidson), *Eastern Shore Indians of Virginia and Maryland* (Charlottesville, VA: University of Virginia Press, 1997). Published in 2008, too late for this study, was her *John Smith's Chesapeake Voyages, 1607–1609*, with the same press. I also did research during the 2004–2005 off-season in the National Museum of the American Indian shortly after it opened in Washington, D.C.

The literature refers to the pre-Columbian residents of the Americas with a variety of terms: Native Americans, Indians, Amerindians, and indigenes, among others. I have not found conclusive any of the various discussions, including that of Mann (pp. 367–372), as to which term is preferred by these peoples themselves, the principal criterion. As such, I employ several as roughly synonymous, although "Amerindian" most frequently.

My basic historical text on Smith Island's Chesapeake basin context from the time of initial contact between Amerindians and Europeans, first as the colony and, later, the state of Maryland, was Robert J. Brugger's masterful *Maryland: A Middle Temperament: 1634–1980* (Baltimore: Johns Hopkins University Press, 1988). John Smith's fascinating accounts of exploration of the Chesapeake Bay in the summer of 1608, including his famous description of the Bay included in Part IV, can be found in *Travels and Works of Captain John Smith* (Edward Arber, ed., New York: Burt Franklin, 1910). The works of Donald G. Shomette are basic regarding the maritime history of the Bay, beginning with his *Shipwrecks on the Chesapeake: Maritime Disasters on Chesapeake Bay and Its Tributaries, 1608–1978* (Centreville, MD: Cornell Maritime Press, 1982).

My knowledge of Bay history was also enhanced by our multiple visits to four museums located not far from Tylerton: the Calvert Marine Museum in Solomons, MD, thirty-five miles northwest near the paleontologically rich Calvert Cliffs; the Chesapeake Bay Maritime Museum in St. Michaels, MD, fifty-five miles north; the astonishing Mariners' Museum in Newport News, VA, sixty-five miles south-southwest; and the Ward Museum of Wildfowl Art in Salisbury, MD, forty miles northeast.

I made regular visits throughout the decade to the Somerset County Library (Princess Anne) and Wicomico County Library (Salisbury); each contains a very helpful "Maryland [Historical] Room." I was also assisted at both the Blackwell Library of Salisbury University and the nearby Edward H. Nabb Research Center for Delmarva History & Culture. I did historical research on Smith Island at the Enoch Pratt Library in Baltimore as well as genealogical work at the National Archives in Washington, D.C.

An extraordinarily rich work regarding the cultural and religious history of Smith Island is Adam Wallace's *The Parson of the Islands: The Life and Times of Joshua Thomas* (Cambridge, MD: Tidewater, 1861, reprinted in 1961). Most of what I learned about the waterman/evangelist Joshua Thomas and his environment was from this book. In addition to Horton's rich memoir, see W. P. Taylor, *A History of Smith's Island* (Wilmington, DE: Hubert, 1910), and Frances W. Dize, *Smith Island, Chesapeake Bay* (Centreville, MD: Tidewater, 1990) regarding the history of Smith Island; for Dize's brief comments about pre-Columbian archeological sites on Smith, see pp. 22 and 192.

William H. Rodgers provided the text and David Harp the photographs for an article entitled "'A Wet and Windy Kingdom,' Smith Island" which appeared in *Maryland Magazine*, Spring, 1979, pp. 2-7. Early in our decade the Welchman Jon Gower quartered at the Inn while doing research, which resulted in his *An Island Called Smith* (Llandysul, Ceredigion, Wales: Gomer Press, 2001), a work including valuable transcripts of his interviews with Tylertonians. An introductory work on neighboring Tangier Island seven miles to the south is Kirk Mariner, *God's Island: The History of Tangier* (New Church, VA: Miona Publications, 1999). The Rass Island of Katherine Paterson's *Jacob Have I Loved* (New York: Harper Keypoint, 1990), 1981 winner of the Newbery Medal, is surely modeled on Smith and/or Tangier islands.

Two-time Pulitzer-winning Stan Grossfeld's interest in the impact of sea level rise resulted in his major photo-article, "An Island Struggles Against Tide, Time," which appeared in *The Boston Sunday Globe*, November 30, 1997, pp. A1, 34–35. A delightful surprise late in my project was publication of William B. Cronin's *The Disappearing Islands of the Chesapeake* (Baltimore: Johns Hopkins University Press, 2005). In addition to my own observation as well as conversations with watermen and guests, my education concerning the perils faced by the Bay was deepened by reading the quarterly *Save the Bay* published by the Chesapeake Bay Foundation and the monthly *The Bay Journal* by the Alliance for the Chesapeake Bay.

Finally, a member of Smith Island's *diaspora* and also a seasonal resident, Gail M. Walczyk, has done extraordinary genealogical work on the bulk of Smith Island's residents since initial European settlement in the 1660s. Her *Smith's Island in 1870* and (with Jennings L. Evans and Frank V. Walczyk) *Graven Inscriptions of Tylerton: Obituaries, Epitaphs and Other Data on the Islanders Buried at Union UME Churchyard, Tylerton MD*, were both published in 1998 by Peter's Row in Coram, NY. For Tom Horton's data on Smith Island demographics in recent decades, see his *An Island Out of Time*, pp. 314-316.

Part III. The Meaning of Place

I seized upon the term *topophilia* ("love of place") after encountering the work of Yi-Fu Tuan in *Topophilia: A Study of Environmental Perception, Attitudes, and Values* (New York: Columbia University Press, 1990).

A list of books I read attempting to arrive at some understanding of the "isle mindset" included, among others, the following: David Guterson, *Snow Falling on Cedars: A Novel* (New York: Knopf, 1995); Barry Lopez, *Arctic Dreams: Imagination and Desire in a Northern Landscape* (New York: Vintage, 2001); Wayne Johnston, *The Colony of Unrequited Dreams* (New York: Random House, 2000); Alistair MacLeod, *Island: The Complete Stories* (New York: Norton, 2001); Richard Nelson, *The Island Within* (New York: Vintage, 1991); Adam Nicolson, *Sea Room: An Island Life in the Hebrides* (New York: Farrar, Straus & Giroux, 2002); Annie Proulx, *The Shipping News* (New York: Simon & Schuster, 1994); Sue Monk Kidd, *The Mermaid Chair* (New York: The Penguin Group USA, 2006); Linda Greenlaw, *The Lobster Chronicles: Life on a Very Small Island* (New York: Hyperion, 2002);

Ernest Shackleton & Frank Hurley (photography), *South:The Endurance* Expedition (New York: Penguin Classics Series, 2004; David Shears, *Ocracoke: Its History and People* (Washington, DC: Starfish Press, 1989); the island studies in Jared Diamond, *Collapse: How Societies Choose to Fail or Succeed* (New York: Viking, 2005); and David Quammen in both *The Song of the Dodo: Island Biogeography in an Age of Extinctions* (New York: Simon & Schuster, 1997) and *The Reluctant Mr. Darwin* (New York: Norton, 2006).

Regarding the audible image of "silent music," see "The Spiritual Canticle" (#14 and #15), *The Collected Works of Saint John of the Cross,* revised ed. (Kieran Kavanaugh, OCD and Otilio Rodriguez, OCD, trs., Washington, DC: ICS, 1991, pp. 525, 535–536); for John's "seas of living fire" quote, see his "Living Flame of Love" (2:10), p. 661. (Note: Fr. Kieran Kavanaugh was my spiritual director in late 1994 when we were discerning whether to launch the Inn project.) See John Frederick Nims (tr.), *The Poems of St. John of the Cross: a Bilingual Edition*, third ed. (Chicago: University of Chicago Press, 1989, p. 7), for a second translation of John's poetry. Those familiar with T. S. Eliot's "The Dry Salvages" found in *Collected Poems 1909-62* (New York: Harcourt, Brace & World, 1970, pp. 191–199), may note the influence of John of the Cross. Copies of *Music of Silence: A Sacred Journey Through the Hours of the Day*, by David Steindl-Rast with Sharon Lebell, Introduction by Kathleen Norris (Berkeley, CA: Seastone, 1998), were on the bedside tables of the inn.

The importance of the *kataphatic/apophatic* distinction arose amid my introduction to the spirituality of St. John of the Cross in 1993. I had become familiar with Paul Tillich's notion of the "self-negating symbol," itself significantly influenced by the Spanish mystic, in my (unpublished) 1968 M.A. thesis at the University of Southern California entitled *A Study of Paul Tillich's Principles of Religious Symbology and Their Application to Jesus Who Is the Christ*. For the formative early contribution to Christian *apophatica*, see *Pseudo-Dionysius: the Complete Works* (Colm Luibheid, tr., New York: Paulist, 1987). Rudolf Otto explores the notion of *mysterium tremendum* in his *The Idea of the Holy* (John W. Harvey, tr., New York: Galaxy, 1965). The image of *Axis Mundi*, found in many religions, is present in the Psalms 48:2 translation "true pole of the earth" found in *Christian Prayer:The Liturgy of the Hours*. (New York: Catholic Book Publishing Co., 1976, p. 751).

My interest in desert spirituality grew in the 1970s as I was able to visit Greek Orthodox monasteries in the Judean hills as well as participate in a week-long trip through much of Sinai including St. Catherine's monastery. I subsequently visited the Baramous Coptic Orthodox monastery at Wadi El Natrun (1983) northwest of Cairo and the monasteries of St. Paul and St. Anthony the Great (1988) in the eastern Egyptian desert. Works which have fed this interest have included the following: Athanasius, *The Life of Anthony* (Robert C. Gragg, tr., New York: Paulist, 1980);

Benedicta Ward, SLG (tr.), *The Sayings of the Desert Fathers*, revised ed. (Kalamazoo, MI: Cistercian, 1984); Douglas Burton-Christie, *The Word in the Desert: Scripture and the Quest for Holiness in Early Christian Monasticism* (New York: Oxford, 1993); and Cyril of Scythopolis, *Lives of the Monks of Palestine* (R. M. Price, tr., Kalamazoo, MI: Cistercian, 1991). A seminal source in my coming to understand both "The Isle Salt Marsh as Apophatic Desert" and "The Sea as the Boundless One" was Bernard McGinn, "Ocean and Desert as Symbols of Mystical Absorption in the Christian Tradition," *Journal of Religion* 74:2 (April, 1994), pp. 155–181.

An excellent source on Carmelite origins in Palestine is *Carmel in the Holy Land* (Silvano Giordano, OCD, ed., photography by Girolamo Salvatico, OCD, Arenzano, Italy: Il Messaggero di Gesù Bambino, 1995). The notion of aging as life's "natural monastery" is developed by Jane Marie Thibault in chapter twelve, entitled "Final Sufferings: Entering into the Passion of Christ," in her *A Deepening Love Affair: The Gift of God in Later Life* (Nashville: Upper Room Books, 1993).

Additional works cited in or consulted for Part III include the following: Pat Conroy, *Prince of Tides* (Boston: Houghton Mifflin, 1986); Robert M. Hamma, *Landscapes of the Soul: A Spirituality of Place* (Notre Dame, IN: Ave Maria, 1999); Paul Tillich, *On the Boundary: An Autobiographical Sketch.* (New York: Scribners, 1966); Jeffrey Johnson, *Harbors of Heaven: Bethlehem and the Places We Love* (Cambridge, MA: Cowley, 2006); and E. F. Schumacher, *Small Is Beautiful: Economics As If People Mattered* (New York: Perennial, 1975).

Part IV. Receiving the Stranger Without: Hospitality

The initial quotation of Part IV is taken from Chapter 53, "The Reception of Guests," *The Rule of St. Benedict in English* (Timothy Fry, ed., Collegeville, MN: Liturgical Press, 1981, p. 73). The Henri J. M. Nouwen quotation regarding "hospitality" is from *The Wounded Healer: Ministry in Contemporary Society* (Garden City, NY: Doubleday, 1972, p. 94); he also discusses this theme in *Reaching Out: The Three Movements of the Spiritual Life* (Garden City, NY: Doubleday, 1975, pp. 45-78). Also cited is *An Interrupted Life: The Diaries of Etty Hillesum 1941–43* (New York: Washington Square Press, 1985). I first encountered the notion of faith as "ultimate concern" in Paul Tillich's *Dynamics of Faith* (New York: HarperCollins, 2001). For his assessment, and novel treatment, of the human "predicament," see Walker Percy's *Love in the Ruins: The Adventures of a Bad Catholic at a Time Near the End of the World* (New York: Ballantine, 1971). For the line "Cure thy children's warring madness," see "God of Grace and God of Glory," *The Mennonite Hymnal* (Scottdale, PA: Herald Press, 1985, p. 434).

For the quote by Abbot Francis Kline, OCSO, see his *Lovers of the Place: Monasticism Loose in the Church* (Collegeville, MN: Liturgical Press, 1997, p. 94). The manner in which the Mepkin Abbey, with Abbot Kline's leadership, sought to acknowledge past residents of their place on the Cooper River in South Carolina was the inspiration for the thrust of chapter 18, "Confession to You: Violated Spirits Past," of this book.

For the "shining like the sun" quotation of Thomas Merton, see his *Conjectures of a Guilty Bystander* (Garden City, NY: Image Books, 1968, p. 157). This quotation is part of Merton's larger discussion of an experience he had at Fourth and Walnut in Louisville, Kentucky, on March 18, 1958, which transformed his monastic self-understanding.

For Mary Maynard Drake's articles (photographs by Bob Maynard Drake) entitled "Silent Music's Serenity: Guests at This B&B Don't Miss the Traffic and Noise One Bit" (pp. 1, 12-13) and "Smith Island, MD: Preserving a Living History of Working Watermen" (pp. 41–44), see *Soundings*, April 2001.

Our single incidence of hate mail was in response to an article reporting on spirituality aspects of the Inn of Silent Music project by Anita Huslin (photographs by Marvin Joseph) entitled "Healing the World a Spirit at a Time," *The Washington Post*, July 9, 2002, pp. B1, 8.

For a spirited account of Joshua Thomas' challenge to the British attack on Fort McHenry the following day (September 13, 1814), see Adam Wallace's *The Parson of the Islands,* chapter X, "Preaching to the Army," pp. 143–154.

For information regarding the history of race relations in the southern part of Maryland's Eastern Shore, I am dependent on Robert J, Brugger's *Maryland: A Middle Temperament*; Joseph E. Moore's *Murder on Maryland's Eastern Shore: Race, Politics and the Case of Orphan Jones* (Charleston, SC: History Press, 2006); and, particularly, John R. Wennersten's *Maryland's Eastern Shore: A Journey in Time and Place* (Centreville, MD: Cornell Maritime/Tidewater, 1992).

My source for the three narratives of blacks on Smith Island (chapter 18) is Jennings Evans. I first read the stories of Miriah Jacobs Parks, George Scott "Kidd" Lee, and Jett and Harriet Sutton in Evans' articles in the *Smith Island Times* after which I sought to learn more about them, and others, in conversations with him. Evans notes that his account of Miriah Parks is partially based on an article shortly after her death in 1910 by Lorrie C. Quinn in the *Crisfield Times* and reprinted in the same in October 1942. In keeping with my pattern throughout chapter 18, I retell these stories in the grammatical first person, in each of the three narratives addressing the person(s) in the second person. Any mistakes in my retelling of these stories are, of course, my own.

Finally, for the text of the penitential rite of the Roman Catholic Mass, twice cited in augmented form in chapter 18, see *The Vatican II Sunday Missal* (Boston: Daughters of St. Paul, 1974, p. 589).

Part V. Receiving the Stranger Within: Hospitalier Self-Care

One of the windmills with which I tilt, perhaps not always necessarily, in Part V is finding a word for us innkeepers based on the same root as "hospitality." A yen for symmetry between the titles of Parts IV and V was part of the challenge. My entertaining of "hospitaller" as the purveyor of hospitality was not well-received by my fastidious editor, who judged the term to be unhygienic, as in "spittle." We finally settled on the Old French "hospitalier," perhaps in hope of gaining some traction from its hint of refinement.

On November 3, 2004, I addressed the annual conference of the Maryland Bed and Breakfast Association, held at the Morningside Inn Bed & Breakfast outside of Frederick, on the theme of "Wholeness and the Innkeeper." The cited article on "emotional exhaustion" among innkeepers is the following: Gary Vallen & Wallace Rande, "The Incidence of Burnout Among Bed-and-Breakfast Owner / Operators," *Journal on Human Resources in Hospitality & Tourism*, 1:2, March 1, 2002, pp. 41–56.

Gerard Manley Hopkins' line, "There lives the dearest freshness deep down things," is taken from his "God's Grandeur," *Poems and Prose*, p. 27; for his "Pied Beauty," which begins with the line "Glory be to God for dappled things," see p. 30. The "Joy is the most infallible sign" quote has been attributed to both Pierre Teilhard de Chardin, S.J. (1881–1955) and Léon Bloy (1846–1917). The Anne Morrow Lindbergh quote is taken from her *Gift from the Sea* (New York: Pantheon, 2005). The Wendell Berry poem, "The Peace of Wild Things," with which chapter 23 concludes, is from *The Selected Poems of Wendell Berry* (Berkeley, CA: Counterpoint, 1999, p. 30). The Frances Poulenc quote, "Above all do not analyze my music—love it!" is from David Dubal, *The Essential Canon of Classical Music* (New York: North Point Press, 2001, p. 606).

My musical fantasy is nourished by memory of an evening in 1991 when, as a member of the Masterworks Chorus, I was able to sing in the Washington Cathedral.

A modest collection of pieces by Karl Barth, reputed to have listened to recordings of Mozart's music each morning *before* beginning his theological writing, is contained in his *Wolfgang Amadeus Mozart* (Clarence K. Pott, tr., Grand Rapids, MI: Eerdmans, 1986).

Although the Roman Catholic tone was not prominent in early Maryland co-lonial history on the Eastern Shore as it was across the Bay, the rendering illegal of Catholic public worship throughout the colony during the century beginning in 1689 left fascinating traces on the Shore. For example, the Jesuits, for purposes of funding an envisioned Georgetown University (founded in 1789), purchased several Eastern Shore plantations. Each would include a space consecrated for worship con-nected to a private home, thus not in violation of the proscription of "public" Catholic worship.

The first of these plantations, in Warwick in Cecil County opposite Baltimore, purchased in 1704, became the Eastern Shore's Roman Catholic center, and remains known today as Old Bohemia. This center birthed several daughter plantations, one of which is Old St Joseph's at Cordova (formerly "Tuckahoe") near Easton, purchased in 1765. Less than sixty-five miles north of Tylerton, Old St. Joseph's, initially a house dating to 1782 with discrete attached chapel built in conformity to Maryland laws, was subsequently enlarged several times. Today it is the second-oldest continuously used house of worship among English-speaking Catholics in the United States.

A second daughter of Old Bohemia is St. Mary's Star of the Sea Chapel in Golden Hill on Meekin's Neck at the north edge of Dorchester County's Blackwater National Wildlife Refuge, thirty-five miles north of Tylerton. There had been Catholics liv-ing on Meekin's Neck as early as 1660. Sharryl and I were able to attend Mass at St. Mary's in 2003. The Roman Catholic parish closest to Tylerton is Holy Name in Po-comoke City, twenty-five miles east-northeast. Its history also dating to itinerations out of Old Bohemia, Holy Name itself now has a mission, St. Elizabeth's, in Westover on Route 413, twenty miles northeast of Tylerton. The parish of which we are a part is St. Francis de Sales in Salisbury, forty miles northeast. Our Diocese is that of Wilmington (est. 1868) consisting of Delaware and Maryland's Eastern Shore. There is no historical evidence of any formal Roman Catholic presence on Smith Island.

For the poignant notion of the "upside-down kingdom" to describe the world-view of Jesus and the Reigning of the One, I am indebted to Donald Kraybill's *The Upside-Down Kingdom* (Scottdale, PA: Herald Press, 2003). The discussion of the nine-teenth-century loss of much of Smith Island's indigenous music is found in chapter 13 of Adam Wallace's work. Regarding the reading gracing the occasion of the inter-ment of Gus, see Judith Viorst, *The Tenth Good Thing about Barney* (New York: Simon & Schuster Children's Publishing, 1971). The Cheri Horton quote is from spouse Tom's *An Island Out of Time*, p. 99. The quote, "Getting old is not for sissies," is widely attrib-uted to actress Bette Davis.

Part VI. The Cosmic Dance as Arena for Adoration

It is important for the reader to note what Part VI is and is not. It is a sampling of one person's prayers growing out of the experience of living in a unique place, particularly as he became increasingly aware of its night sky component. My principal commitment in writing this section, particularly chapters 29-31, was to be truthful to the experience I had during our decade in that place. Thus, rather than a *Summa*, to say nothing of *Credo*, Part VI is a series of windows into the prayer of one person's inimitable spiritual path.

Serving as both inspiration and model for the combining in prayer of the first and second grammatical persons with the interrogative mode was Karl Rahner, SJ, in his *Encounters with Silence* (James M. Demske, SJ, tr., Westminster, MD: Christian Classics, 1984).

During the year bookended by the Advents of 2004 and 2005, each including a week at the Mepkin Trappist Monastery, I was reading Dante Alighieri's *The Divine Comedy*. Astonished by his fanciful and inexhaustibly rich integration of scholastic theology and Ptolemaic cosmology, I began to realize that at some level in my prayer life I was also being drawn into a synthesis between my faith as a Catholic Christian and modern cosmology. And amid the vast differences between Dante's effort and my own was the fact that, in contrast to his "sense of choice" in his imagery, which I judged to be *sight* in addition to the written word, my own, in addition to the written word, was the *audio*, more specifically, music. While admitting that even the naming of this inspiration may well smack of *hubris*, I argue that it is also the case that reading great literature, from the Pentateuch to the latest Pulitzer, invariably nudges us toward fresh ways of hearing the music, and so it was for me.

The reference to Dante's glimpsing of the human image in the divine is from the final canto of the *Comedy* (33:106-46); the words forming the heading for Section F in chapter 30, "O Love that Moves the Sun and Other Stars," are from the work's final line (33:146). Inspiration for the notion that not only the entire cosmos, but none less than the One, awaited Mary's exercise of agency (Lk 1:38), is credited to a homily on the Blessed Virgin Mary by Bernard of Clairvaux, OCist (1090–1153).

My amateur foray into astronomy was nurtured at a number of springs: conversations with scientist guests, reading of introductory astronomy materials (see brief list in Part II above), the donation of a fine telescope to the Inn by two ophthalmologist guests, my subsequent purchase of a serious set of binoculars, and the burgeoning access to space information and photography via the web.

But more important to me were sources gravitating toward the cosmogenesis/spirituality interface which included the following: Rich Heffern, "Spirituality and the Fine-tuned Cosmos," pp. 1–2, 4, 6–7, and "'Promise' of the Universe," pp. 3, 5, *National Catholic Reporter*, December 12, 2003; Brian Swimme, *The Hidden Heart of the Cosmos: Humanity and the New Story* (Maryknoll, NY: Orbis, 1999); Brian Swimme and Thomas Berry, *The Universe Story: From the Primordial Flaring Forth to the Ecozoic Era—A Celebration of the Unfolding of the Cosmos* (New York: HarperSanFrancisco, 1992); Thomas Berry, *The Dream of the Earth* (San Francisco: Sierra Club Books, 1990), and *The Great Work: Our Way Into the Future* (New York: Bell Tower, 1999); the works of John F. Haught, particularly his *God After Darwin: A Theology of Evolution* (Boulder, CO: Westview Press, 2000), in dialogue with the thought of Richard Dawkins, a British evolutionary biologist who is an atheist; Owen Gingerich, *God's Universe* (Cambridge, MA: Harvard University Press, 2006), and *The Book Nobody Read: Chasing the Revolutions of Nicolaus Copernicus* (New York: Penguin Group, 2005); Elaine M. Prevallet, SL, *Making the Shift: Seeing Faith Through a New Lens: A Cosmological and Evolutionary Faith Perspective* (Nerinx, KY: Elaine M. Prevallet, 2006); Dava Sobel, *Galileo's Daughter: A Historical Memoir of Science, Faith, and Love* (New York: Penguin, 2000); and three works by Jared Diamond: *The Third Chimpanzee: The Evolution and Future of the Human Animal* (New York: HarperPerennial, 1993); the Pulitzer-winning *Guns, Germs, and Steel: The Fates of Human Societies* (New York: Norton, 1997); and *Collapse: How Societies Choose to Fail or Succeed*.

For a discrete nod toward the heliocentric on the part of John of the Cross (in 1586!), see "The Living Flame" (4:4), *The Collected Works,* p. 709; John had studied four years at the prestigious University of Salamanca which had an astronomy chair. For the text of Pope John Paul II's "Truth Cannot Contradict Truth" delivered October 22, 1996, to the Pontifical Academy of Sciences, see www.newadvent.org/library/docs_jp02tc.htm (accessed February 11, 2009). M. Basil Pennington, OCSO, *Lectio Divina: Renewing the Ancient Practice of Praying the Scriptures* (New York: Crossword, 1998) is a good introduction to this tradition.

My indebtedness to the mystic saints is rarely as great as with their images for the One, the issue of the divine names. See *The Dialogue of St. Catherine of Siena* (Algar Thorold, tr., Rockford, IL: Tan Books, 1974); see pp. 118, 134, 178, 192, 238, 261, 277, 325, and 333 for examples of her use of the image "Sea Pacific" for the One, and for her employment of the terms "mad" and "Loving Madman," see pp. 76, 91, and 330–334. For the use of the term *veriditas* ("greening power") for both Creator and creation, see *Hildegard of Bingen: Scivias* (Jane Bishop, tr., New York: Paulist, 1990). The "all manner of thing shall be well" quote of Julian of Norwich first appeared in her *Sixteen Revelations of Divine Love*; two decades later she rewrote and expanded this text which is available as *Julian of Norwich: Showings* (James Walsh and Edmund Colledge, trs., New York: Paulist, 1988).

While the divine name "Furnace" (of Love) is implicit in several writings of John of the Cross, especially "The Living Flame," it is explicit in his Carmelite descendent, Thérèse of Lisieux, in her *Story of a Soul* (John Clark, tr., Washington, DC: ICS, 1976, pp. 198–200); Catherine of Siena, in her *Dialogue* (p. 248), has the words "the furnace of My love" in the mouth of the One.

The "Hound of Heaven," an improbably rich divine image for me dating back to 1965 and appearing several times in chapters 29–31, comes from Francis Thompson's *The Hound of Heaven* (Mount Vernon, NY: Peter Pauper Press, 1978); the quotation "Is my gloom, after all, / Shade of His hand, outstretched / caressingly?" is on p. 26.

For an example of Teresa de Jesús' use of the exclamation "Oh, what blessed madness, Sisters!" for the One, see *The Collected Works of St. Teresa of Avila*, vol. 2 (O. Rodriguez, OCD, and K. Kavanaugh, OCD, trs., Washington, DC: ICS, 1980, p. 396); for her statement that she "would want to be all tongues so as to praise the Lord," see her "Life" (16:4, vol. 1, 1976, p. 149). The source for Teresa's comment beginning with, "If this is the way you treat your friends," reportedly offered by her amid a wagon mishap while crossing rushing water, is uncertain.

The Augustine quotation beginning with "You have made us for Yourself" is taken from *The Confessions*, I:1; that with "O Beauty most ancient and most new" from X:27. For the variant of Descartes' *Cogito ergo sum* ("I think, therefore I am"), I am most grateful to Fr. Kenneth E. Grabner, CSC.

The phrase "lost in wonder, love and praise" is from the Charles Wesley hymn "Love Divine, All Loves Excelling," *The Mennonite Hymnal*, p. 76; for J. S. Bach's choral arrangement of "Jesus, Joy of Man's Desiring," see p. 599; for the hymn "O for a Thousand Tongues to Sing" (also Charles Wesley), see p. 104.

The cited hymns or songs found in *Worship: A Hymnal and Service Book for Roman Catholics*, 3rd ed. (Chicago: GIA, 1986) include "I received the Living God," Richard Proulx, p. 735; "Gather Us In," Marty Haugen, p. 665; "What Wondrous Love Is This," p. 600; the Latin/English carol "O Come, All Ye Faithful/*Adeste Fideles*," including the words *Veníte Adorémus,* p. 392; "There's a Wideness in God's Mercy," p. 595; and "Joy to the World," including the phrase "And heaven and nature sing," p. 399.

The entire text of Palestrina's *Alma Redemptoris Mater* is available at the following: http://www.cpdl.org/wiki/index.php/Alma_Redemptoris_Mater (accessed February 7, 2009). Georg Friedrich Handel's "Hallelujah Chorus" and "Worthy Is the Lamb" are choral pieces concluding parts II and III, respectively, of his oratorio *Messiah* composed in 1742.

The two quotes of Irenaeus of Lyons, "The glory of God is a human being fully alive" (*Gloria Dei vivens homo*) (IV:20,7), and "our Lord Jesus Christ . . . became what we are, that he might bring us to be what he is himself" (Preface to V), are taken from *Irenaeus Against Heresies* (Whitefish, MT: Kessinger, 2004), vols 4 and 5, respectively. The quotation from John of the Cross beginning with "In giving us his Son" is found in "The Ascent of Mount Carmel" (22:3), *Collected Works*, p. 230; for his discussion of the image "silent music," including three occurrences of the word "symphony," see his commentary on "The Spiritual Canticle" (#14/15:25–27), pp. 535–536. For another treatment of the role of relinquishment in the Incarnation, see Søren Kierkegaard [Johannes Climacus, pseud.], *Philosophical Fragments* (Howard V. Hong and Edna H. Hong, eds. & trs., Princeton, NJ: Princeton University Press, 1985, pp. 26-30), for the parable of "the king and the maiden."

For an introduction to John Polkinghorne's thought, including an annotated listing of his major publications, see Lyndon F. Harris' "Divine Action: An Interview with John Polkinghorne," from http://www.crosscurrents.org/polkinghhorne.htm (accessed February 7, 2009). Fr. Ronald Rolheiser, OMI, employs the figure of being kissed into being in *The Restless Heart* (New York: Bantam, 2006).

For a translation by Kythera Ann of the text Chief Seattle delivered to his people in his native Salish language in 1854, see the website of the School for Spiritual Integrity, http://visit.elysiumgates.com/connected.html (accessed February 11, 2009). For the source of the Stephen Hawking query, "Why does the universe go to all the bother of existing?" see his *A Brief History of Time: From the Big Bang to Black Holes* (New York: Bantam, 1988, p. 174).

For the Georges Bernanos quote, see his *The Diary of a Country Priest* (Pamela Morris, tr., New York: Image Books, 1974, p. 233).

Additional works cited in Part VI include the following: Albert Camus, *The Stranger* (Stuart Gilbert, tr., New York: Vintage, 1946); Matthew Fox, *Original Blessing* (New York: Penguin Group, 2000); T. E. Lawrence, *Seven Pillars of Wisdom: A Triumph* (New York: Anchor Books, 1991); C. S. Lewis, *The Problem of Pain* (New York: HarperCollins, 2001); William Paley, *Natural Theology* (Knight, Knight & Eddy, eds., New York: Oxford University Press, 2006); and J. B. Philips, *Your God Is Too Small: A Guide for Believers and Skeptics Alike* (New York: Simon & Schuster, 2004). The quote from the Roman Catholic Mass concluding the prayer "O Beautiful Dreamer!" (chapter 31) is taken from the Eucharistic Prayer of Reconciliation I.

I. General Index

A

Abba ("Daddy"), 321–322, 325, 332, 340–341, 345, 358, 362–363, 365, 371, 373, 376, 379–380

"Abrahamic faiths" (Judaism, Christianity, Islam), 15, 85, 137, 139, 159–167, 331, 389

Abyss (image of divine), 143–144, 373

Acceptance (of innkeepers), 101, 286–287

Accomack: tribe, 66; county (VA), 28, 69, 71

Admiral, 192–193

Aging, 289–293. *see also* Jane Marie Thibault

Ajacán (Spanish Virginia), 65, 205

Alcohol (as issue), 117, 186, 199, 251–252

Alfie (cinema), 281, 347

Alwine, Sanford, 14, 86, 130

Amatus sum ergo sum ("I am loved, therefore I am"), 325, 402

Amen Corner, 255

American Friends Service Committee (AFSC), 25, 157

Amerindian history: pre-Clovis, 57–58; Clovis, 59–60; Archaic, 60; Woodland, 60–61, 92; post-contact, 61–68, 91–92, 222

Andrew, William, 213

Andromeda galaxy, 35, 380, 382

Annemessex: tribe, 61; river, 42

Anthony of the desert, 138, 395

Anthropic Principle, 363

Apokatástasis ("restoration"), 150, 155, 273

Apophatópia ("apophatic place"), 135

Appreciations, 18

Arcadia (mid-Atlantic coast), 64

Armenian Massacre, 367

Arminianism, 276–277

Armwood, George, 213

B

Asparagus (wild), 50

Assateague, 64–65, 125

Associated Mennonite Biblical Seminary (AMBS), 157, 291

Athanasius of Alexandria, 395

Attentiveness, 30, 298–299

Augustine of Hippo, 15, 144, 356, 374, 390, 402

Auschwitz, 349, 367

Axis Mundi ("Pole of the Earth"), 120, 333

B

Babbi Yar, 365

Babette's Feast (cinema), 197–199, 272. *see also* Isak Dinesen

Bach, Johann Sabastian, 263, 402

"Backwards talk" (Tylerton), 86

Baltimore, Lord, 67–68, 283

Barrington, Judith, 389

Barth, Karl, 262, 266, 398

Bautista de Segura, Juan, 65, 205

The Bay Journal, 394

"Bean Snuckers" (North Enders), 105

"O Beautiful Dreamer!" (prayer), 379–380

Beauty: personal as ephemeral, 289–290; nature as sustaining, 253–259

"O Beauty Herself!" (prayer), 354–356, 383

Beethoven, Ludwig von, 262, 269

Benedict of Nursia/Benedictines, 138, 157, 163, 184, 309

Bernanos, Georges, 382, 403

Bernard of Clairvaux, 372, 400

Berry, Thomas, 302, 345, 401

Berry, Wendell, 259, 398

Bethlehem (as event), 148, 153, 304, 310, 325, 327, 359, 371

I

J

K

N

II. Scripture Index

Matthew (Mt): 1:1–17, 161. 1:23, 151. 2:2, 331. 2:13–23, 161. 5:48, 365. 6:9–13, 306, 321. 6:10, 184, 292, 378. 17:1–13, 150, 257. 25:31–46, 161. 25:35, 163. 26:29, 155. 27:46, 312, 335.

Mark (Mk): 1:12, 137. 4:38–41, 108, 144. 9:1–13, 150. 9:24, 359, 369. 14:25, 155. 14:36, 321. 15:34, 312, 367. 16:15, 338.

Luke (Lk): 1:34–35, 366. 1:38, 312, 400. 1:43, 330. 1:46–55, 362. 2:1–7, 148, 161. 2:34–35, 332. 3:23–38, 161. 4:14–30,162. 5:8, 328. 5:12–16, 162. 6:6–11, 162. 7:1–10, 162. 7:36–50, 162. 10:25–37, 162, 226, 248, 329. 11:2–4, 306, 321. 13:10–17, 162. 14:1–6, 162. 15:11–32, 348–349, 357–358, 367, 375. 16:13, 338. 17:11–19, 162. 19:1–10, 162. 22:18, 155. 22:42, 366. 23:27–31,162. 23:40–43, 217. 24:10–11,162.

John (Jn): 1:1, 371. 1:5, 271. 1:1–14, 148–149, 306, 312, 325, 329–330. 2:1–11, 198–199, 289. 3:16, 373. 4, 314. 4:7–26, 144. 6, 148. 6:39, 373. 6:44, 319. 10:15–18, 332. 14:9, 150, 312. 17:21, 381. 17:24, 342. 21:18, 291.

Acts of the Apostles (Acts): 6:13, 15. 7:58, 15. 9:2, 148. 10, 162. 10:2, 162. 10:6, 265. 13:16, 162. 15, 162.

Romans (Rom): 1:20, 310, 313. 8:15, 321. 8:18–25, 150, 306, 338, 348, 366, 372. 8:26, 283, 365. 8:28, 293.

1 Corinthians (1 Cor): 1:23, 332. 2:9, 151, 293, 340, 364, 377. 6:19, 250. 9:27, 226. 11:26, 155. 15:20–28, 149, 306, 376, 378. 16:22, 327.

2 Corinthians (2 Cor): 4:4, 150, 312, 332. 5:17, 184. 8:9, 136, 312.

Galatians (Gal): 1:17, 137. 4:6, 321. 6:15, 184.

Ephesians (Eph): 1:10, 306, 376, 378. 3:19, 381. 5:22–33, 372.

Philippians (Phil): 2:5–11, 136. 2:7, 183, 226, 312, 332.

Colossians (Col): 1:15, 150, 312, 332. 1:17–20, 148, 306.

Hebrews (Heb): 1:3, 261, 313, 326, 333, 336, 378. 4:15, 335. 12:1, 204.

James (Jas): 1:18, 149–150.

2 Peter (2 Pt): 1:4, 381. 3:13, 107, 155, 306, 348.

1 John (1 Jn): 1:1, 150, 334, 341. 3:2, 381. 4:16, 314, 323.

Apocalypse (Apoc): 5:6, 378. 5:9, 274. 5:12–13, 383. 7:17, 368. 10:6, 265, 274. 14:3, 274. 20:14, 379. 21:1–5, 144, 306, 339, 359, 369, 379-380. 21:23–25, 261, 379. 22:1–2, 348, 379. 22:5, 379. 22:20, 327.